*Great Racehorses in Art*

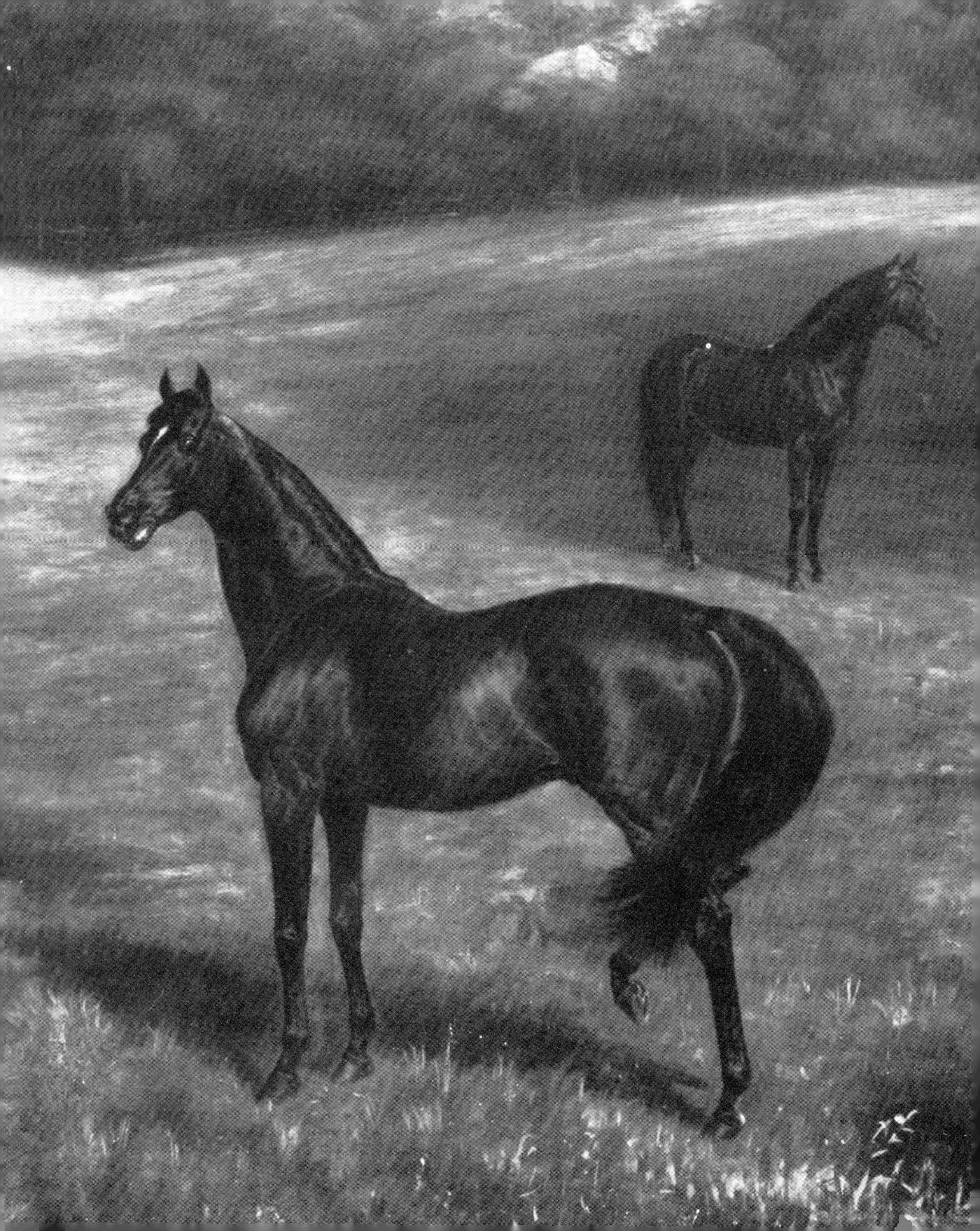

# *Great Racehorses in Art*

JOHN FAIRLEY

Foreword by

CAPTAIN JOHN MACDONALD-BUCHANAN

PHAIDON · OXFORD

*For Theodora, Beatrice, and Chloe – who loved Shergar*

Phaidon Press Limited, Littlegate House, St Ebbe's Street, Oxford
First published 1984


British Library Cataloguing in Publication Data

Fairley, John
Great racehorses in art
1. Racehorses 2. Painting
I. Title
758'.3 ND1385

ISBN 0-7148-2319-8

Printed in England by Jolly & Barber Ltd, Rugby, Warwickshire

FRONTISPIECE
Lynwood Palmer: *The Duke of Portland's Six Stallions* (detail showing St Simon, with St Serf in the background). See p. 139

# Contents

# Foreword

## by Captain John Macdonald-Buchanan

Within the vast field of international art over the last three centuries, the one area that now appears uniquely British, which was formulated and developed in these islands, and which has maintained its position and popularity during virtually the whole of the period, is that usually referred to as Sporting Art.

From the beginning it displayed a peculiar and easily recognizable 'Englishness', seeming to represent the standards and enthusiasms of the leisured or moneyed classes of those times. Some few men might have their wives painted, particularly if they were distinguished enough or rich enough to afford the great portrait painters of their day. However, practically every man amongst them would have his favourite horses painted, whether by good or indifferent artists. This in itself would appear an unlikely quirk elsewhere than in this country!

These people developed a taste for scenes depicting their various pleasures, pastimes, and sports, whether fishing, shooting, hunting, cockfighting, or whatever; and, in addition, there appeared a particular penchant for scenes of coaching, during its brief heyday. All these facets formed an extraordinary genre and, for the most part, it has been centred around the horse.

The tradition stretches from Wootton and Seymour, through Gilpin, Stubbs, and Marshall, Landseer, Ferneley, and Herring, down to Munnings and Lynwood Palmer, Gilbert Holiday and Lionel Edwards, right on to the present day when works by Edward Seago and Susan Crawford adorn many of the same walls as their predecessors. Occasionally, great artists in their own right (and not particularly in this art-form) have lent lustre to these ranks. The prodigious genius of Stubbs stands out, and in modern times Munnings is world ranked.

These are all British artists, but there have also been great masters from overseas, such as Delacroix, Degas, and Toulouse-Lautrec. Many lesser Continentals also

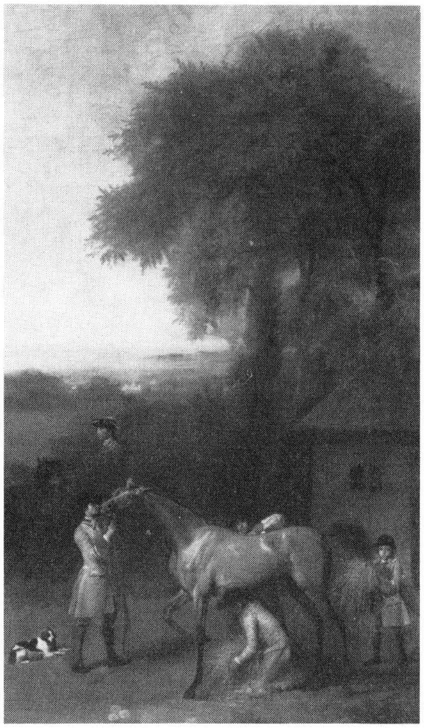

George Stubbs: *The Duke of Richmond's Horses Exercising* (detail). See p. 14

followed the tradition, yet even they appear to have possessed the desire to paint in a very English manner – de Dreux and Agasse are obvious examples. These standards also extended to America and the Antipodes, where many fine artists, such as Martin Stainforth and Henry Koehler, have continued the tradition.

The fascination of such pictures comes from seeing the equestrian heroes and heroines of the past represented on canvas, and it is inevitable that very many of these will be racehorses. The great names with which we are familiar stand before us, and we are able to appreciate the qualities of these horses, and their physical appearance and idiosyncrasies.

It is my opinion that John Fairley has encompassed all this within his book. It certainly breaks new ground and is fascinating to study. There are many great horses here and many great artists. There are also (and of equal interest) several great horses painted by less than great artists; similarly there are less than great horses painted by superb artists! What does it matter?

By allowing us a glimpse of the great names of the racecourse together with the great names of the studio the author has brought to life three centuries of racing. Added to which his descriptions and narrative continually provide both excitement and interest. The book is written not only with great enthusiasm but also with great authority. He reveals so many details and facts which enliven the illustrations for us. I have discussed much of the text and many of the pictures with him, and I found our discussions enthralling. I believe that he has managed to convey this same fascination to the pages of his book.

Inevitably some people will question why such and such a horse has not been included, while others will be convinced that some other horse should never have appeared at all. In the same fashion, many will decry certain artists, whereas some will be disappointed by the absence of another. They miss the author's purpose – surely it is to show the enormous wealth of fine pictures that have been painted both in order to represent these great horses and as works of art in themselves. In this the author has undoubtedly succeeded, not only through his understanding and discernment of the art-form and the artists, but equally in his knowledge of the horses themselves and their achievements.

John Fairley's interest in racing is well known; his sensitive production of television programmes concerning the sport is proof positive. But his comprehension and fine appreciation of Sporting Art, particularly as it concerns racing, is a revelation.

As I write, good horses are even now stamping their names upon the records and history of the Turf. Fortunately there does still appear to be a sufficiency of good artists, proud owners, and discerning patrons to allow future generations to see these horses suitably represented upon canvas and not in photographs alone.

Racing people and enthusiasts for Sporting Art alike will, I am certain, appreciate this fine work, and future generations must stand indebted to the author.

John Macdonald-Buchanan

# *Introduction*

Racing is founded on history – on sire lines and families, on the great performances of the past, on traditions, customs, and comparisons. From the beginning there have been outstanding artists who have devoted themselves to recording that history, and as Sir Walter Gilbey, writing nearly a hundred years ago in his *Animal Painters of England*, pointed out: 'If we are not wedded to our own opinions concerning equine characteristics, we can learn much from pictorial records.' Yet it is not easy to get to see the paintings of the great thoroughbreds.

The finest collection is in the Jockey Club rooms at Newmarket, locked away, except on rare occasions, from all but the 121 members. The Société d'Encouragement in Paris and the Australian Jockey Club in Randwick have some interesting pictures, mainly in private rooms. Paul Mellon has generously given a fabulous collection to the Yale Center for British Art at New Haven, Connecticut, and also to the Tate Gallery in London, but at the time of writing most of his racehorse paintings are still in his private possession. The Woodward Collection at the Baltimore Museum of Art has been consigned to the cellars for the last three years – all but a handful of pictures – and shows no sign of emerging into the light. The old Duke of Portland's pictures at Welbeck are now seen only by young soldiers trooping to lectures down 'horse corridor'. Many fine individual paintings are in private houses. Even Stubbs's marvellous picture of Whistlejacket has been withdrawn from Kenwood House in London, and now hangs out of public view.

There remains the annual pleasure of the autumn exhibitions of sporting art in London, which usually offer a brief chance to see some fine racing pictures before they disappear onward into private hands. But until recently only the splendid collection at the National Museum of Racing at Saratoga Springs in New York State, under the enterprising direction of Mrs Elaine Mann, offered the chance to see a fair sample of racing's great thoroughbreds – those enshrined in America's 'hall of fame'. In 1983, there was the welcome opening in England of the National Horseracing Museum at Newmarket, with some interesting pictures. The British Sporting Art Trust is striving valiantly, with notable gifts from Paul Mellon and the late Mrs Ambrose Clark, to establish a public collection of sporting art, but it seems likely that for many years to come racing's artistic heritage will remain largely scattered and inaccessible. It is the modest hope of this book to afford a coherent glimpse of that heritage.

The plan of the book, after an introductory historical sketch, is to show examples of work by the major artists of the thoroughbred racehorse, in a chronological way, selecting where possible studies of horses who have made a notable impression on the history of the Turf. It has been necessary to amend a number of the descriptions by which paintings have been known to their owners or sold in galleries and auction rooms. The sources for fuller studies of the artists, where available, are given in the Bibliography, and the family relationships of the horses over a period of 300 years, and their major racing triumphs, are identified in the Selective Blood Lines and lists of Classic Winners.

Private individuals, such as Kenneth Watt of Tattersalls, Lord Zetland with his vast Landseer picture of Voltigeur, and M. Philippe Gund, patron of André Marchand, have been most generous in allowing their paintings to be published for the first time. Indeed, the very great majority of works in this book are not available for public view. The owners have therefore been especially kind in allowing the reproductions to be made. They are acknowledged individually at the end of the book.

Particular thanks must go to the Stewards of the Jockey Club and to Mrs Elaine Mann at Saratoga, to the London galleries of Richard Green, Frost and Reed, and Messrs Ackermann, to the Tryon and Moorland Gallery, to Miss Margie Christian of Christie's, to Beverly Carter and Duncan Robinson of the Paul Mellon Collection and the Yale Center for British Art, to Jill Barron for research help, and to the staff of the London Library.

Finally I must thank Captain John Macdonald-Buchanan, a far-seeing Senior Steward of the Jockey Club and a notable connoisseur of sporting painting, who has kindly written a foreword to this book.

# *The Racehorse in History and Art*

Across two centuries and more, in the pictures of John Wootton and James Seymour, it is possible to sense the awed excitement of men who have discovered a new god – the thoroughbred racehorse.

In the space of only forty years, from 1687, there had arrived in England the three Eastern stallions who were to be the foundation of thoroughbreds everywhere: the Darley Arabian, the Byerley Turk, and the Godolphin Arabian. Nor were they alone. We know of more than 170 named Arabians who were recorded in the first Stud Book. The earliest known stallion to be imported from the East, the Markham Arabian, appeared in England in 1616. His admirers included King James himself, who bought him for £154. At first there were dissenters. Gervase Markham wrote in his treatise *Cavallarie* of 1617: 'The true English horse, him I meane that is bred under a good clime on a firme ground, in a pure temperature, is of tall stature and large proportions; his head though not so fine as the Barbaries or the Turkes yet is lean, long and well-fashioned. For their endurance I have seen them suffer and execute as much and more than ever I noted of any foriane creation.' But the tide was not with the conservatives, nor was the evidence of the racecourse. The horsemen of the day seem quickly to have realized that here was a magic draught to instil a wonderful speed and stamina in the native racehorse. As the deeds of their progeny surpassed all dreams, there came, too, an urge to record for ever, on canvas, the creatures who achieved such miracles: Bay Bolton, Squirrel, Crab, and Flying Childers, 'the fleetest horse that was ever bred in all the world'. So it is that, from the very beginning of the thoroughbred racehorse, we have portraits of the great champions, the early pictures replete with that astonished veneration recorded in the match books of the time.

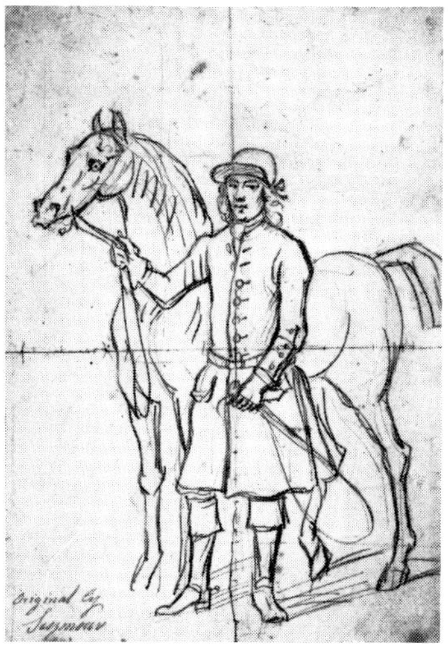

James Seymour: *Sketch of a Racehorse held by a Groom*. Pencil on washed mount, 27.5 × 19.5 cm. Royal Library, Windsor Castle

And what supernatural creatures John Wootton's thoroughbreds are! In his pic-

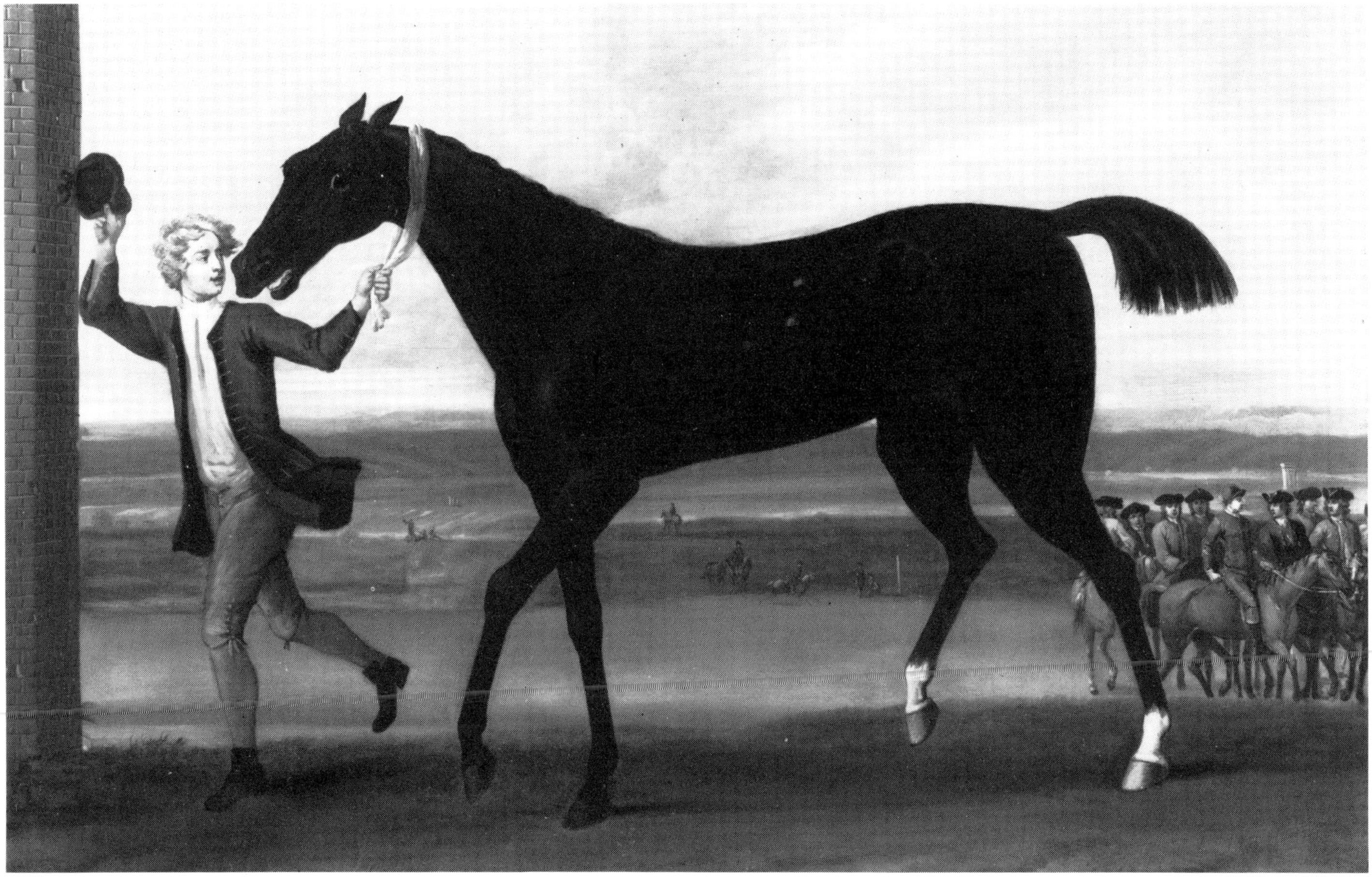

John Wootton: *Black at Newmarket (The Duke of Rutland's Bonny Black).* 1715? Oil on canvas, 76.2 × 123.2 cm. Paul Mellon Collection, Yale Center for British Art, New Haven, Conn.

ture *Black at Newmarket*, the fair-haired boy leading the black horse by a scarf is like a young angel who has harnessed the devil himself. His portrait of the famous grey, Lamprey, shows the horse standing with an Olympian grandeur beside the work-aday and slightly grubby figures of his connections, who remain intent on one of those eternal bouts of expostulation between jockey, owner, and trainer, while a bemused Negro boy looks on (see p. 49). Wootton could be a careful, even meticulous painter and his human figures are closely observed, but his horses were designed to overwhelm and belittle the men around them. Clearly, the worship of the thoroughbred had already begun. James Seymour's paintings too are acts of obeisance. The horses, huge and elaborately caparisoned, are attended by impassive acolytes or surrounded by humble altar boys, straw in hand, bowed at their feet. These pictures were no more intended to be anatomically accurate than was a Gothic altarpiece. They are the undisguised icons of a new faith.

In the middle of the eighteenth century came one of those periods when man, nature, and circumstance conspire to nurture a flowering of creativity. Newton had laid the foundations of the new scientific age of enlightenment, and a spirit of inquiry and experimentation was rife in England. Watt was developing the steam-engine. Priestley was isolating oxygen from the gases in the atmosphere. Disciples were copying 'Turnip' Townshend's new scientific agriculture from his estates in East Anglia. Robert Bakewell, breeding back continually to his finest stock, had shown how to refine superb strains of sheep and cattle. Lind and Hanway were launching the infant science of nutrition. In sport and art alike, the search for perfection of form was stimulated by a new degree of scientific understanding about the systems of life. Half a dozen of England's greatest painters were born in that extraordinary fifty years: Gainsborough, Reynolds, Romney, Turner, Constable, and the man who was to transform the world of animal painting, George Stubbs.

Born in Liverpool in 1724, Stubbs was imbued with the spirit of his age. He moved to Yorkshire when he was 20 years old and set about the study of anatomy. He attracted the attention of a York surgeon, Dr John Burton, who was engaged in writing *An Essay towards a Complete New System of Midwifery*. Burton asked Stubbs to engrave the illustrations, a skill he had learnt from a Leeds house-painter of his acquaintance. Eighteen drawings engraved on copper by Stubbs eventually accompanied the volume. Stubbs had already established a reputation in the north of England as a painter of animal and human portraits. But a determination to devote himself to mastering the skills of painting led him to abandon his clientele and go first to Italy to study, and then, on his return, to apply himself for a period of two years, when he was already 32 years old, to the study of the anatomy of the horse. With extraordinary singleness of purpose, he installed himself in a farmhouse at Horkstow in Lincolnshire, accompanied by his lifelong partner, Mary Spencer, where, remote from any opposition to his gruesome enterprise, he set about dissecting carcasses of horses in the utmost detail. He installed an arrangement of slings and pulleys which permitted him to hold the horses in different positions so that he could analyse the movement of sinews and muscles. The work was conducted with the

George Stubbs: *Two Drawings for 'The Anatomy of the Horse'*. 1758–9. Pencil, 36.8 × 49.5 cm (l.), 36.8 × 18.4 cm (r.). Royal Academy of Arts, London

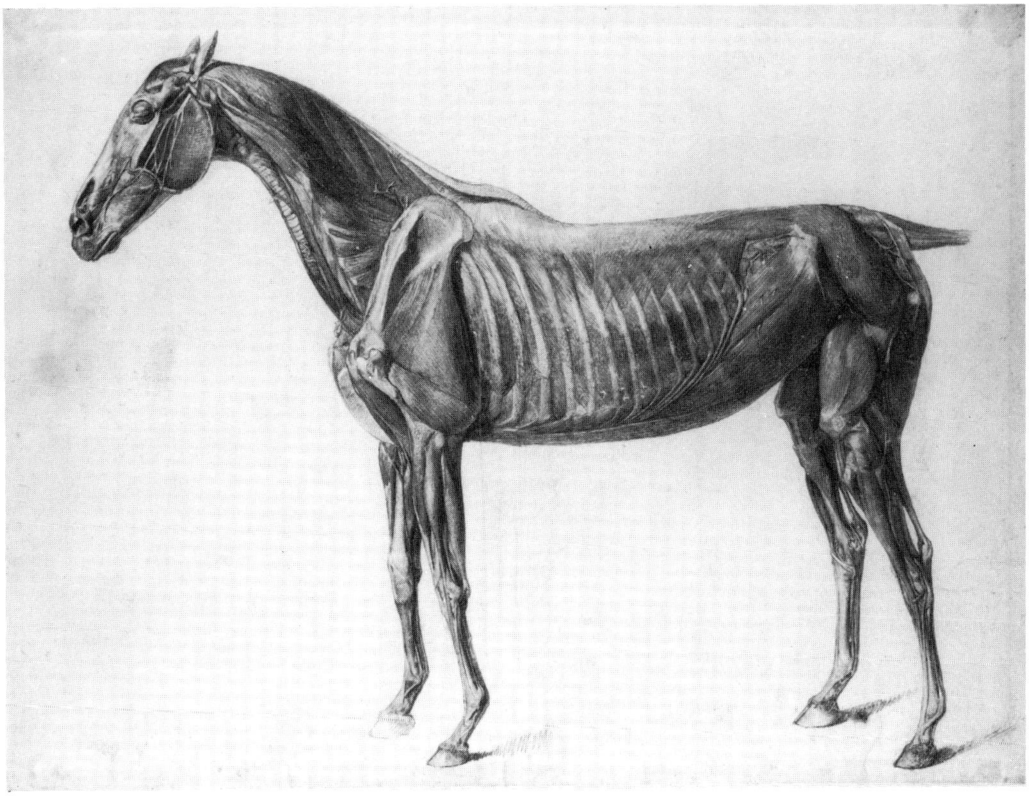

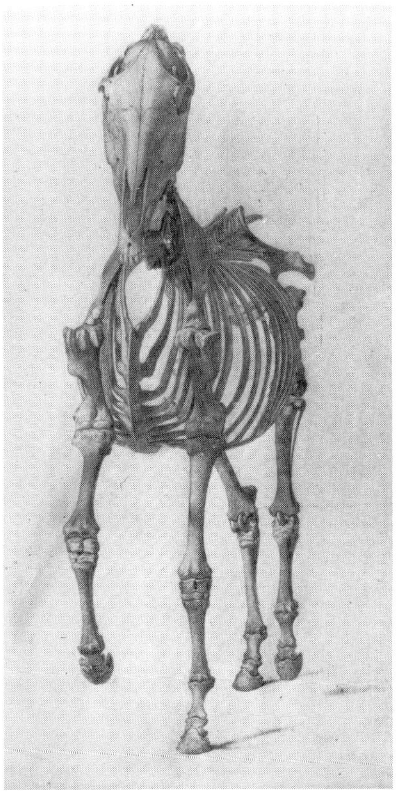

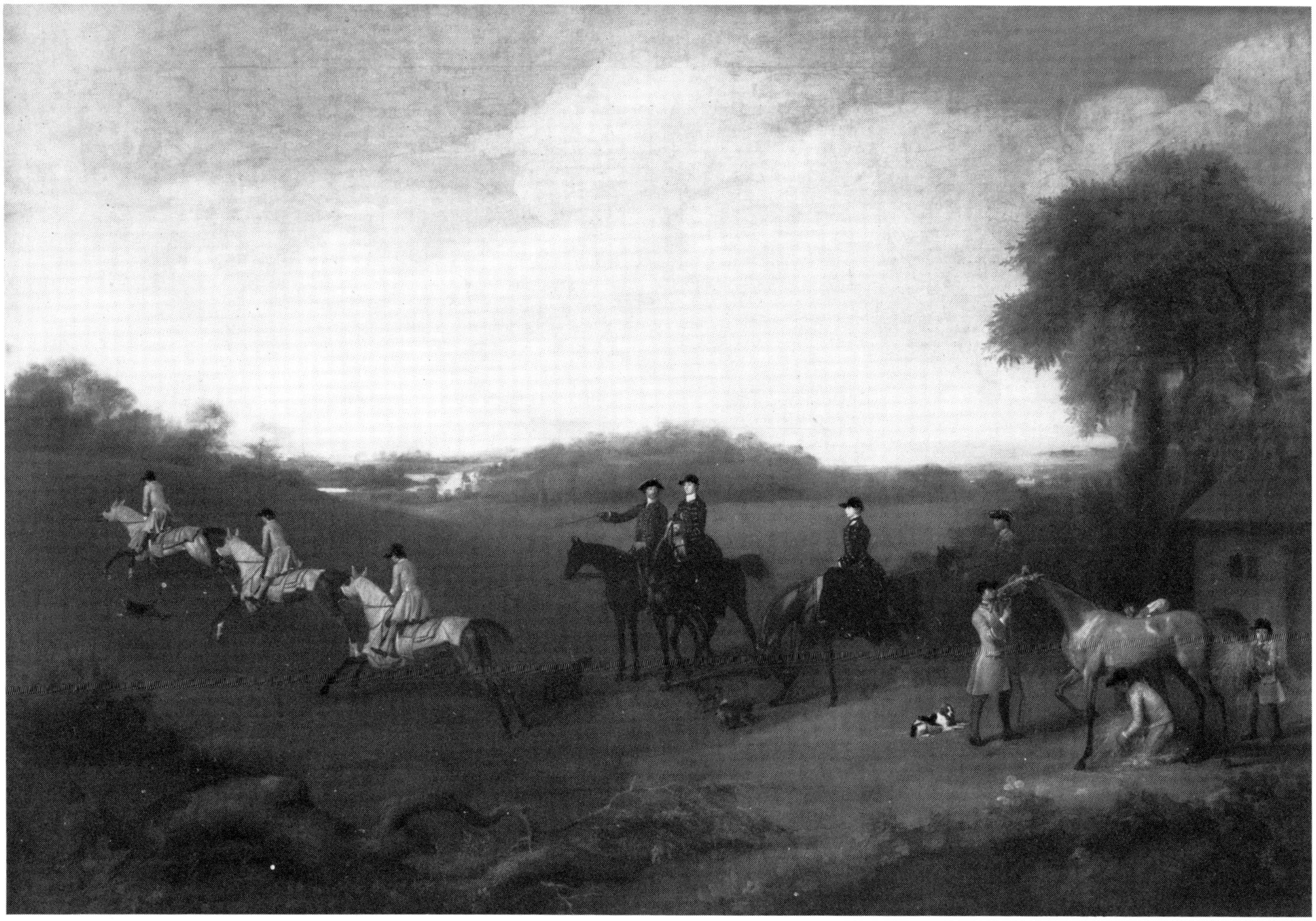

George Stubbs: *The Duke of Richmond's Horses Exercising*. 1760–1. Oil on canvas, 127.6 × 205.1 cm. Goodwood House, Chichester

most rigid precision. The resulting studies, showing the dissection at every stage down to the basic skeleton, were published in 1766 as *The Anatomy of the Horse*.

Stubbs emerged from this retreat to a racing world that was ready to appreciate his genius. The sportsmen of the 1760s, Lords Grosvenor, Portland, and Rockingham among them, were no longer content to have merely artistic impressions of their favourite horses. They were connoisseurs, and were eager for portraits which recorded the subtleties of form which they saw in their animals, as well as the vigour and the glory. Stubbs found immediate success. In 1762 he went to Eaton Hall and painted *The Grosvenor Hunt*. From Goodwood there came *The Duke of Richmond's Horses Exercising*, and at Wentworth he painted the life-size picture of Whistlejacket (see p. 58). These pictures are not only anatomically precise, with the tendons, muscles, and surface veins faithfully rendered, but they also pulsate with life. The grey horse bridling at the sight of the stag at bay in *The Grosvenor Hunt* and the foal suckling in the picture of *Mares and Foals by a Stream* still create a sense of wonder today. To have seen them during that first decade of George III's reign must have been a revelation.

OPPOSITE
George Stubbs: *The Grosvenor Hunt* (detail). 1762. Oil on canvas, 149.9 × 241.3 cm. Private collection

Stubbs was not alone. Sawrey Gilpin had come down from Carlisle to study painting at Samuel Scott's school in Covent Garden. He was soon taken up by the

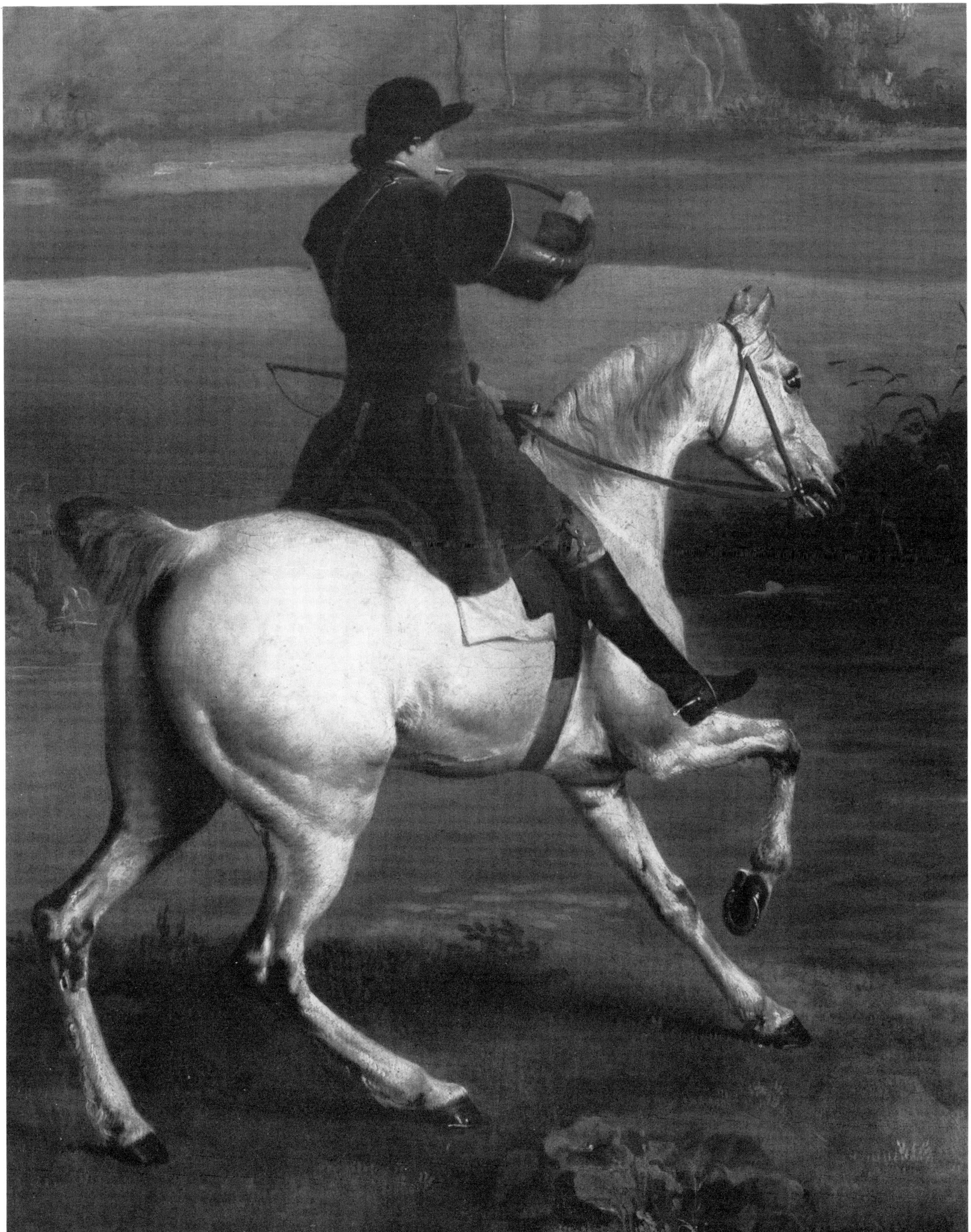

Duke of Cumberland and he remained in demand to the end of his long life. A contemporary wrote: 'Mr Gilpin is inferior to Mr Stubbs in anatomical knowledge, but is superior to him in grace and genius.' It is not necessary to adopt this judgement wholeheartedly to appreciate the splendour of his portrait of Highflyer (see p. 67). The work of George Garrard too, a pupil of Gilpin's, was felicitous enough to elicit a commission from Sir Joshua Reynolds. Stubbs himself turned away from racehorse pictures for the best part of twenty years, concentrating on his enamels, his work with Josiah Wedgwood, and his studies of more exotic animals, like leopards, lions, and cheetahs. He returned to the subject, apparently out of financial need,

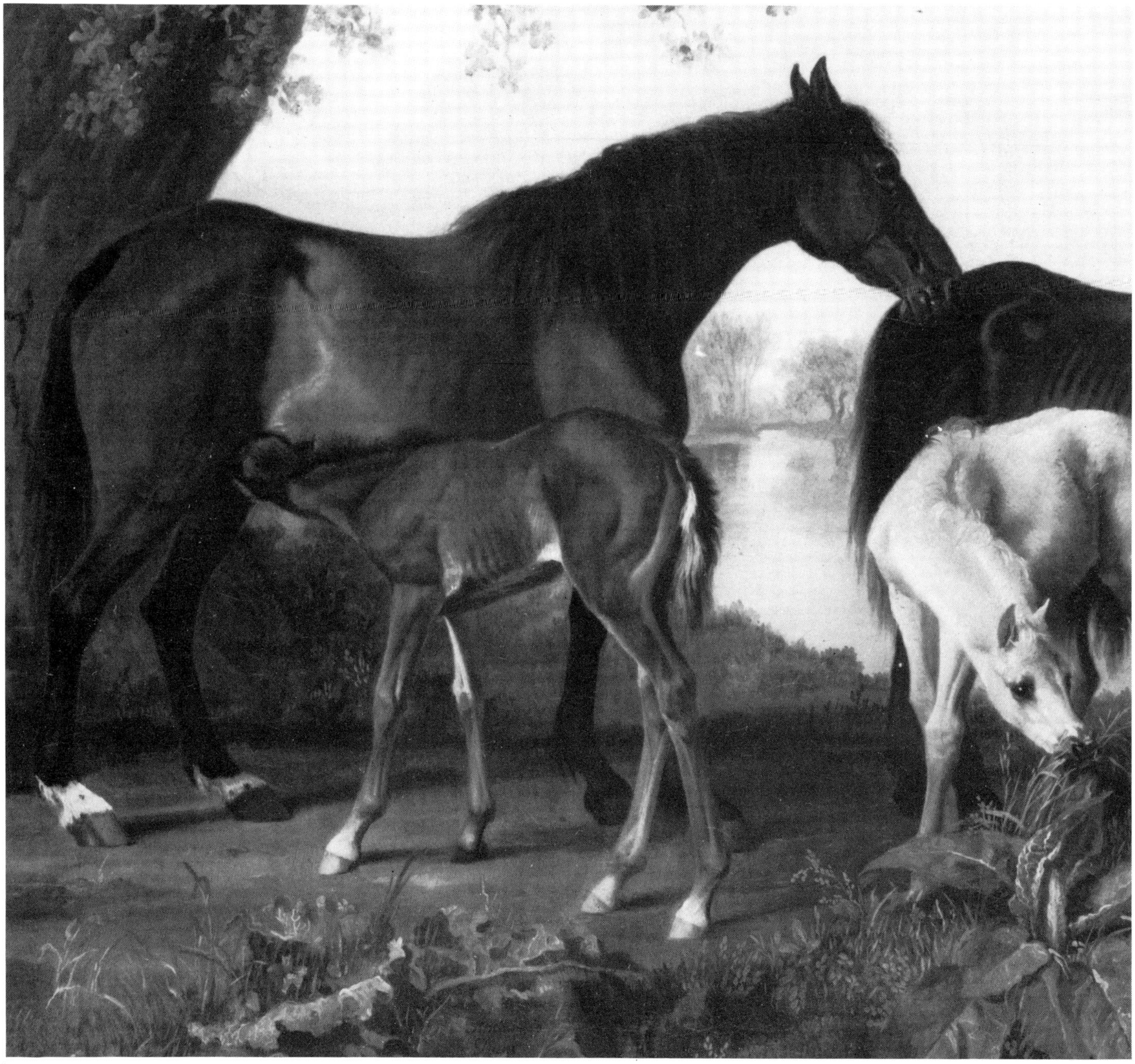

George Stubbs: *Mares and Foals by a Stream* (detail). 1763–4. Oil on canvas, 59.7 × 100.3 cm. Euston Hall, Thetford

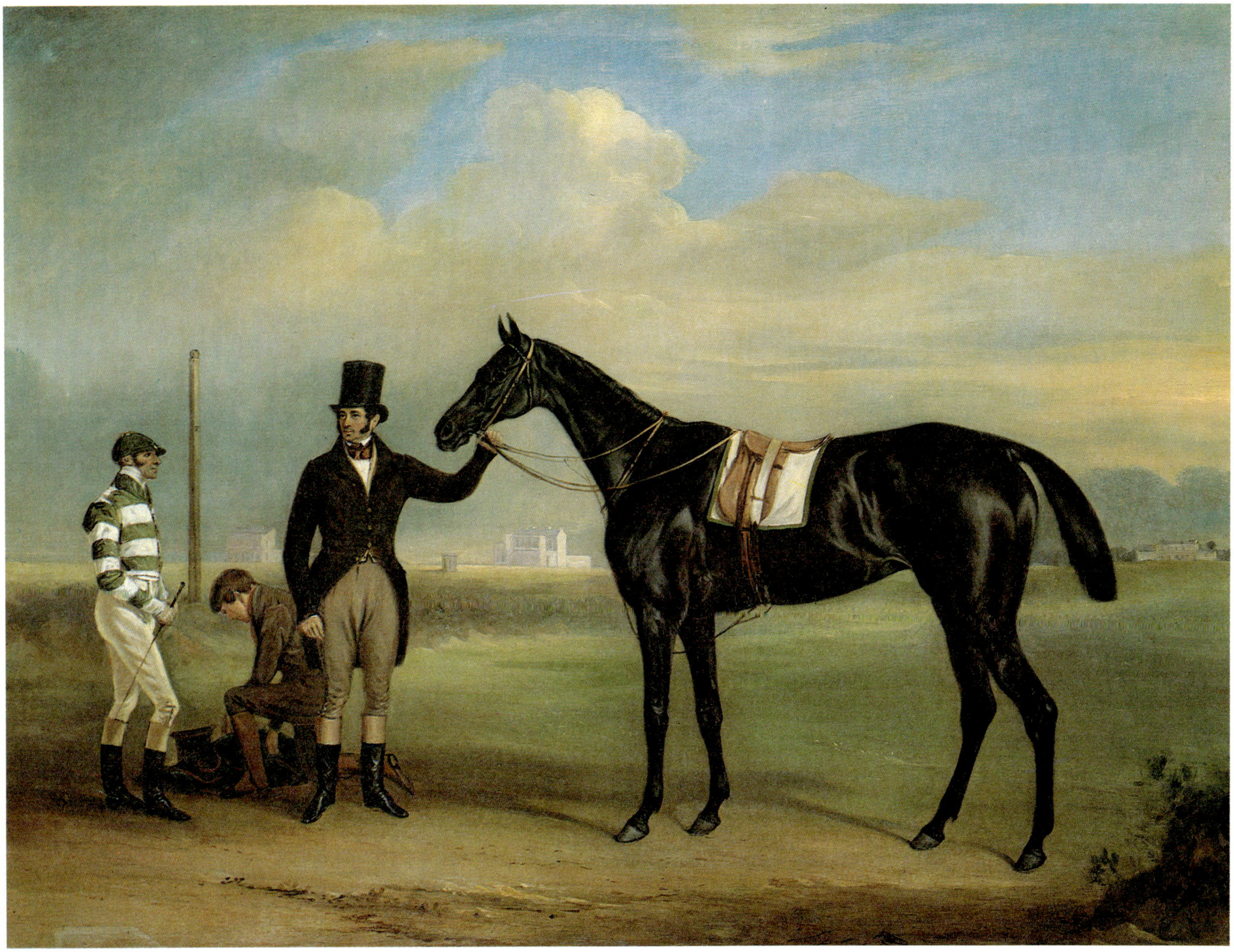

John E. Ferneley: *Pussy, with her jockey 'Old' John Day, held by her owner Mr T. Cosby*. 1834. Oil on canvas, 81.2 × 107.2 cm. Private collection

with the series of sixteen portraits of racehorses produced for the *Turf Review* in 1794.

The heirs of Stubbs – Ben Marshall, J. F. Herring, John E. Ferneley – inherited the most confident years of British racing. From being an aristocratic sport, thoroughbred racing became the concern of a wide public. Racing had always seemed immune to the politics of the nation. Cromwell and the Stuarts alike imported Arab horses. The great Classic races were established when the thoughts of the nation's leaders might well have been diverted towards the revolution in America or the deeds of Dr Guillotine's machine in France. The Napoleonic Wars caused scarcely a ripple, indeed, racing flourished as never before. Newspapers sprang up chronicling the events of the Turf and carrying prints of all the leading horses of the day. It was a profitable time to be an equestrian artist. Herring painted twenty-six consecutive winners of the St Leger, and thirty-four in all, for reproduction as engravings, and was able to maintain himself in some affluence to the end of his days on his 30-acre estate at Meopham Park in Kent. Ferneley made a good living without having to move from Melton Mowbray in Leicestershire, though racehorses were only an occasional subject. For this was also the heyday of the country gentleman, with hunts, such as the Quorn and the Pytchley, replete with thrusters keen to see themselves and their mounts immortalized on canvas. Marshall had sixty pictures reproduced in the *Sporting Magazine* and also ran a flourishing studio school in London, through which passed Abraham Cooper and Ferneley.

The sporting artists of the first half of the nineteenth century were part of an uproarious circus which encompassed the most reckless gambling, unabashed chicanery by owners and jockeys, and a search for glory on the Turf which rewarded few and ruined many. William Day, the jockey, quoted in his memoirs a description of social life at Doncaster the night before the 1832 St Leger:

> To see the Duke of Cleveland's white sardonic countenance, and Gully's threatening overcharged brow, with Crockey's satanic smile and working jaw, surrounding the table was to view a picture worthy the pencil of Rembrandt. Old Ord, of Beeswing notoriety, mounted the table, being howling drunk as usual and unshaved for a fortnight, and denounced the whole gang as a crew of robbers and miscreants, for whom the gallows would be too good. Then old Jemmy Bland, an atrocious 'leg' of the ancient top-booted semi-highwayman school, and old Crockey got set by the ears like two worn-out mastiffs, and had a few words through their false teeth.

Unfortunately, there was no Rembrandt around to depict these scenes. We must look to Marshall for a flavour of the distinctive life-style of the men who made their living from the Turf: the crumpled figures clustered round the horses, hats and faces alike, battered and bent. In his studies of jockeys we see the weasel mien and hatchet features of the men who openly gambled both for and against their mounts, and almost as openly 'pulled' them.

Marshall was a skilled anatomical observer, but his horses frequently look as though they have been subjected to the most extreme degree of sweating and wasting, which was certainly in vogue at the time, though frowned upon by some distinguished men of the Turf, such as Sir Charles Bunbury. It was Herring and Ferneley who perfected the art of portraying the wonderful texture and lustre of a racehorse's skin. Herring's superb picture of Memnon (see p. 100), the 1825 St Leger winner, and Ferneley's of Pussy, the 1834 Oaks winner, both painted against cloudy skies, are supreme evocations of the thoroughbred at the height of its powers, coat gleaming, muscles tuned, ready for the moment of trial. In the middle years of the nineteenth century, Harry Hall took over the role of journeyman painter of each year's champions. When working on a large enough scale, as in his admiring picture of the French champion Gladiateur (see p. 129), Harry Hall could produce fine pieces, but there is a wearisome repetition in his innumerable horses in stables which dulls the appreciation of his talent.

From the very early days of the thoroughbred, there had been attempts to portray the racehorse not only at rest, before and after the contest, but also in action, in the throes of the race itself. Tillemans's pictures of this type are remarkably successful. His ebullient, even hilarious picture of the start of the King's Plate on the Round

Course at Newmarket, probably 1725, is also perhaps the most informative visual record we have of the early days of racing. In amongst the comic cameos of spectators being tossed boots over breeches from their hacks, there are some wonderfully surprising details. Can that really be the starter, his red and black flag at the ready, squatting at the top of a pole like some twentieth-century entrant for the *Guinness Book of Records*? There is the drummer and his boy apparently summoning the five contestants to the start. One jockey is just mounting, on his own – no leg up in those days! The ladies watch from their carriages, while the more staid among their menfolk cluster behind the racehorses. But already a number of young bloods have started hurtling their mounts down the course ahead of the runners, a practice which was to be a bane of racing for nearly 200 years, until the enclosed racecourses and the internal combustion engine finally put paid to it. The custom of wearing colours is obviously well established, and the rubbing-down house already built. Indeed, Newmarket was to change little for another 150 years.

Pictures of the great encounters of the Turf were always in demand. J. N. Sartorius recorded the famous matches between Rockingham and Dungannon, and Kitt Carr and Lurcher. Henry Alken junior specialized in scenes of Derby Day at Epsom. But the excitement and atmosphere of these works is blemished to the modern eye by a fatal flaw: the absurd rocking-horse action of the galloping horses. It has been claimed that this convention was handed down through the ages and across the continents from ancient China. Nevertheless, it is astonishing that men who travelled, worked, and disported themselves on horseback all their lives were not able to work out, if not from the look, then from the feel of the action under them, how a horse actually cantered and galloped, in what order and with what motion the feet were placed on the ground. Stubbs himself painted one of the most ludicrous versions in his picture of Baronet (see p. 64). Even his first and finest portrait of Gimcrack is diminished by the cartoon quality of the racehorses in action in the background.

Illumination arrived with the advent of photography. The camera, perceived at first as a devilish machine which would obliterate portrait painting – the artist Edward Troye actually gave up work in despair – in fact became a source of revelation. In 1872 Eadweard Muybridge took a series of photographs in California which were greeted with stunned astonishment by horsemen and artists alike. These were the pictures published as 'The Horse in Motion'. Muybridge was financed by Leland Stanford, a former Governor of California and one of the builders of the

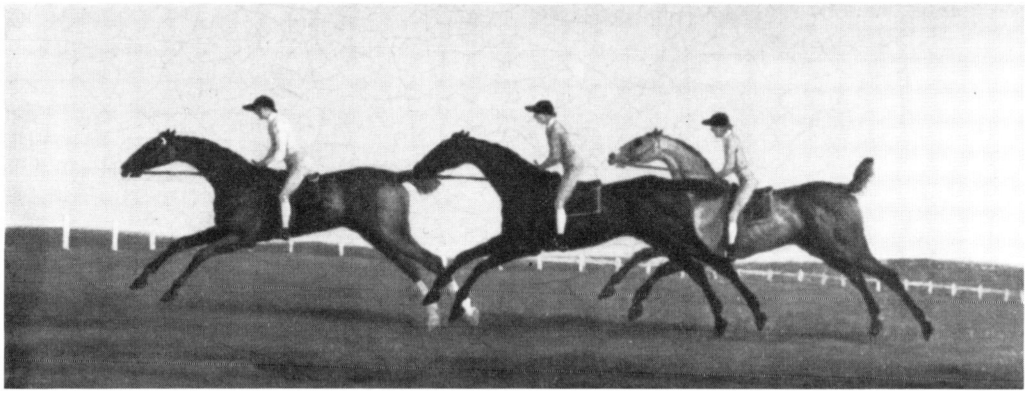

George Stubbs: *Gimcrack* (detail).
See p. 60

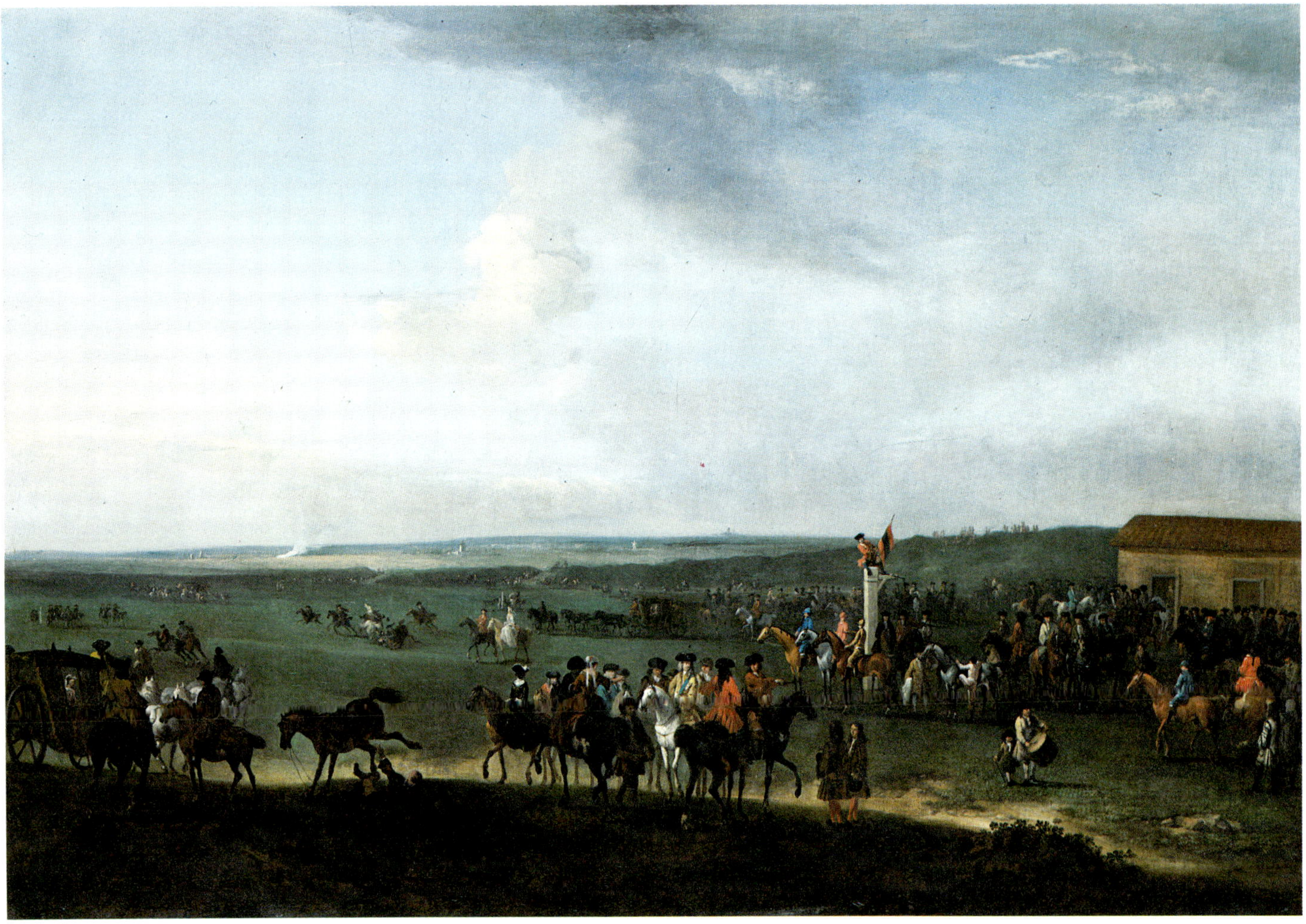

Peter Tillemans: *Racing for the King's Plate at Newmarket. c.*1725. Oil on canvas, 87 × 99.7 cm. Paul Mellon Collection, Yale Center for British Art, New Haven, Conn.

Central Pacific Railroad. Stanford was watching some of the trotting horses on his Palo Alto ranch near San Francisco, so the story goes, when he became involved in an argument about their action. Stanford maintained that the horses did, at some point, have all four feet off the ground. As disputes among horsemen often do, reasoned disputation degenerated into a wager; Stanford backed his opinion with $25,000. Whether Stanford's interest was pecuniary or more disinterestedly scientific, he employed Muybridge to resolve the matter. Muybridge set up a series of twenty-four cameras beside the race-track. Each one in succession was triggered by the horse breaking a thread, so that a consecutive strip of photographs was obtained. Stanford was proved right. Trotting horses do remove all four feet from the ground at the same time. Muybridge also took sequences of the other gaits of the horse. These demonstrated that 2,000 years of convention could be wrong. The rocking-horse gallop does not happen. A galloping horse never has all four feet off the ground when its legs are outstretched.

In order to display the results of his work, Muybridge invented what he called a 'zoopraxiscope': basically a wheel on which he mounted his transparencies, so that, when revolving, it produced a moving picture of the horse in action. With this

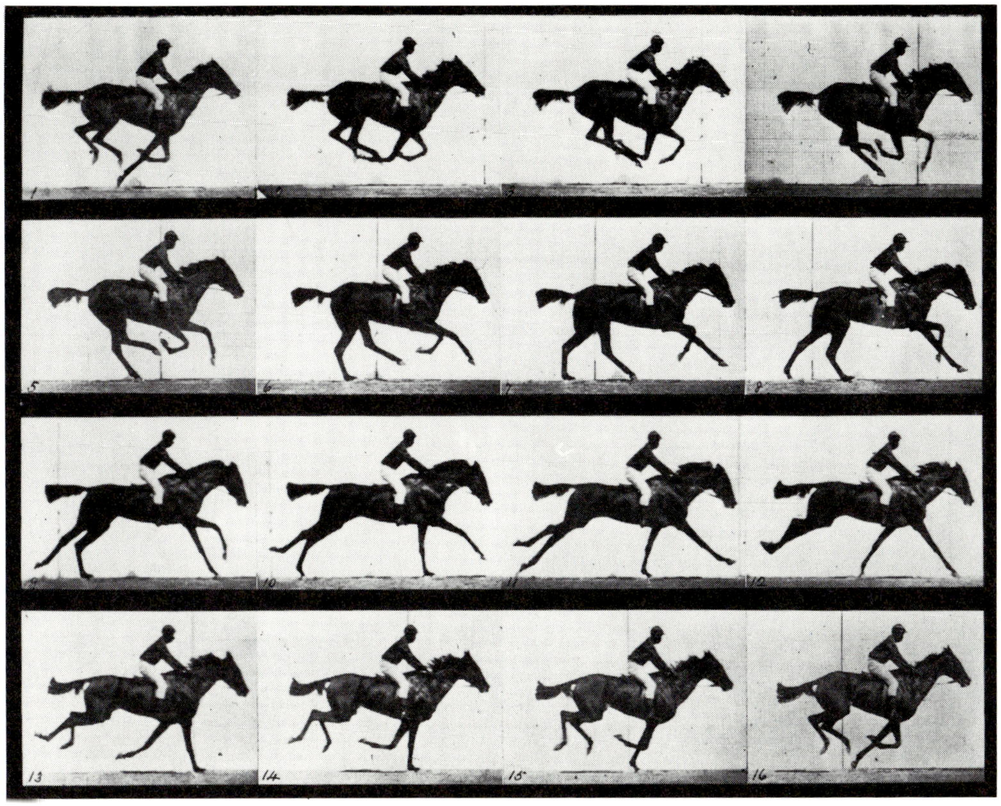

Eadweard Muybridge: *A Galloping Horse in Motion*. Published in *Animal Locomotion*, 1887. Eadweard Muybridge Collection, Kingston upon Thames Museum

device he set out to tour the east of America and then Europe, including France, Germany, and England. Private gatherings of artists were organized to view the photographs, and some of the Impressionists, particularly, seem to have been interested. (Muybridge followed his work on horses with photographs of the human figure in motion.) Degas, who had been fascinated by the atmosphere of the racecourse in the 1860s and early 1870s, painting scenes at Longchamp and copying English sporting prints, seems to have been stimulated by seeing the Muybridge pictures. From 1880

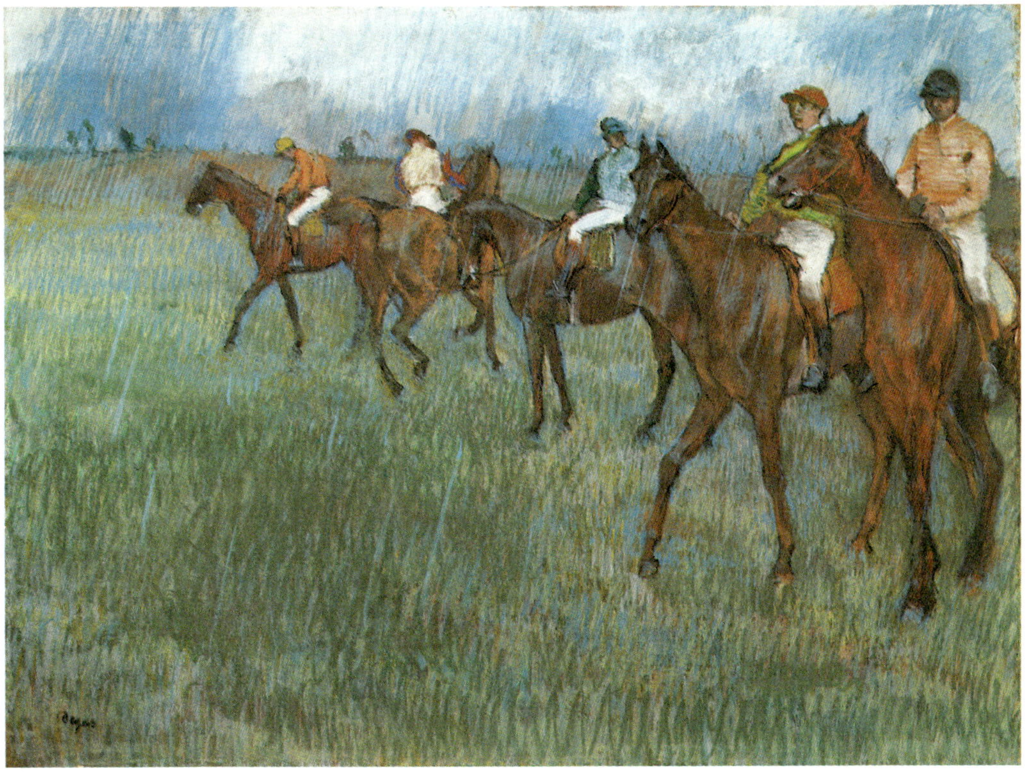

Edgar Degas: *Jockeys in the Rain*. *c*.1886. Pastel on paper, 47 × 65 cm. Glasgow Art Gallery and Museum

he returned to the race-track as a subject and produced accurate studies of horses in movement, such as the beautiful rendering of horses edgily milling about at the start in *Jockeys in the Rain*. Just as Stubbs's understanding of the anatomy of the horse had transformed equine portraiture more than a century before, so Muybridge's photographs inaugurated a theme which still dominates the art of painting racehorses today. The desire to capture the supreme excitement of the thoroughbred world, horses in action, giving their all on the race-track, became at last a feasible ambition for the painter.

Alfred Munnings was the first great English exponent of this synthesis of old skills and new insight. He had worked hard at his calling, hunting down an original edition of Stubbs's *The Anatomy of the Horse*, making drawings from Rosa Bonheur's *Anatomical Horse*, copying from an equine skeleton in the local museum, then going to London to work from the bones of St Simon in the Natural History Museum and Eclipse at the Royal Veterinary College. But Munnings was also a romantic. Contemplating the mortal remains of Eclipse, he wrote:

> Think of that famous horse's skeleton, once covered and articulated with tendon, muscle and nerve, all under the rich dark chestnut coat, groomed and polished day after day throughout his short span. That skull had once contained the brain and racing instincts of Eclipse. His eye had moved in and looked out from the dark socket. His lips had covered and been drawn over those teeth, had played with the bit and sneered when smelling something queer, and had played afterwards with many a mare at stud.

Munnings was fascinated with the 'electricity' in thoroughbreds. The nervous pageantry of racing – stripping the champions for action in the paddock, leading them prancing and highly keyed past the stands, the shifting tensions at the start – is a recurring theme of Munnings's work. John Skeaping, a generation younger than Munnings, was drawn repeatedly to the very thick of the action on the race-track. Whether with the brush, as in *Heavy Going at Arlington Park*, or in bronze, as with his sculpture of the finish of the 1974 Travers Stakes, *Hanging to the Left* (see p. 171), he loved the high drama of the contest itself. Though there are skilled portrait artists working today, such as Susan Crawford and Carolyn Alexander, it is still the Noble Contest on the track itself which is the elusive quarry of the present generation.

Among the artists who painted the thoroughbred in America, Edward Troye was the first to make for himself not only a successful livelihood, but a reputation that has lasted down to the present day. Many of his paintings were lost at the time of the Civil War, but there are still fine examples of his work which survive. Born in Switzerland, Troye had learned his skills in England, and, though obliged by an exotic life-style to work hard, he seems to have been imbued with a sense of the historic value of his pictures. There are echoes of Stubbs's *Turf Review* series in Troye's project to publish *The Race Horses of America* in the last years of his career (reissued in a handsome edition by Alexander Mackay Smith in 1981). He had great natural ability, and faults of youth and inexperience are scarcely apparent in an early picture like *American Eclipse* (see p. 93). The paintings of his mature years, such as the portrait of *Asteroid at Stud*, are confident and luxurious enough to match anything produced by his contemporaries in Europe. Troye was not, of course, alone. Im-

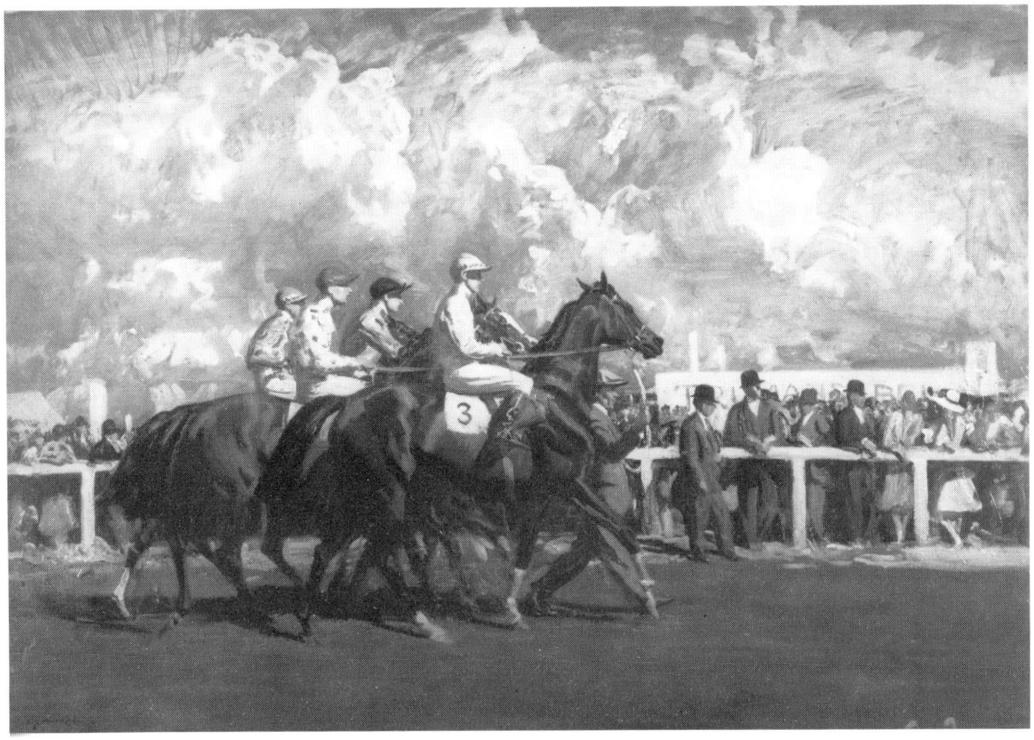

Sir Alfred Munnings: *Going out at Epsom. c.*1958. Oil on canvas, 86.4 × 125.7 cm. Private collection

migrants and visitors, like Henri Delattre and Alvan Fisher, were working at the race-tracks on the East Coast. Delattre had a rather primitive, but vigorous style, as seen in his picture of the match between Mac and Zachary Taylor at Philadelphia in 1848. Alvan Fisher from Dedham, Massachusetts, is one of the earliest American

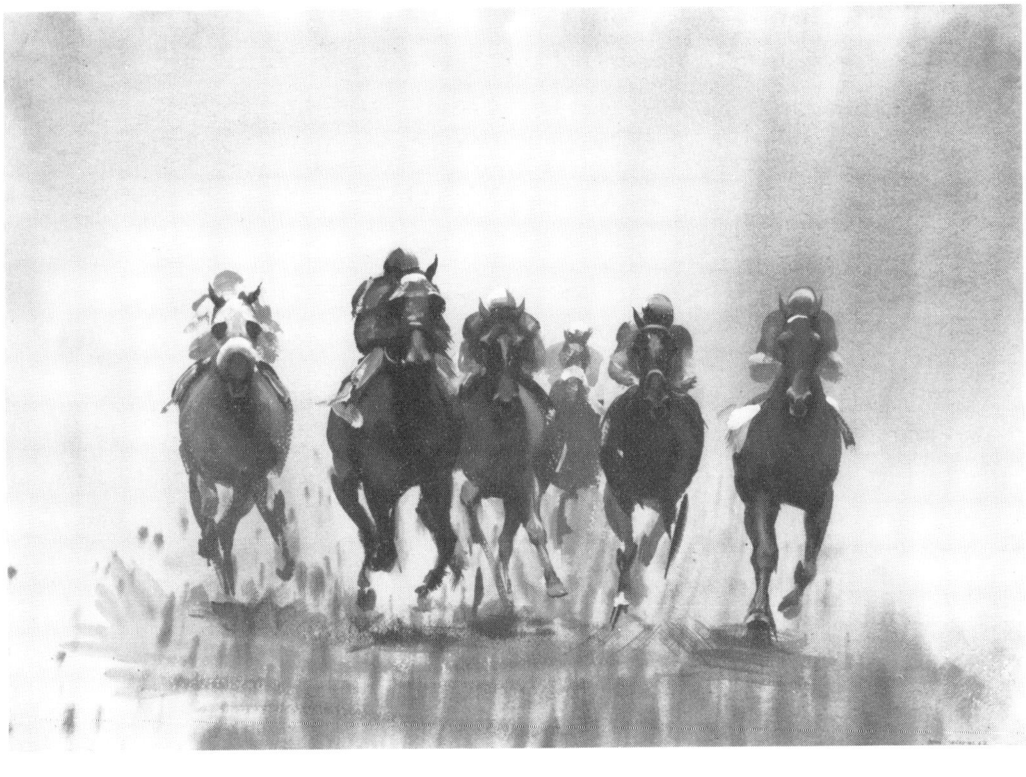

John Skeaping: *Heavy Going at Arlington Park.* 1967. Gouache, 54.6 × 74.9 cm. Private collection

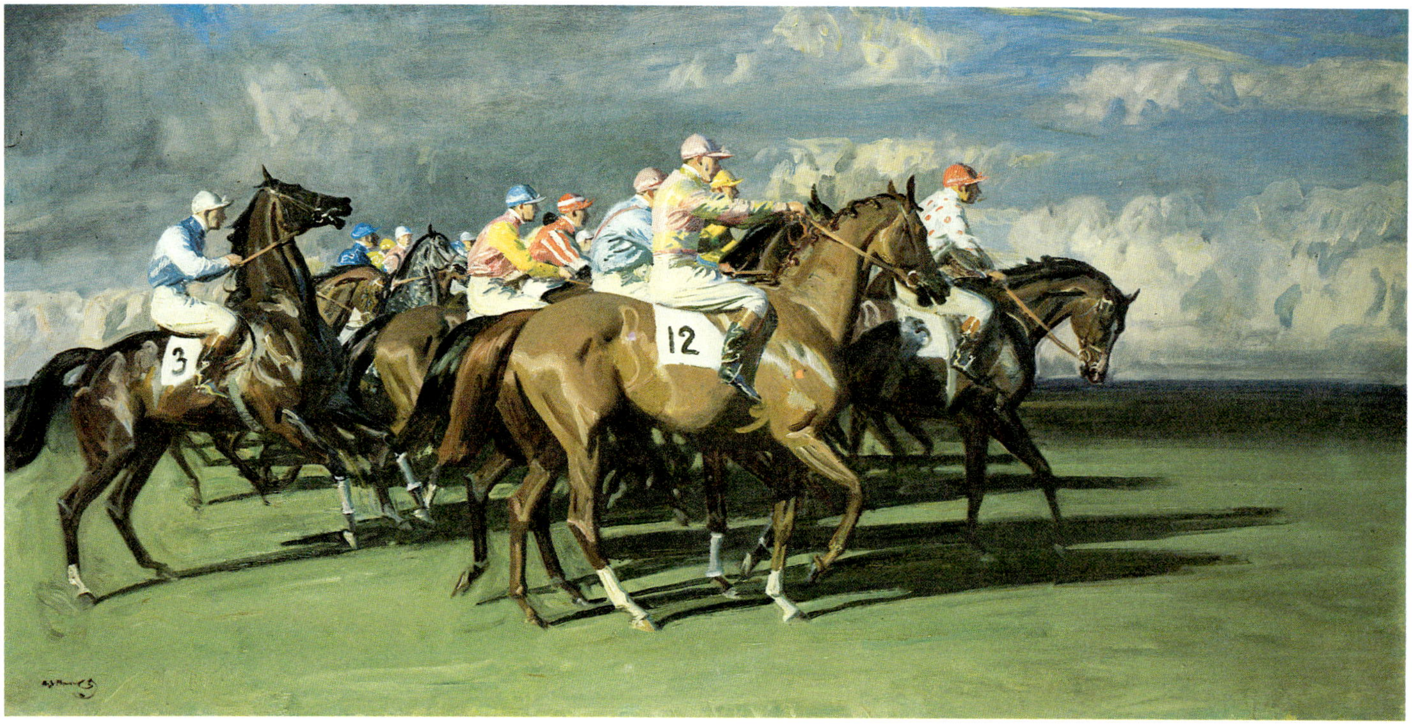

Sir Alfred Munnings: *Start at Newmarket*. *c*.1937. Oil on board, 91.5 × 183 cm. Private collection

sporting artists whose signature has survived (see p. 93). There are also renderings of the general racing scene from the mid-nineteenth century. Charles Severin composed illuminating pictures of race-meetings in the 1840s which are detailed and exact, down to the man checking his betting slip, yet full of drama, as shown by the print of Peytona's defeat of Fashion at the Union Course on Long Island, New York, in 1845.

In the present day, a New Yorker, Richard Stone Reeves, is probably the most sought-after painter of the thoroughbred horse in the world. But the reputations of those artists who worked in America during the eighty years or so between the ascendancies of Troye and Reeves have been overshadowed. It has been their misfortune that the great dramas of animal painting in their time lay far to the west, in the frontier sagas of Fanny Palmer, Karl Bodmer, George Catlin, Frederic Remington, Arthur Fitzwilliam Tait, and the chroniclers of the Indian Wars. Furthermore, some of the great American collectors of sporting art, such as William Woodward and Paul Mellon, have concentrated on English painters.

However, there are special qualities in the American racehorse painters of that time. Henry Stull's amused, almost caricaturist's eye produced memorable images of horses in action, as in his portrait of Hanover at the gallop (see p. 146), the like of which are not to be found in Europe. Gean Smith, working in Chicago and New York, then Galveston in Texas, was more at home with the trotters and the sulkies, but nevertheless he left a record of thoroughbred champions, such as Imp, that stretches across forty years. Franklin B. Voss, as keen a foxhunter as there was in Maryland during the early years of this century, became almost an artist in residence to the Whitneys and the Vanderbilts. His pictures are infused with the warmth and affluence of the paddocks around Baltimore.

OPPOSITE ABOVE
Edward Troye: *Asteroid at Stud*. 1870. Oil on canvas, 64.8 × 79.4 cm. Private collection

OPPOSITE BELOW
Henri Delattre: *Mac and Zachary Taylor*. 1850. Oil on canvas, 70.5 × 111.1 cm. Private collection

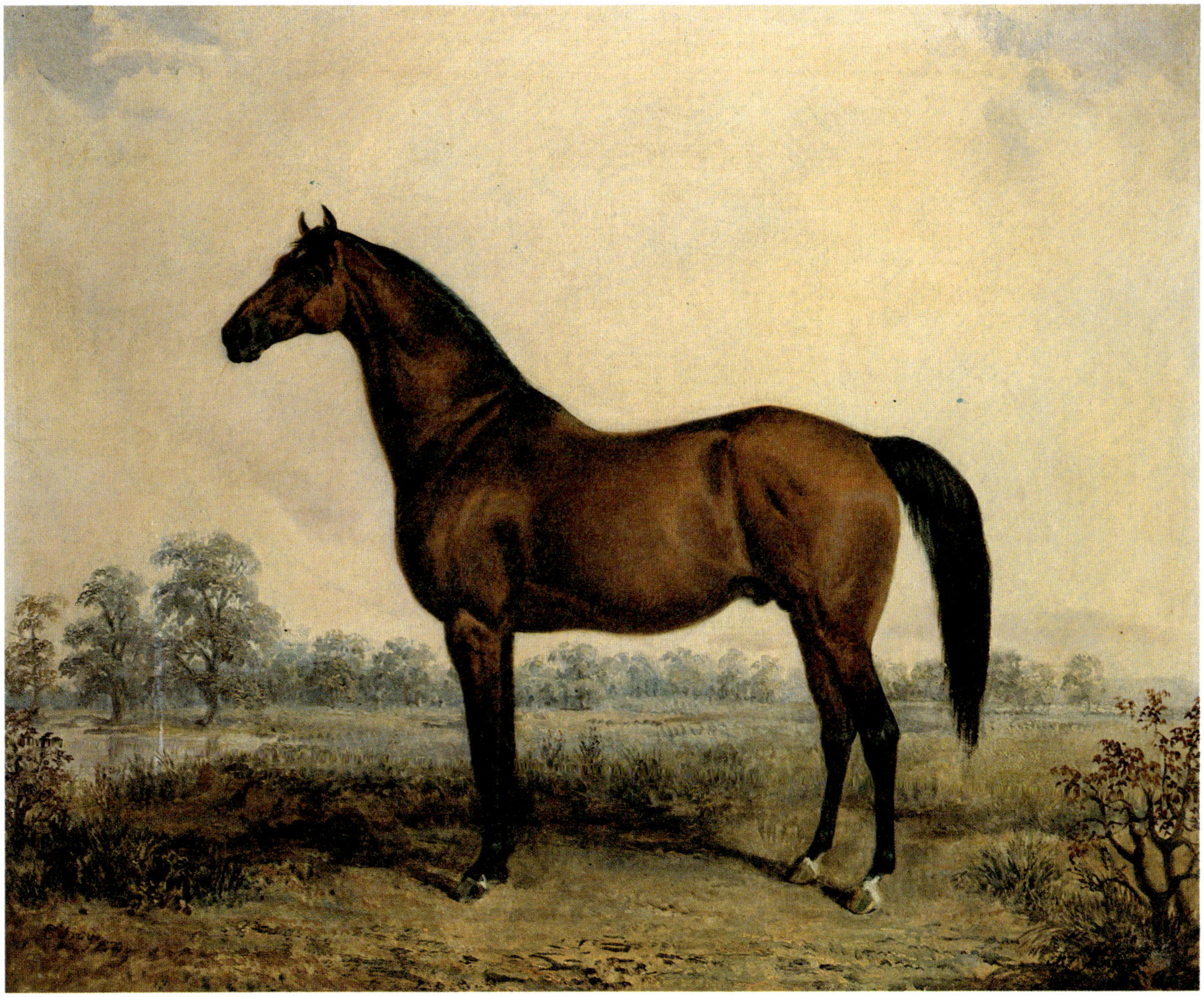

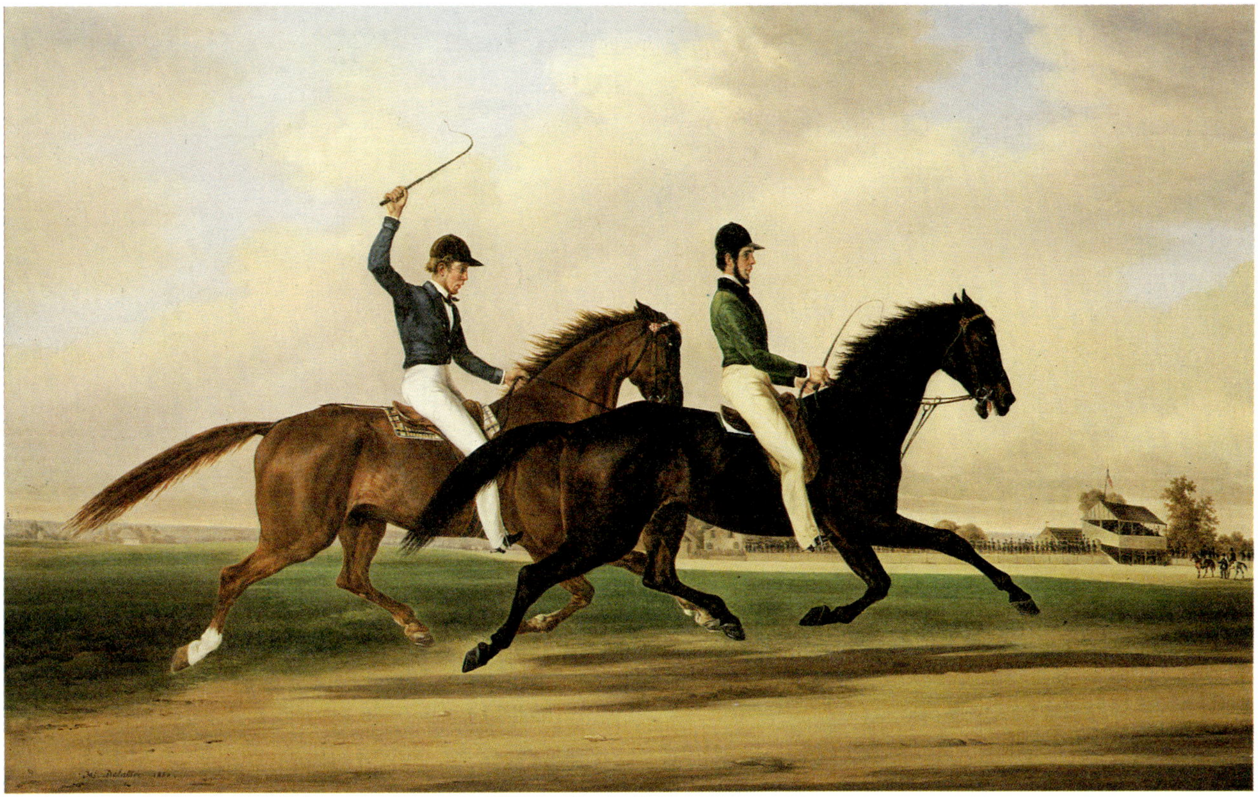

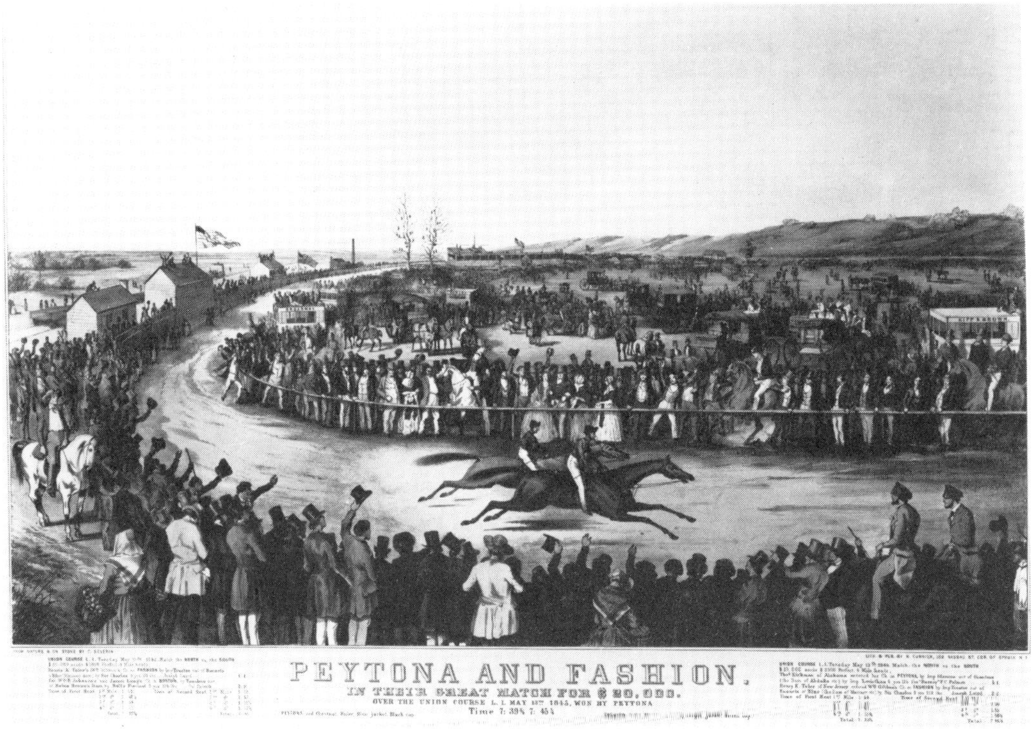


Charles Severin: *Peytona and Fashion*. Lithograph by N. Currier, 1845. Harry T. Peters Collection, Museum of the City of New York

Voss was a friend of Alfred Munnings, and today it is clear that the separate traditions of American and British horse painting have merged as effectively as the bloodstock industries on either side of the Atlantic, with Koehler, Reeves, and the ladies of the 'British School' at home equally in Newmarket, Suffolk, and in Lexington, Kentucky.

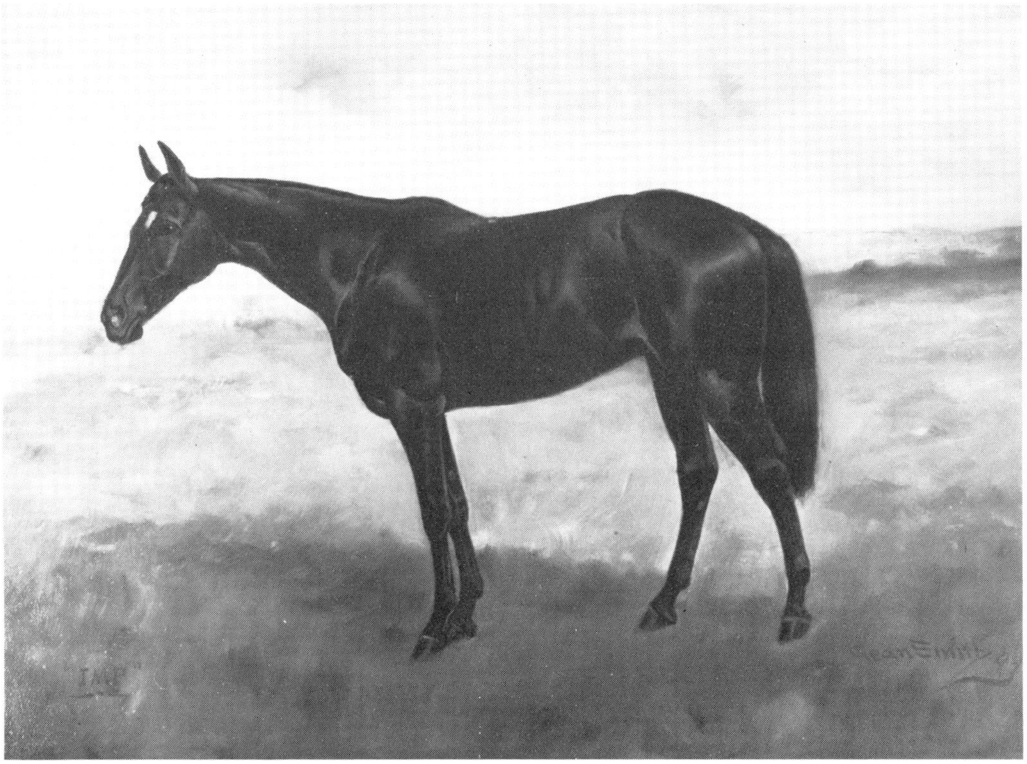

Gean Smith: *Imp*. 1894. Oil on wood, 38.1 × 55.9 cm. National Museum of Racing, Saratoga Springs, NY

No doubt horses have been raced against each other from the first moment that men climbed upon their backs, whether it be in ancient China, on the plains of Tartary, or in the great hippodrome of Byzantium. But the records of organized racing along the lines by which thoroughbreds are tried today date back only to the seventeenth century. There is an account of a cup race at Richmond in North Yorkshire in 1662, and there were certainly races at Hyde Park in London during the same era. Oliver Cromwell had an eye for a horse. He imported the stallion known as Place's White Turk, who appears in Matchem's pedigree and thus in Derby winners such as Airborne and Santa Claus in recent years. But it was the Restoration and the arrival of King Charles II which launched the era of racing in something like its modern form.

King Charles restored the palace at Newmarket, part of which is still extant behind the High Street. The stables which once housed the King's horses are still in use today as part of trainer Bruce Hobbs's yard. Newmarket must have been a roistering place, with Lady Castlemaine's gambling hell in full swing – she was said to have won £15,000 one night and lost £25,000 the next – and Nell Gwynn installed just across the road. The King himself was a furious competitor on the Heath. In 1671 he won the Plate, and again in 1674. 'I do assure you the King won by good horsemanship,' wrote Sir Robert Carr. Charles does not appear to have maintained a royal stud, but the importation of Arab horses certainly revived. John Evelyn records in his diary the presence of the King when three Arabs were brought over from Hamburg: 'They trotted like does, as if they did not feel the ground.'

Already in King Charles's time we hear of the man who was to be 'Keeper of the Running Horses' to four sovereigns, Tregonwell Frampton. Frampton should properly be regarded as the first royal trainer in the modern sense. Indeed, he presided as acknowledged arbiter of Turf matters over the transition of racing from its seventeenth-century character of relatively informal meetings of gentlemen into the harbinger of modern organized sport, with regular meetings and agreed rules.

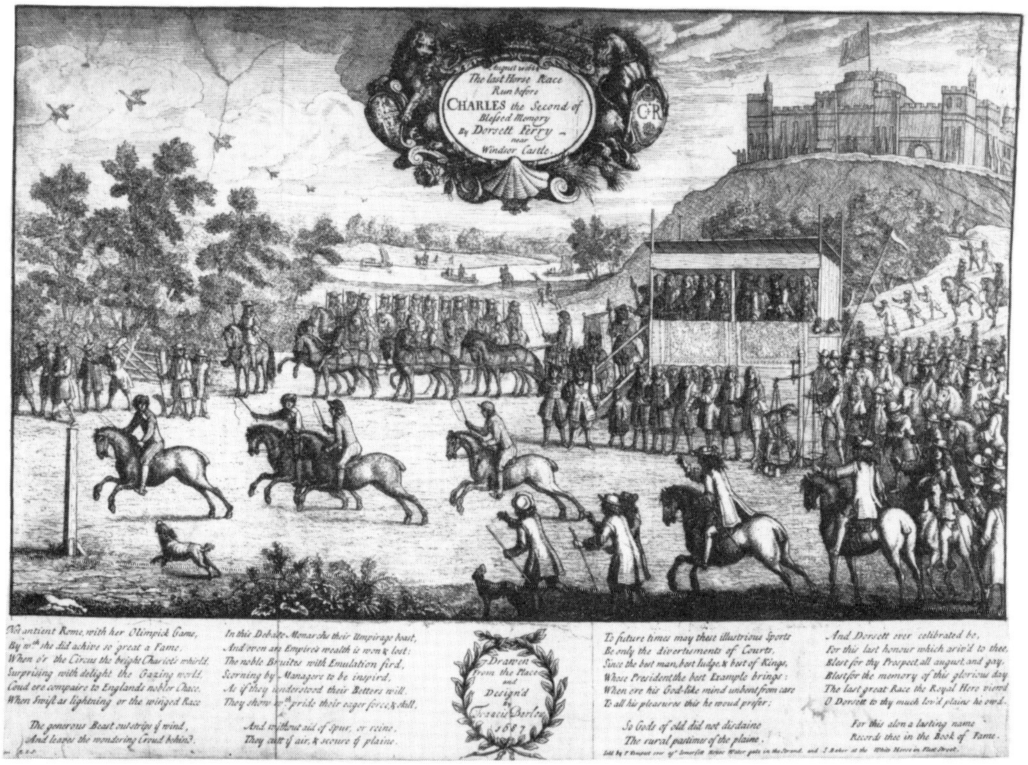


Francis Barlow: *The Last Horse-race run before Charles II by Dorsett Ferry near Windsor Castle, 24 August 1684.* Engraving, 1687, 22.4 × 37.1 cm. The British Museum, London

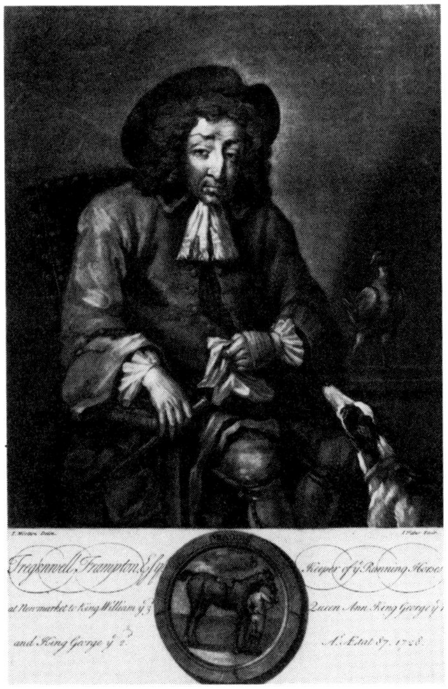

John Wootton: *Tregonwell Frampton and Dragon*. Mezzotint by John Faber, *c.*1728, 39 × 25.5 cm. The British Museum, London

Frampton had a modern enough cast in other ways. He was a renowned 'plunger', or betting man. He had a ruthless attitude to his charges, having, according to the rumours of the town, gelded a fine stallion called Dragon in order to qualify him for a match. The story has been discounted, but the reputation of the hard man remains. He was up to every trick: 'pulling' horses, colluding with rivals, disguising weights and performances in trials.

Frampton, who came from Dorchester in Dorset, was already past 50 years old when he was given charge of King William III's horses. He was to retain the job through the reigns of Queen Anne and George I, and into the reign of George II. Old-fashioned in dress, to the point of eccentricity, he was prone to wander up to court at any time he fancied and demand to see the monarch. But there has frequently been a special dispensation for those who have had care of the royal racehorses; Edward VII demanded daily reports on his Derby hopefuls and put aside all other business when the important priorities of Epsom required consideration. Queen Anne was an early exemplar. She was mad on the horses. As well as maintaining the royal interest in Newmarket, she travelled wherever there was good racing to be had. Anne is chiefly remembered today as the founder of Royal Ascot, giving a plate worth 100 guineas for the first meeting in 1711, and attending herself with a large party from the court.

Frampton was instrumental in setting up a legendary betting race of the time. He had matched one of the Queen's horses against Old Merlin, a celebrated racer owned by Sir William Strickland, whose descendants in Yorkshire own racehorses to this day. Frampton inveigled Old Merlin's trainer into allowing a secret trial. Frampton put his horse in with 7 lb. overweight and still ran Old Merlin to a length. Confident of defeating the Yorkshire horse at level weights, Frampton and the fast company who seemed to share his 'secret' all plunged into the betting ring up to the hilt. Unfortunately, they had not reckoned with the Yorkshiremen indulging in an identical subterfuge. Old Merlin won. Such were the cries of pain and anguish from fleeced London gentry that an Act of Parliament was passed limiting the stake in any bet to £10. No doubt this measure was as honoured in the breach as every other attempt down the ages to curb the gambling instinct. Frampton died in 1728, about a year before the Godolphin Arabian, last of the three prepotent Arabians, arrived in Britain. But he had lived to see the first evidence of the extraordinary impetus which they were to give to English bloodstock. Flying Childers, a son of the Darley Arabian, had come to Newmarket in 1722 and beaten a horse called Fox, who up till then had been considered one of the best horses in training. Flying Childers gave him a stone and distanced him. That must have provided food for contemplation down at Heath House, Frampton's headquarters in Newmarket.

Tregonwell Frampton, in his person, had contained the regulation of racing. But such narrow definitions could not last, racing was becoming too popular and widespread. In 1737, John Cheny published his *Historical List of all Horse Matches Run, and of all Plates and Prizes Run for in England of the Value of Ten Pounds and Upwards in 1736, Containing the Names of the Owners of the Horses that have Run as Above and the Names and Colours of the Horses also, with a list also of all the principal Cock Matches of the Year above and who were the Winners and Losers of Them.* For half a guinea annually, Cheny undertook to provide subscribers with a similar service for the next seven

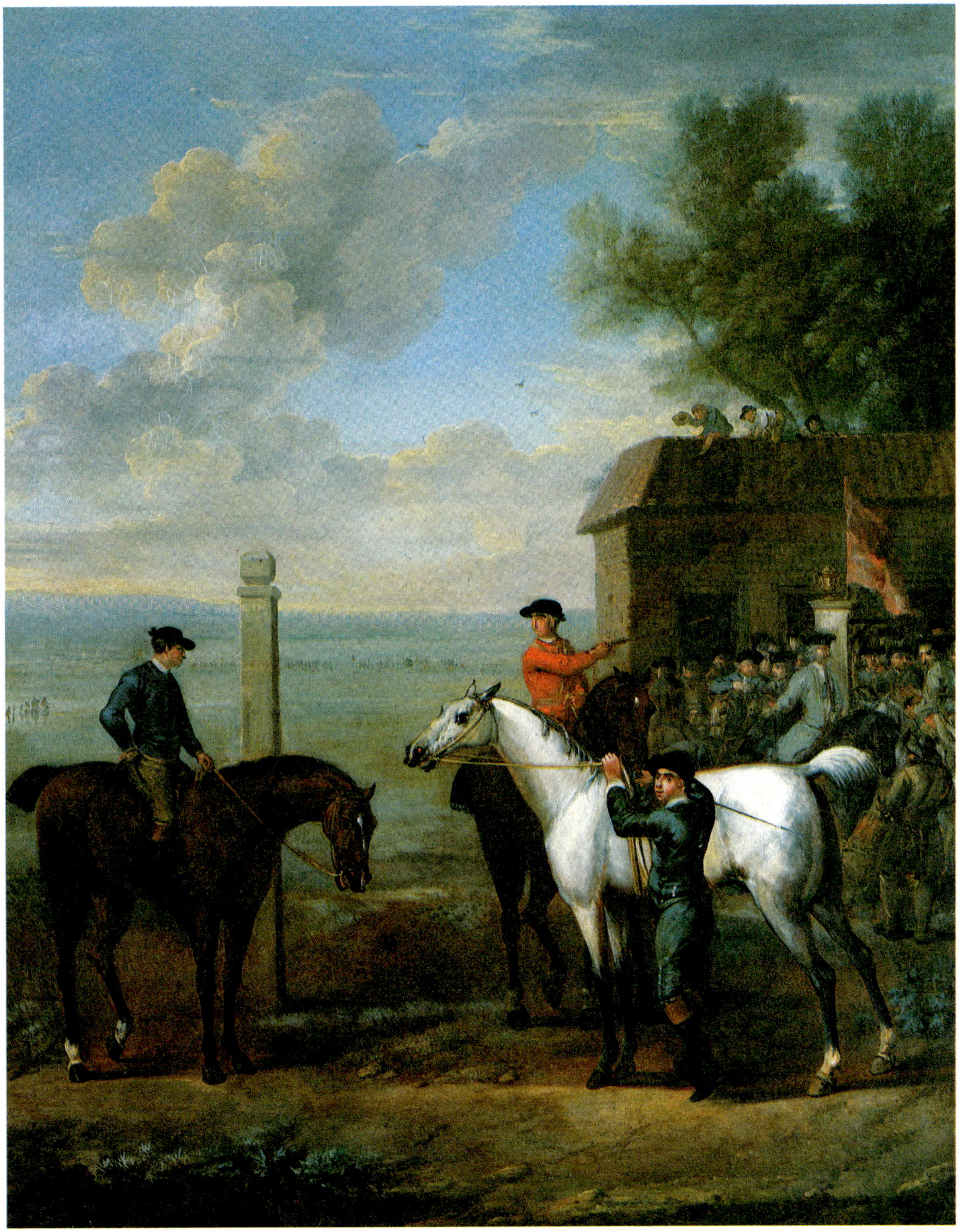

John Wootton: *Racehorses, with Jockeys up, by the Rubbing-down House on Newmarket Heath.* Oil on canvas, 123 × 99 cm. Private collection

years. Cheny's subscription list was headed by eighteen dukes, twenty-three earls, and numerous baronets. He listed 148 'places of sport', including Finchley, Moreton-in-the-Marsh, and Haverfordwest. There were over 1,200 horses in training and the stakes could be enticing. On 27 April at Newmarket, for instance, there were seven starters for 'The Great Stakes of 800 guineas for four-year-olds.' The race was won by the Duke of Devonshire's grey horse Flesham. By contrast, a fortnight earlier, there had been humbler fare at Boroughbridge in Yorkshire: 10 guineas for horses of 14 hands carrying 9 stone, 'to give or take if higher or lower'. Mr Firbank's bay mare Mashamshire Molly took the stake by winning both heats.

Throughout this period, most racing was conducted in heats of 3 or 4 miles – the best of three – with older, even aged horses taking part. The four-year-olds in the Newmarket race would have been regarded as utter infants, at the very lowest age at which they should be allowed to race. The gruelling weight-for-age scale, enshrined in an Act of Parliament of 1740, prescribed 10 stone for five-year-olds, another stone at six, and 12 stone at seven years, though even greater weights had been common at the beginning of the century. Racing in heats was an elaborate process which could take the best part of an afternoon to complete. In such long races, tactics played a crucial role, and professional grooms took over the job of riding from the gentleman owners. After each heat the horses would be allowed a respite of twenty minutes to half an hour. Like boxers between rounds, they were earnestly massaged, rubbed, and cosseted by the boy handlers – the rubbing cloths and twists of straw are a recurring feature in contemporary paintings – before being returned to the fray. On Newmarket Heath, the rubbing-down house was the centre of activity and the focus of many paintings by Stubbs, Wootton, and Seymour. In the picture by Wootton shown here, the trophy is displayed atop the pole beside a flag, as the jockeys and officials, drummer boy at the ready, prepare for the next heat.

In 1745, when the advance of Bonnie Prince Charlie and his army might reasonably have occupied the attention of the nation's legislators, Parliament still found time to enact a statute about the conditions of plate races, to modify the earlier Act of 1740. Around 1750, racing men themselves seem to have felt a need for stricter control over the conduct of racing and the access to Newmarket Heath, as well as over the activities of parvenus and blackguards. Thus the Jockey Club was born. It must be accounted a uniquely successful venture. More than 200 years later, it is still a self-perpetuating club of enviable exclusivity, with scarcely more than 100 members governing a multi-million-pound industry by fiat. The coffee room where the members first met in 1752 is still part of the Club's rooms at Newmarket, though now consigned to the use of the handful of women members.

From the beginning, the Jockey Club seized the initiative. The members knew what they wanted and were in a position to impose their wishes on the denizens of the Heath. By 1758, they were ruling that riders who did not declare overweight should be disqualified. They decided to settle races in a single running, rather than in heats. In 1759, they opened races to public participation. In 1762, they agreed on specific colours for members' jockeys. The pace of change and regulation did not slacken in the early years of George III's reign, as the Club entered its second decade. In 1769, there was a series of new promulgations. Entries had to be given to the Keeper of the Match Book. The age of horses had to be certified in writing. And the election of Stewards was decreed. These men – Sir Charles Bunbury, Lord Bolingbroke, and Mr Jenison Shafto were Stewards in 1770 – were certainly no conservatives. In the very year that Eclipse's exploits on Newmarket Heath were marking the high point of the first century of thoroughbred racing, the Stewards were officially sanctioning the innovation which was to alter racing for ever. They gave their blessing to contests for two-year-olds. Taken with the subsequent decision that 8 st. 7 lb. was to be the highest weight a horse should carry, this marked a complete reversal of the traditional practice in which horses of mature years – Eclipse did not race until he was 5 years old – carried up to 12 st. in 4-mile heats.

Throughout the early years, the argument by which those who concerned themselves with such niceties had justified racing was that it helped to develop speed and stamina in an animal whose performance was important to the nation in war and commerce. The pace and endurance of the Byerley Turk himself was reputed to have saved the life of Captain Robert Byerley at the Battle of the Boyne when he found himself surrounded by King James's cavalry. From 1770 onwards, such considerations seem to have been summarily ejected by those at the helm of the Jockey Club. Two less exalted factors were in their mind. First, 'dash' racing was much more exciting. Second, it was a much more attractive betting medium. The welfare of the breed was clearly a long way down the list of priorities. Indeed, by 1786 they had authorized the ultimate mischief of yearling racing.

These mutations were not, however, the unpopular impositions of a small group of dictatorial men at Newmarket. On the contrary, they seem to have been widely

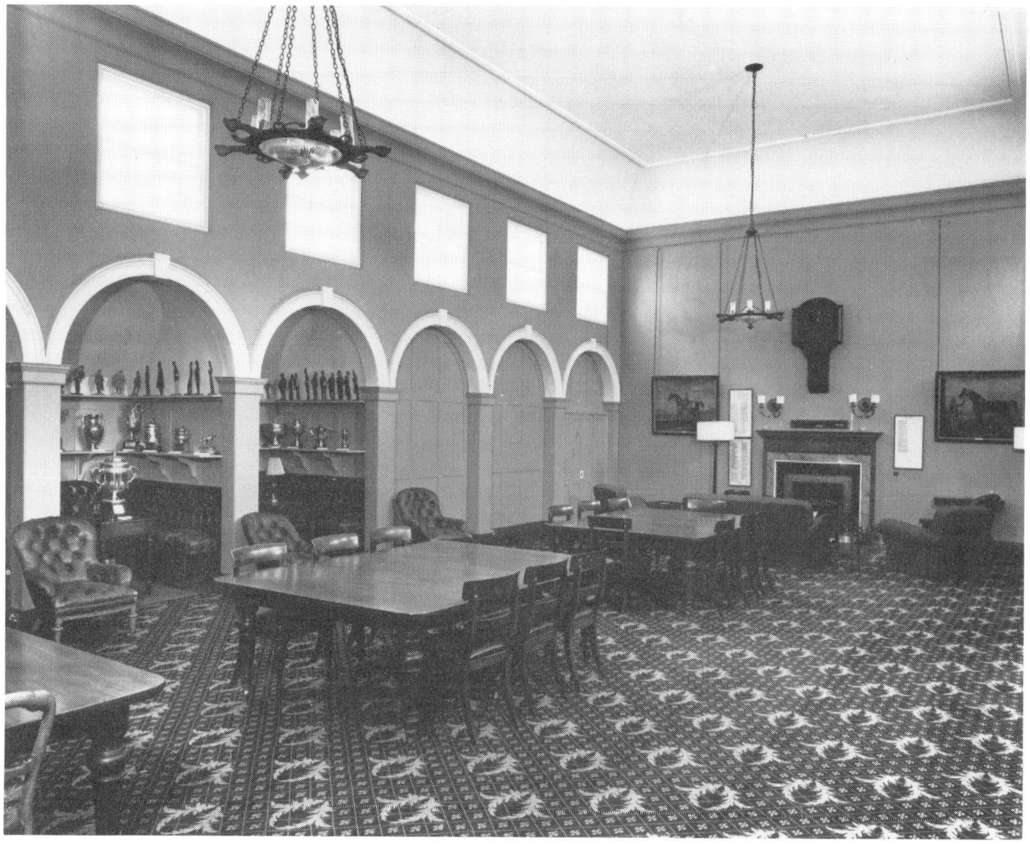

The coffee room at the Jockey Club, Newmarket, as it looks today

welcomed, even in the broad acres of Yorkshire. In 1776, the Yorkshiremen introduced, at Doncaster, Colonel Anthony St Leger's race for three-year-olds over 2 miles (reduced to just above $1\frac{3}{4}$ miles in 1813) that was to become the first Classic. The race for a 25-guinea sweepstake, with colts carrying 8 st. and fillies 7 st. 12 lb., was won by Lord Rockingham's filly Alabaculia – an early indication of the success of fillies against colts in the autumn contests, which is noticeable even today. This was, in fact, the first race for three-year-olds ever run at Doncaster, and the local town council, who administered the course then as now, were sufficiently encouraged at the prospects to order a new track to be laid out, with new stands, on the Town Moor. More than 200 years later, the St Leger remains the final Classic of the English season.

In 1778, Sir Charles Bunbury and Lord Derby, carousing one night at the Earl's house, The Oaks, on Epsom Downs, concocted a race of $1\frac{1}{2}$ miles for three-year-old fillies only. The first running of the Oaks took place the following year. The same two gentlemen were also responsible for originating a race for three-year-old colts and fillies called the Derby, first run in 1780 over 1 mile (increased to $1\frac{1}{2}$ miles in 1784). The undulating left-hand course on Epsom Downs soon became established as the supreme test for a racehorse, and Derby Day itself evolved into a unique unofficial public holiday enjoyed each year by hundreds of thousands of people from all walks of life, a phenomenon epitomized in W. P. Frith's famous painting.

The pattern of three Classic races for three-year-olds, and two more for fillies only, was not completed until some years later. The Two Thousand Guineas, for three-year-old colts and fillies over a mile at Newmarket, and the One Thousand Guineas, for three-year-old fillies only, over the same course, followed in 1809 and 1814 respectively. Mr Christopher Wilson won both inaugural Guineas races with Wizard and Charlotte – a notable feat, as he had also owned Champion, who was, in 1800, the first horse to win both the Derby and the St Leger. But it was not until 1853 that a horse captured the 'Triple Crown'. West Australian was the first three-year-old to show that he could beat his contemporaries over a mile in the spring at Newmarket, take the Derby at $1\frac{1}{2}$ miles in the summer, and still be good enough in September to win over more than $1\frac{3}{4}$ miles in the St Leger. The style of the Classics

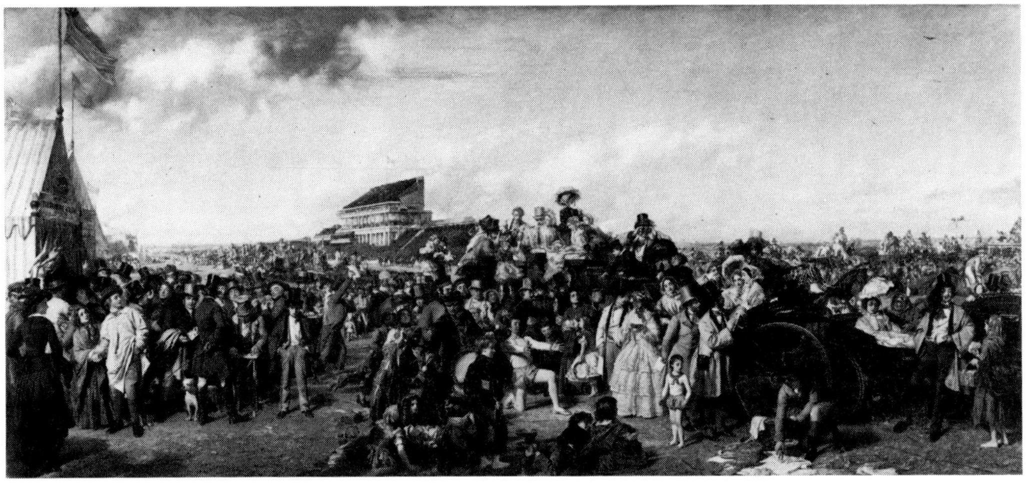

William Powell Frith: *Derby Day*. 1856–8. Oil on canvas, 101.6 × 223.5 cm. The Tate Gallery, London

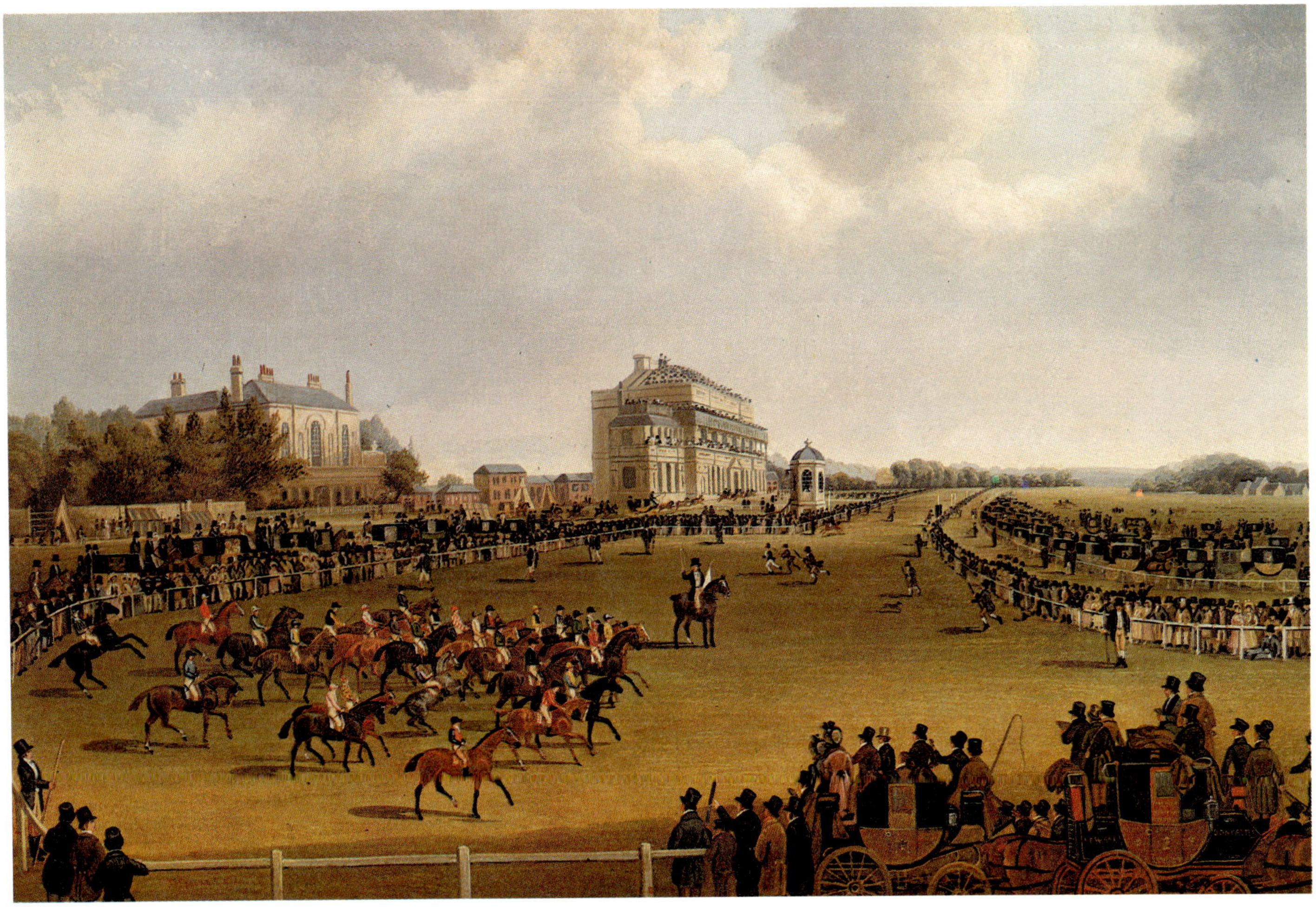

James Pollard: *The Start of the 1830 St Leger*. Oil on canvas, 49.5 × 75 cm. Private collection

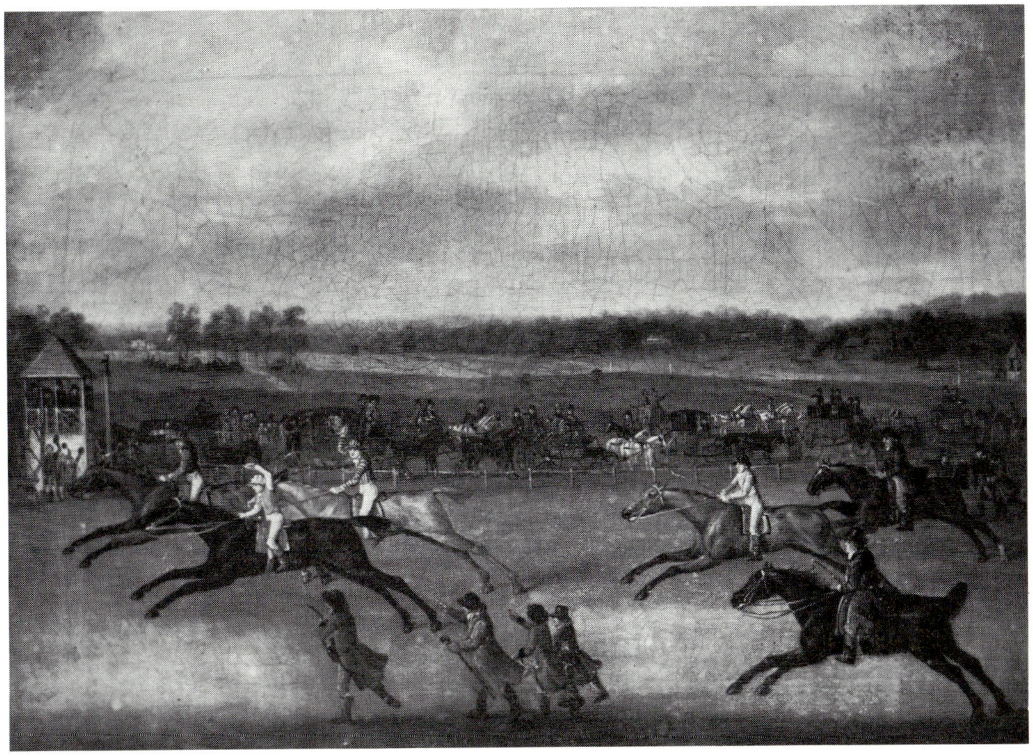

J. N. Sartorius: *The Finish of the 1791 Derby: the Duke of Bedford's colt by Florizel (later named Eager) beating Lord Foley's Vermin and Lord Egremont's Proteus*. 1792. Oil on canvas, 41.3 × 55.2 cm. Brodick Castle, Isle of Arran

– young horses carrying low weights over short distances in once and for all 'dashes' – was repeated at every level of racing, so that within fifty years it was hard to find any trace of the old ways. The 1824 Racing Calendar shows a few encounters still being run off in heats at country tracks where there was clearly a shortage of runners, at Beadnell in Northumberland and Wells in Somerset, for example.

A search for an era immune to the fever of wagering would surely be vain, but the last years of the eighteenth century and the beginning of the nineteenth saw the fever reach the level of an epidemic. With fashionable girls' schools teaching whist and casino, E. O. tables (a basic form of roulette) to be found on every racecourse, and bets on any and every capacity of a racehorse – Gimcrack was bought specially to be taken to France to contest a wager on how far he could run in an hour – it sometimes appears that the whole nation was perpetually entombed in a Hogarthian gambling hell. The 1824 Calendar records the rise of handicap racing to meet the cravings of frenetic gamblers. With horses assigned different weights according to their apparent abilities, in order to make their chances as even as possible, the outcome of a race became enticingly uncertain to the betting man. At the Newmarket spring meeting, there were three consecutive handicap races on the Tuesday. The handicapper must have been very pleased with the tribute to his expertise in the last race: Lord Darlington's Whisker, a four-year-old on 7 st. 7 lb., dead-heated with Mr Meynell's five-year-old Ajax, on 8 st. 4 lb. Whisker won the run-off. The betting was recorded: '2–1 against the winner, 5–2 against Spermaceti, 3–1 against Ajax; after the dead heat 5–4 on the winner, who won easy at last'.

There was also heavy betting on the St Leger that year, with twenty-three runners quoted at every price from 17–4 against the favourite, Streatham, right out to 40–1 against Tarandus. This was Jerry's year (see pp. 99–100); he was quoted at 9–1. The staid pages of the Calendar indulged in a description of how the race gave almost everyone a run for their money:

> Soon after starting, Streatham took the lead and made severe running, keeping about two lengths ahead until after passing the Red House where Canteen headed him. Brutandorf then made his run, but was soon beaten. About the distance The Miller of Mansfield came in front, but could not maintain it and Canteen appeared to be winning when Jerry came suddenly up on the outside about half-way within the distance and won tolerably easy by about two lengths. The Miller ran third and Streatham and Brutandorf were fourth and fifth. It was altogether a most beautiful race, the whole keeping close together all the way and even at the last, they were all well up with the exception of Mr Gascoigne's filly, which was thrown out at the start and Serab, which was pulled up after going about two hundred yards.

J. F. Herring: *John Mytton of Halston, Salop*. 1828. Oil on canvas, 61 × 73.7 cm. Private collection

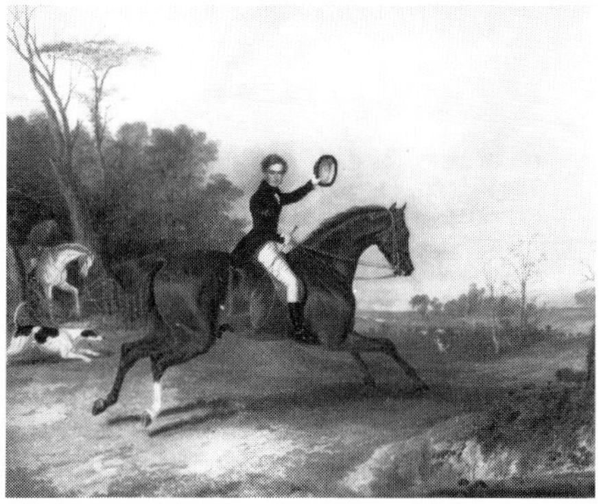

Clearly, a good time was had by all. And if excitement was still required, there was always the cockpit. A typical note after the racing results records: 'A main of cocks was fought between Dr Bellyse (Phillips, feeder) and Mr Walker (Merryweather, feeder) for 10 sovereigns a battle and 200 the main which was won by the former as follows: Phillips 21M 6B, Merryweather 12M 7B.'

One of the runners in that 1824 St Leger was Oswestry, owned by John Mytton. Mytton was the most celebrated of the innumerable characters who were ruined by the excesses of the nineteenth-century Turf. Once MP for Shrewsbury, High Sheriff of Shropshire and Merioneth, and an officer in the yeomanry, he was forced to flee to that resort of all contemporary debtors, Calais, returning only to die in the King's Bench prison in London. He was reviled, as the fallen are, in the popular press, but his friend Charles Apperley ('Nimrod') wrote a revealing and sympathetic life of a man whom he dubbed 'a satire on humanity'. Mytton was certainly a satire on the fashionable world of St James's and Newmarket. 'He was a very dangerous man with a dice box in his hand,' wrote Apperley, who continued:

> Wine gave him courage which generally tells at hazard. I am afraid to say what was supposed to have been the amount of bank notes that were one night blown out of his carriage on his road from Doncaster races, but I have reason to believe it was several thousand pounds. I have seen him when he has been going a journey, take a lot of bank notes out of his travelling desk and rolling them into a lump, throw them at his servant's head. I picked up one of these lumps some years since in the plantations at Halston, containing £37 which had been there some days by its appearance. It was hard to say which were the better stocked, Mr Mytton's wardrobe or the Halston cellars. I once counted a hundred and fifty-two pairs of breeches and trousers in the former, with a proportionate accompaniment of coats, waistcoats etc.

Mytton's fate was shared in that era by many for whom hunting, racing, shooting, and gambling were a full-time and exclusive occupation. Squire George Osbaldeston, perhaps the greatest sportsman of his day, reflecting in old age, said:

> Mine has been a life of plunder; no man has been so persecuted, robbed and cheated by stewards and gentlemen who professed to be friends, by trainers, jockeys and betting men who live by plunder and make it their study. It is a well known fact that at the present time, five or six of the betting men have £400,000 or £500,000 among them and many others of the same class £30,000 or £40,000. Several of the jockeys also have £30,000; one has £40,000; one or two of them £20,000 though only twenty-two years old. As it is impossible that they could have realised these sums by their profession alone, it is a natural conclusion that they have 'worked the oracle' as they call it and are confederates with the betting men.

Osbaldeston, first-class shot, expert rider, and hunting man, was also a habitual duellist. One of the men he called out was the young Lord George Bentinck. Fortunately, His Lordship was only shot through the hat (see p. 110) and thus survived to become the great reformer of the Turf in the 1840s.

Lord George was not universally admired. William Day noted that His Lordship was not beyond some sharp practice himself. Day wrote: 'There is no doubt that many of his lordship's horses, with his knowledge, ran unprepared, for the purpose of deceiving not only the world at large, but his friends also, in order that on a future and fixed occasion, he might reap alone the full reward of this policy.' Some things in racing never change! Day continued: 'He won more over Crucifix when she won the Oaks than over any race [see pp. 114–15]. On this occasion he seriously crippled the ring, which amongst other little accomplishments he sincerely hoped and tried to break.' But Lord George did reform himself, and racing too, with his energetic pursuit of the Running Rein scandal which engulfed the Derby of 1844. This race set some kind of record for chicanery. Ratan, William Crockford's horse, was doped, as well as 'hooked up' by his jockey, Sam Rogers – retribution for past misdeeds by

J. F. Herring: *The Start of the 1844 Derby*. Oil on canvas, 102.9 × 209.5 cm. Brodick Castle, Isle of Arran

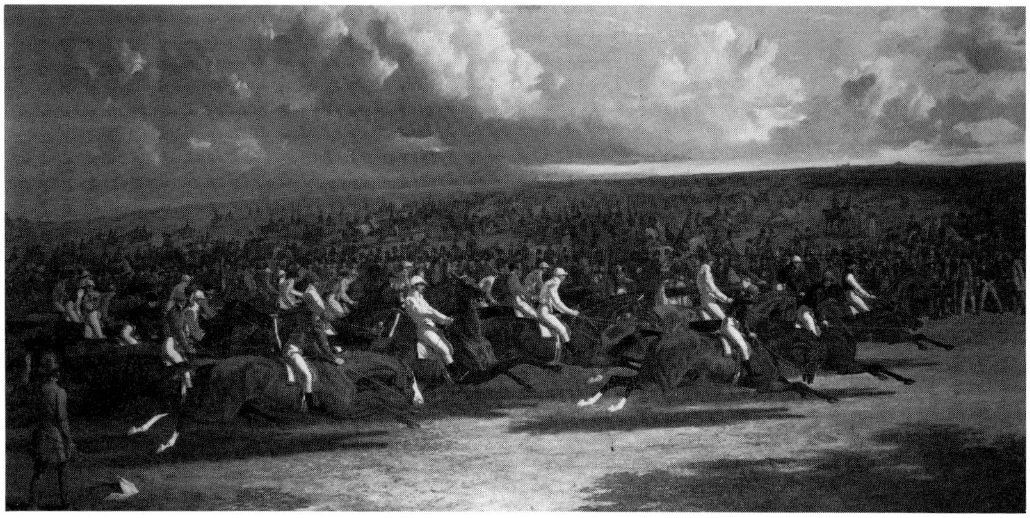

Crockford. Another horse, Leander, was discovered afterwards to be at least 4, if not 6 years old. Running Rein himself, who actually won the race, was a 'ringer'. He was in truth a four-year-old named Maccabeus.

Bentinck laid about him in the most energetic fashion after this Derby. He encouraged Colonel Jonathan Peel, the owner of the second horse, Orlando, to object to the winner and provided a great deal of the evidence with which the Colonel won the subsequent lawsuit; Lord George had first suspected Running Rein when he appeared, allegedly as a two-year-old, the year before at Newmarket. Not content, His Lordship also exposed Sam Rogers's betting book to the assembled fancy on the steps of the Spread Eagle at Epsom, thereby initiating the process by which Rogers was 'warned off'. In this case, the noble zeal may have been intensified by the considerable sums laid by Lord George himself on Ratan. A subscription of £2,100 was raised from the public by way of testimonial to Lord George for his endeavours on behalf of the punter. However, as his trainer John Kent put it, 'The Hercules of the Turf, having cleansed the Augean stables, refused to accept anything, either in the form of plate or money.' It was eventually appropriated for 'the advantage of trainers and riders of good character'.

George Thompson: *Admiral Rous and George Payne*. Oil on millboard, 37.5 × 29.2 cm. National Portrait Gallery, London

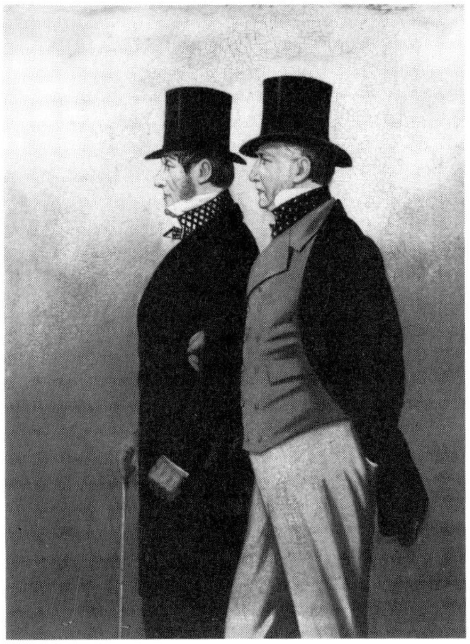

Already, however, there was an even more indefatigable and incorruptible figure waiting to take over as the 'Napoleon of the Turf'. Admiral Henry John Rous, being neither a serious gambler nor a considerable owner of horses, was patterned to be a pillar of rectitude. His reputation was founded on his skill as a handicapper, and his weight-for-age scale is still the basis of modern handicapping. His book *On the Laws and Practice of Horse Racing*, published in 1850, codified the customs and ordinances of 100 years of Jockey Club hegemony, and remains an invaluable source book. But the knowledge he acquired in the process of assessing horses – it was a rare morning when he was absent from the gallops on Newmarket Heath – was also employed in steering blackguards away from the Turf. The Admiral certainly needed a powerful personality to dominate an age of individualists like the Earl of Glasgow, who would materialize without warning at his stables in Middleham, demand trials of his horses, and then have the losers shot, or Francis Villiers, Senior Steward elect of the Jockey Club in 1855, who ran off to France owing £100,000.

From 1830 onwards, Flat racing in England was obliged to share the affections of the public with the new sport of steeplechasing. The Irish had been racing over 'country' since at least 1752. The first recorded steeplechase proper in England took place at St Albans, organized by some officers of the Household Cavalry. Captain MacDowall, riding a grey, was the winner. The new form of racing rapidly achieved popularity. Before the end of the decade, Cheltenham had established for itself an eminence in steeplechasing which it has never surrendered and the eponymous Captain Becher had fallen off Conrad into his brook at Aintree during the first running of the world's toughest steeplechase, the Grand National. Aintree has always provided the stuff of legends. Lord Poulett changed his jockey on The Lamb in 1868, on the strength of a dream, and won. The New Zealand horse Moifaa swam ashore from a shipwreck on his way to England, but still managed to win in 1904.

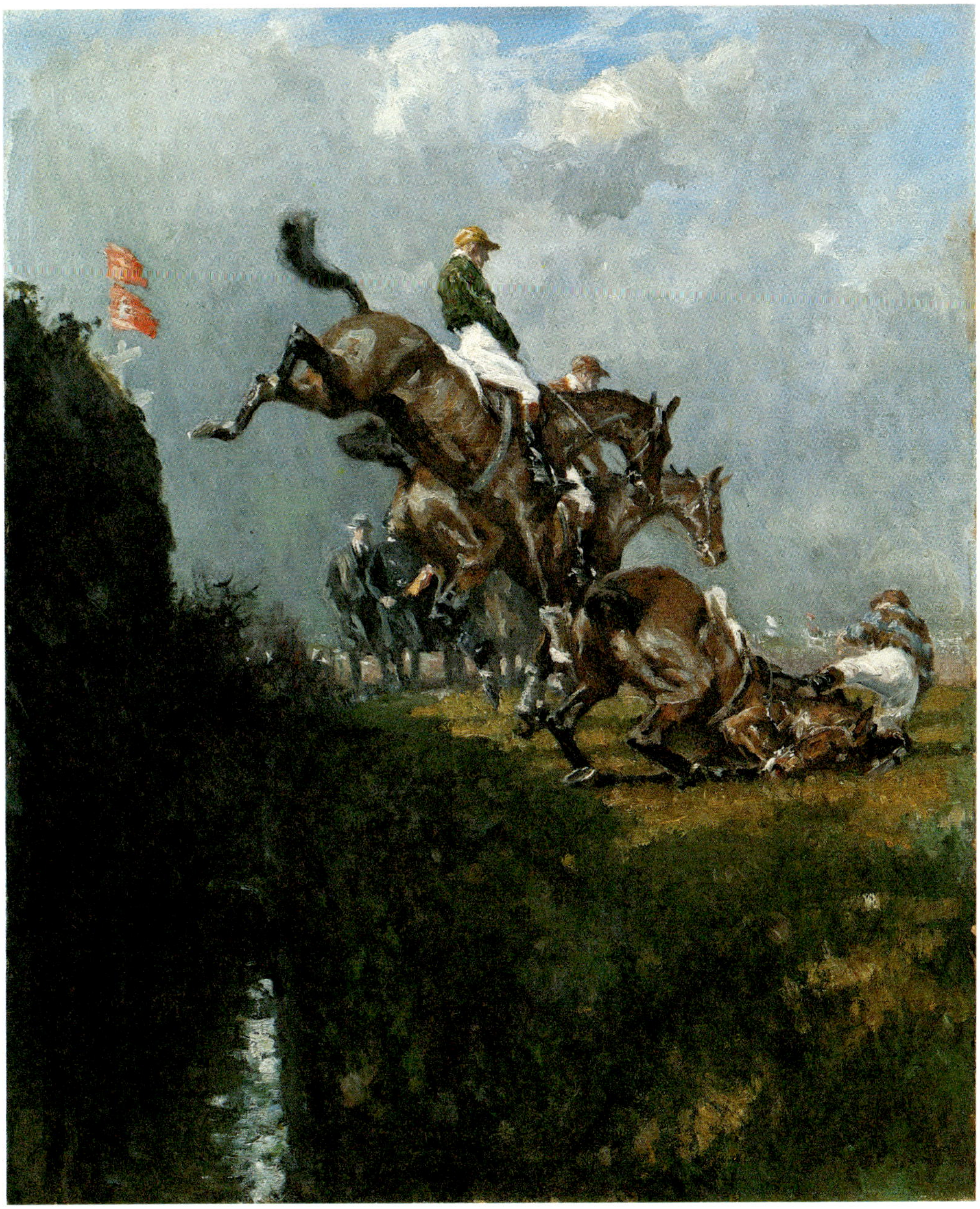

Gilbert Holiday: *Becher's Brook in the Grand National of 1921: (l. to r.) Fred Rees on Shaun Spadah, Mr Harry Brown on The Bore, and Capt. G. H. Bennet falling from Turkey Buzzard.* Oil on canvas 76.2 × 60.9 cm. Private collection

James Pollard: *Northampton Grand Steeplechase*. Etching and aquatint by H. Pyall, 1833, 35.2 × 42.8 cm. Private collection

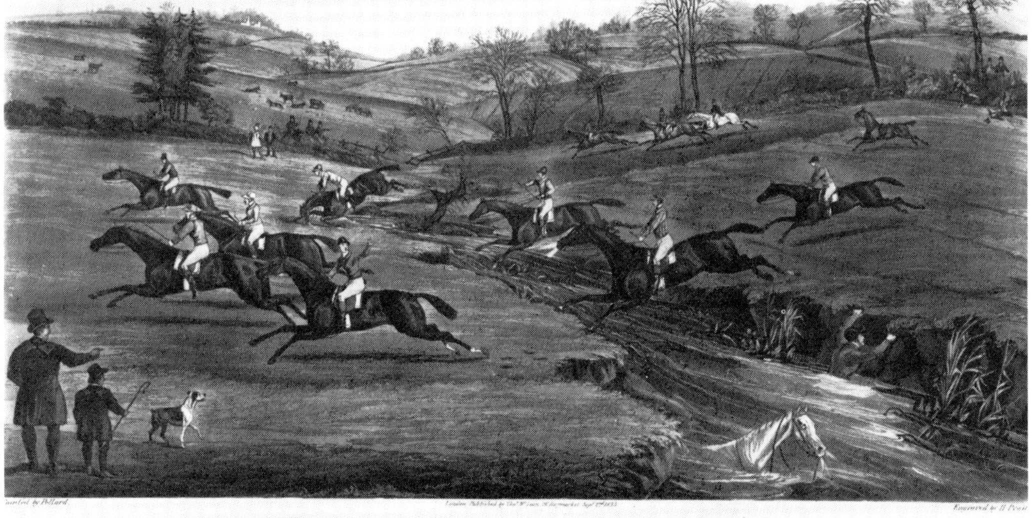


The Prince of Wales won with Ambush II in 1900, but the Queen Mother had probably the worst luck ever seen at Aintree when her horse Devon Loch fell down, for no apparent reason, fifty yards from the winning-post in 1956. Two American amateurs came over with the specific ambition to win the National in 1965 and 1980, and both succeeded; Tommy Smith on Jay Trump beat the favourite in 1965, and Charlie Fenwick won on Ben Nevis fifteen years later. The saga continues with Bob Champion, newly recovered from cancer, winning on Aldaniti in 1981, and a 48-year-old grandfather, Dick Saunders, the victor on Grittar in 1982.

The second half of the nineteenth century saw the establishment of the thoroughbred beyond the confines of the two countries where it had been cherished from the beginning, Britain and America. The French, through the Société d'Encouragement, planned a deliberate campaign to match the qualities of the English horse. In 1865, they succeeded superbly when Gladiateur crossed the Channel to win the Epsom Derby. In Canada, racing was stimulated by the arrival of bloodstock fleeing the perils of the American Civil War. In Australia, the first Melbourne Cup was run in 1861, though the Melbourne Jockey Club dates back to 1838. The 1890 Cup was won by Carbine, who was subsequently bought by the Duke of Portland and exported to England, where he enjoyed an outstanding career as a sire. In 1900, the Duke was able to invite Lynwood Palmer down to the Welbeck stud to paint a collection of stallions beyond compare: St Simon, Carbine, Donovan, Ayrshire, St Serf, and Raeburn (see p. 139). Donovan and Ayrshire were Derby winners. Raeburn was the sole conqueror of the 1893 Triple Crown winner, Isinglass. St Serf, a son of St Simon, got two Classic winners. And St Simon himself, who was never beaten, never indeed extended, is perhaps the only horse fit to stand beside Eclipse in the pantheon of the thoroughbred.

The First World War disrupted racing and only substitute Classics were run at Newmarket. This deprived a fine horse, Gainsborough, sire of Hyperion, of full honours. In the years between the wars, the two outstanding rivals on the Turf were Lord Derby, who owned Hyperion, and the Aga Khan, who owned some fine scions of The Tetrarch's line. As the Second World War approached, the Aga Khan, shrewd to the point of ruthlessness in business, sold his three Derby winners, Blenheim, Bahram, and Mahmoud, to the United States for more than £100,000, thus, in the view of many racing people, finally shifting the balance of supremacy in the bloodstock world to America.

In the inter-war years in Italy, Federico Tesio was following a cerebral approach to breeding, based on the most intense study, which was to produce not only some great racehorses, but the most potent sire line of the post-war era. Nearco was foaled in 1935. He beat the English and French Derby winners and went on to sire Dante, an English Derby winner, and, above all, Nasrullah, an outstanding sire. Shirley Heights, Sir Ivor, Nijinsky, Mill Reef, Roberto, and Golden Fleece are all descendants in the male line of Nearco, and all winners of the English Derby. Nearco's grandson Northern Dancer, bred in Canada, has outstripped all his contemporaries as a sire of Classic horses. After the war, Tesio produced Ribot, another of the great horses of this century (see p. 189). He was unbeaten in three seasons' campaigning in England, France, and Italy. In 1961, he too was exported to the United States.

The Aga Khan leading in Mahmoud, with Charlie Smirke up, after his victory in the Derby of 1936

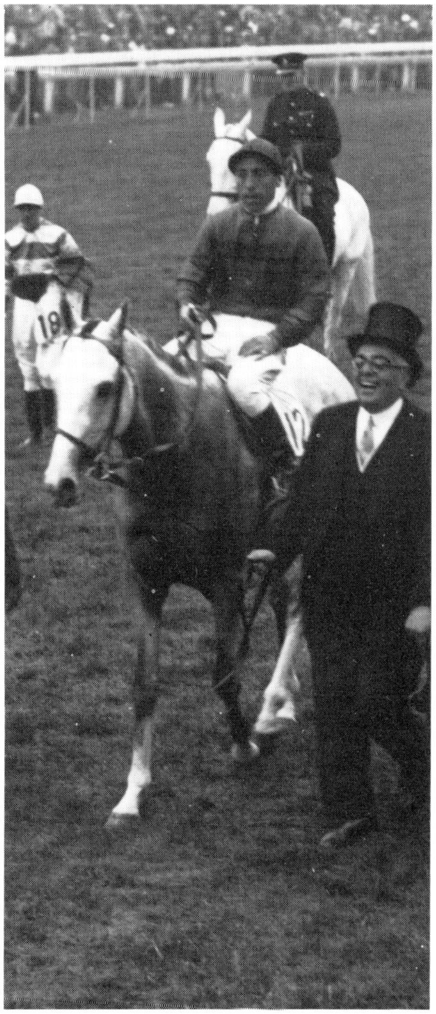

Racing arrived in America virtually with the Mayflower. The first consignment of running horses of which we have records had the misfortune to arrive before a hard winter. They were eaten. Early colonial America offered only hard-won territory to the settlers. The country was covered in scrub and forest which had to be cleared yard by yard before the land was fit for cultivation. Each acre was precious. There was certainly no room for racing on open ground in the way that the sport was developing in England. But the unquenchable urge that men have to try their horses for speed against others was not to be denied. The streets of the small towns and settlements were simply commandeered for the purpose, despite attempts by the local communities to curtail the practice. So developed the most characteristic face of racing in America, in which the greatest premium was put on sheer speed over quite short distances and the ability to get away to a flying start – the quarter-horse is the pride of the South and West to this day. Philadelphia still has a Race Street as a legacy of these competitions in the 'City of Brotherly Love'.

The principal exception to this rule was New York where, within months of the seizure of the town from the Dutchman Peter Stuyvesant in 1664, Governor Richard Nicolls was encouraging racing out on Long Island. Here was a great grass plain where, according to topographer Daniel Denton, 'you shall find neither stick nor stone to hinder the horses' heels or endanger them in their races'. The Governor's track lasted for more than 100 years, supported by such luminaries as Lewis Morris, one of the signatories of the Declaration of Independence, and the Delancey family, and rivalled by tracks in such unimaginable spots as what are now Greenwich Village and Brooklyn. It was Virginia, however, that became established as the home of the thoroughbred breeder. Two outstanding stallions were brought over

OPPOSITE ABOVE
W. S. Hedges: *A Race-meeting at Jacksonville, Alabama*. 1841. Oil on canvas, 50.1 × 85.2 cm. Private collection

OPPOSITE BELOW
Gerry Cranham: *Churchill Downs on Kentucky Derby Day*. May 1979

from England, Janus in 1756 and Fearnought in 1764. As the Virginians acquired more space and the exhausted tobacco fields had to be turned over to grass, racing on contemporary English lines developed, with contests run in heats over distances of 3, 4, or 5 miles. The Tayloe family of Mount Airy, Virginia, became the arbiters of the Turf. Colonel John Tayloe III had a fantastic run of success in the years across the turn of the century, with his stable winning 113 of their 141 starts. It was he who in 1784 imported Gimcrack's son Medley, first of the four great stallions which were the foundation of nineteenth-century American racing. Among Medley's descendants were Hanover and Domino.

Medley was followed in 1786 by Shark (see pp. 70–1), a son of Marske, Eclipse's sire. Shark's winnings in England were recorded as '£15,507, eleven hogsheads of claret and a cup worth 120 Guineas', as well as the Challenge Whip at Newmarket, all of which did not apparently suffice to keep his proprietor, a scurrilous pamphleteer named Charles Pigott, out of the Sumpter prison for debt. Shark was sold off at Tattersalls and dispatched to Benjamin Hyde in Fredericksburg, Virginia. Messenger, a son of Mambrino imported in 1788, was owned by, among others, Henry Astor, and became a noted sire of trotters as well as Flat racers. Diomed, winner of the first English Derby, did not arrive in the, now United, States until he was 21 years old, dispatched with no great recommendation by James Weatherby to his client Colonel John Hoomes of Virginia. Diomed flourished. He died ten years later after siring some notable horses, including Haynie's Maria and Sir Archy. The 'Famous Four' were, however, the last notable importations from England for almost thirty years. Sentiment against the Old Country hardened in the years after the Revolution, culminating in the war of 1812, and everything British became anathema.

This repudiation of the fashions of Albion coincided with the decline of long-distance racing in England. The old contests run in 4-mile heats – so recently the stage for the likes of Gimcrack and Highflyer – were eclipsed by the new short

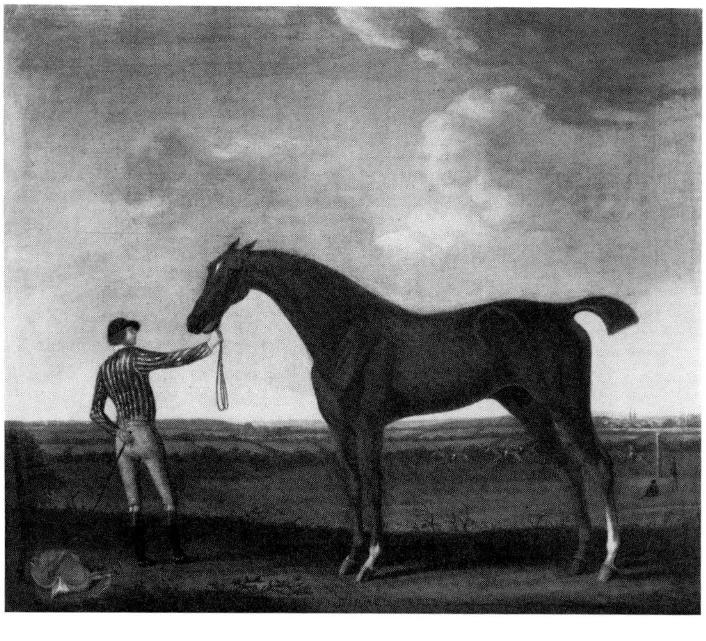

F. Sartorius: *Diomed*. 1780. Oil on canvas, 63.5 × 76.2 cm. Jockey Club, Newmarket

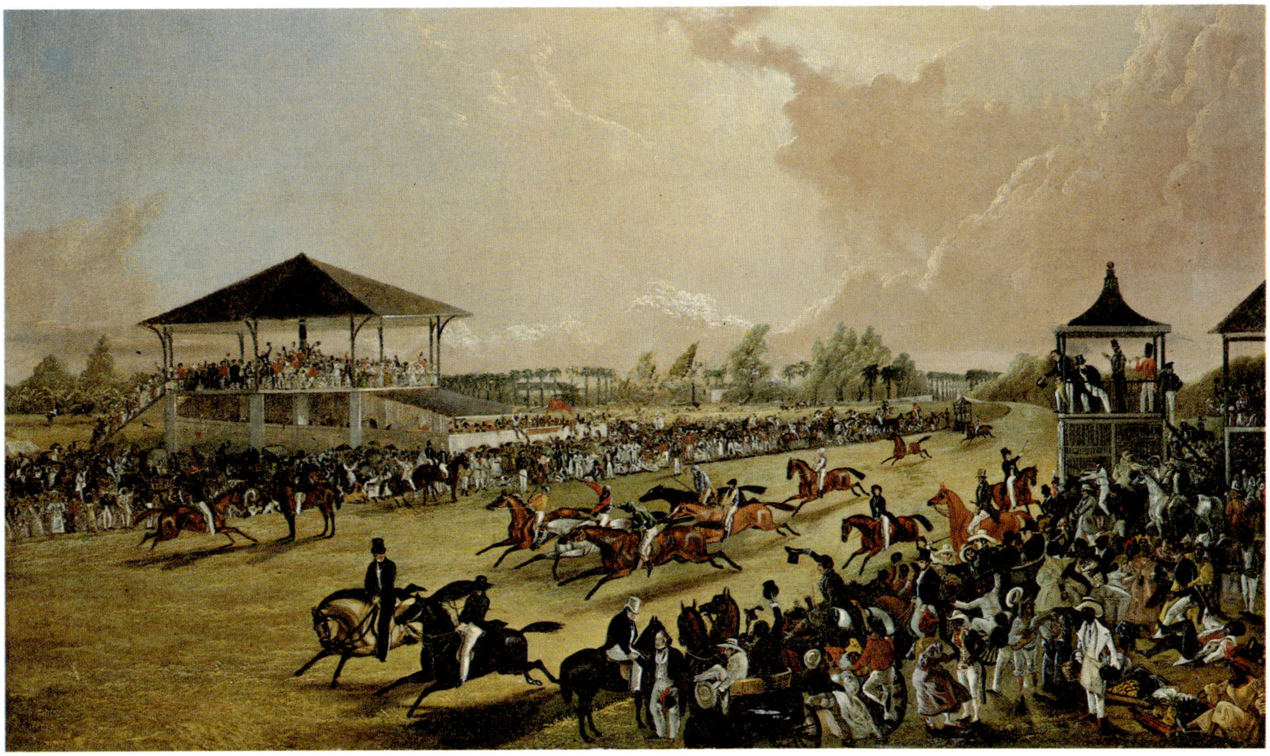

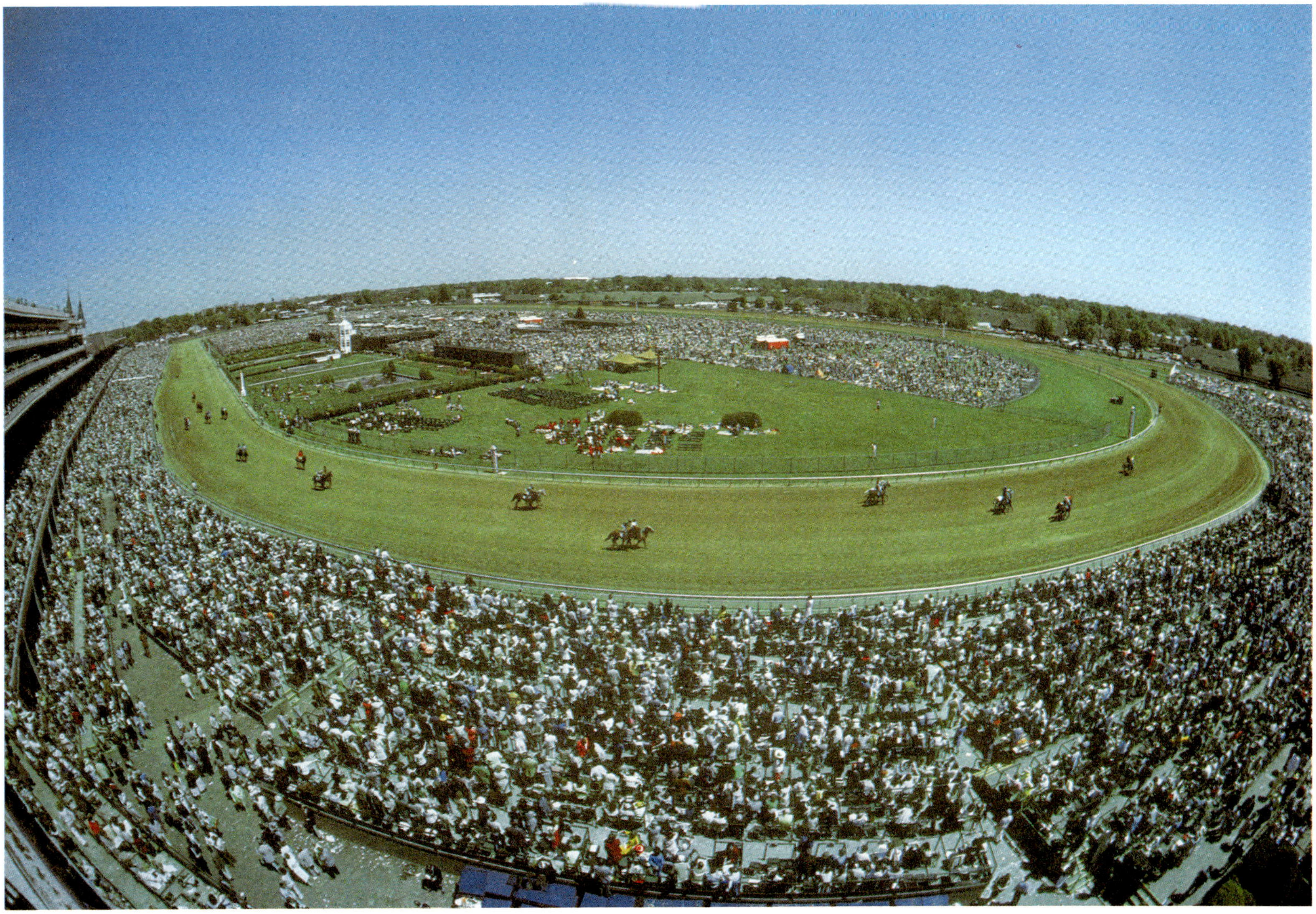

'dash' races for three-year-olds, which were to become the Classic races of the Turf. America would have none of this. The long race, for mature horses, remained the lodestar of equine excellence. A race advertised at Lexington in 1789 set out the conditions: entry was 'free for any horse, mare or gelding, weight for age, three-mile heats, the best two in three; one quarter of an hour allowed between heats for rubbing'. When the Union Course opened in 1821 in New York, it introduced another feature which was to characterize American racing. The track was 'skinned' in order to give a dirt surface. Turfites, already possessed of that distinctive American obsession, timing, noticed that it rode much faster than grass.

Right up to the period of the Civil War, long-distance racing continued to dominate the scene. Lexington's feats in his maturity against Sallie Waters and Lecomte during the 1850s were all over distances of 4 miles. Such matches had almost vanished in England. The Civil War devastated racing in its American heartland of Virginia, Maryland, and Kentucky, but even in the post-war years, as race-tracks were established across the nation, the traditional ways persisted. When the Californians wanted to attract the best horses in 1873, the prize of $20,000 in gold was still for a race run in 4-mile heats. But the tide was turning. Within two years, without much fanfare, the first Kentucky Derby was run on Churchill Downs. The new men who came into racing preferred the thrills and excitement of the short races. Pierre Lorillard, the most successful racehorse owner in America at that time, said: 'I don't want to race anything but two and three-year-olds. You get tired of the same old horses. I had rather race two-year-olds than any other class.' Above all, the public, flocking to the tracks in great numbers in the heady days of the eighties and nineties, wanted a fast and furious gambling medium. The 'dash' races fitted the bill.

In 1894, it was estimated that $1 million a day was passing through the hands of the bookmakers at the Brighton Beach track near Coney Island in New York. The puritan ethic was affronted. The same forces which were to triumph with the Prohibition legislation tried a preliminary canter on the race-tracks. Gambling was successfully eliminated in many states, particularly New York. By 1910, what became known as the 'blackout' had descended. Some of the famous studs and stables were sold off. James Ben Ali Haggin sold 150 horses to Argentina and Germany in 1909. Ed Corrigan's ninety-odd horses each fetched an average of only $250 at auction. The English Jockey Club, in ruthless fashion, rubbed salt into the wound with the so-called 'Jersey Act', which ruled that no animal could be registered in the Stud Book unless its ancestors also graced those august pages, thereby disqualifying a vast proportion of American thoroughbreds. There were those who saw this piece of chicanery as pique at the success of American horses in Europe. Iroquois had won the Derby back in 1881 for Mr Lorillard, but 1908 saw Rubio win the Grand National, Norman win the Two Thousand Guineas, and Rhodora win the One Thousand Guineas, all for American owners. The same year, William Vanderbilt won the Grand Prix de Paris with Northeast and dead-heated for the French Derby with Sea Sick. Xenophobia ruled. It had already chased home the American jockey Tod Sloan after he had scandalized – and revolutionized – English racing with his monkey-crouch riding style, perched high over the horse's withers (see p. 152).

After the First World War matters improved in America. *Pari mutuel* (totalizator) betting had established itself as a way of circumventing the gaming laws. In 1920 there were 4,000 horses in training, a modest enough total across the country, though it included two superstars in Sir Barton, the first horse to win the Triple Crown of Kentucky Derby, Belmont, and Preakness, and Man o' War, who broke every American record from 1 mile to $1\frac{5}{8}$ miles. There were good horses in the period between the wars, but, financially at least, they were not golden years. The continuing rivalry with the trotters divided the loyalties of horsemen, as it does to this day, with trotting enjoying a degree of popularity unimaginable to English racegoers. The Depression kept a damper on expansion. It was not until the Second World War and after – there were 20,000 horses in training by 1948 – that the next boom came, initiating a period of almost uninterrupted growth towards the million-dollar races and the multi-million-dollar bloodstock sales of the present day.

In the years since the Second World War, thoroughbred racing has become a truly international business. Sha Tin, built out into the sea in Hong Kong, is probably the most opulently equipped racecourse in the world, and its patrons the most frenetic gamblers. Japan is now running rich international races. New Zealand has produced horses of the highest class. Even the Soviet Union has keenly contested racing at the Moscow Hippodrome, with punters clutching fistfuls of rouble tote tickets like any denizen of Aqueduct or Ascot. Air travel for horses means not only that they can be shipped over to race for the Arlington Million in Chicago, then onward to Paris for the Arc, or Tokyo for the Japan Cup, but also that breeding is no longer confined by frontiers; Her Majesty The Queen sent her superb St Leger winner Dunfermline to a stallion in the United States.

Syndicates like that of Robert Sangster and Vincent O'Brien are able and willing to pay \$3–4 million for an untried yearling in Kentucky and ship him to whichever part of the world seems to offer the best opportunities. Sangster races and breeds in France, Australia, America, and Ireland, as well as England. Success on the racecourse has allowed him to command extraordinarily high prices for his stock. Storm Bird, a son of Northern Dancer, won only as a two-year-old, yet he was syndicated for \$30 million. Sangster's system is a global adaptation of the methods of men like the Duke of Portland a century ago, who realized that if the breeding of stock was impeccable and the horses could be trained to win some important races, then their value as stallions would far exceed anything the animals could earn on the racecourse. Today that philosophy is being extended to brood-mares. But the mysteries of breeding racehorses still entice all sorts and conditions of men and women to enter the quest for a Classic winner.

All logic suggests that the three great sires who are the only progenitors of thoroughbreds the world over cannot have been the three best Arabs or Turks that ever lived. Their stumbling, fortuitous journeys to England by way of the battlefields and the byways of seventeenth- and eighteenth-century Europe are evidence enough. Small wonder, then, that racing men have had a recurring dream that they could return to the desert and find, somewhere, the new Arab blood which would infuse vigour into the contemporary thoroughbred as the Darley Arabian, the Byerley Turk, and the Godolphin Arabian did two and a half centuries ago. Somewhere out there must be the blood of Pegasus himself! This vision dates back to the earliest days. Indeed, there are 174 different Eastern stallions mentioned in the first edition of the Stud Book in 1793. Eclipse himself had in his pedigree such names as the Lister Turk, D'Arcy's Yellow Turk, Hutton's Bay Barb, Hutton's Grey Barb, and the Oglethorpe Arabian. D'Arcy's White Turk occurs six times in Eclipse's antecedents, so, although his direct male line has long died out, he can be assumed to have had a great influence on the mighty Eclipse, and thereby on the superb stock of Eclipse's line. But much of the imported blood disappeared within two or three generations. The Alcock Arabian, for example, produced Crab and, via Spectator and Marc Antony, the Derby winner Aimwell, but then faded from the sire lines. There is a picture of King George III's racehorses which includes a coloured horse, a strain completely vanished today, except on the trotting tracks.

Jacques-Laurent Agasse's magnificent picture of the Wellesley Grey Arabian is testimony to the continuing dream. The splendid animal, almost white, a naked boy at his head, struts across the dunes to his far-away destiny, leaving the camel caravans and the tents for the green pastures of England. It is a powerful evocation of the mirage. The Wellesley Grey Arabian (also painted by Ben Marshall) was imported via India by the Duke of Wellington's youngest brother, Henry. There is no doubt that he was intended as a sire of racehorses for he was advertised as standing in Hertfordshire – 'Any gentleman enquiring at the Green Dragon, Cheshunt, will be directed to the house' – and a note, written at about the same time as Agasse's painting was completed, recorded that he had already got winners of a number of short races at Newmarket.

Across the Atlantic in the 1850s, Edward Troye's friend and patron Keene Richards was struck by the Arabian chimera and set off for the Middle East to buy direct from the bedouin sheikhs. The expedition was profitless as far as fast horseflesh was concerned, but it did produce some fine paintings from Troye. In the 1870s in England, some enthusiasts matched their pure-bred Arabs against thoroughbreds in a series of specially organized races, only to find them humiliatingly defeated. Today, the racing of Arab horses still goes on in England and the United States. They make a beautiful sight, galloping across the Wiltshire Downs with manes

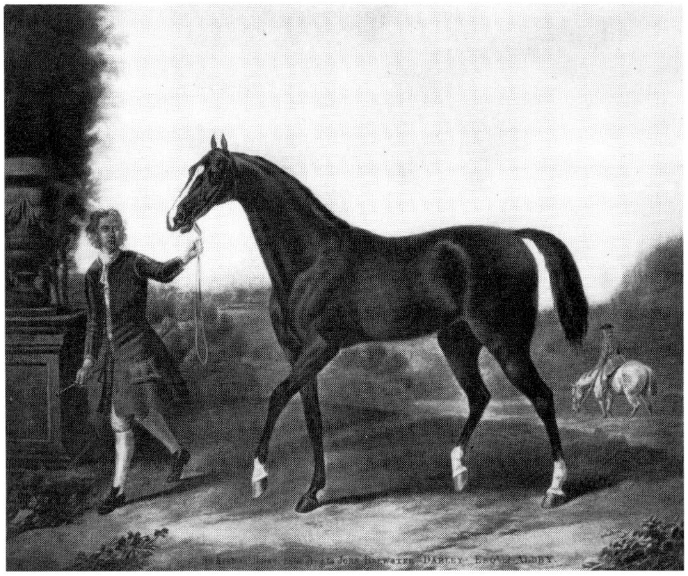

BELOW LEFT
John Wootton: *The Darley Arabian.* Copper engraving, *c.*1720, 28 × 35 cm. Private collection

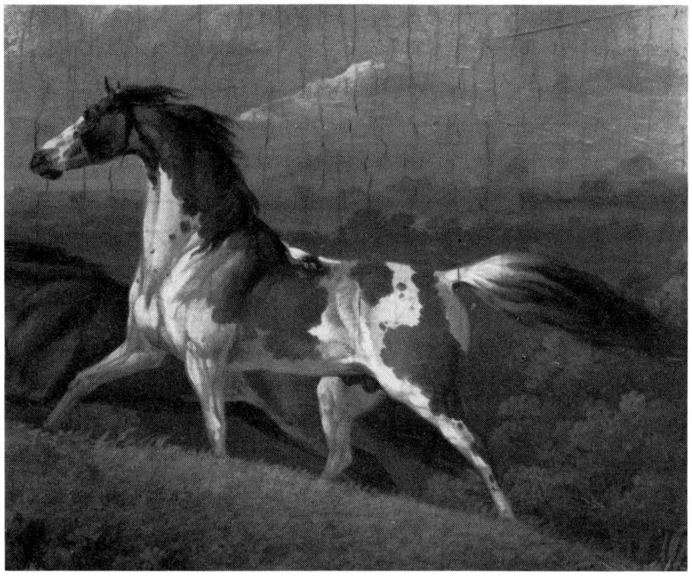

BELOW RIGHT
Follower of George Stubbs: *King George III's Racehorses* (detail showing King of Trumps). *c.*1790. Oil on panel, 22.5 × 27.8 cm. Sudley Art Gallery, Liverpool

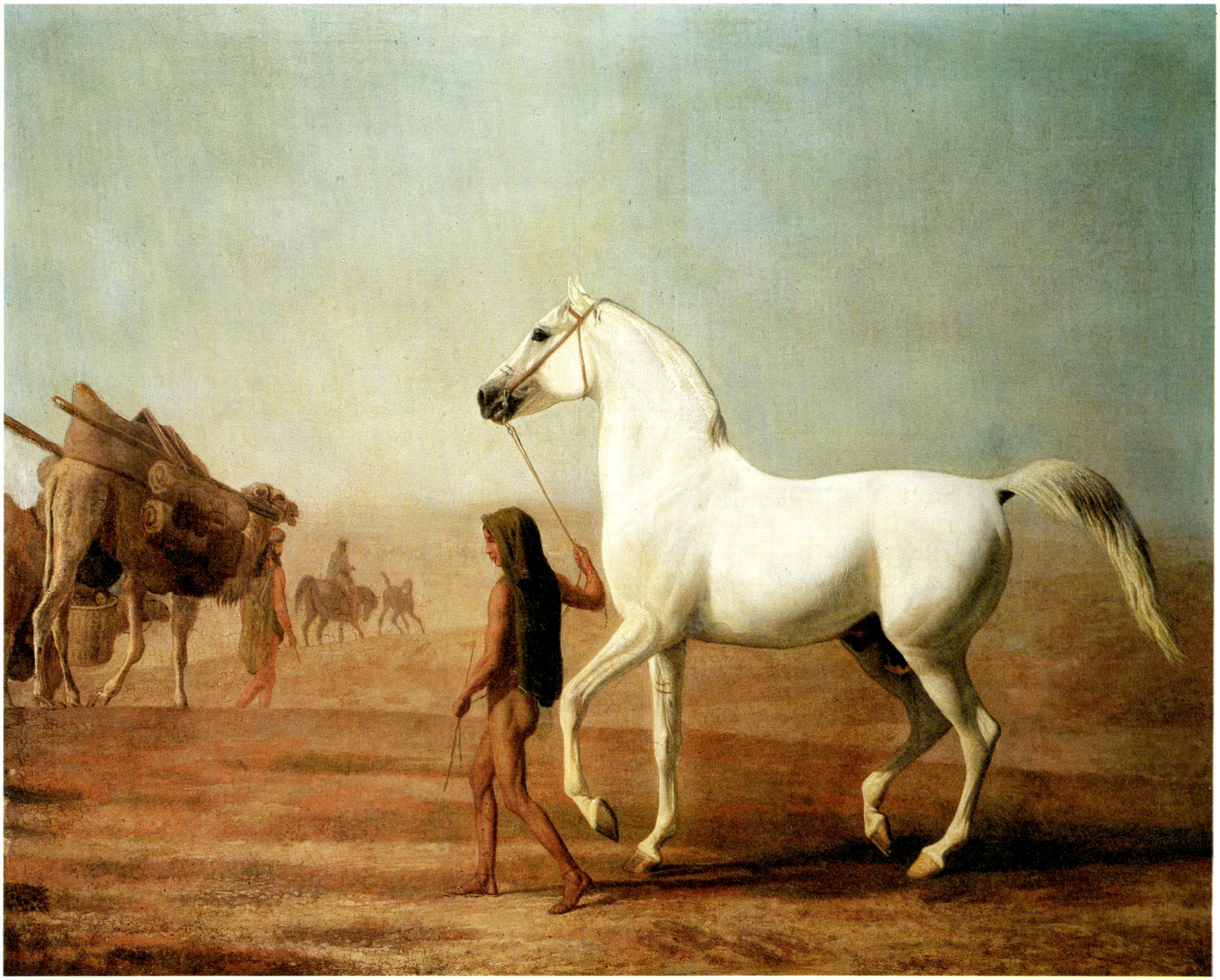

Jacques-Laurent Agasse: *The Wellesley Grey Arabian.* 1810. Oil on canvas, 101.9 × 127 cm. Paul Mellon Collection, Upperville, Virginia

streaming and tails held high, but no one now suggests that they can match the thoroughbred for speed and endurance.

It is curious, though, that while the athletic performance of humans seems to show a steady improvement under the influence of better diet, improved training methods, and modern scientific research – the 4-minute mile now seems positively pedestrian – there has been no such improvement in the thoroughbred racehorse. Taking the 'ultimate piece of wood' – Tesio's name for the winning-post at Epsom – as the yardstick, it is clear that there has been only the slightest improvement in the performance of Derby winners over the last sixty years. The record time has stood for almost half a century; even Golden Fleece in 1982, the fastest Derby winner since the war, could not match the time of Mahmoud in 1936. According to the figures worked out by Dr J. R. Pattison, there has been an improvement of only a second or two, on average, in the winning time since before the First World War. Even that may be attributed to horses reaching maturity rather earlier, or simply being foaled earlier. Nor have horses grown appreciably in size, though they do seem to have altered somewhat in shape, for example a more sloping croup (the top of the body between loins and tail) in response to the demands of shorter races. It would now be truly freakish to find a horse of only 14 hands 1 inch as Gimcrack was 200 years ago. But Hyperion was hardly a hand bigger, and he was good enough to dominate his generation in the 1930s.

There are various theories about this lack of progress. Dr Pattison believes that the gene pool has probably reached its optimum. Federico Tesio, perhaps the most brilliant and innovative thoroughbred breeder of all time, believed that there is in the thoroughbred a 'quality' or 'electricity' or 'nervous energy' which is dissipated in racing or breeding and can only be recovered through rest over a long period. He noted that no direct sire line had succeeded in producing more than three generations of Derby winners before it retreated from the front rank for a time. He ascribed the failure of good race-mares to sustain the highest quality through a number of generations to the same loss of 'electricity' on the racecourse. But this does not explain why the improvements in nutrition, which have had such a remarkable effect not only on human performance, but also on the breeding of cattle and sheep, have had no similar impact on the racehorse. Nor have the elementary methods of interval training made an effective contribution on the gallops of Newmarket or Kentucky. Such application of science as there has been seems to have concentrated on the malign purposes of the dopers, the anabolic steroid men, and the blood changers. It remains to be seen whether the geneticists, the nutritionists, and the physiologists can produce another St Simon or Eclipse to astonish the racing world.

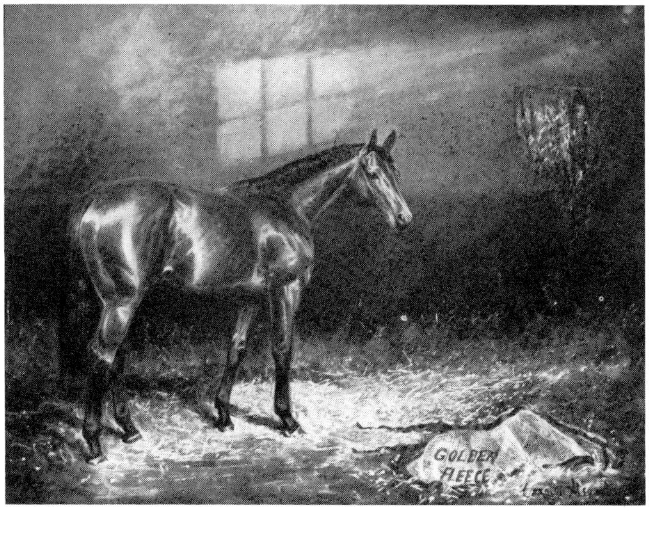


Carolyn Alexander: *Golden Fleece*. 1983. Oil on board, 45.7 × 61 cm. Private collection

# *Great Racehorses in Art*

# John Wootton

*c.1678–1765*

Lamprey
Victorious
Basto

John Wootton is one of the first artists whose portraits of racehorses have come down to us. Indeed, the picture of Lamprey was painted even before the Godolphin Arabian, one of the three foundation sires of the thoroughbred horse, had arrived in England. A tradition of painting racing scenes already stretched back to King Charles II's reign, but Wootton founded a custom which persists to this day when he betook himself to Newmarket for the express purpose of painting the famous racers of the time. He found it a prosperous enterprise. Charging 40 guineas for a large picture, and 20 for a more modest effort, he flourished sufficiently to establish himself in later years at Cavendish Square in London (even then a smart address), where Queen Caroline herself condescended to see his work.

Wootton was well connected from his youth. Henry, Duke of Beaufort, to whom he may have been page, sent him to Rome to study. He had already been a student of John Wyck, the splendid Dutch painter of battle scenes and hunting panoramas, who lived in London. His work was soon recognized by the 'quality' for what Horace Walpole called its 'consummate skill, animation and truth'. The literal truth, particularly the size of horses, may have been exaggerated by Wootton, though the boy grooms who make the horses seem colossi were often of minuscule stature; there are records of grooms riding at $3\frac{1}{2}$ stone. But the purpose of Wootton's portraits was not to give a precise anatomical record, but rather to convey the triumphal glory of these early champions. The portraits of the two greys, Lamprey and Victorious, are painted from a low angle, so that they seem to have stepped down from Mount Olympus.

Many of the figures in Wootton's paintings are shown with their heads turned away, suggesting that Wootton himself was none too confident with human portraits. Yet, there are striking faces in these pictures. The handsome and confident jockey carrying the saddle behind Victorious is a most assured and attractive rendering of the proud rider. Similarly, there are some powerful portraits among the figures in the Lamprey picture. The suggestion has been made that these are by another hand. This seems by no means certain. There is a sureness about the Victorious picture which suggests no need of assistance. Though we do know that Hogarth painted the faces in one of Wootton's hunting pictures for the Prince of Wales; the two men were paid separately.

Wootton was regarded as 'a capital master in the branch of his profession to which he chiefly devoted himself,' which included a wide variety of country and sporting scenes. Landseer was said to admire his picture of a partridge hunt at Badminton beyond any rival. Towards the end of his life he concentrated increasingly on landscapes. Wootton was past 80 when he died, though he seems to have given up painting some years earlier; the

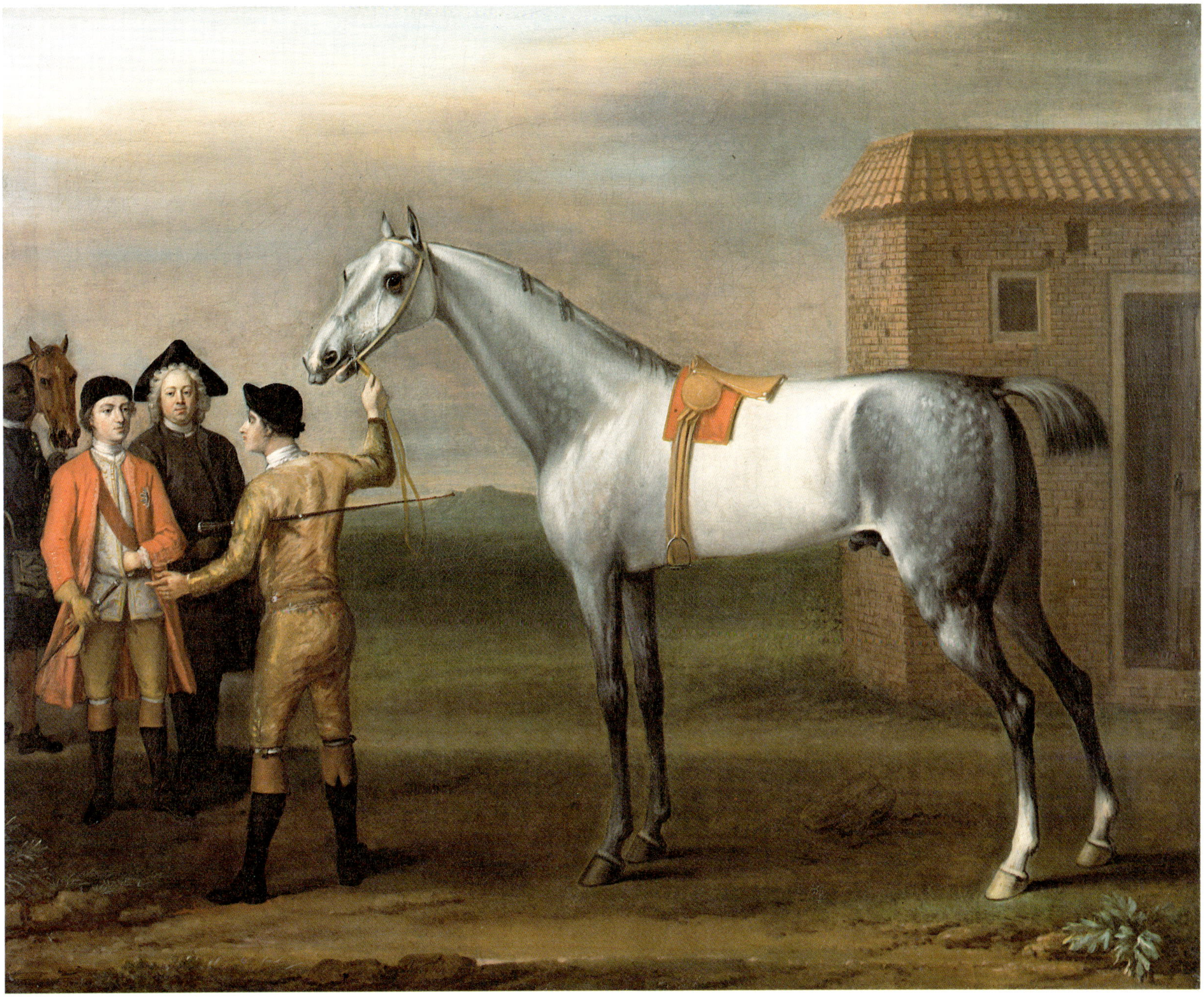

John Wootton: *Lamprey, with his owner Sir William Morgan (in the red coat).* 1723? Oil on canvas, 104 × 125.7 cm. Paul Mellon Collection, Yale Center for British Art, New Haven, Conn.

contents of his 'noble painting room' at Cavendish Square were sold off in 1761, four years before his death.

There must have been something odd about Lamprey, either he was unusually good or he was unusually difficult. He won every race in his first season at Newmarket in 1722, yet he was sold on each time. Thomas Panton bought him out of Yorkshire, won a 200-guinea match against a filly belonging to the Duke of Somerset, and promptly sold him on to Mr Neale. For Neale he won a King's Plate and was then sold on to Sir William Morgan. Perhaps it was all just good business. Lamprey served Sir William well, being still unbeaten when he defeated Lord Halifax's Sophonisba over 4 miles for 200 guineas at Newmarket at the end of 1725. However, by 1728, Lamprey was in the ownership of a Mr Howe and running down the field in a couple of races.

Lamprey was by Grey Hautboy, and was a full brother to Bay Bolton. He is said to have been killed shortly after he went to stud, but he did sire a son who made something of a mark in Ireland, Young Lamprey.

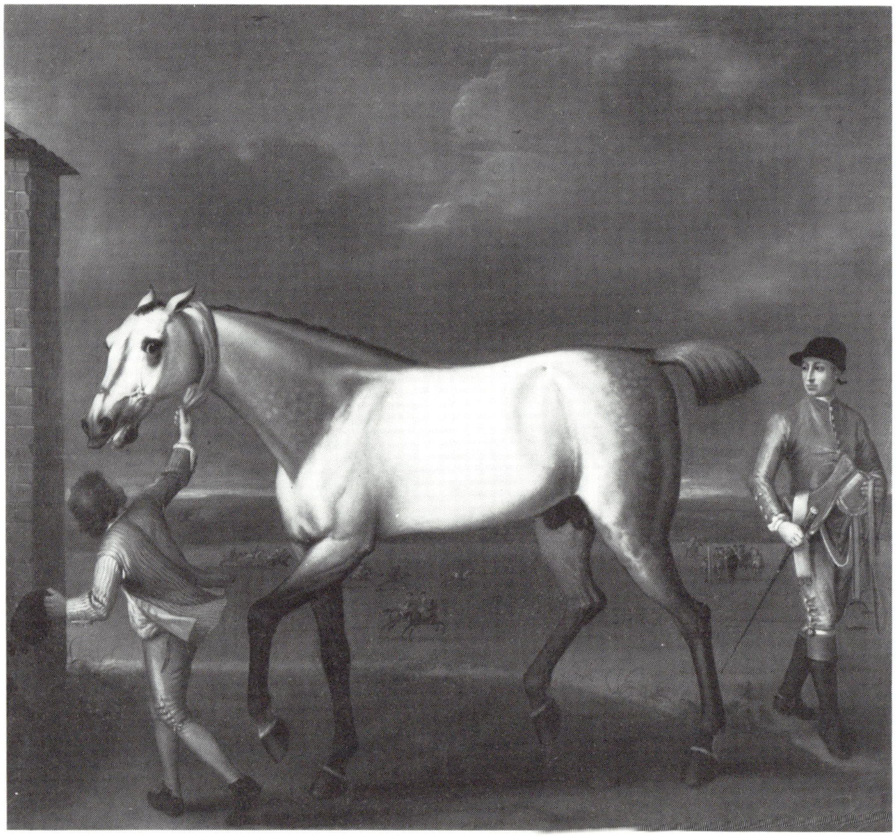

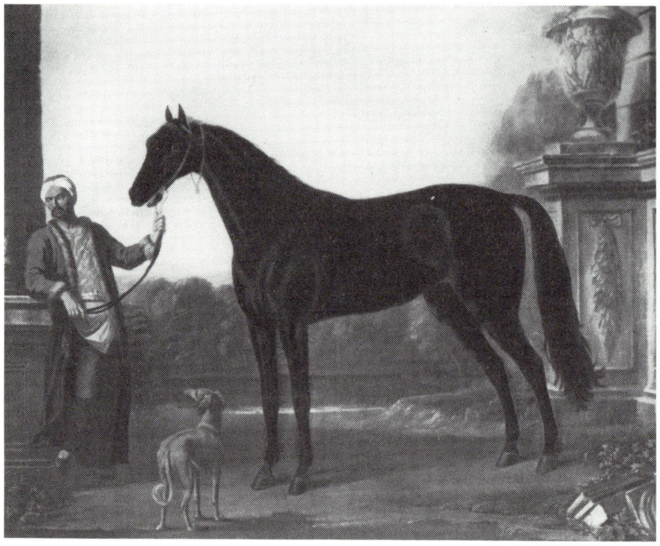

John Wootton: *The Byerley Turk*. Engraving, 1718, 27.9 × 34.9 cm. Private collection

John Wootton: *Victorious*. *c*.1725. Oil on canvas, 287.7 × 324 cm. Paul Mellon Collection, Yale Center for British Art, New Haven, Conn.

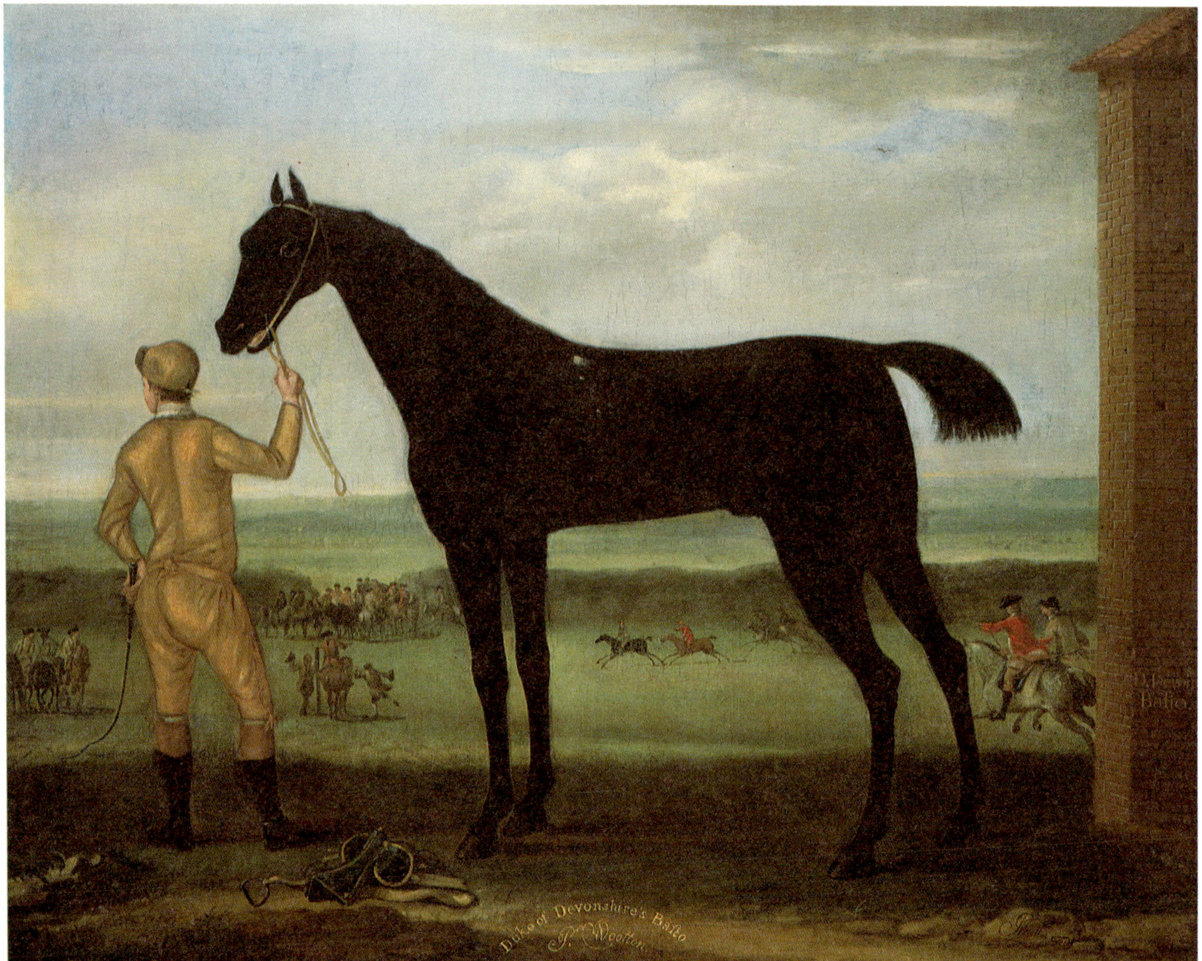


John Wootton: *Basto*. After *c*.1710. Oil on canvas, 101 × 127 cm. Private collection

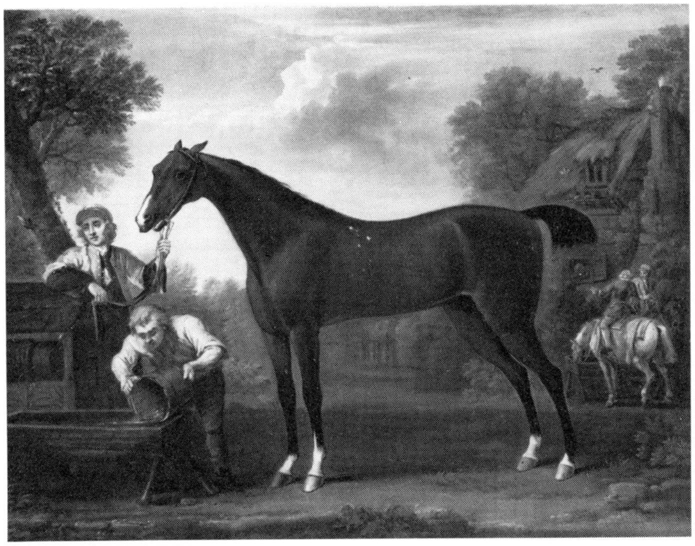

John Wootton: *Flying Childers*. 1735. Oil on canvas, 104 × 129.5 cm. Private collection

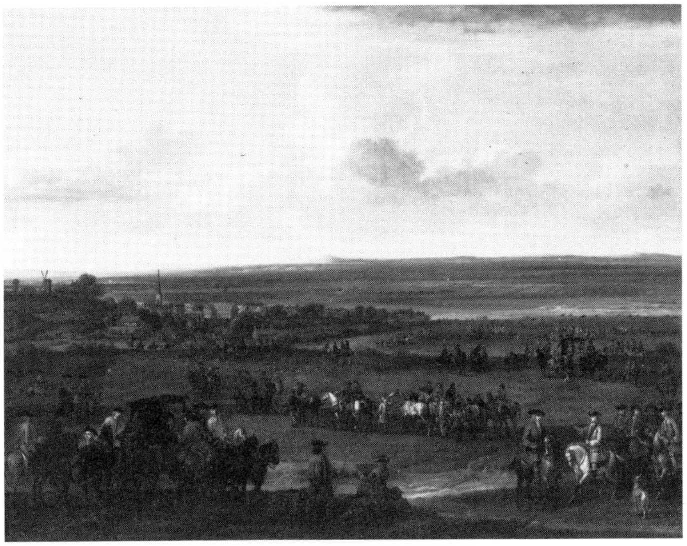

John Wootton: *George I at Newmarket*. 1717. Oil on canvas, 127.3 × 170.3 cm. Paul Mellon Collection, Yale Center for British Art, New Haven, Conn.

It is fair to surmise that the Duke of Hamilton bought the magnificent dappled grey Victorious from Lord Milsintown on the basis of his looks – and one victory – and then, as many a horseman after him has done, repented at leisure. There is an air of desperation about his programme. Victorious was taken down to Guildford, up to Nottingham and Lincoln, was beaten by Crab at Newmarket and by the Duke of Bolton's son of the Oxford Bloody Shouldered Arabian, managed to collect a 40-guinea plate at Huntingdon, was walked all the way up to Hambleton in Yorkshire, and still lost, but then redeemed himself on the Duke's home ground in Scotland, winning at Cupar and Peebles. The Duke's persistence was rewarded, for Victorious, who was by Ruffler, was a fair sire, with his progeny still running good-class races twenty years later.

The picture of Basto, probably by Wootton, would seem to be an early work and it certainly has not the forceful and finished quality of the Lamprey and Victorious portraits. Basto was a formidable racehorse and sire for the Duke of Devonshire. He was bred near Ferrybridge in Yorkshire, by Sir William Ramsden, and was said to follow the colour of his dam, Bay Peg, although in this picture he looks very like his sire, the Byerley Turk. Foaled in 1702, Basto won many good matches at Newmarket in the years 1708, 1709, and 1710, beating Earl Godolphin's Squirrel, the Marquis of Dorchester's Brisk, and Lord Raylton's Chance. He sired a number of good horses before dying at the Duke's estate, Chatsworth, in 1723. A dozen of his progeny made their mark during the reigns of Queen Anne and King George I. However, it was not Basto's line, but that of his contemporary, Partner, which was to perpetuate the Byerley Turk as one of the three tail-male ancestors of the modern thoroughbred.

Wootton painted a version of Flying Childers which was only brought to light by Richard Green, the London dealer, in the mid-1970s. The picture had been acquired under the impression that it was Matchem. But cleaning revealed some overpainting, and underneath was an unmistakable Flying Childers, with his four white feet and his white nose, which can be well compared with the Seymour picture (see p. 53).

Wootton's scenes of Newmarket are tremendously informative. His picture of George I mounted on a grey horse watching the racers being exercised at Newmarket contains a wealth of detail, including a self-portrait of Wootton, apparently, sketching the scene, with his telescope beside him. The shabby figure in the carriage would appear to be the ageing Tregonwell Frampton, the royal trainer. Compared with later times, the horses are not excessively rugged up, but the endless strings cantering away into the remote distance show that the Heath was going through one of its flourishing phases. The whole scene is rather straightfaced, however, and there is little sign of the amused eye for the rumbustious which is evident in Peter Tillemans's wonderfully lively *Racing for the King's Plate at Newmarket* (see p. 20).

# *James Seymour*

*1702–1752*

## Flying Childers
## Crab

Flying Childers raced only five times, but his victories at Newmarket in the 1720s made him the first popular hero of thoroughbred racing, with inns in England named after him to this day. He was painted certainly by Peter Tillemans and by John Wootton and at least three times by James Seymour for his owner the Duke of Devonshire and for Sir William Jolliffe.

This picture, by Seymour, most probably gives the nearest impression of what the first great English racehorse actually looked like, for Wootton is accused of exaggerating the size of his horses in deference to the illusions of their owners, and Tillemans, too, is thought to have erred on the side of fineness in line and conformation. Seymour, on the other hand, was considered to be meticulous in recording the contours of a horse. Even here, however, the looming power of the animal against the three grooms may be creating a false impression. Flying Childers was only $14\frac{1}{2}$ hands high, even smaller than his sire, the Darley Arabian, and was noted by the fancy of the time as compact and short-backed. Nonetheless, he was fast enough to do 4 miles on the Round Course at Newmarket in 6 minutes 48 seconds, carrying 9 st. 2 lb.

Flying Childers, a bay very like his sire, but with an extra white sock and a smaller blaze, shows the white scars of saddle sores, a common and faithfully recorded blemish seen on pictures painted well into the twentieth century. Indeed, he may have acquired them going about the business of post-horse to Leonard Childers of Doncaster, who bred him from a mare called Betty Leedes, and then used him to carry letters from his home at Carr House.

James Seymour had a more than professional interest in the Turf. Born in London and raised in a house frequented by Wren and Lely, he was left a considerable fortune by his father, a banker. But James was a legendary gambler and it apparently did not take him long to lose it all backing horses, a consequence which encouraged him to turn to painting them professionally. Seymour had a notoriously sharp wit and quick temper. He walked away from a lucrative commission to paint a room at Petworth House after a dinner-table row with his host, the Duke of Somerset. However, his patrons continued to support him, paying some princely sums, even £100, to commission him, though he was often characterized as an idle and unreliable sprig.

For all that, Seymour was the most important link between Wootton and Stubbs, modifying the primitive style with some careful studies and detailed backgrounds, as is evident in this painting of Flying Childers. He seems to have worked from finished sketches made in a pocketbook, from which his concern for anatomical precision is apparent. Very few of his drawings have survived.

Seymour was a busy painter and among his host of

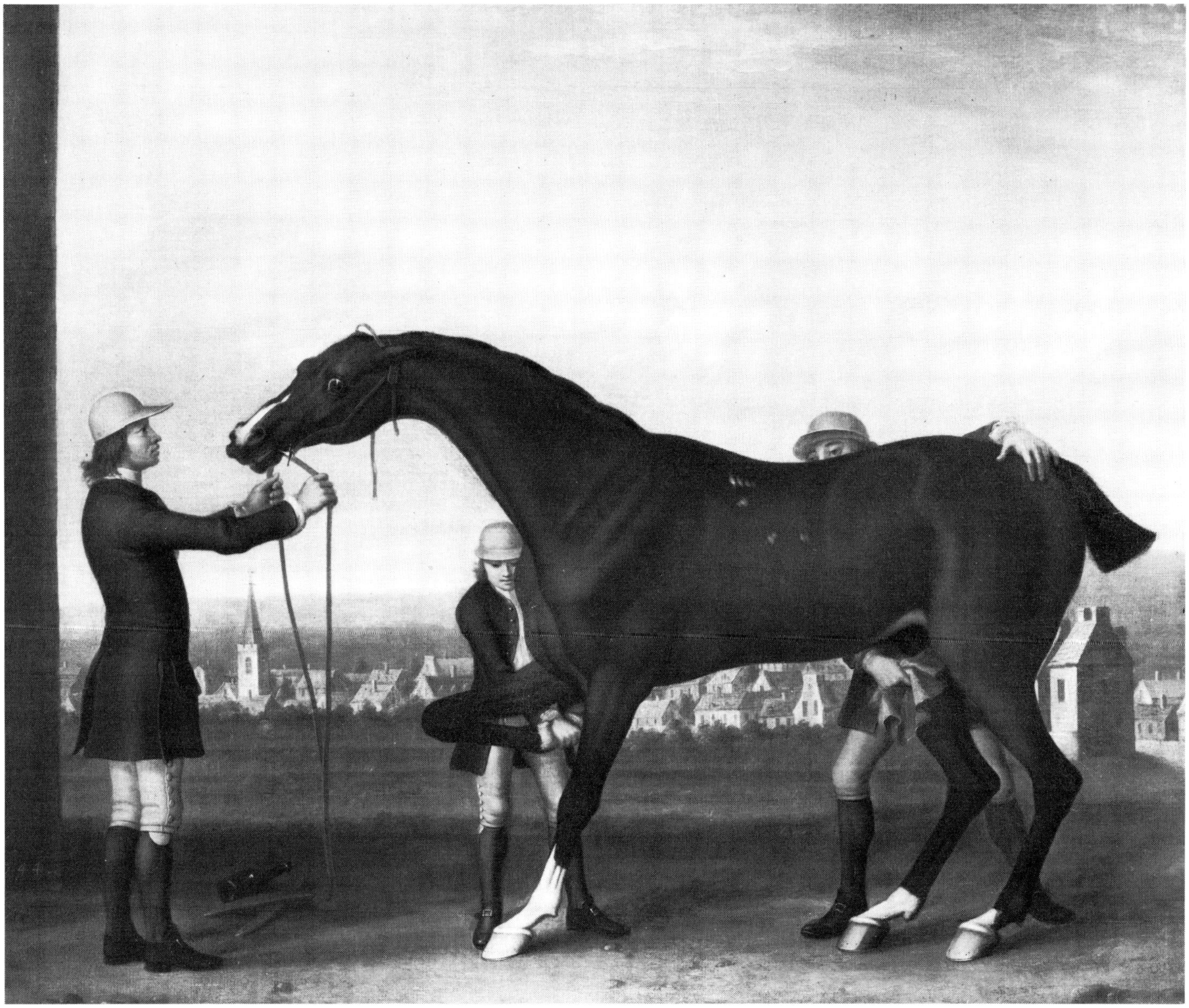

James Seymour: *Flying Childers*. After 1722. Oil on canvas, 60 × 71 cm. Private collection

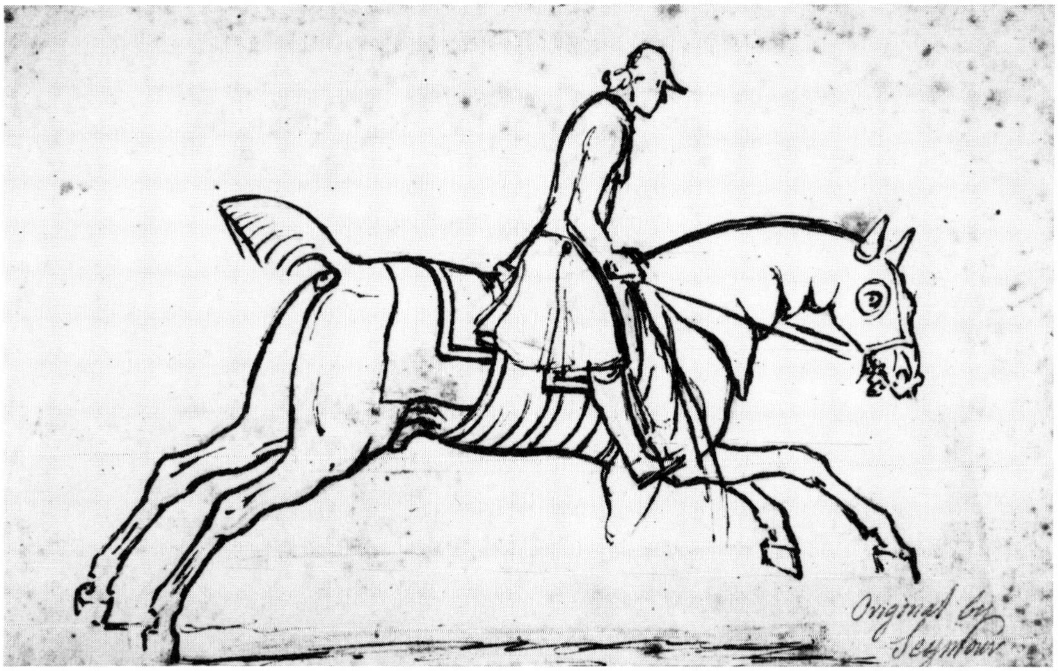


James Seymour: *Sketch of a Galloping Racehorse with a Groom mounted*. Pen over pencil with washed mount, 16.8 × 27.3 cm. Royal Library, Windsor Castle

racehorse pictures are Bajazet, a son of the Godolphin Arabian, Spanking Roger, a son of Flying Childers, Squirrel, a son of Snake, Bay Bolton, Fearnought, Lamprey, Moorcock, Old Scar, Conqueror, Babraham, Young Cartouche, Bonny Black, Lath, Carlisle, Second, Creeping Molly, Betty, Volunteer, and Sportsman. He also painted a famous study of the Bloody Shouldered Arabian. Seymour's first known work, a portrait of Old Partner, was a racehorse picture, but he soon became adept at a range of sporting and animal work, including pictures of cattle, fox hunting, and greyhound coursing.

There being no Messrs Weatherby's about in the first half of the eighteenth century to regulate the naming of horses, it is not always easy to identify the animals in early pictures. Portraits allegedly of Matchem by Seymour have been seen about in London galleries recently, when

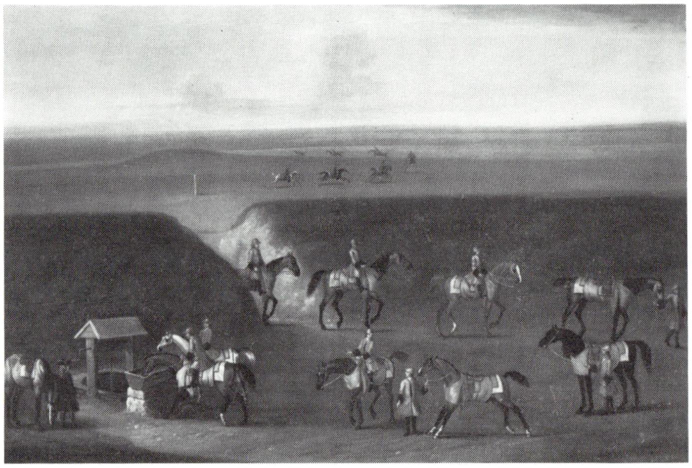

James Seymour: *A View of Newmarket Heath at the Well Gap in the Devil's Ditch, with Horses Watering*. Oil on canvas, 79.4 × 121.9 cm. Private collection

James Seymour: *Crab*. 1752. Oil on canvas, 91.5 × 114.5 cm. Private collection

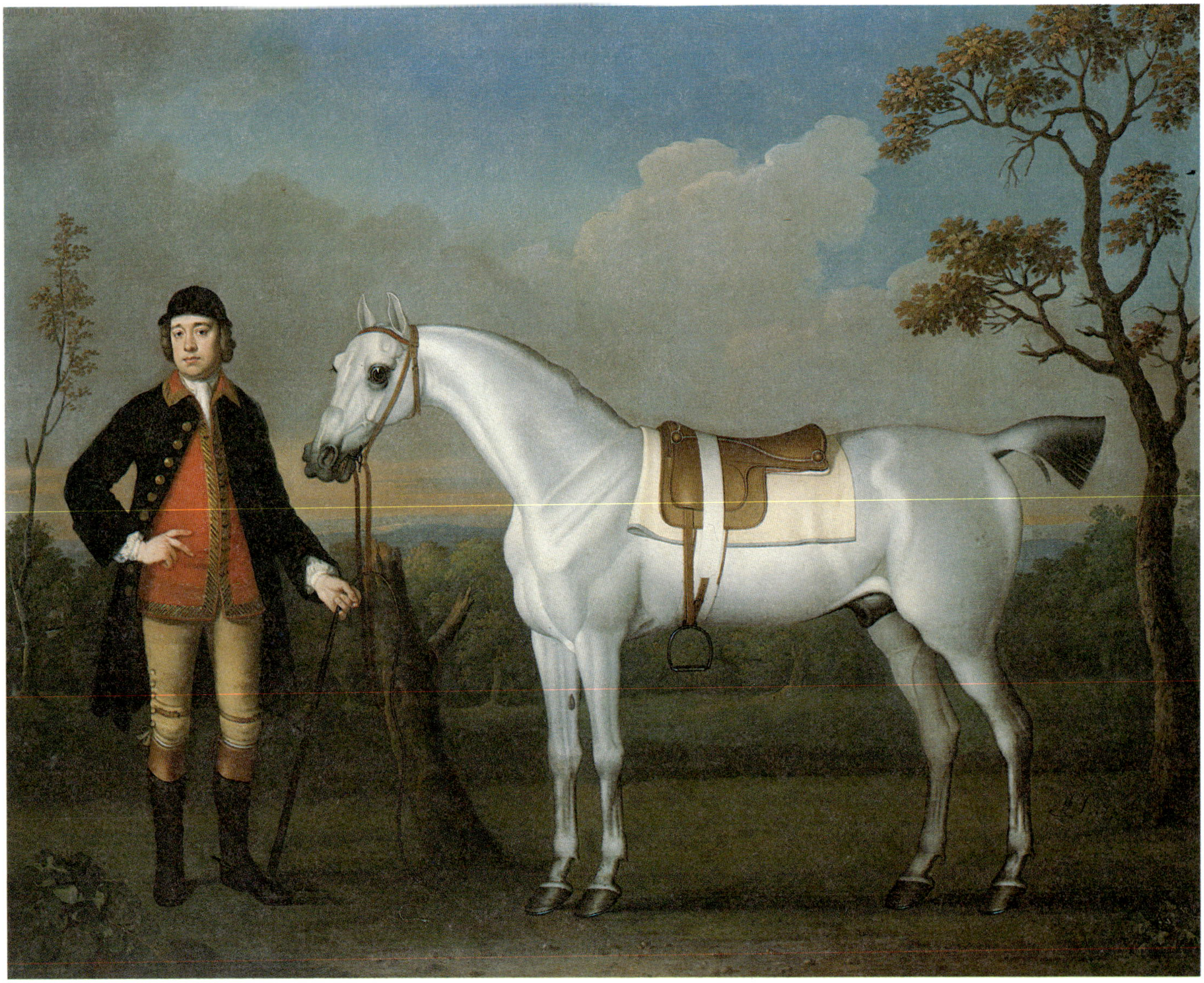

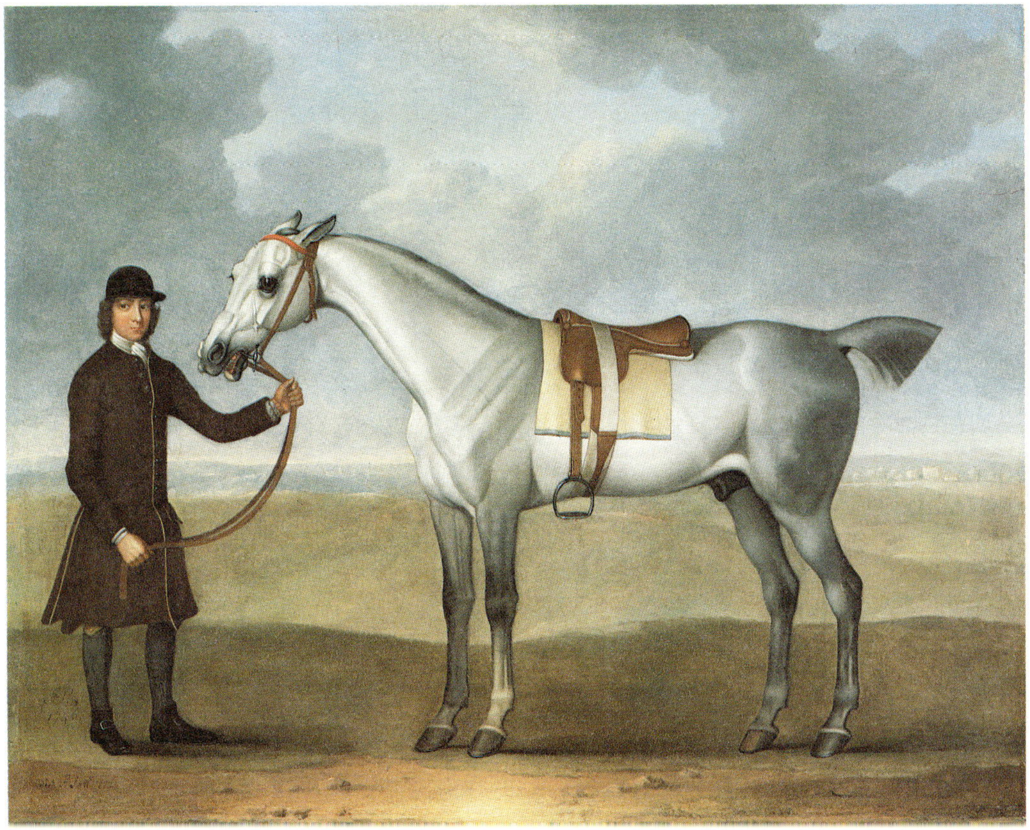

James Seymour: *Crab*. 1746. Oil on canvas, 51 × 63.5 cm. Private collection

Matchem did not race till after Seymour's death. In particular the portraits of Crab by Seymour offer plenty of room for confusion.

There is a most handsome and fully finished work dated 1752 of a Crab who may be the son or even the grandson of the original Crab, a son of the Alcock Arabian. In 1750, Lord Portmore won a King's Plate with a 'grey horse Crab, by Crab', and this is probably his likeness. The horse is fit, compact, and eager in appearance. The trees, the broken stump, the groom, the evening light are most carefully done to produce a worshipful portrait, demanding if not the reverence of Wootton's work, then at least a sober homage. There is another Seymour picture of Crab dated 1746. The horse is a more commanding animal and the background is comparatively skimped, but there remains the abiding impression that these, still novel, scions of Arab blood demanded veneration from the owners who commissioned their portraits.

Crab, the son of the Alcock Arabian, beat the Duke of Bolton's Cleopatra in a match for 500 guineas at Newmarket in 1728 and won a King's Plate, beating the Duke of Cumberland's Victorious, the following year. He was then sold on to the Duke of Ancaster, who ran him more than a dozen times at such unlikely spots as Chipping Campden. Lord Portmore had a six-year-old grey named Crab running in 1742, and another six-year-old Crab in 1750. It is reasonable to assume that they are both sons of the original Crab, who is said to have died in 1750. These would seem to be three different horses if not three generations of the Alcock Arabian line of greys, all called Crab, which produced the Derby winner of 1785, Aimwell, though he was a bay.

Seymour also produced some busy contemporary scenes of Newmarket, including the picture at the Well Gap in the Devil's Ditch showing a string of horses watering, all clearly with grooms in one livery, while another group canters beyond the dike. These records of early Newmarket must have already had an antique charm by the end of the eighteenth century, for a number of them were engraved and published as prints at that time, apparently with some success.

# *George Stubbs*

*1724–1806*

## Mambrino
## Whistlejacket
## Hambletonian
## Gimcrack
## Eclipse
## Godolphin Arabian

Across two centuries, the power and magnificence of the great grey stallion Mambrino still course through Stubbs's most splendid picture. The massive crest and shoulders, the unmistakable arrogance of the Arab lineage, the blood almost palpable in the veins, the tension in the skin, the strutting pose as he dominates the landscape combine to form as enthralling a portrait as any in the history of the thoroughbred. All Stubbs's painstaking labours for *The Anatomy of the Horse*, and his enduring attachment to grey horses, came to no grander fruition than in the painting which now hangs at Garrowby Hall in Yorkshire, scarcely thirty miles from where the horse was bred by Mr John Atkinson of Scholes in 1768.

Mambrino's career brushed against the most celebrated figures in the golden age of racing. He passed from Yorkshire, the cradle of the thoroughbred, to Lord Grosvenor's ownership at Hare Park, Newmarket, there to carry His Lordship's colours in a series of matches against the horses of Charles James Fox, most shining of the Talents and a devotee of the Turf. 'The Druid' (Henry Dixon) left an affectionate portrait of Fox: 'He was a macaroni of the first water, and not only rejoiced in red-heeled shoes but undertook a journey from Lyons to Paris with the Earl of Carlisle for the sole purpose of buying waistcoats, which formed their sole theme there and back. He was a heavy bettor and a constant visitor to Newmarket, where his portly frame was ever to be seen on his hack, tearing wildly past the judge's chair, close up with the leading horses.'

Mambrino was first matched against Fox's brown horse Pyrrhus, for a purse of 2,000 guineas, in the spring of 1774. With Pyrrhus's owner on one side 'riding at full speed, whipping, spurring and blowing as if he would have infused his whole soul into his favourite racer', and Pyrrhus's jockey deliberately bumping Mambrino and knocking him half-way across the course, the match took on a desperate note. The two horses were locked together to the last, with Mambrino eventually going down by a neck.

The next spring, after winning the Newmarket King's Plate, he came up against 'the terrible horse Trentham', another crack owned by Charles James Fox and his partner Lord Foley. Trentham, by Sweepstakes, won eleven races off the reel and beat 'the most capital horses in England'. The bay and the grey lined up on the Heath for the Jockey Club Plate. The first running resulted in a dead heat, and so, in the relentless custom of the day, the race was rerun. Mambrino triumphed – a tribute to the extraordinary toughness which, it was to transpire, he would hand on to his stock.

Mambrino was still racing at the age of 9, when he

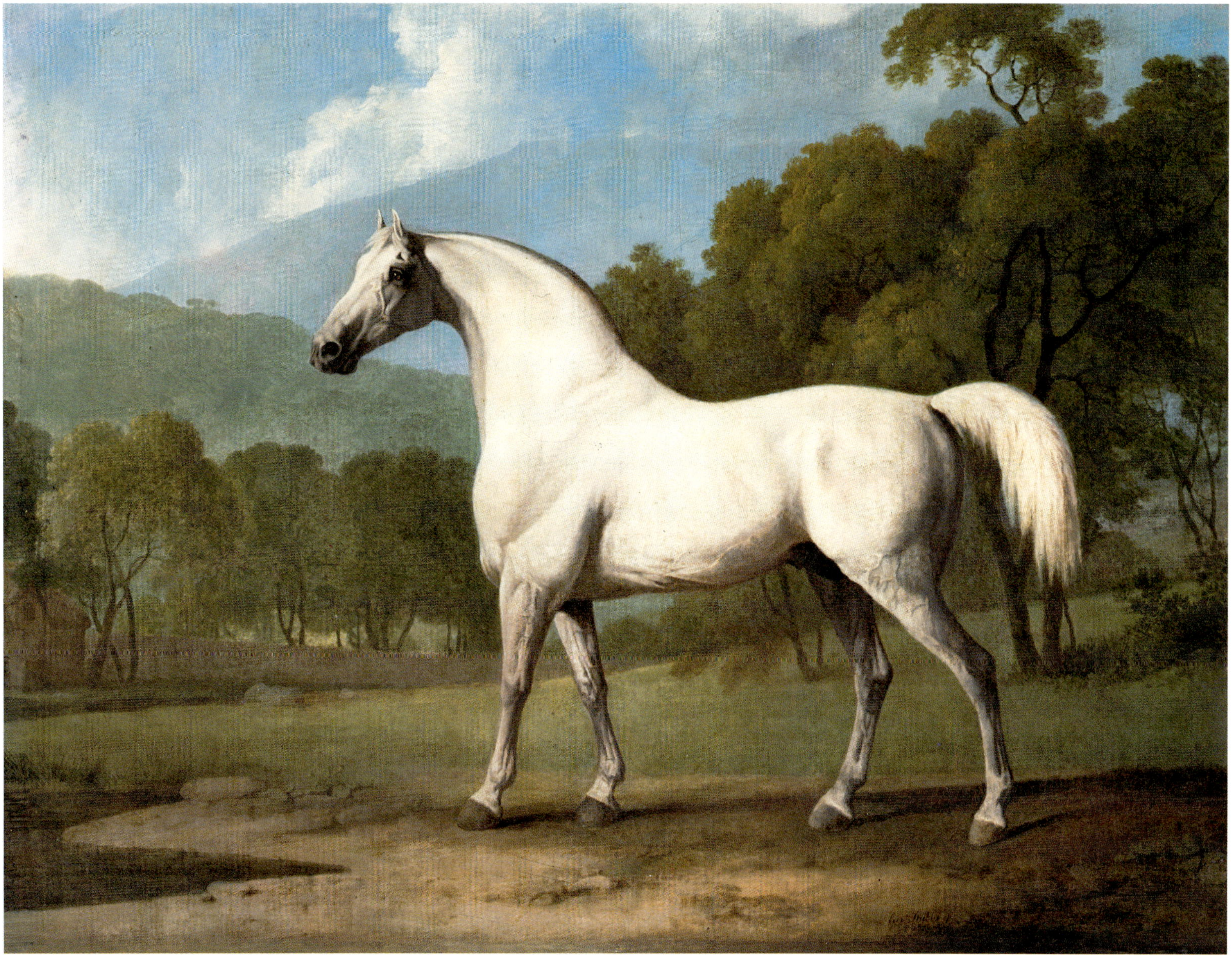

George Stubbs: *Mambrino*. 1779. Oil on panel, 63.5 × 76.2 cm. The Halifax Collection

was matched against Shark, but then went to stud at Balsham in the company of three distinguished contemporaries, Gimcrack, Sweetbriar, and Sweet William. His special place in the history of racing comes through his son Messenger, another grey. Messenger was exported to America and was to be found standing for £5 at Mr Philip Platt's 'in the neighbourhood of the townships of Newton and Flushing on Long Island in the State of New York'. For this modest fee, America received the blood which was to become the cornerstone of the trotting breed.

A first sight of Stubbs's portrait of Whistlejacket is awe-inspiring. All the fire and drama of the thoroughbred stallion flash out of this life-size picture: the hoofs flailing, nostrils wide, eye askance, the chestnut coat gleaming, mane and tail flying. Whistlejacket is said to have been roused to fury by the vision of himself, and to have attacked the canvas – and the painter. The purity of the picture against its plain background heightens the impact, but it seems this was fortuitous. Lord Rockingham, Stubbs's patron, had apparently intended a landscape and a figure of the King to be added by other artists, but eventually decided to leave it plain, whether

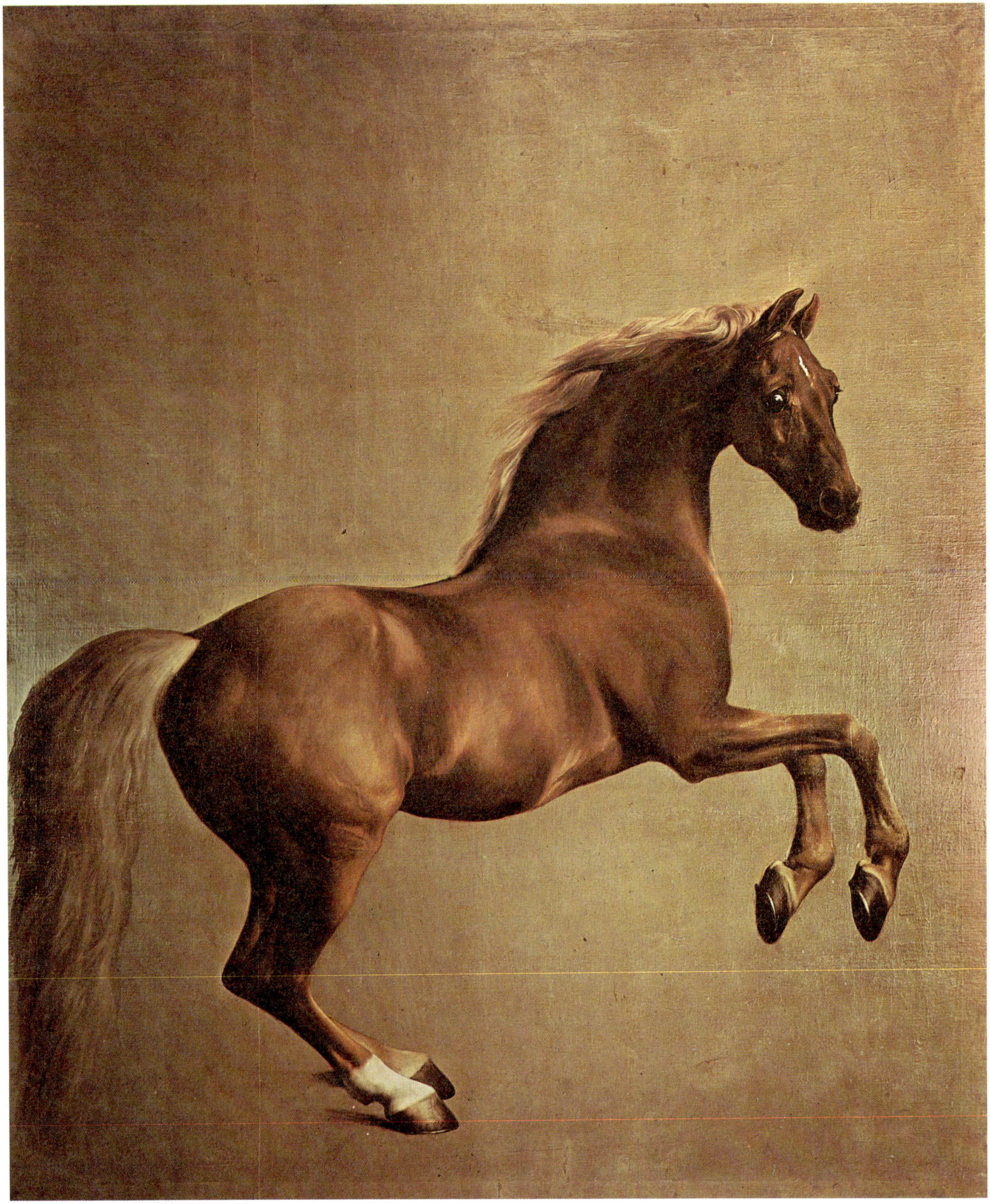

out of aesthetic discrimination or political animosity to George III's new policies is unclear.

Whistlejacket has a deceptively modern look in this picture, which tends to undermine the authenticity of all those small-headed, thin-necked, narrow-quartered renderings of eighteenth- and early nineteenth-century horses. It is not hard to imagine him being provoked into rearing and showing his paces at some late twentieth-century county show.

Whistlejacket originally belonged to Sir William Middleton, a Northumberland Member of Parliament who had also owned the celebrated racers Squirrel and Camilla. Sir William ran him in the Jockey Club Plate of 1756, but he was beaten by the Duke of Ancaster's Spectator, a son of Crab. He was then sold to the Marquis of Rockingham – twice Prime Minister – who was a great supporter of Northern racing. He was responsible for the new grandstands at Doncaster and York, won the first St Leger with Alabaculia, and owned Bay Malton, who, in his heyday around 1766, broke the four-mile record at York and was so fast that no horse could be found to take him on. Lord Rockingham's great adversary on the Turf was a Yorkshire landowner, Sir Charles Turner. Sir Charles's Brutus had, to Rockingham's great chagrin, given 7 lb. and a beating to his horse Remus in a 500-guinea match at Newmarket in 1757. Whistlejacket seems to have been purchased for the express purpose of avenging that defeat.

The contest took place on the Knavesmire at York in 1759. The two leading jockeys of the day were engaged, Whistlejacket having the benefit of John Singleton, and Brutus being ridden by Thomas Jackson, 'bred up at Black Hambleton,' as it said on his gravestone, 'and crowned with glory at Newmarket'. But not at York. The race was 4 miles and the stake 2,000 guineas. Jackson was held to be the epitome of the Yorkshire style of dash and forcing jockeyship, whereas Singleton, though also a Yorkshireman, had imbibed the subtler arts of the Newmarket 'waiting style'. The race ran to plan, with Singleton waiting till he was in sight of the grandstand to get Whistlejacket home a comfortable winner.

There are few more humbling moments for the horse-lover than the sight of a brave horse stripped down at the end of a race. He has given his all. The eyes roll at once in triumph and exhaustion. The flanks heave. The ears lie back on the neck. Every vein stands out on the sweated skin like the marbling on old porcelain. The animal shifts and strains as he is washed or rubbed down. The catharsis of the race is over. The onlooker is left only with wondering admiration.

Stubbs painted two inspired pictures of these private, almost sacramental moments on the racecourse. The first was of Gimcrack on Newmarket Heath in 1765. Then, over thirty years later, he painted Hambletonian after his defeat of Diamond in a match at the Craven meeting in 1799. Every fibre of Hambletonian testifies in this picture to the ordeal he has been through. The mouth is slack and the tail wildly splayed. He is threshing around as though the discipline of being held is beyond his endurance. The stable-lad has a sympathetic hand on his

LEFT
George Stubbs: *Whistlejacket*. 1761–2. Oil on canvas, 325 × 259 cm. Private collection

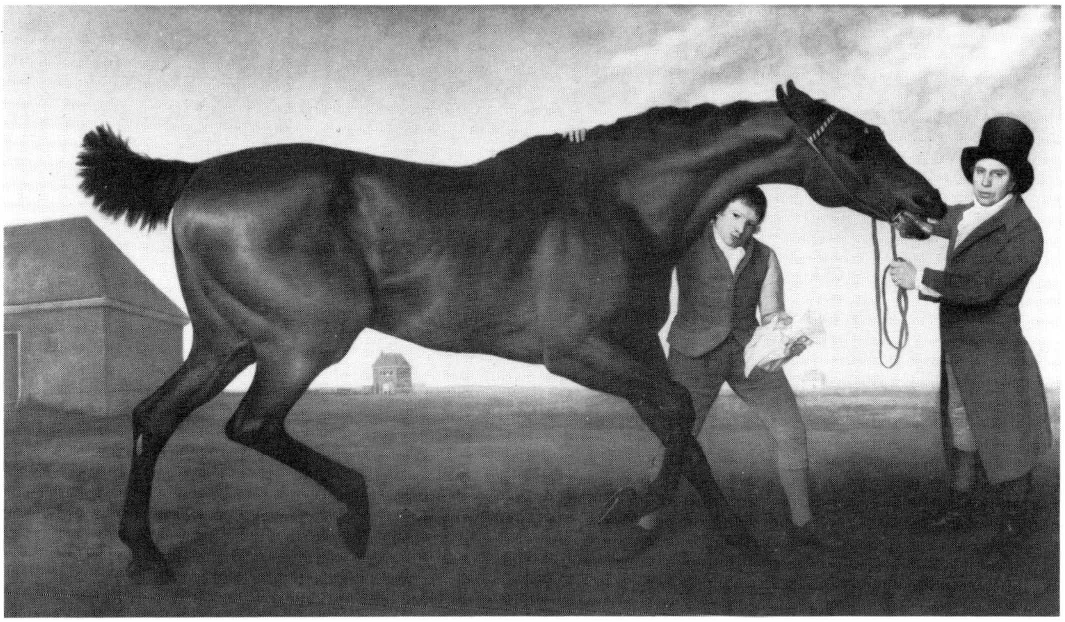

RIGHT
George Stubbs: *Hambletonian*. 1799. Oil on canvas, 209.5 × 367 cm. Mount Stewart, Co. Down

neck. The trainer seems almost in shock. It is a huge and emotional picture.

Hambletonian, a bay son of King Fergus, belonged to Sir Henry Vane-Tempest when he was matched against Mr Joseph Cookson's Diamond for 3,000 guineas. Hambletonian was so named because he won his first race at Hambleton in Yorkshire. Sir Charles Turner bought him in a job lot with Beningbrough and Oberon from an ex-stable-boy, John Hutchinson. Hambletonian immediately won two sweepstakes for Sir Charles at York, and then went down to Doncaster to win the St Leger for him. Indeed, the horse was to win seventeen of his twenty races. He was sold to Sir Henry Vane-Tempest in 1796.

Hambletonian came to the match of 1799 a fresh horse, not having raced in 1798, whereas Diamond had had a hard season. Diamond was a son of Highflyer, much more lightly built than his rival. Hambletonian had Frank Buckle in the saddle: 'to praise his riding would be to gild gold,' said 'The Druid', 'his shape and seat were exquisite'. And indeed, Buckle seems to have managed to steal some ground in the early stages as they passed the Ditch on the Beacon Course at Newmarket. But then the smaller horse, receiving 3 lb. with Dennis Fitzpatrick in the saddle, got away up the hill. Hambletonian took back the lead until the last half-mile when Diamond came at him again. The battle which then ensued must have been unusually cruel. For though it was an age when the whip and the spur were employed with abandon, the thrashing which both horses received that day lived on for many a year in the memory of those who saw it. Hambletonian got up in the final strides to win by less than a length.

Sir Henry Vane-Tempest is often said to have determined never to race Hambletonian again. But he did, in fact, send the stallion out at the York August meeting of 1800 to beat Dion and Timothy. Hambletonian retired to stud at Middleham in North Yorkshire, unbowed by his exertions, and sired more than 140 winners before his death at the age of 27 in 1818. He stands in the direct line from Eclipse through to St Simon and Diamond Jubilee.

The study of Gimcrack being rubbed down after a race more than thirty years previously, in 1765, is less emotive. It is an intriguing picture, with the horse composed rather than distressed, and the stable-lad, jockey, and trainer relaxed and confident after victory.

George Stubbs: *Gimcrack*. 1765. Oil on canvas, 101.6 × 193 cm. Jockey Club, Newmarket

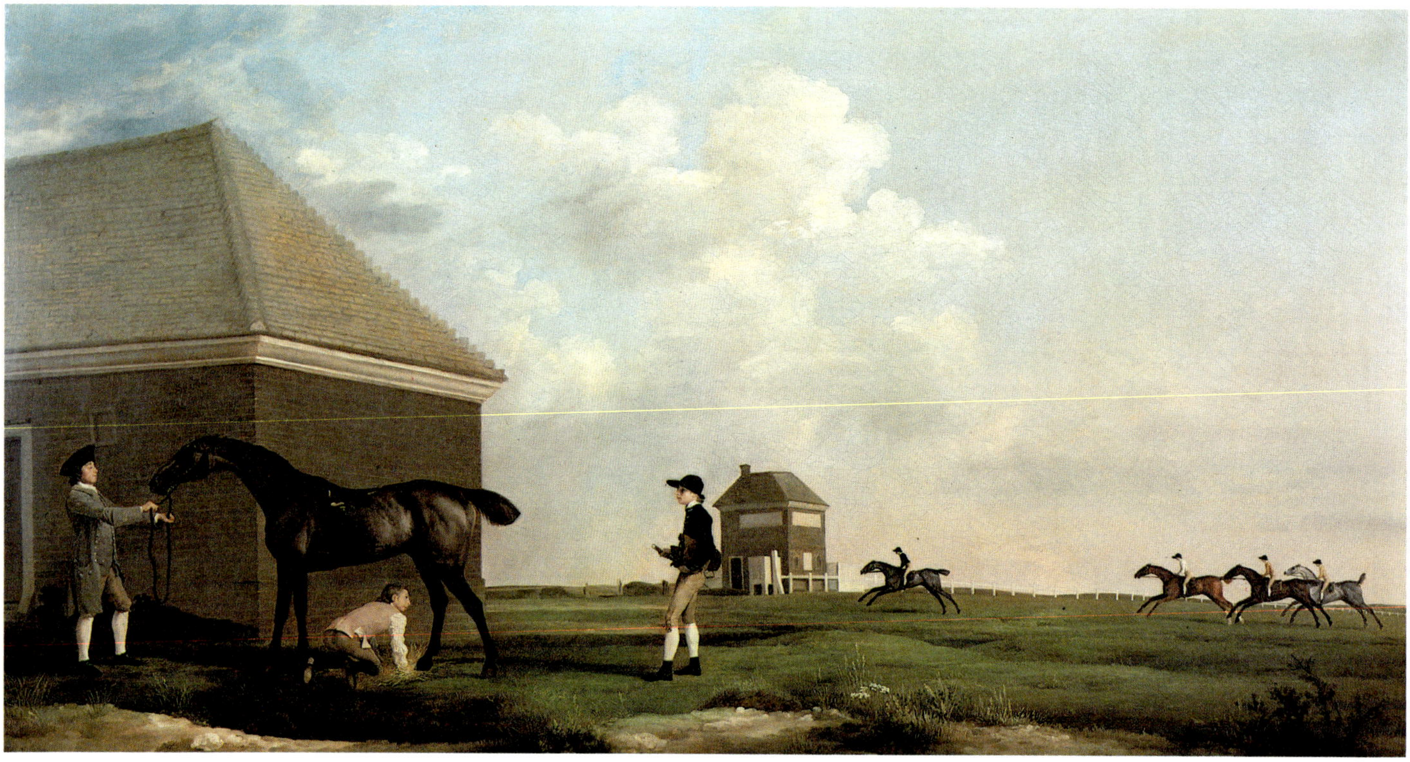

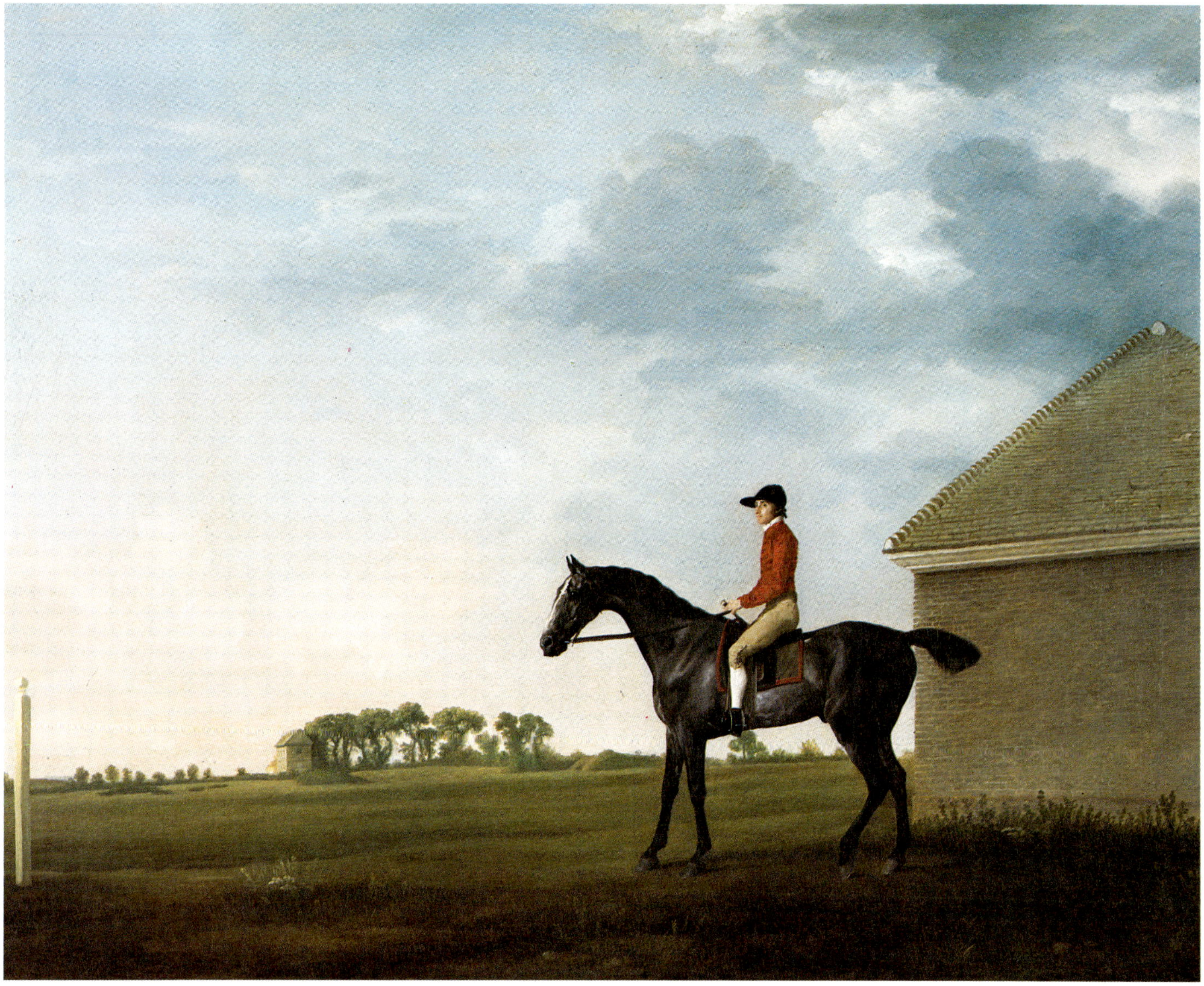

George Stubbs: *Gimcrack*. *c*.1765. Oil on canvas, 100.3 × 127 cm. Fitzwilliam Museum, Cambridge

In the background is a version of the race itself, with Gimcrack winning quite easily. We know Stubbs made the most careful preliminary studies of landscape and background before completing these Newmarket paintings. He then seems to have eliminated all extraneous detail before laying out the final work on quite strict, almost geometric lines.

Gimcrack was painted at least three times by Stubbs. He was a dark grey at first, but he lightened rapidly. By the time Lord Halifax's picture was painted he was almost white. This was 1770, when he was 10 years old. He still looks fit to run for his life, with the almost

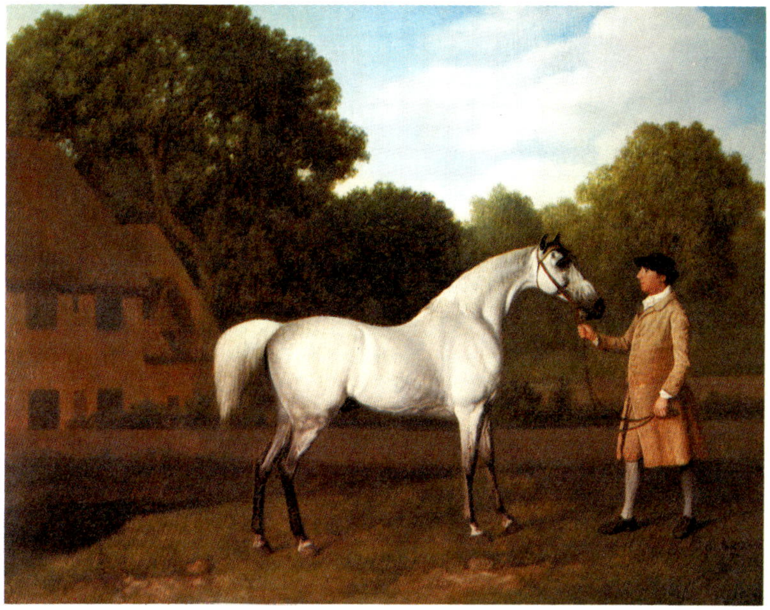

George Stubbs: *Gimcrack*. 1770. Oil on canvas, 84 × 110.5 cm. The Halifax Collection

miniature neatness which so endeared him to his followers, though he has not a pretty head and rather a big nose. 'The sweetest little horse that ever was,' Lady Bunbury called him. Indeed, he was really only a pony, measuring 14 hands 1 inch. Bred at Murrel Green in Hampshire, he was by Cripple who was a son of the Godolphin Arabian. The grey colour must have come from Crab through the dam's side.

Gimcrack won twenty-six of his thirty-six races for a succession of owners, including Stubbs's patrons, Lord Bolingbroke and Lord Grosvenor. One of Gimcrack's proprietors was a Frenchman, Count de Lauraguais, who bought him specifically to take to France in order to win a wager that a horse could cover 22½ miles in an hour. Gimcrack crossed the Channel and obliged. He returned to England and eventually retired to stud at the age of 11. His admirers had already founded the Gimcrack Club, which endures to this day and holds an annual dinner at which the winning owner of the Gimcrack Stakes at York is required to opine on the current state of Turf affairs.

In the auspicious year of 1764, when the moon eclipsed the sun, the mysterious arbiters of genetic power produced a horse who was to surpass all others as a racehorse and a sire, and was to be a fit subject for the greatest painter of the thoroughbred horse. Eclipse, a son of Marske out of the mare Spiletta, was in the male line of the Darley Arabian. He was bred by the Duke of Cumberland, and on the Duke's death was sold at auction to a Smithfield butcher, William Wildman. With an unexceptional pedigree, as it seemed at the time, and a ferocious temperament, Eclipse may have looked an unpromising purchase. But Wildman was a patient man, and finally produced Eclipse as a five-year-old for his first race at Epsom in 1769.

Among the crowd that day in May was a noisy Irish gambler, Captain Dennis O'Kelly. O'Kelly was shrewd and courageous, and an outstanding judge of a horse. It took him only one sight of Eclipse in action to change his fortunes for life; previously, in a roistering career, he had been a sedan-chair carrier, spent time in prison for debt, and eventually turned to gambling, financed by a lady of the town, Charlotte Hayes. After Eclipse had won the first of the three 4-mile heats in untroubled fashion, O'Kelly knew he had seen an outstanding horse and immediately announced his famous bet, 'Eclipse first, the rest nowhere.' So it happened. In the second heat Eclipse distanced his rivals, leaving them more than a furlong behind at the finish.

O'Kelly determined to buy Eclipse. At first he took a half-share from Wildman, and then in 1770 acquired the horse outright. Eclipse won eighteen races and was never extended. Indeed, seven were walk-overs, for most owners were unwilling to take him on. When he did have opponents, their chances were considered so derisory that he would start at 10–1 on. Eclipse, a chestnut with a white blaze and one white foot, was a remarkable success at stud, siring the winners of 862 races, including three Derby winners, Young Eclipse, Saltram, and Sergeant. O'Kelly lived in style for the rest of his days, thanks to Eclipse, who he reckoned had earned him more than £25,000.

O'Kelly owned two other famous horses that appeared in Stubbs's *Turf Review* series: Volunteer, a chestnut, who was the sire of Eagle, and Dungannon (see also pp. 72–4), who was second in Saltram's Derby and won a string of races, including the Craven Stakes and the King's Plate of 1786 at Newmarket. Stubbs's picture of Dungannon shows him accompanied by a sheep, marked with Dennis O'Kelly's initials; the two animals were reputed to be inseparable.

The Godolphin Arabian (also called the Godolphin Barb) is one of the three sires to whom all thoroughbred racehorses can be traced back. He was a brown horse, apparently from Yemeni stock, who seems to have been presented to Louis XV of France by the Bey of Tunis in 1731, when he was 7 years old. He was acquired by Mr Edward Coke of Longford Hall in Derbyshire, along with a crop of legends, including the story that he had been pulling a water-cart in Paris.

As far as the records show, the Godolphin Arabian never raced, and when Mr Coke died in 1733 he bequeathed him along with all his bloodstock to Earl Godolphin. There he covered the mare Roxana to produce Cade and through him Matchem. His line has never been as luxuriantly successful as that of the Darley Arabian, but it has been doggedly persistent, throwing

---

OPPOSITE ABOVE
George Stubbs: *Eclipse*. 1770. Oil on canvas, 100.3 × 131.4 cm. Jockey Club, Newmarket

OPPOSITE BELOW LEFT
George Stubbs: *Dungannon*. 1793. Oil on canvas, 101.6 × 127 cm. The Halifax Collection

OPPOSITE BELOW RIGHT
George Stubbs: *The Godolphin Arabian*. c.1750. Oil on canvas, 36.8 × 43.2 cm. Woodward Collection, The Baltimore Museum of Art

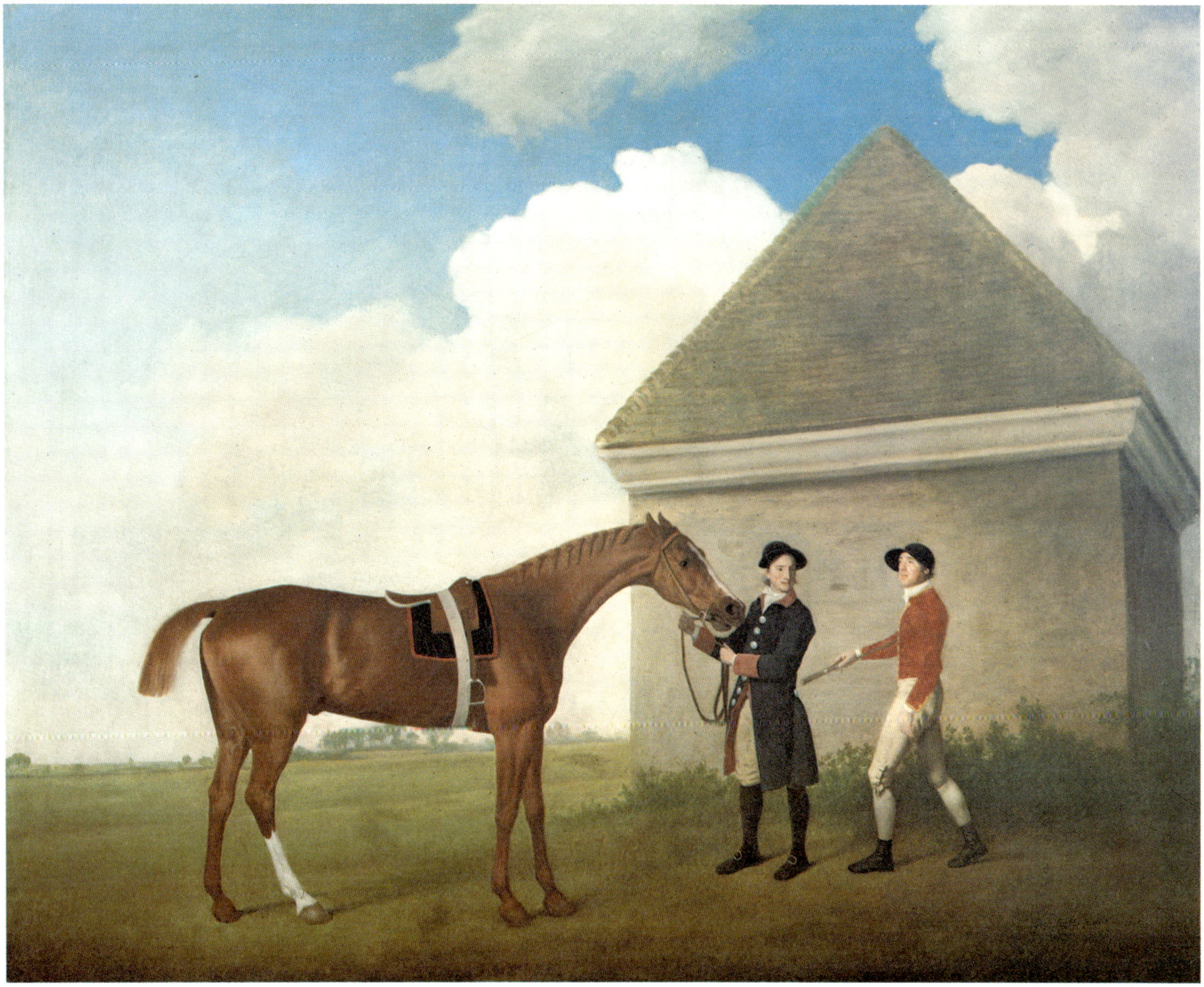

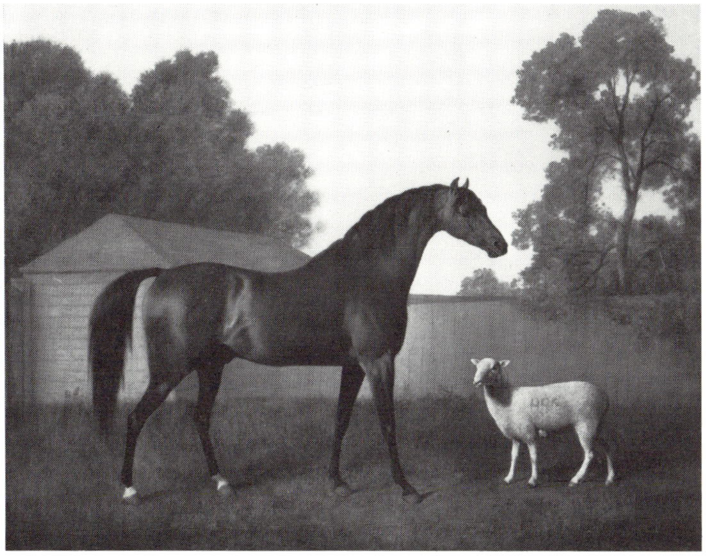

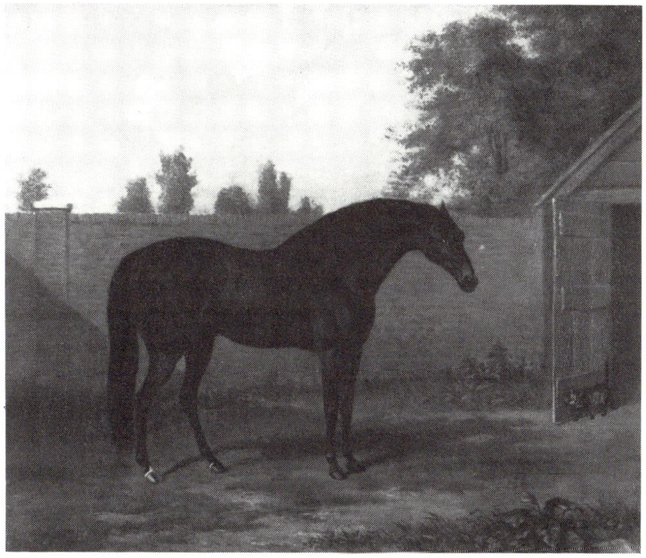

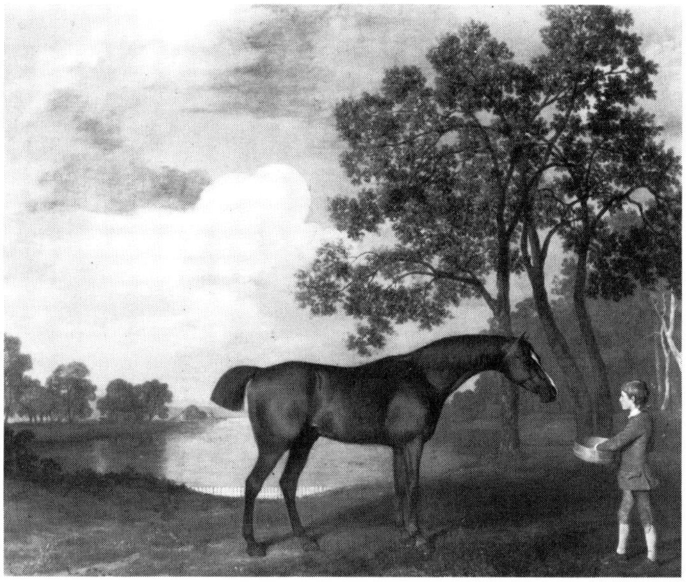

George Stubbs: *Pumpkin*. 1774. Oil on panel, 80 × 99.7 cm. Paul Mellon Collection, Upperville, Virginia

up West Australian in the middle of the nineteenth century, Airborne and Santa Claus, Derby winners in England another century on, and Man o' War in the United States.

There is no doubt from Stubbs's picture that we are seeing a mature stallion of beautiful quality, the neck full and arched, fine legs, and a handsome head. The tabby cat, Grimalkin, was supposed to be his constant companion. This portrait was probably executed not long before the Godolphin's death in 1753, by which time his grandson was beginning the exploits on the racecourse which were to help establish the Godolphin line.

It was not only the anatomical accuracy, the emotional realism, and the mature colours which made Stubbs seem so novel and appealing to the English patrons of the 1760s. He also introduced new settings and groupings for his horse pictures. The Mares and Foals are the most celebrated, but his picture of Pumpkin is a truly charming and endearing study which must have seemed revolutionary to connoisseurs of the day. The boy in his red coat concentrating on tempting the stallion; the horse himself, tentative, but not hostile; the classic landscape fading away to the left across the lake; all the intensity of the picture, including the three big trees, focused into the extreme right of the canvas – it is a splendid moment from the high era of English country life. Pumpkin, a son of Matchem owned by Thomas Foley, was a tough racehorse who won sixteen of his twenty-four starts. In 1776, he beat Mambrino and Trentham in a 200-guinea sweepstake. There are two other pictures of him by Stubbs, with the jockey William South up.

Not all of Stubbs's pictures are as felicitous as the Pumpkin study. It has to be confessed that his picture of Baronet, the Prince of Wales's horse, with Sam Chifney up, has an almost comic look. Chifney is shown gazing insouciantly out to his left while the horse careers onwards, all four feet off the ground, apparently travelling downwards to the nether regions.

Baronet, who remained unbeaten, did not race until he was 6 years old, when he won the Oatlands Stakes of 1791 at Ascot. His rider was the elder Sam Chifney, originator of the celebrated 'Chifney rush' by which he and his son stole innumerable races. This was achieved, so Chifney described, at the end of the race 'when the horse's mouth should be eased of the weight of the rein. When horses are in great distress they cannot face the visible manner of pulling. They must be allowed to ease themselves an inch at a time as their situation will allow. This should be done as though you had a silken rein as fine as a hair and were afraid of breaking it.'

Sam Chifney's riding of another of the Prince's horses, Escape, was shortly to cause the Royal Personage to withdraw from racing altogether. Escape, beaten into last place of four at the Newmarket October meeting of 1791, turned out the next day and won easily at 5–1, with Chifney having had a bet of 20 guineas. In fact, it seems certain that Escape had merely been in need of a

George Stubbs: *Baronet, with Sam Chifney senior up*. 1794. Oil on canvas, 100.5 × 125 cm. Private collection

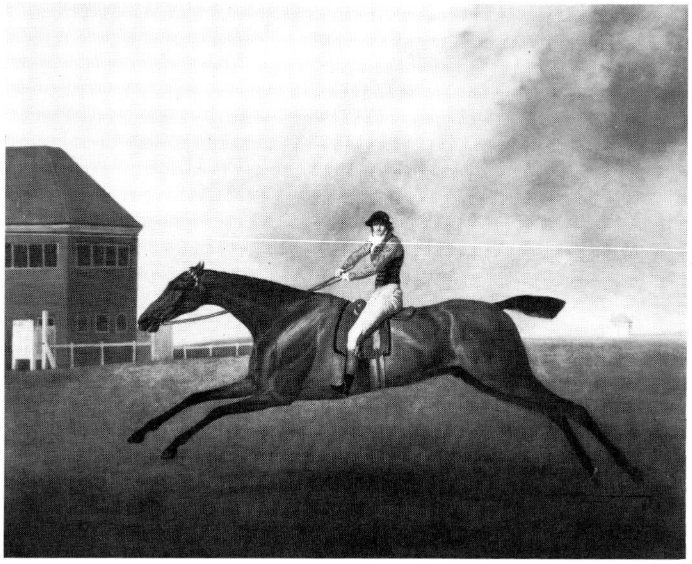

gallop on the first day, and that Chifney, a fine judge of a horse, had realized that this was the case. Certainly this was the Prince of Wales's opinion. But Sir Charles Bunbury and the stewards took a more baleful view and advised the Prince that 'if Chifney were suffered to ride the Prince's horses, no gentleman would start against him'. The Prince refused to condemn Chifney and promptly disposed of his stud and gave up racing. He never returned to Newmarket.

George Stubbs was born in Liverpool in 1724. He secured himself a job at Knowsley Hall, the home of the earls of Derby, by the device of copying a picture by the artist Hamlet Winstanley and sending it to him. Winstanley was himself engaged in copying some of the works at Knowsley. This seems to have been all the tuition that Stubbs ever received, and it did not last long. He left after a quarrel, saying that he would in future 'look into nature for himself and copy her only'. Before he was 20, he had won a gold medal from the Liverpool Society for the Encouragement of the Arts for a model of a horse.

In 1744 he left for Yorkshire, where he engraved the illustrations for an essay on midwifery by a York doctor. He made a trip to Italy, but then settled in Lincolnshire where he received some commissions from Lady Nelthorpe. In a cottage at Horkstow he set out upon the immense labour of drawing and dissecting carcasses in order to produce *The Anatomy of the Horse* (see pp. 13–14). His work had already attracted the attention of a London dealer, Parsons, and in 1760 Stubbs entered upon the most successful decade of his career, painting for Lord Grosvenor at Eaton Hall, the Duke of Richmond at Goodwood, and the Marquis of Rockingham at Wentworth. Stubbs also became friendly with the Wedgwoods and his work was reproduced on their porcelain.

In the early 1780s, however, he fell out with the Royal Academy over the requirement to present a diploma picture. From then onwards his fortunes, though not his talents, went into decline. In 1794 the Turf Gallery in Conduit Street, London, exhibited pictures of sixteen famous racehorses painted by Stubbs for the *Turf Review*. The horses portrayed were the Godolphin Arabian, Marske, Eclipse, Dungannon, Volunteer, Gimcrack, Mambrino, Sweetbriar, Sweet William, Protector, Shark, Baronet, Pumpkin, Bandy, Gnawpost, and Anvil. They were intended as the first subjects in an ambitious series of prints, to be engraved by Stubbs's son, George Townley Stubbs, which would show 'Every Horse of Note since the year 1750'. The project collapsed, yet some of Stubbs's finest work, such as the Hambletonian portrait, dates from these last years when he was in his 70s. Stubbs died in poor circumstances in 1806.

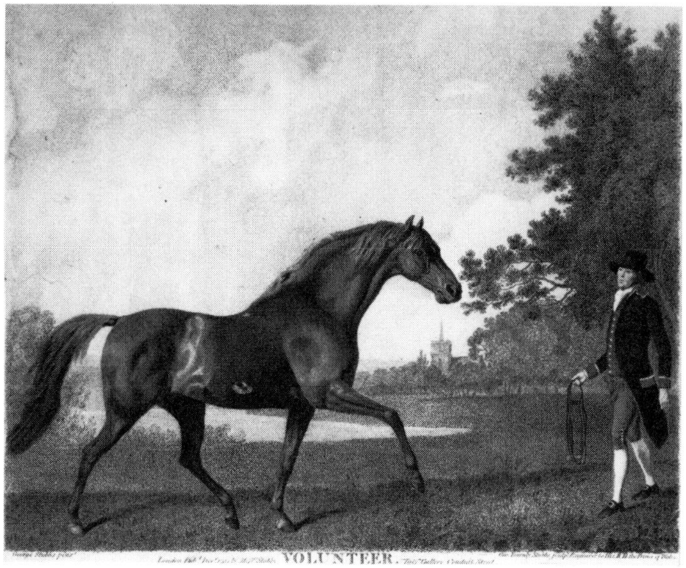


George Stubbs: *Volunteer*. Stipple engraving by George Townley Stubbs, 1794, 20.1 × 25.1 cm. Private collection

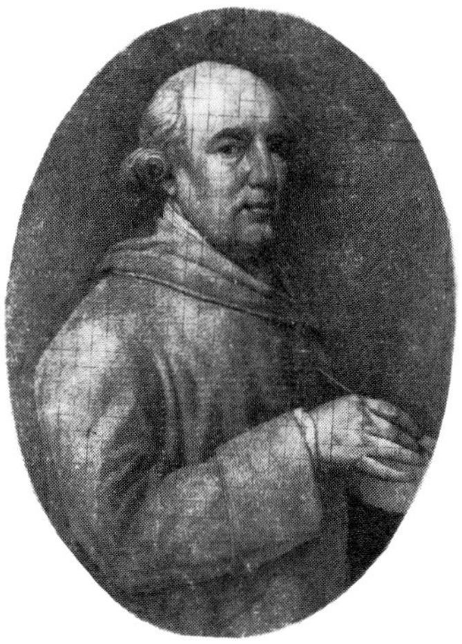

George Stubbs: *Portrait of the Artist*. 1780–1. Pencil on paper, 30.5 × 22.9 cm. Paul Mellon Collection, Upperville, Virginia

# *Sawrey Gilpin*

*1733–1807*

## Highflyer

The obituary in the *Sporting Magazine* was plain enough:

HERE LIETH
The perfect and beautiful symmetry
Of the much lamented
HIGHFLYER
By whom and his wonderful offspring
The celebrated TATTERSALL acquired
A noble fortune
But was not ashamed to acknowledge it
In gratitude to this famous
STALLION
He called an elegant mansion he built
HIGHFLYER HALL

Almost two centuries later the fortune that was based on Highflyer still flourishes at Tattersalls' sales paddocks in Newmarket. For Highflyer must have been one of the hardest-worked and most lucrative stallions in history. Richard Tattersall was reckoned to earn up to £15,000 a year for Highflyer's services. As another contemporary wrote, 'He had more mares every season than any horse should cover. Mr Tattersall's love of money would reject none. He was worn out in the service of venery before his time and was buried in his own paddock, shod and unskinned.'

Highflyer, a son of Herod, in the line of the Byerley Turk, had been bought by Richard Tattersall from Viscount Bolingbroke when His Lordship was in slightly straitened circumstances. The bill of sale still survives whereby, 'in consideration of two thousand five hundred pounds of lawful money', Tattersall acquired 'all that my bay horse called High Flyer, now in training under the care of Thomas Robson of the Valley near Newmarket'. John Lawrence, the celebrated author and gossip, wrote not long afterwards, 'Mr Tattersall laid hold on Highflyer, in order to repay himself, which he effected by going down in the night to Newmarket, seizing the horse, and, as my informant phrased it, "clapping a double lock upon him".' The year of 1779 was a good one for Tattersall. Five months after acquiring Highflyer he opened the establishment at Hyde Park in London which, removed later to Knightsbridge, was to serve as sale ring, betting hall, and meeting-place for generations of racing men.

Highflyer was bred by Sir Charles Bunbury and was never beaten on the racecourse. He raced at Nottingham, York, and Lichfield as well as Newmarket and won £9,336 in stakes. Tattersall put him to stud at a fee of 15 guineas, which was much increased by the time of his death in 1793. Highflyer's great stud rival was Eclipse, but Tattersall had a theory that Eclipse's daughters would make the perfect match with his own stallion. He proceeded to buy up every Eclipse mare he could find. Three of Highflyer's sons, Noble, Sir Peter Teazle, and Sky-

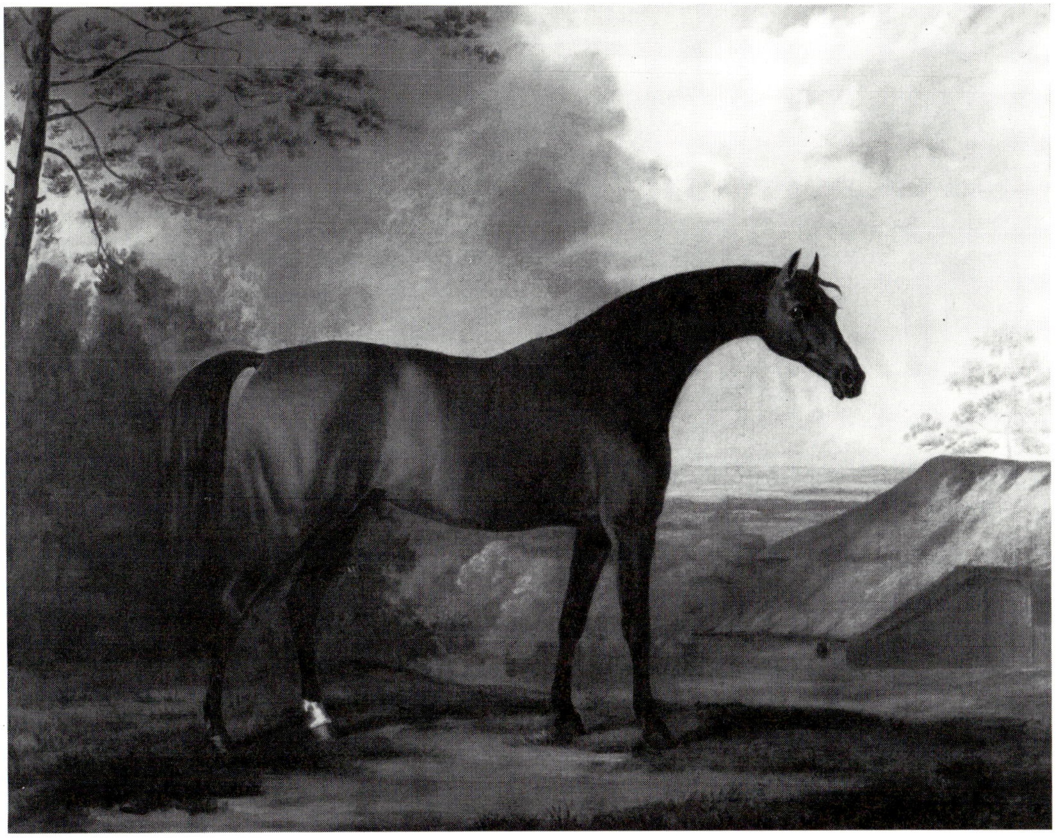

Sawrey Gilpin: *Highflyer*. After 1779. Oil on canvas, 86.3 × 111.7 cm. Tattersalls, Newmarket

Thomas Beach: *Richard Tattersall (1724–95) with Highflyer in the Background*. 1787. Oil on canvas, 125 × 98.3 cm. Tattersalls, Newmarket

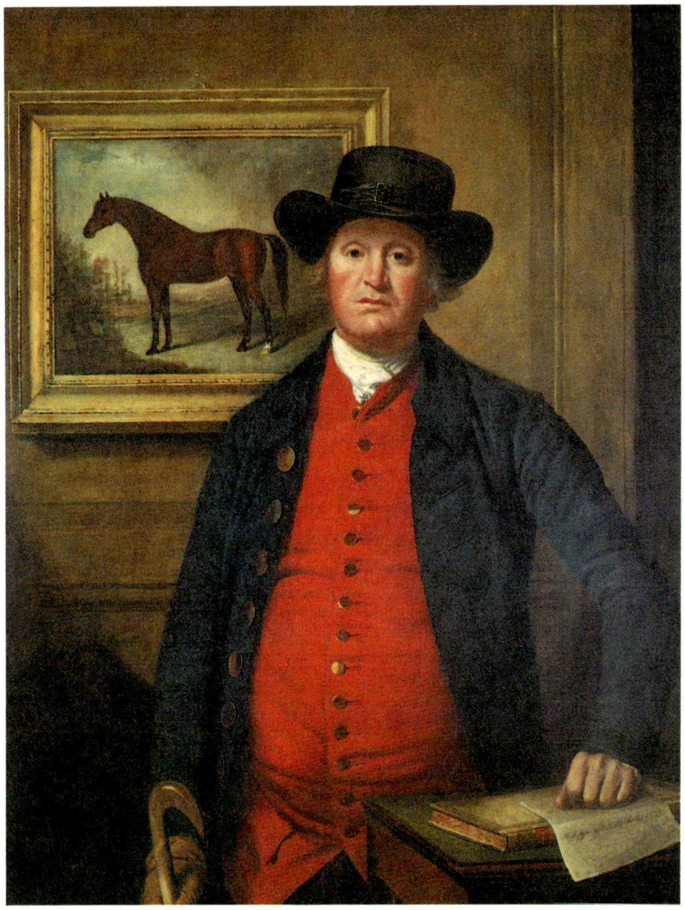

scraper, won the Derby in four years in the 1780s and he is ancestor in tail male of more than twenty Derby winners. Through his daughter Grey Highflyer, who bred Hambletonian, lies the descent which produced Voltigeur, Galopin, and St Simon.

Sawrey Gilpin was one of the more accomplished of Stubbs's contemporaries. He was brought up in Carlisle. At the age of 16 he was sent down to London to study boat and river painting under Samuel Scott. He soon, however, seems to have been attracted to the horse and wagon scenes around Covent Garden. His horse painting came to the notice of 'Butcher' Cumberland, the royal duke who had defeated Bonnie Prince Charlie's army at Culloden. This was the beginning of a lifelong patronage from various members of the Hanoverian family.

According to the *Sporting Magazine*, Sawrey Gilpin was 'justly admired for the great truth and spirit of the composition and extreme chasteness of colouring'. He was President of the Society of Artists and co-operated with many of his fellow painters, providing the cattle in a picture of Turner's and working with Zoffany and Marlow. Gilpin painted a number of racehorses, including Herod and Sir Peter Teazle, but he also had a great fondness for literary and historical scenes. He had two other notable patrons, Colonel Thomas Thornton, for whom he painted *The Death of the Fox*, and Samuel Whitbread of the brewing family.

# George Garrard

*1760–1826*

## Tandem

George Garrard's racehorses invariably appear burdened with a doleful look, particularly inappropriate in the case of Tandem, who had a wonderful career on the Turf and an extremely productive life at stud.

Tandem belonged to Mr Shafto and was by Syphon, who was a son of Squirt, the grandsire of Eclipse. Foaled in 1773, he made his début as a four-year-old on the middle 2 miles of the Beacon Course at Newmarket in the July meeting. Receiving over a stone from Lord Abingdon's Oxonian, he beat him; he was never again to be treated so leniently, but he went on winning. In 1780, in the Jockey Club Stakes, he finally came up against a better horse in the famous Pot-8-os and was defeated at level weights. Mr Shafto then sold him to Mr Wastell and Tandem resumed his winning ways. When he was retired to stud he sired a stream of winners. His tough qualities must have been appreciated, for many leading owners sent their mares to him, including the Duke of Grafton, Sir Frank Standish (frequently), the Duke of Norfolk, and Lord Egremont.

George Garrard was a student of Sawrey Gilpin and married the artist's daughter Matilda. Garrard's family traced back to Marcus Garrard, who came from Bruges to be painter to Queen Elizabeth I in the sixteenth century. George Garrard travelled with Colonel Thomas Thornton and contributed the illustrations for his *Sporting Tour of Scotland*. He also produced the attractive prints of Improved British Cattle, which are now highly prized. Garrard's most faithful patrons were the 8th Duke of Hamilton, who owned twelve of his works, and Samuel Whitbread the brewer. About 1802 he seems to have given up painting in favour of sculpture and modelling, only returning to it twenty years later, just before his death.

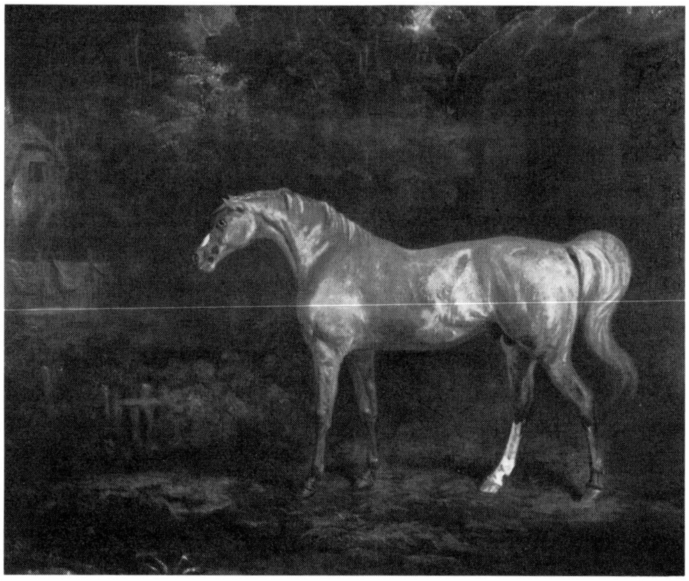

George Garrard: *Eclipse*. After *c*.1780. Oil on canvas, 101.6 × 126.9 cm. Tattersalls, Newmarket

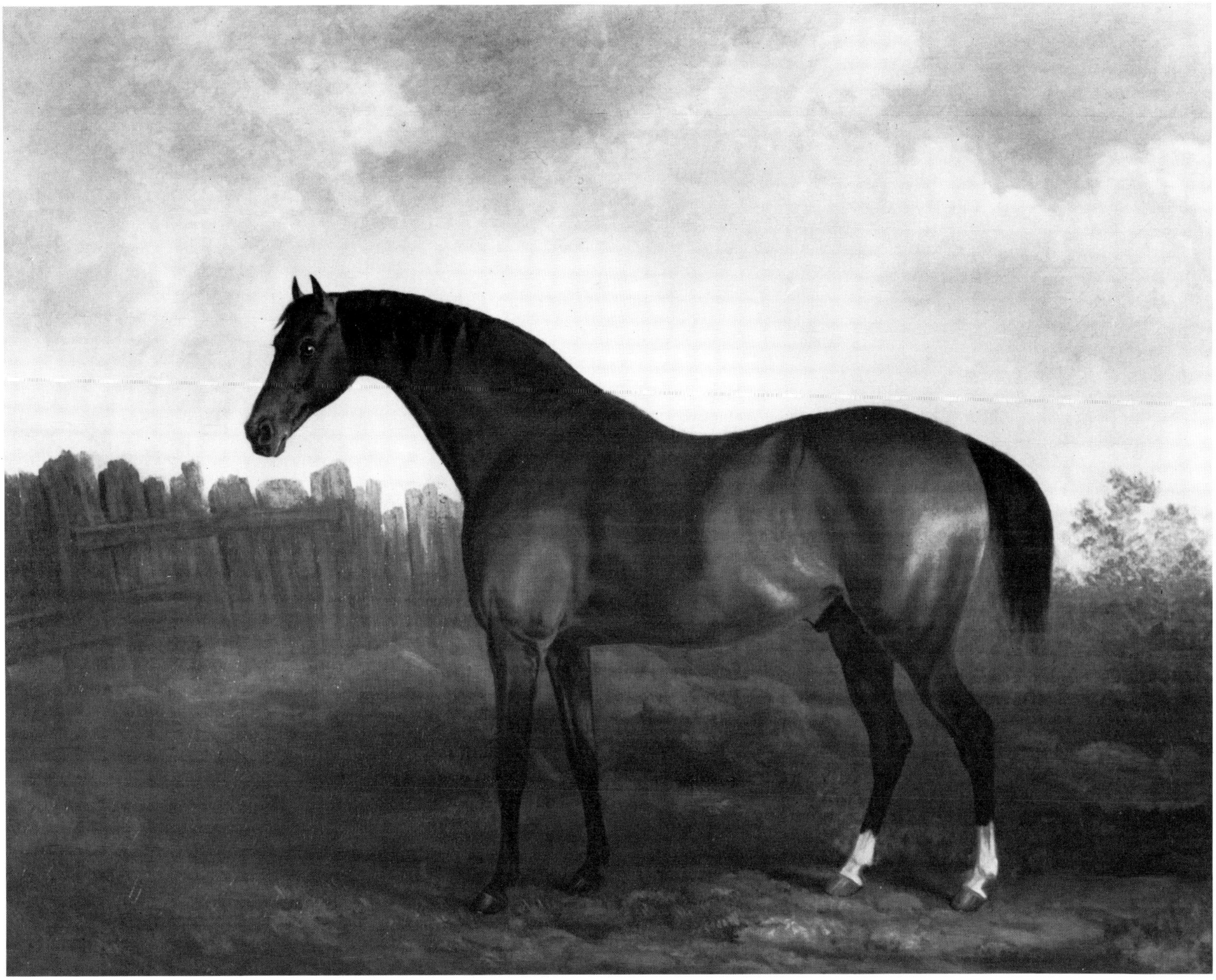

George Garrard: *Tandem*. After *c*.1780. Oil on canvas, 85 × 110.4 cm. Tattersalls, Newmarket

# *John Boultbee*

*1753?–1812*

Gohanna
Shark

Gohanna was defeated by Waxy in the Derby of 1793, in which seven of the thirteen horses were by Pot-8-os, the bizarrely-named son of Eclipse. Gohanna was by Mercury and was described by 'The Druid' as a 'plain hunter style of horse'. He and Waxy, one of the seven 'potatoes', ran a series of tough matches against each other in the following years, with Gohanna winning when receiving 3 lb. and Waxy the victor when they were at level weights. The two horses were very close in ability.

'He was put to all kinds of mares,' said 'The Druid' of Gohanna, 'and got great power on a short leg, and if they exceeded fifteen-one it was beyond the average. They had broad foreheads, small noses, and a very prominent eye, and were uniformly speedy and staying.' Gohanna belonged to Lord Egremont, a remarkable scion of the Percy family. He had a huge stud, spent, it is said, £20,000 a year on charitable institutions, was a patron and collector of Turner and Constable, and still managed to leave his successors twice the fortune that he inherited. It may be relevant to mention that he was unmarried.

John Boultbee was one of twin brothers, both painters, who came from Leicestershire and were taught by Sir Joshua Reynolds. Leicestershire at that time was in its heyday: Robert Bakewell was developing the new breeds of sheep and cattle, and the great hunts, such as the Quorn, with thrusters like William Coke, were at their zenith. John Boultbee painted for both the Cokes and Robert Bakewell, but he soon acquired a grander patron in King George III himself. The King gave Boultbee a residence in Windsor Park and commissioned him to paint a number of his favourite animals. Boultbee's most celebrated picture is the portrait of the great Durham Ox, which was engraved in 1802 and became one of the most successful prints of the day. His studies of hounds and hunters were also very popular.

John Boultbee produced some copies in oils of Stubbs's thoroughbred pictures, including one of Shark (see also p. 40), a brown son of Marske, who belonged to the shady and venomous Charles Pigott. Shark started racing when he was only 2 years old, in 1774. Four years later he retired, after a defeat at Newmarket, with twenty-six races under his girth, including contests with Mambrino and most of his other notable contemporaries. He earned more than £15,000 on the racecourse. Boultbee also painted Highflyer for Richard Tattersall, posed in front of Highflyer Hall, the establishment which the stallion's exertions, on the racecourse and after, had earned for the famous bloodstock auctioneer.

---

RIGHT
John Boultbee: *Shark, with his trainer Price.* After 1775. Oil on canvas, 27.3 × 37.5 cm. Paul Mellon Collection, Upperville, Virginia

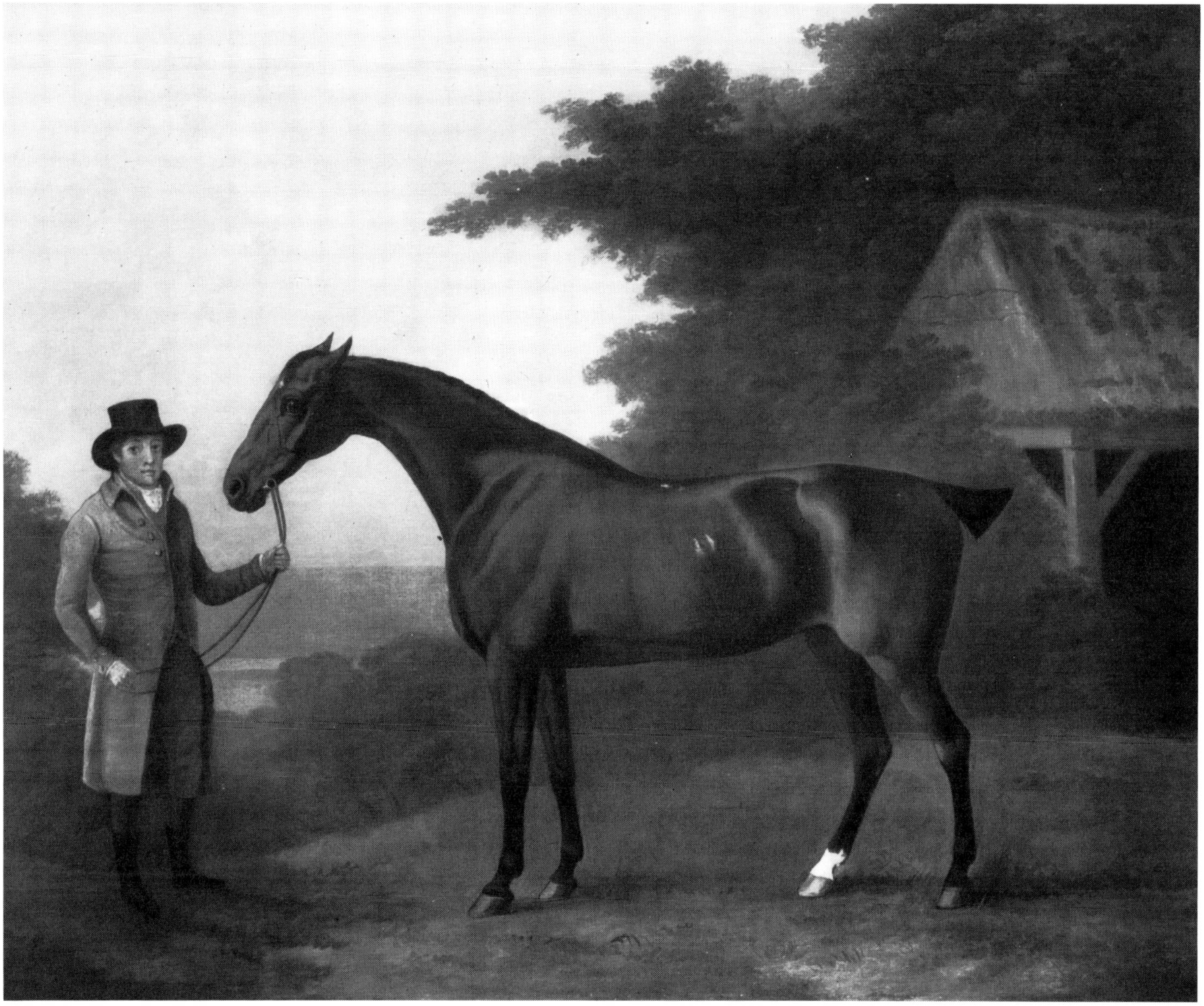

John Boultbee: *Gohanna*. 1804. Oil on canvas, 61 × 75.6 cm. Private collection

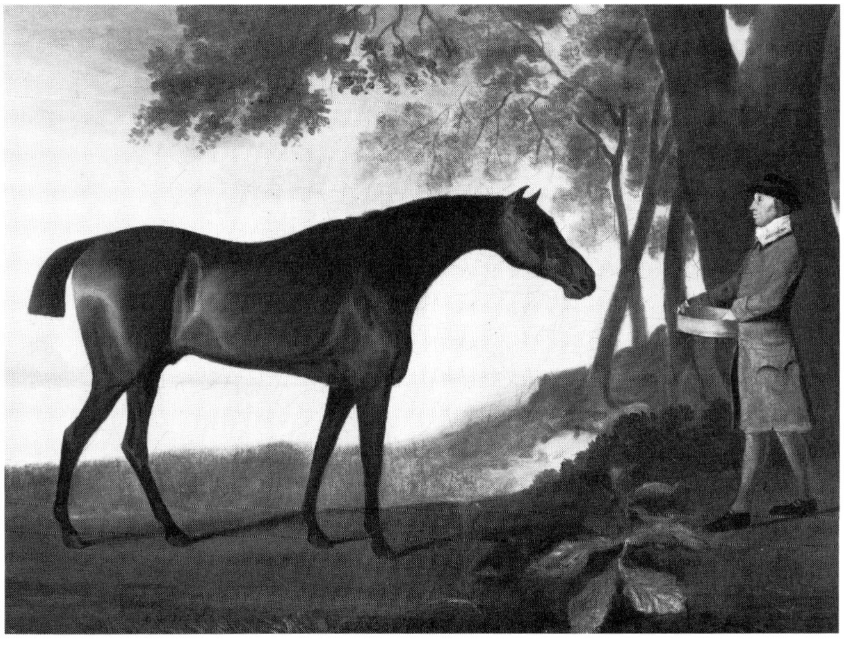

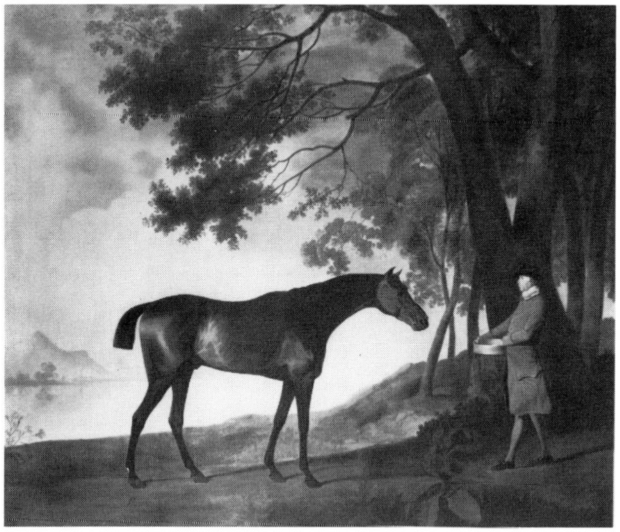

ABOVE
George Stubbs: *Shark, with his trainer Price*. 1775. Oil on panel, 81.9 × 99.7 cm. Private collection

# J. N. Sartorius

*1759–1828*

## Dungannon and Rockingham
## Lurcher and Kitt Carr
## Creeper and Dragon

The Sartorius family were the first of the family dynasties of English sporting painting. Unlike the Ferneleys, the Marshalls, and the Herrings, it was not the first generation which monopolized the talent. John Nost Sartorius was the grandson of the first Sartorius to paint in England.

Of all the historic rooms in the Jockey Club at Newmarket, the ambience of glories long ago is keenest in the card-room, where Gladiateur's tail lies beside a writing-desk and silver candlesticks adorn the tables – the weary loser would retreat sighing 'The game's not worth the candle.' But above all, the walls are hung entirely with the pictures by J. N. Sartorius of great contests and fine horses of two hundred years past: Dungannon beating Rockingham, Lurcher beating Kitt Carr, and Creeper beating Dragon.

Looking at this rich collection, it is not hard to see why J.N. has always been valued, even though he learnt little from the labours of Stubbs and cared less for Marshall and the anatomists. For J.N. knew the excitements of racing thoroughbreds, and could leave the thrill on canvas to endure for two centuries, despite the rocking-horse gallops and the emaciated animals. *Dungannon beating Rockingham* is a wonderful action picture: the whips flying, the eager, determined cast to the horses' heads, Dungannon stretching out his neck to the post as though a photo-finish camera were present, both riders furiously driving for the line.

Dungannon (see also p. 63) had run second in the 1783 Derby, Saltram's year. He was by Eclipse and belonged to Dennis O'Kelly. He proved to be a tough competitor and won a series of matches at Newmarket. When O'Kelly took him up to Nottingham in 1784, no one could be found to start against him and he walked over on successive days. He was 6 years old when he came up for the Rockingham match. Rockingham, a year younger, had won the Jockey Club Plate in 1785 and then beat the Prince of Wales's Hardwicke in a 300-guinea match at the Newmarket second spring meeting. Obviously, the Prince must have been impressed, for the next month we find Rockingham running in the Prince's colours and beating Clayhall in a 500-guinea outing. At the October meeting Rockingham went down to another of O'Kelly's horses, Soldier, while Dungannon continued winning. The exchanges between O'Kelly and the Prince which produced the Dungannon versus Rockingham match can be imagined.

The contest took place on 1 May 1786 at Newmarket, with Dungannon carrying 8 st. and Rockingham carrying 7 st. 8 lb. over the Beacon Course on the Heath. As Sartorius's picture so vividly shows, Dungannon got up to win in the tightest of finishes. The Prince, it would appear, was not amused. Before the season was out he had sold Rockingham on to Mr Bullock. And Mr Bullock passed him on to the teenage Lord Barrymore, for whom

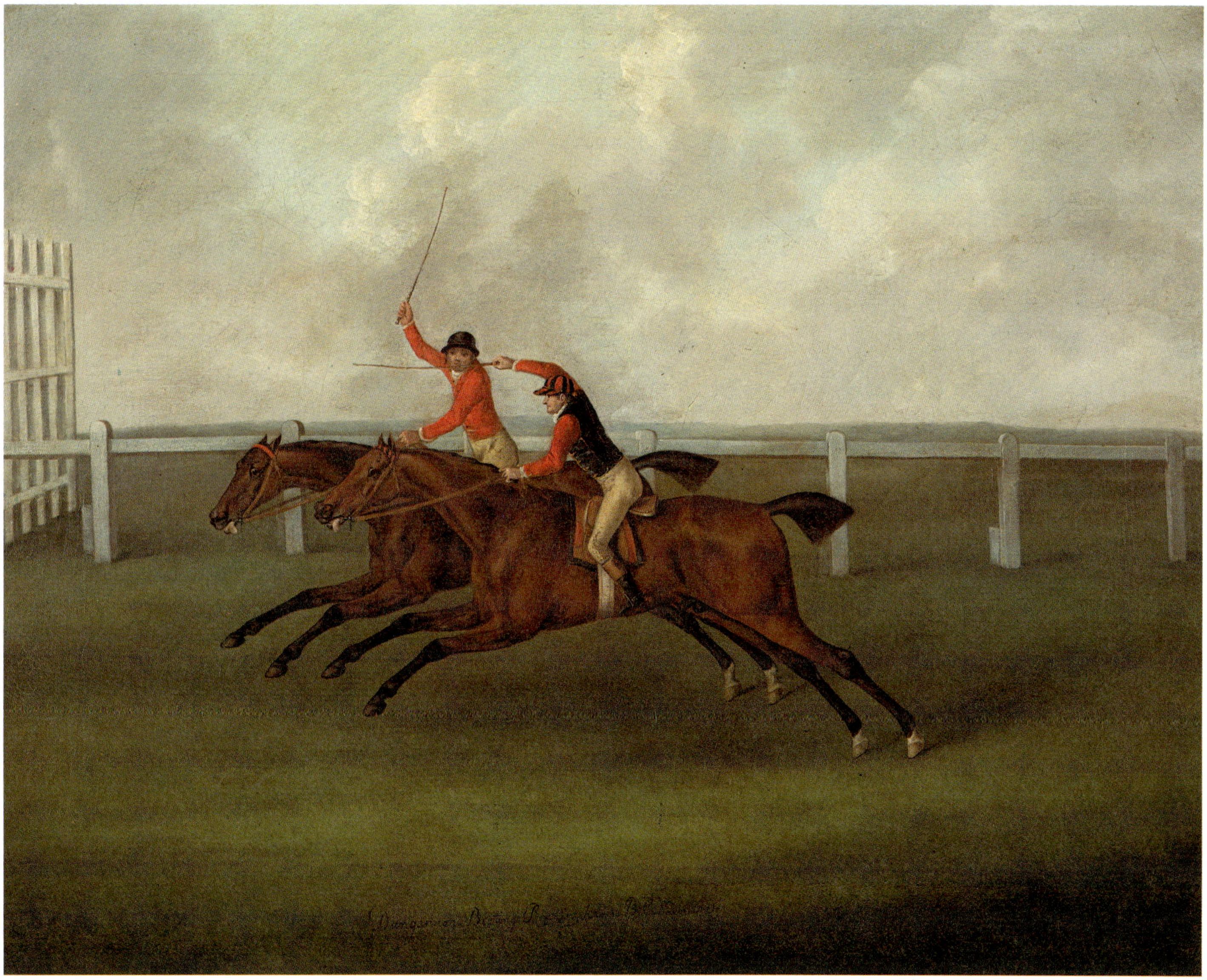

J. N. Sartorius: *Dungannon beating Rockingham at Newmarket*. 1786. Oil on canvas, 69.2 × 87.6 cm. Jockey Club, Newmarket

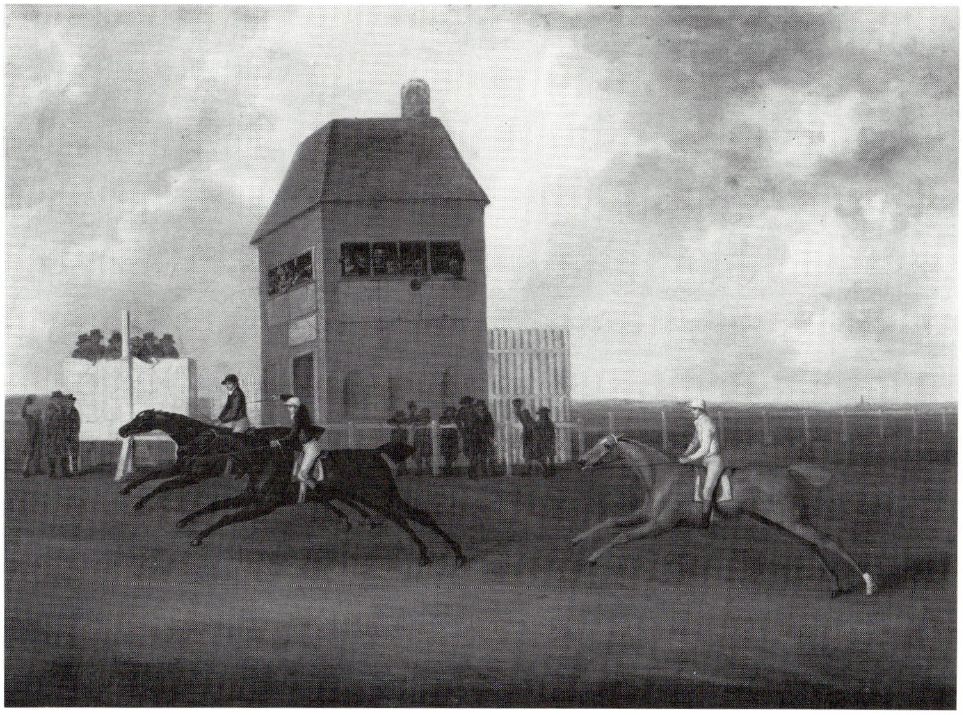

J. N. Sartorius: *Lurcher beating Kitt Carr and Ormond at Newmarket*. 1793. Oil on canvas, 74.3 × 104.7 cm. Jockey Club, Newmarket

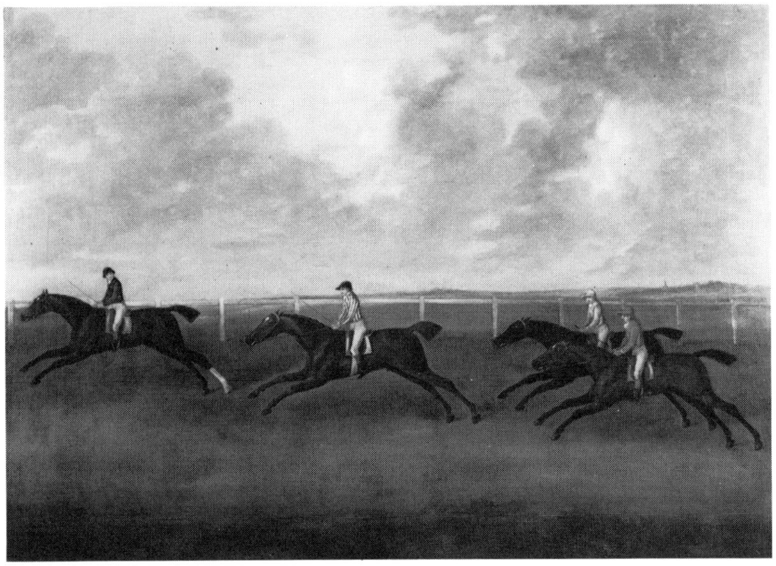

J. N. Sartorius: *Creeper beating Dragon, Vermin, and Pipator*. 1792. Oil on canvas, 74.3 × 105.4 cm. Jockey Club, Newmarket

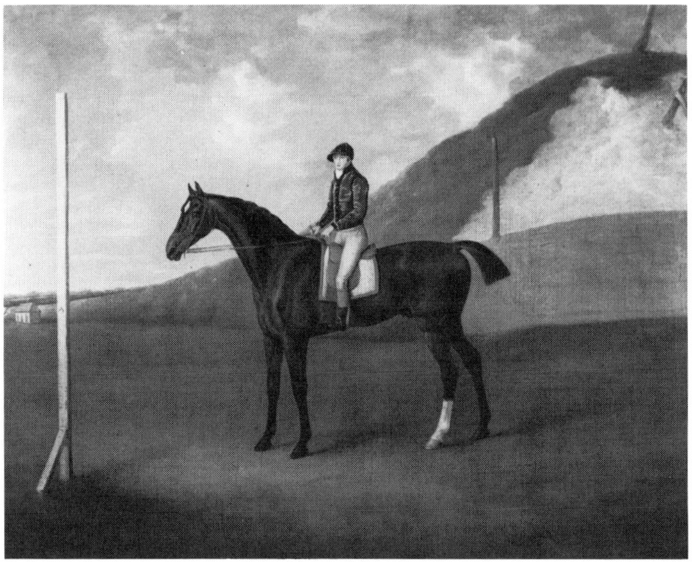

J. N. Sartorius: *Creeper*. 1793. Oil on canvas, 69.8 × 90.1 cm. Jockey Club, Newmarket

he won the Jockey Club Plate of 1788. Two days later His Lordship rode him to win a match against Stargazer. Rockingham was then deemed to have done enough and was retired to a successful stud career. Dungannon, after his defeat of Rockingham, won the Whip at Newmarket, a trophy originally given by King Charles II and into which hairs from the mane and tail of Eclipse were woven. Dungannon, too, then retired to stud.

Lurcher was one of Dungannon's sons and belonged to Mr Wilson. He obviously had an easier race than his parent, beating Sir Frank Standish's Kitt Carr and Mr Wentworth's chestnut Ormond in a 500-guinea sweepstake over the 'Ditch in' course at Newmarket. Creeper also belonged to Mr Wilson and the contest with Dragon was by way of being a revenge match. Dragon belonged to the Duke of Bedford and, though a year younger, had defeated Creeper for the Whip in 1792 at level weights. Pipator had been third. Clearly honour had not been satisfied and all three, plus Lord Foley's elegantly named Vermin, turned out a fortnight later at the Houghton meeting for 200 guineas. Creeper, this time getting 6 lb. from Dragon, beat him, with Lord Clermont's Pipator again last.

Though J. N. Sartorius could paint quite a handsome portrait, as he did of Creeper and Eclipse, his heart was clearly in the cut and thrust of the race and the scenes on the course. He did not lack for exalted patrons; they included the Prince of Wales, Lord Derby, Sir Charles

J. N. Sartorius: *Eclipse*. 1790. Oil on canvas, 68.6 × 91.4 cm. Jockey Club, Newmarket

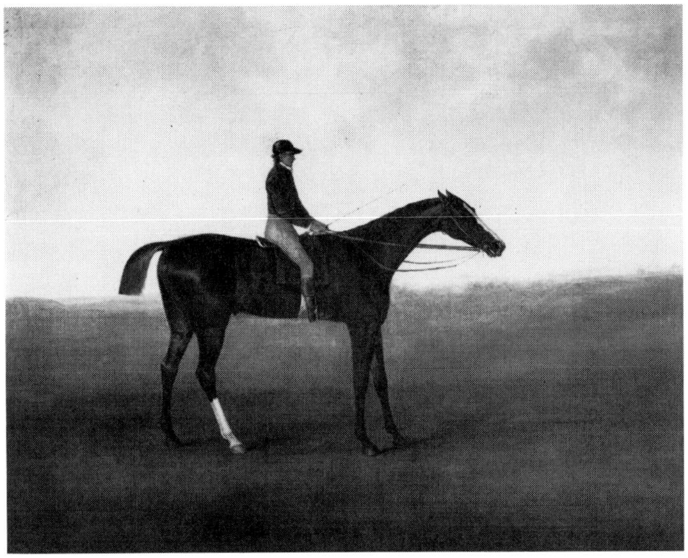

F. Sartorius: *Eclipse*. After 1770. Oil on canvas, 87 × 116.4 cm. Private collection

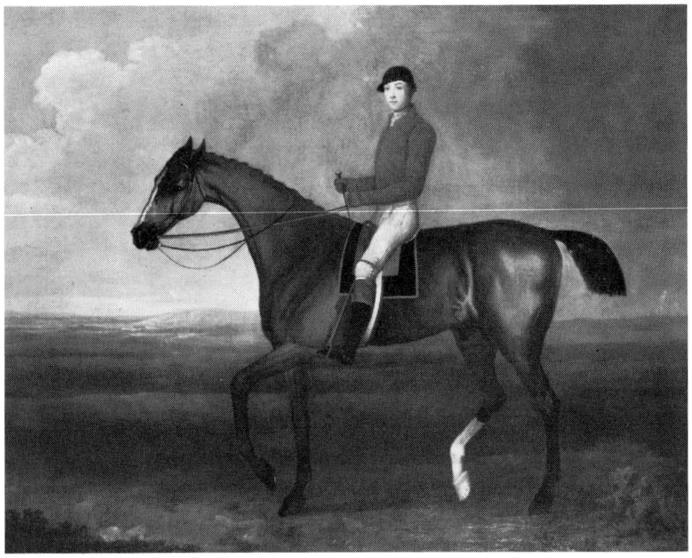

Bunbury, and Charles James Fox. Though contemporaries described him as 'a painter of distinguished merit', his work was written off as 'tame and pretty' by the twentieth-century critic Walter Shaw Sparrow, with the admonition, 'J.N. should have seen that his rocking-horse gallops were too stiff and too ugly to be tolerated.' Be that as it may, he has left us a uniquely vivid and valuable record of racing in his time.

J.N.'s father, Francis Sartorius (1734–1804), might more properly be in receipt of such strictures as are justified. The picture of the grey Jason winning at Newmarket, assumed to be by Francis, has a primitive look, not only in comparison with his son's work, but also with his predecessors like Peter Tillemans. The horses are in identical poses, the whips at identical angles. His horse portraits, too, have a flatness and uniformity which has kept their prices low in the sale-room, even in these days when the early sporting painters are highly valued. But they do have a considerable place of record and he was undoubtedly the fashionable painter of the time. It is said that Francis Sartorius painted more pictures of Eclipse than all his contemporaries put together, and more pictures, too, of winners on the Turf than any other artist in the latter half of the eighteenth century.

His picture of Diomed (see p. 40), the first English Derby winner, is in the Jockey Club at Newmarket. Diomed, owned by Sir Charles Bunbury, was unbeaten as a three-year-old, did not race at four or five, and then won a purse at Guildford. Unremarkable at stud in England, he was sold off to America, where he founded the most potent line which produced, in tail male, Sir Archy, Boston, and Lexington.

Francis Sartorius's own father, John Sartorius (*c.*1700–80), was a horse painter who came to England from Nuremberg, and J.N.'s son John Francis Sartorius (*c.*1778–1831) kept up the tradition. Thus there are four generations of the Sartorius family whose work is known in England.

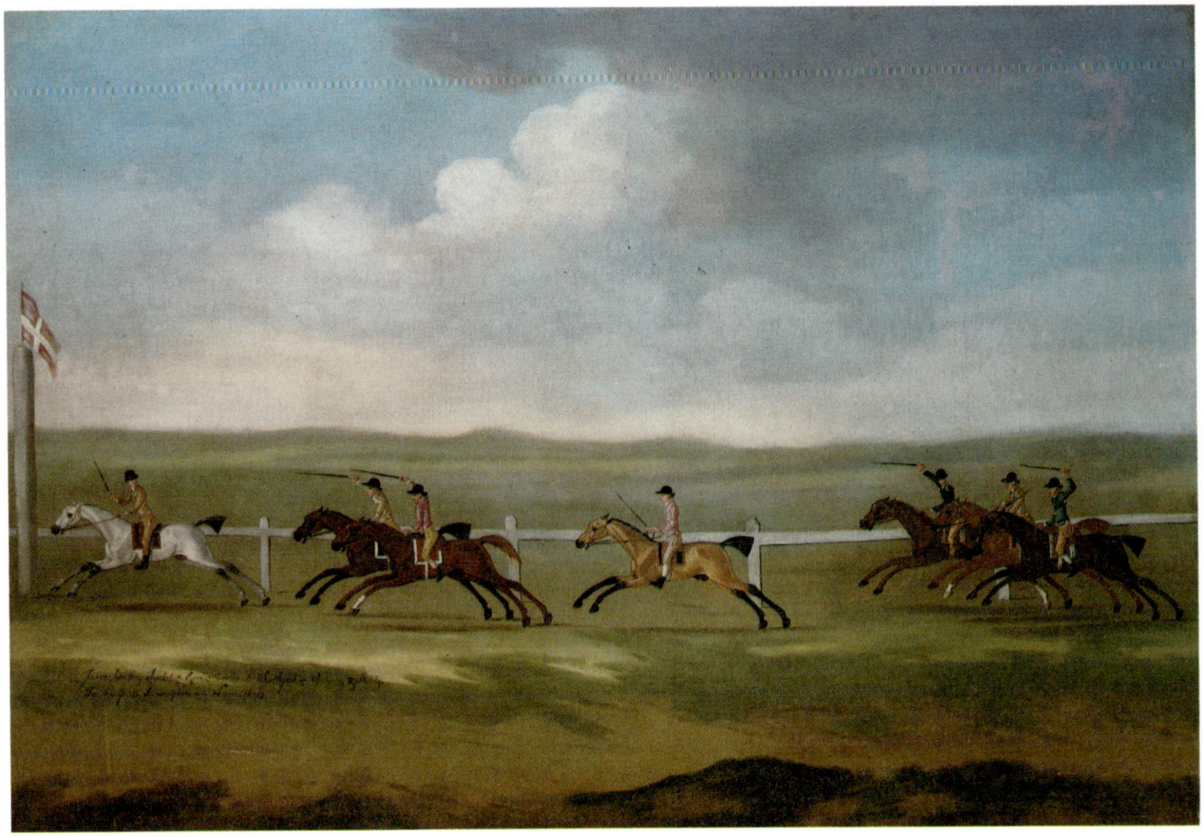

F. Sartorius: *Jason beating Spectator, Rover (Jessamy?), Brilliant, Whistlejacket, Venture (Forester?), and Stately at Newmarket.* 1757. Oil on canvas, 84.5 × 124.5 cm. Private collection

# *James Ward*

*1769–1859*

## Eagle

James Ward's picture of the bay stallion Eagle flaunts the unabashed masculinity of one of America's celebrated imports, who came to Virginia sometime after 1809 and had a considerable influence on the American thoroughbred. There is a vivid three-dimensional quality about this assertive portrait; the horse stands, with the breeze ruffling his mane, monarch of all he surveys. The careful and precise painting of the flowers in the foreground, the thick, almost palette-knife strokes of the trees and the plants nearby, the points of activity in the distance – three horses are frolicking far away down the hill – and the rippling heavily muscled horse himself freeze a dynamic moment of life.

Eagle was bred by Sir Frank Standish of Duxbury in Lancashire, and inspired superlatives all his life. The sight of him is said to have imbued Admiral Rous with his love of the thoroughbred. And even when he was 28 years old, and at stud near Lexington in Kentucky, his owner, S. Cooper, felt able to assert, 'Eagle combines more power, beauty and speed than any horse on earth, more even than human minds can imagine.'

Eagle started as evens favourite for the Derby of 1799, and was confidently expected to emulate his full brother, Spread Eagle, who had won a second Derby for Sir Frank four years before. However, Eagle could only manage third to the stable's second string Archduke, a brown colt by Sir Peter Teazle. This disappointment does not seem to have diminished the attraction of his magnificent presence. Colonel Henry Mellish, the great sportsman and Peninsular War hero, paid 800 guineas for him in 1803. When the Colonel, one of the Turf's most legendary betting 'plungers', finally had to sell his stud, Eagle fetched 1,200 guineas.

Ward himself thought the painting one of his best works. 'Eagle will ever fly over the heads of my highest soarings,' he wrote in 1848 to his friend Thomas Garle, who owned the painting. In one of the annotated catalogues of the 1810 Royal Academy Exhibition, at which the picture was shown, there is the note, 'I never saw so well painted a horse.' Another enthusiast, Lord Ribblesdale's son Thomas Lister, wrote to his father that the picture of Eagle 'is beyond all conception and raises my awful veneration for that artist beyond all bounds'.

James Ward was born in 1769 and lived to be 90. At 13 years old, he was apprenticed to a London engraver, John Raphael Smith. His sister Anne married the painter George Morland, and Ward became entranced by Morland's style, to the point that many of Ward's early paintings are thought to be attributed, to this day, to Morland. By the time he painted Eagle, however, Ward had developed an individual style which made him perhaps the premier animal painter of his day. A disastrous commission to execute a gigantic allegorical painting for the British Institution in 1815 sent his career on a downward

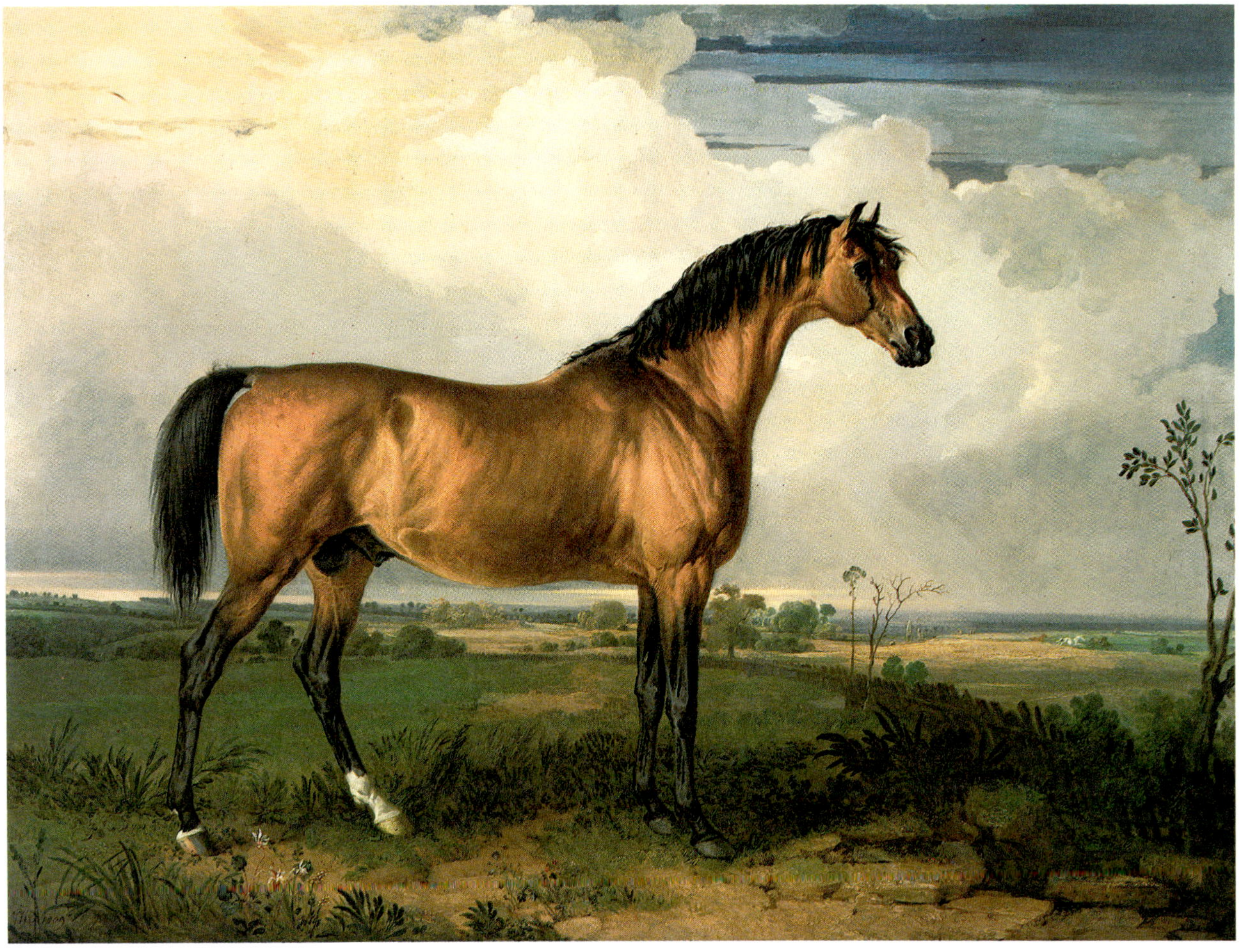

James Ward: *Eagle*. 1809. Oil on canvas, 90.8 × 122 cm. Paul Mellon Collection, Upperville, Virginia

path. He had the galling experience of seeing his pictures knocked down in the sale-room for a third or a quarter of the sums he had previously received for commissions. Even though he was still at work in 1856 at the age of 86, his reputation was not restored in his lifetime.

Ward is known to have produced more than 800 paintings in his long and industrious life, but scarcely a dozen are of thoroughbreds; these include Mameluke, Smolensko, and Dr Syntax. But his preference was for commoner creatures, cows, sheep, pigs, or for romantic and dramatic pictures like *L'Amour de Cheval* and the apocalyptic contest between darkness and light in *Stallions Fighting on a River Bank*.

Eagle was a famously idle horse and it took Sam Chifney senior to get the best out of him. Chifney, with his renowned 'loose rein' style of riding (see p. 64), was regarded with incredulity by his contemporaries. But, as 'The Druid' wrote, 'Paganini had not more complete mastery over a violin than the father [Chifney] acquired over a horse's mouth, however hard and unformed,' and he recounted how the Prince of Wales and his friends came down to see how Chifney would handle a horse called Knowsley who had run away with every jockey who had sat on his back. Chifney was given a fierce curb bridle, but he said, 'Take that silly gimcrack thing away and bring me a plain snaffle.' Knowsley duly won, in full control, on a slack rein.

Eagle's problem was the very opposite. No one could make him try. After the Derby, Chifney advised the Duke of Dorset to buy him from Sir Frank Standish. Sir Frank thankfully unloaded Eagle, while advising the Duke in return not to back him, as 'no jockey could make him go'. Chifney, riled, told the Duke before the King's Plate at Newmarket that not only would he win, but Eagle would not be touched 'with whip or spur'. In 'The Druid's' account, 'The other jockeys were so fully aware of Eagle's sluggishness that they positively walked the three miles and a quarter of the Round Course, and then came along as hard as they could split for the last three furlongs. However, these tactics did not answer, as Eagle could not withstand the masterly bit pressure which was at once brought to bear on him, and won a very fine race by a neck without being touched by whip or spur.'

# *Edwin Cooper*

*1785–1833*

## Eleanor

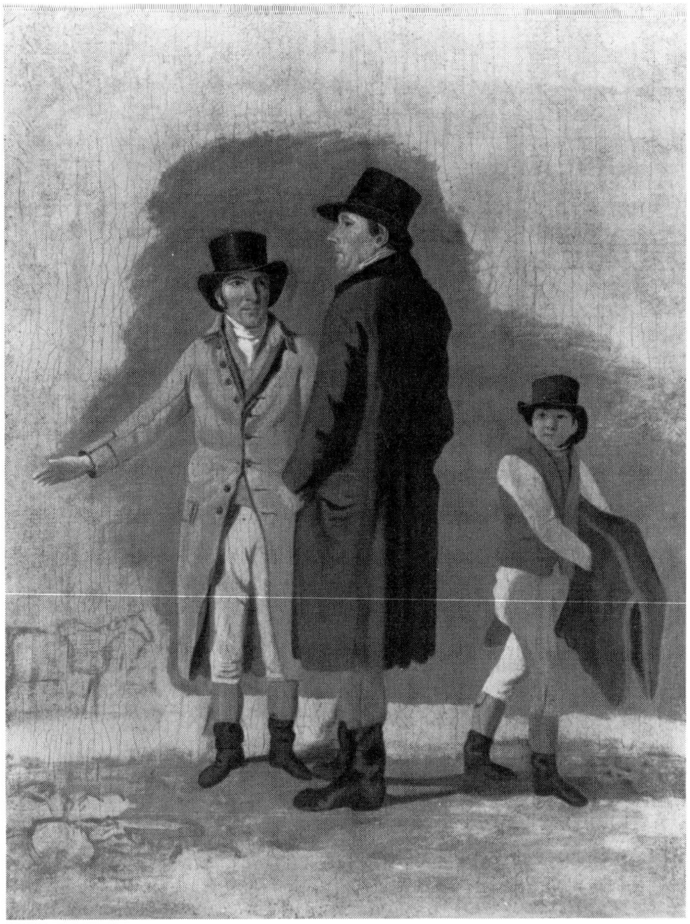

'Depend upon it, that Eleanor is a hell of a mare,' said Cox, her trainer, as he lay dying in the week before the 1801 Derby. She was to prove him right in the most spectacular style. First, with Saunders riding, she won the Derby, easily beating a colt by Fidget. Then, only twenty-four hours later, she was produced for the Oaks, and again trotted up to win.

Eleanor, by Whiskey out of a mare called Giantess, belonged to Sir Charles Bunbury, the 'Perpetual President' of the Jockey Club, who, together with the Earl of Derby, had originated the Derby Stakes twenty-one years before. Bunbury was an advocate of light training as opposed to the fearful rigours of sweating rugged-up horses for ten miles or more, which was the prevailing fashion at the time. But that does not seem to have prevented him from expecting a great deal from his horses. Apart from her two trips round Epsom on consecutive days, Eleanor ran another forty-four times before she was allowed to retire at the end of the 1805 season. In all she won twenty-nine races.

Certainly Edwin Cooper's portrait of her shows an animal that has not been allowed the luxury of any spare flesh. Apart from the jockey in the Bunbury colours, presumably Saunders, it is not clear who the other figures in the picture are. None of them bears any resemblance to the lively portraits of Bunbury and Cox in Ben Marshall's study for his picture of Eleanor and

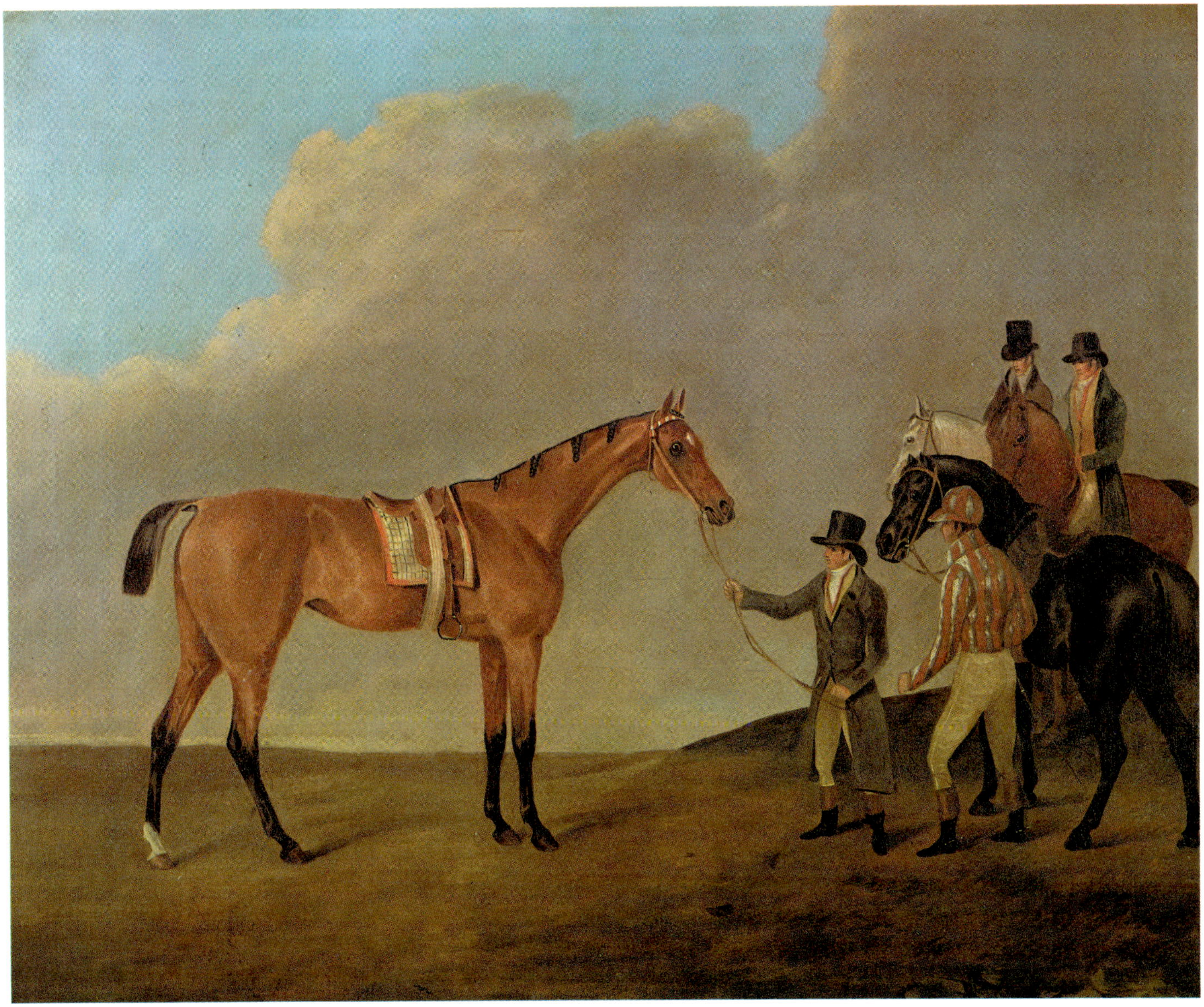

Edwin Cooper: *Eleanor*. 1801. Oil on canvas, 59.7 × 73.6 cm. Jockey Club, Newmarket

Surprise. As Cooper was only 16 when Eleanor won her two Classics, and still only 20 when she retired, there might still be grounds for thinking that the work was copied from Marshall. The two were certainly painting at Newmarket together for a dozen years or more, and may even have shared a studio and the same house. But it seems more likely that this was one of Cooper's first commissions.

Cooper came from Bury St Edmunds – Bunbury was MP for Suffolk – and we know that word spread quickly of the local boy who was something of a horse-painting prodigy. The Duke of Grafton commissioned him in 1802 when he was 17, and, by the time he was 18, Cooper's picture of the Duke of York's Grey Arabian was being exhibited at the Royal Academy. As is apparent from the Eleanor painting, humans received much less attention from Cooper than horses. Indeed, he often used other artists to paint in the faces. Although reputedly in later life a prodigious drinker who could not paint 'until he had mastered the contents of a bottle of port', Cooper seems to have been extraordinarily industrious. His biographer, Desmond Taylor, has catalogued 400 of his works, which must have helped sustain a merry life but a short one. He died in debt at the age of 48.

Ben Marshall: *Study of Sir Charles Bunbury (c.) and Cox (l.) for 'Eleanor and Surprise'*. 1801. Oil on canvas, 47 × 36.8 cm. The Tate Gallery, London

# *Clifton Tomson*

*1775–1828*

## Altisidora

Of all the great horses which graced Mr Richard Watt's paddocks at Bishop Burton in the East Riding of Yorkshire – Tramp, Blacklock, Manuella among them – it is Altisidora whose name still endures on the village inn sign, as the last reminder of the days when the stables of the nearby Hall housed the cream of English bloodstock. Altisidora was a brave filly who won the St Leger in 1813, the first year that the Doncaster course was reduced from 2 miles to just under 1 mile and 7 furlongs. As became almost the custom in the St Leger, there were ten false starts before they got away. But Altisidora, who started favourite, soon settled and after a brief tussle in the straight with Cameleopard and Tiger won comfortably enough from a field of seventeen.

She went on racing until she was nearly 6 years old and her story is a parable of the unending joys and calamities of horse-racing. She was bred by Mr W. N. W. Hewett, a Yorkshire landowner who also bred Tramp; both were offspring of the stallion Dick Andrews, and jointly the means by which an important line of the Darley Arabian was rescued from obscure neglect down among the hunting mares of the English West Country. The spring of 1812 saw Mr Hewett with the kind of hand that owners have dreamed of since thoroughbred racing began. He had a filly, Manuella, of such quality that all her connections were confident she could win not only the Oaks, but also the Derby, though she had never set foot on a racecourse. He had Manuella's full sister Altisidora, by Dick Andrews out of Mandane, a mare who was to go on to produce two more celebrated horses in Lottery and Brutandorf. He also owned Tramp, winner of four Gold Cups, and Petuaria.

In the days before the Derby of 1812, Mr Hewett backed Manuella with every penny he had. And he also made his fatal mistake. He 'jocked off' his local Richmond rider, William Peirse, in favour of the fashionable up-and-coming jockey of the time, the younger Sam Chifney. Chifney blatantly stopped the filly in the Derby so that she finished way down the field behind Octavius. Mr Hewett was ruined. Chifney coolly went out the next day and laid £2,000 to £100 that Manuella would win the Oaks, which she duly did in a canter, with Peirse riding. Hewett did not have a single bet on her. Before settling day, he fled to France with his sons, and his

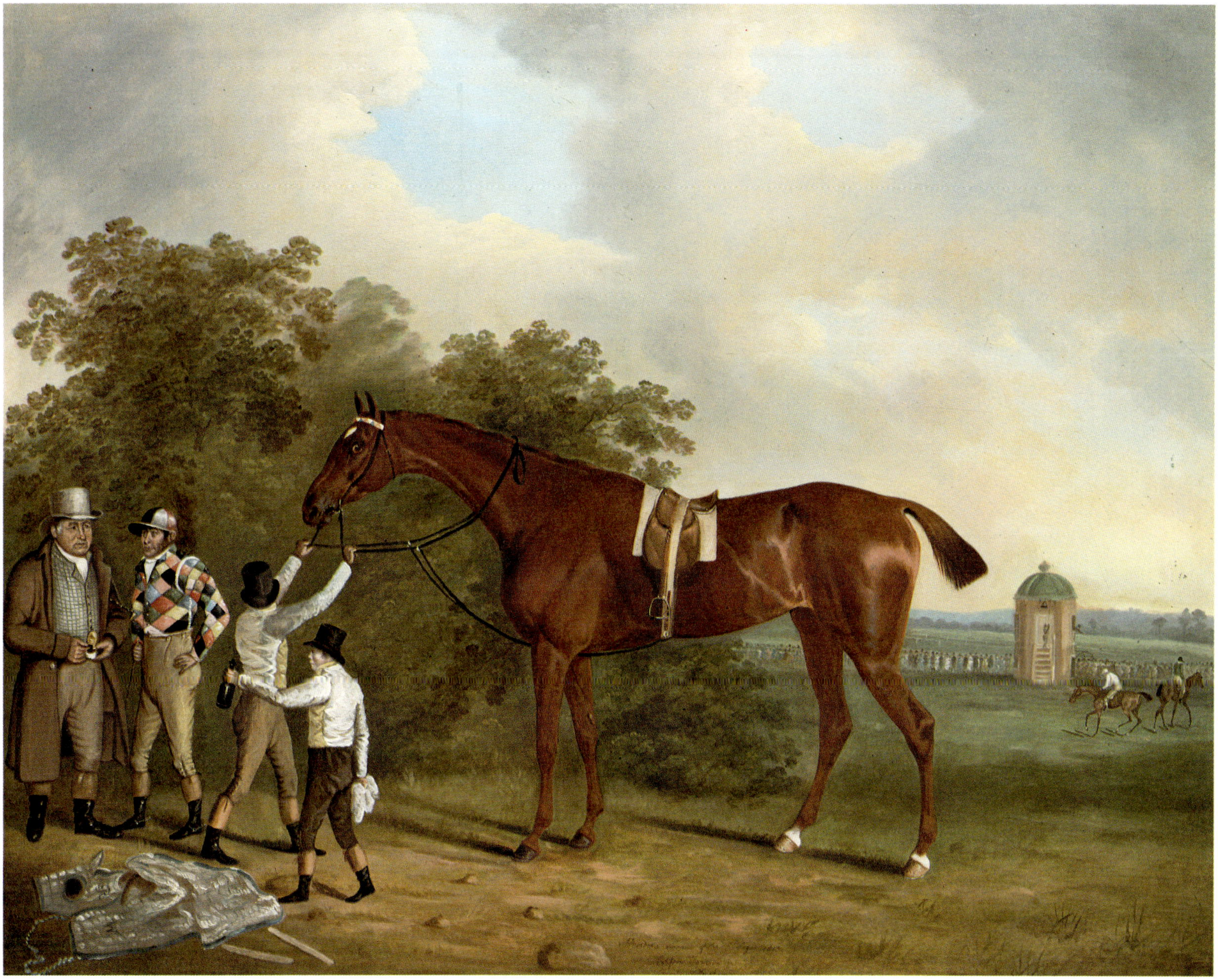

Clifton Tomson: *Altisidora, with her jockey John Jackson and trainer Tommy Sykes*. 1814. Oil on canvas, 101.6 × 127 cm. Private collection

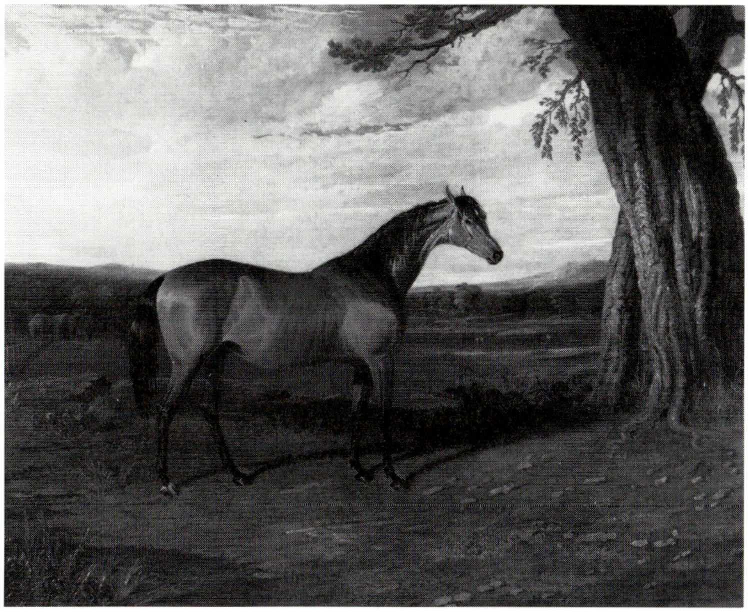

J. F. Herring: *Manuella*. 1825. Oil on canvas, 101.6 × 127 cm. Private collection

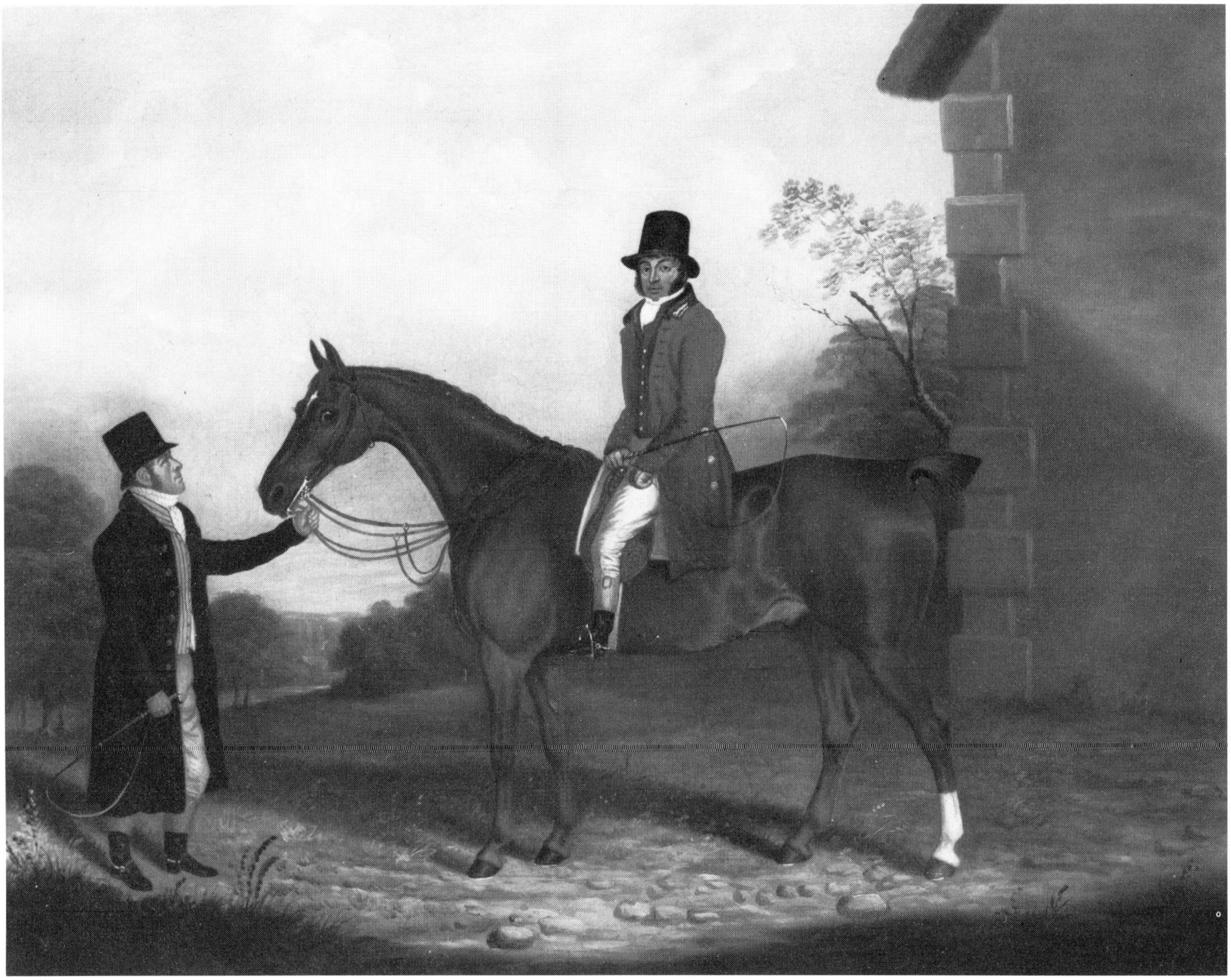

Clifton Tomson: *Mr Richard Watt on Harlequin*. 1821. Oil on canvas, 71.1 × 91.4 cm. Private collection

property was sold up. Richard Watt bought all his bloodstock in one lot, including the two-year-old Altisidora, and thus removed one of the most significant single purchases in racing history to the undulating pastures of Bishop Burton.

Altisidora raced successfully for two more years after her St Leger victory, until two defeats by Filho da Puta in the Richmond Cup and the Doncaster Club Stakes persuaded Mr Watt to retire her to stud. Watt went on to win three more St Legers, but the death of Altisidora marked the ebbing in the tide of his fortunes, just as her purchase had been the beginning of his great days on the Turf. Altisidora was in foal to the prepotent Blacklock when she fell into a ditch at the bottom of one of the Bishop Burton paddocks and, in struggling to get out, died. Her owner died soon after and was buried in the local church.

'The Druid', visiting Bishop Burton some twenty years later, found one old brood mare, Birthday, still there, and stables 'on whose doors the plates of Memnon, Blacklock, Barefoot, Rockingham, Altisidora, Muta and a host of other winners still hang as silent tablets of the luck of other days. Our attendant told us how of yore the mares and foals would come dashing wildly altogether down the hill, through the valley and up the opposite one like a charge of Cossacks, till Mr Watt and his grooms fairly looked on trembling, lest some of their brave little bits of Tramp, Blacklock or Lottery blood should be rolled head over heels down the steep. The shorthorns of a neighbouring farmer quietly browse on it now; but we would fain hope that the thoroughbred traditions which still linger fondly round it, will ere long be potent to drive these intruders from the spot and people it with bloodstock, not inferior to those on which John Jackson in the harlequin so often rode back in triumph to scale.' It was not to be.

The painting of Altisidora shows John Jackson, wearing the striking harlequin colours, together with trainer Tommy Sykes. Altisidora is a chestnut with the long, lean, and expressive head of her sire, Dick Andrews. The artist, Clifton Tomson of Nottingham, was almost unknown until Gerald Pendred published the result of his researches in 1978. But in his day he was spoken of in company with Ferneley and the elder Herring. Tomson produced three paintings of the 1813 St Leger: the start, the finish, as well as this large portrait. There is certainly a primitive touch to his style, but this picture is a fine centre-piece reflecting the quality of the big mare who remained the pride of old Richard Watt till the end of her days. Tomson also painted Altisidora's dam Mandane for Watt, with her foal Captain Candid, as well as Cerberus.

Tomson's most famous picture is probably that of Lord Byron's dog Boatswain, but he painted many racehorses, including Orville (winner of the 1802 St Leger), Filho da Puta, Eleanor, Blacklock, Lottery, Memnon, Dr Syntax, Swap, Tarrare (winner of the 1826 St Leger), The Duchess, Sherwood, Thunderbolt, Brother to Smolensko, Tramp, St George, Brother to Vivaldi, Citizen, Pipeling, Cinnamon, Moorcock, Sir Solomon, Hyale, and an Eclipse mare. Tomson died at the age of 53 in September 1828, having lived all his life in Nottingham.

# Ben Marshall

*1767–1835*

Mameluke
Zinganee

Ben Marshall was a fine painter of horses, but the special and spicy flavour of his pictures often stems from the human characters who surround them. For Marshall had almost a caricaturist's eye for the qualities of that racy sector of humanity who congregate in the vicinity of horses: the wary self-assurance of the stable-lad, the conspiratorial conversation of owner and trainer, intent on pulling a coup, the aplomb of a successful jockey.

Mameluke and his connections were a fine subject for concocting a vigorous tableau. For the villainy surrounding his run in the 1827 St Leger seems to have set the celebrated bookmaker William Crockford (of Crockford's Club) on his road to fortune. Mameluke was publicly supposed to belong to the Earl of Jersey, but Crockford discovered that he had been secretly purchased by John Gully, the famous ex-prize-fighter and Champion of England. Gully, himself a bookmaker, confidently backed Mameluke with Crockford to win £45,000. The horse had already won that year's Derby. Crockford, however, knowing that Mameluke had an evil disposition, bribed the other St Leger jockeys to jostle and harass him at the start.

The scene at Doncaster degenerated into a shambles even by the standards of that unruly era. There were seven false starts and when the field was eventually allowed to go, Mameluke was facing entirely in the opposite direction. Even so he got up to be second. Gully

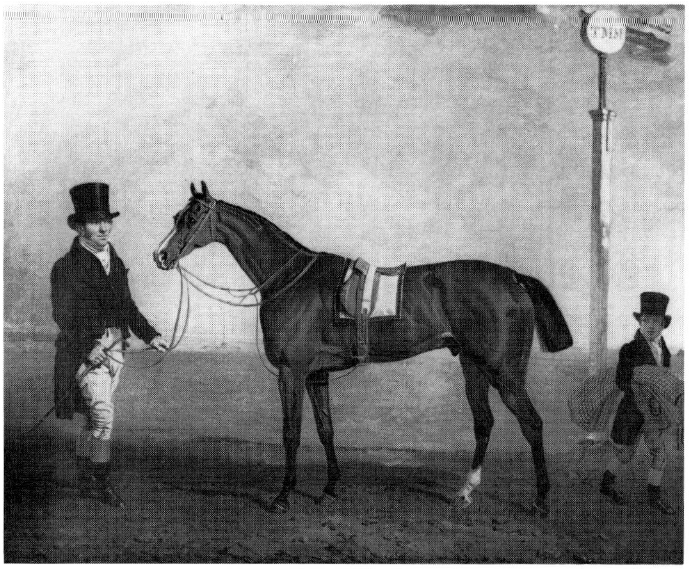

Ben Marshall: *Mameluke held by his owner John Gully (?) at Newmarket*. 1828. Oil on canvas, 71.1 × 91.4 cm. The Halifax Collection

waited seventeen years for his revenge, nobbling Crockford's horse Ratan in the 1844 Derby (see pp. 35–6); two days later, Crockford collapsed and died with the words, 'I have been done, that was not Ratan's right running.'

In this, the version of Marshall's painting owned by Lord Halifax (there are certainly three others), Mameluke's huge, powerful quarters stand out, but he has rather

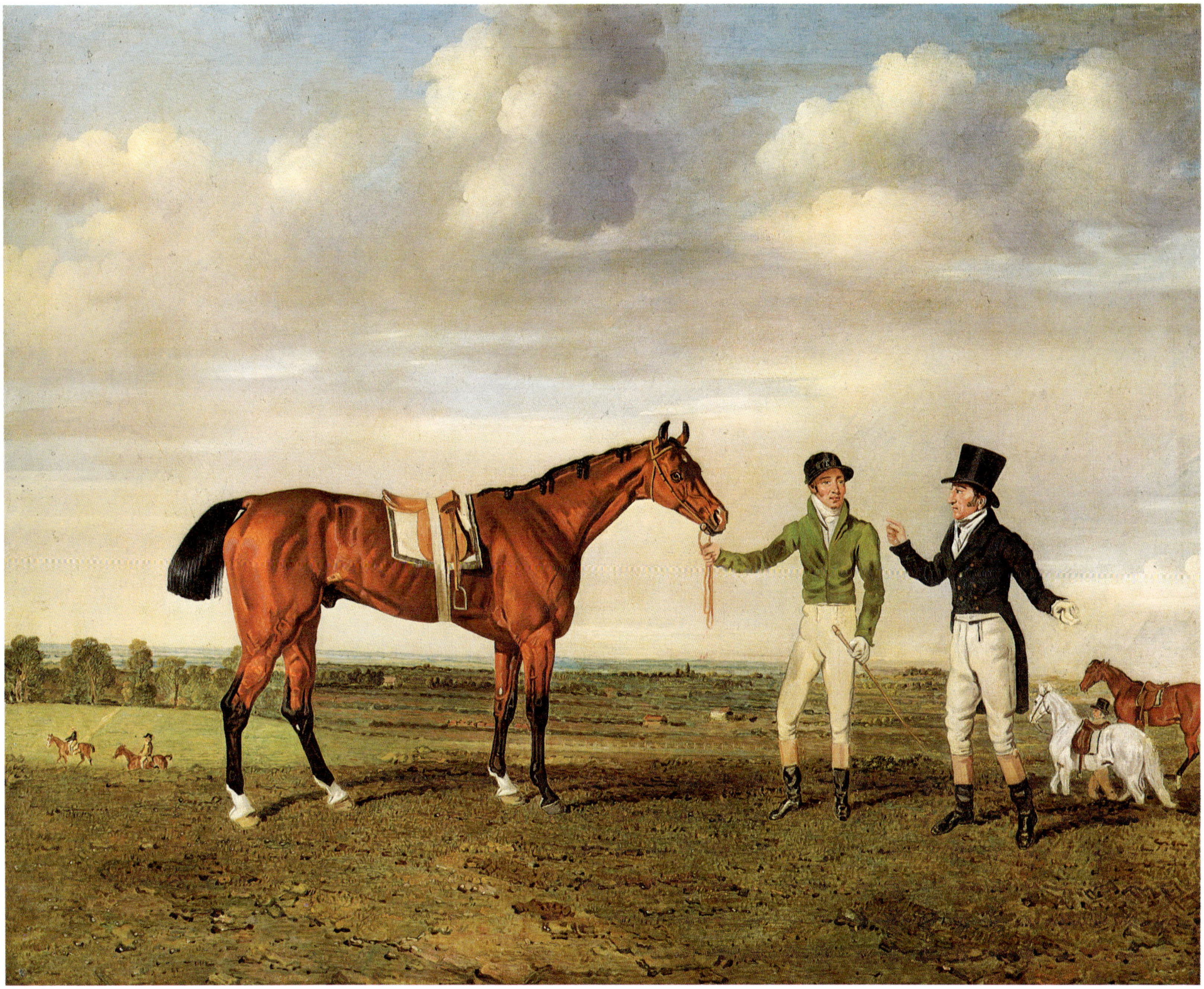

Ben Marshall: *Zinganee held by Sam Chifney junior, with his brother Will, the Trainer*. After 1829. Oil on canvas, 103 × 125 cm. Private collection

a sorrowful look, belying the notorious foul temper. Nor does Gully – if it is he – betray much mark of his previous career as a pugilist. Mameluke was eventually to go to stud in America, but before he set sail he was involved in an epic Ascot Gold Cup in 1829, which was won by another of Marshall's subjects, Zinganee.

The field for the Gold Cup included the 1828 Derby winner, Cadland, and the runner-up, The Colonel (see pp. 96–7), as well as an Oaks winner, Green Mantle. Even twenty-five years later, Henry Dixon was able to assert in his memoirs, 'Such a carnival, as far as carriages were concerned, has never been seen at Ascot either before or since. The carriages were nearly twenty deep by the side of the cords and the verderers declared that "nearly half a mile of them" never reached the course at

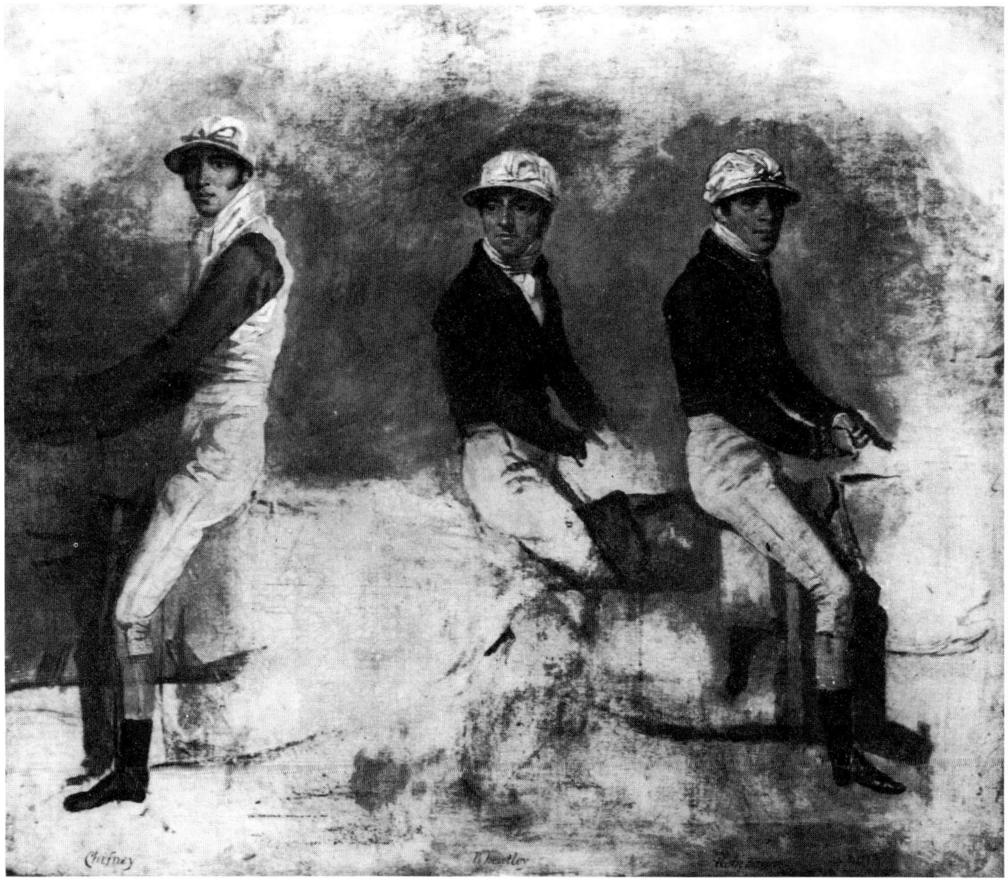

Ben Marshall: *Study of Three Jockeys: (l. to r.) Sam Chifney junior, William Wheatley, and Jem Robinson.* *c.*1818. Oil on canvas, 50.8 × 61 cm. The Halifax Collection

all.' Zinganee was owned by the Chifney brothers and Sam rode him. He lay about seventh until three-quarters of a mile out when 'Zinganee suddenly went through his horses like a minie-ball, Mameluke still hanging on to his quarters until half way up, when he could live the pace no longer, and Sam landed the Bretby colours – amid loud shouts enough to scare every faun and dryad from the shade of Herne Oak for life – a clever first by two lengths.'

In Marshall's picture of Zinganee, Sam is wearing the Bretby colours alongside his brother Will, the trainer. The Chifneys were famous for tough training, and Zinganee, hardly a pretty horse in the first place, shows every sign of the hard work and wasting to which he was subjected. But he is keen-eyed and beautifully muscled. Zinganee passed from the Chifneys to Lord Chesterfield and then to the King's ownership without again reaching such heights. He was put to stud in England, again without much success, and was finally dispatched to the United States in the wake of Mameluke.

Zinganee is definitely the star of Marshall's picture and the portrait of Sam Chifney is unusually feeble. Undoubtedly Marshall had some difficulty capturing Sam's likeness. There is a study of three jockeys, Chifney, Wheatley, and Robinson, in which Marshall has produced a most distinctive account of the latter two, but again gives only a rather featureless rendering of Chifney.

It is an endearing quality of Marshall's painting that he shows quite plainly where his interests and sympathies lie. In the portrait of Banker, who won the Oatland

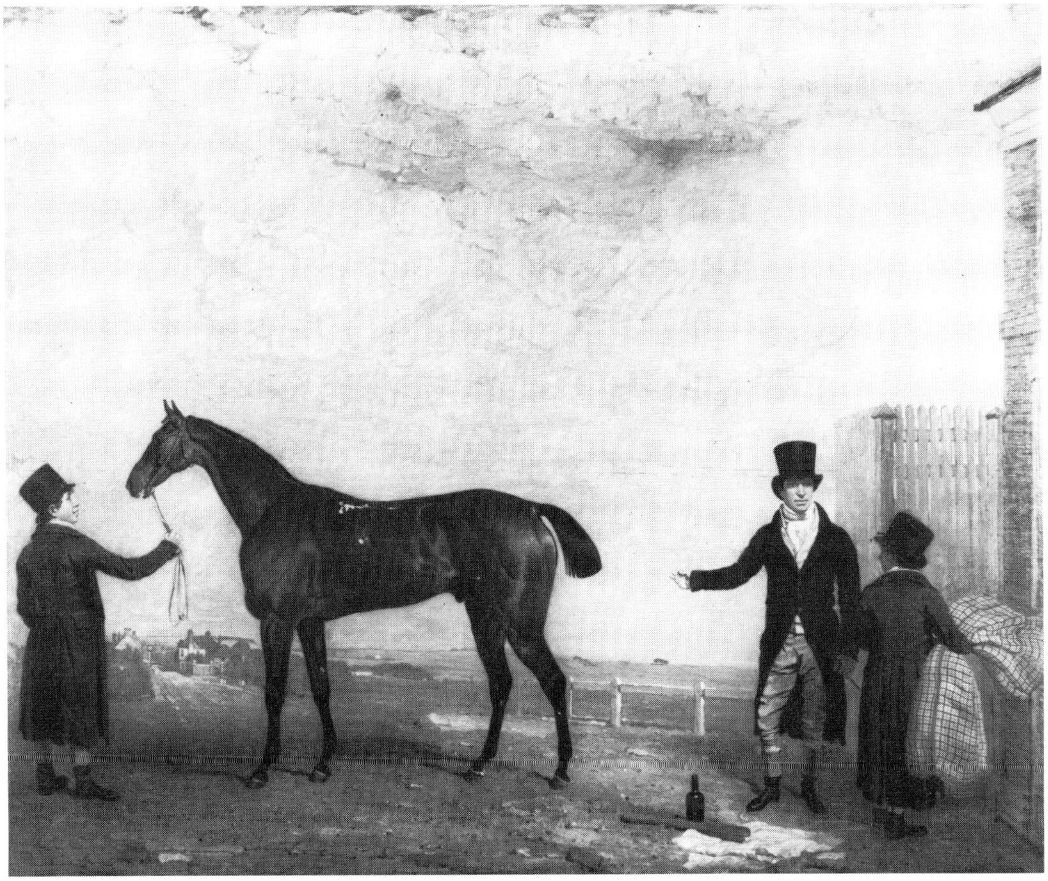

Ben Marshall: *Banker, with his trainer William Butler*. 1821. Oil on canvas, 99.5 × 125 cm.
The Halifax Collection

Stakes in 1820, Marshall clearly had not much time for the horse. A bay colt bred by the Duke of York, it is presented as a characterless animal, almost lost in what is, in any case, a curiously disproportioned picture. All the figures are set in the bottom half of the canvas against an unconvincing sky. But it is redeemed by the splendid, jolly, curly-haired stable-lad who is holding the horse. Banker was later sold to the eccentric gambler John Mytton, but did little to delay that unfortunate man on his journey to a debtor's prison and death at the age of 38 (see pp. 34–5).

Ben Marshall was born in Leicestershire and moved to London, where he was primarily a portrait painter. From there he departed for Newmarket with the legendary remark, 'I have a good reason for going. I discover many a man who will pay me fifty guineas for painting his horse who thinks ten guineas too much to pay for painting his wife.' He had been inspired to take up animal painting after seeing Sawrey Gilpin's *The Death of the Fox* at the 1793 Royal Academy Exhibition.

In an active career of more than forty years, Marshall painted many of the celebrated racehorses of his time, including Sam, Phosphorus, Copperbottom, Jasper, Precipitate, Badger, Emilius, Longwaist, Priam, Diamond, Grey Diomed, Sailor, Euclid, Champion, Sorcerer, Cockfighter, Middleton, Surprise, and Eleanor. There was undoubtedly a 'Marshall school', with Abraham Cooper one of his notable pupils, and Ferneley another. But his son Lambert Marshall was his closest follower, though the inherited talent ran somewhat thin.

# *John E. Ferneley*

*1782–1860*

Priam
Rowton

Priam, a great grandson of Diomed, the first Derby winner, won his own Epsom Classic in 1830, thus rewarding the Chifney brothers for a remarkably percipient piece of judgement. Like Vincent O'Brien and James Delahooke in the present era, there are some men who can look at an unmade yearling colt and spot a Classic horse of two years hence, and then be prepared to back their opinion with a great deal of money. Will and Sam Chifney were certainly blessed with that same flair.

They saw Priam as an unbroken yearling when he came up to Newmarket to be sold out of Sir John Shelley's stud, just before the July meeting of 1828. By all accounts, they were taken greatly with the colt the moment they set eyes on him. Consequently, Mr Tattersall found himself presiding over one of the epic bidding battles of the Newmarket sale ring. There were plenty of contestants in at first, for Priam was by Emilius out of Cressida, good though not yet celebrated blood. As the bidding went past 500 guineas, all dropped out except for the Chifneys and the stable, who were keen to keep him. Finally, at 950 guineas the connections gave in and Priam was knocked down, before an awestruck throng, to the Chifneys for 1,000 guineas.

The brothers never even tried him until he was a three-year-old. He won at the Newmarket Craven meeting, and then was walked via London to Epsom, including a parade through Piccadilly and down Sloane Street. With only one race to his name and John Gully, the bookmaker, plunging on Little Red Rover, Priam was allowed to start at 4–1. The system of starting at that time called for a false start to be declared if any horse was clearly left when the 'Go' was shouted. The opportunities for chicanery were legion, and in 1830 it was only after thirteen previous attempts that the Derby field was permitted to run. Even then, according to the *Sporting Magazine*, Priam was 'dancing on his hind legs at the post' as the other twenty-two contestants took off. But it took him only a quarter of a mile to catch up and he won by a comfortable 2 lengths.

Priam was beaten in the St Leger by Birmingham, in a race run during thunder and lightning on ground which was already a quagmire from days of continuous rain. He was a tough horse. Two days later, he came out and

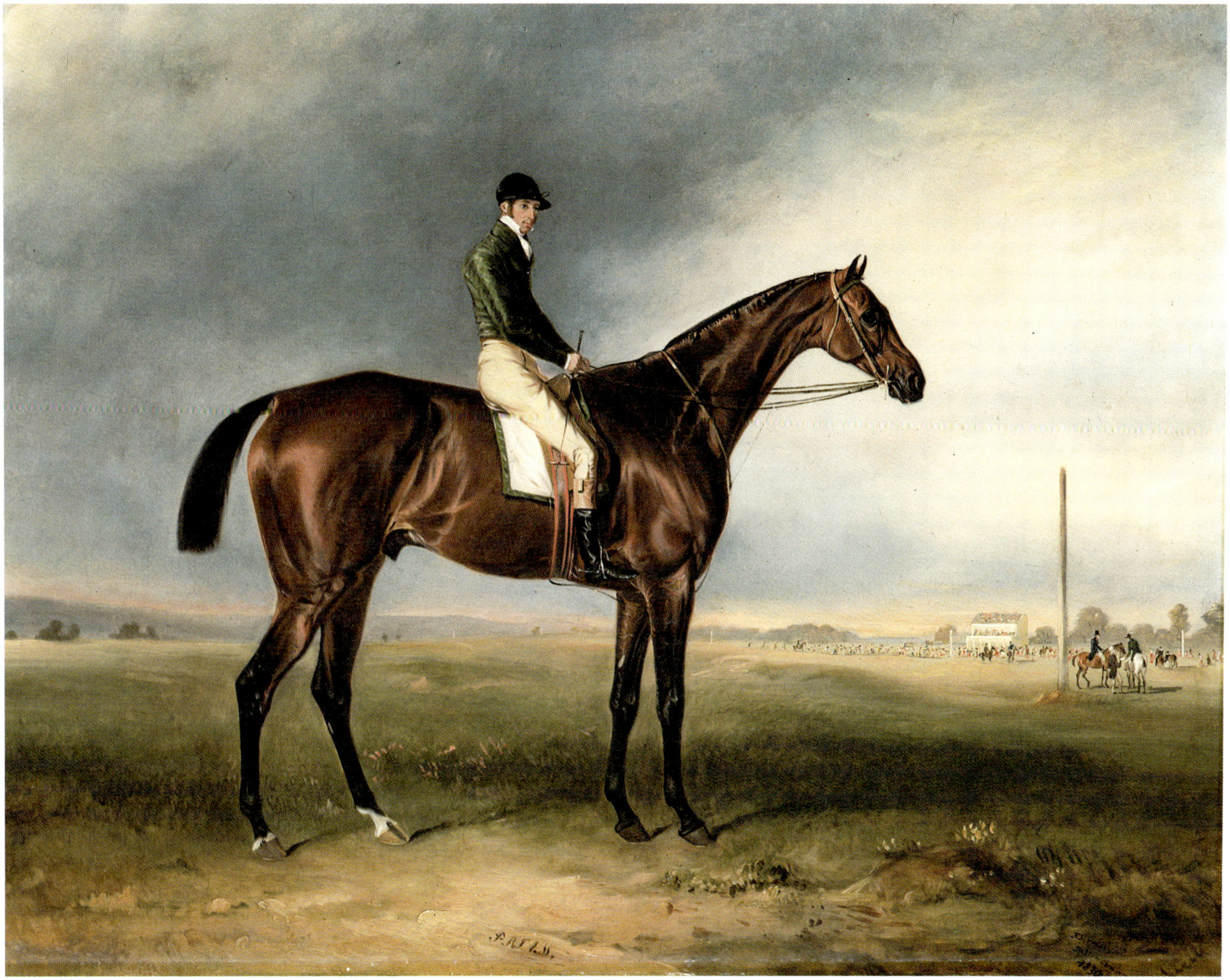

John E. Ferneley: *Priam, with Sam Day up*. 1830. Oil on canvas, 78 × 100.5 cm. The Halifax Collection

won a match of 500 guineas aside against Retriever over $1\frac{1}{2}$ miles. As a four-year-old, he was sold to Lord Chesterfield, and won a fierce match against the five-year-old Ascot Gold Cup winner Lucetta. He gave 16 lb. and a beating to his contemporary Augustus, winner of the Two Thousand Guineas, in another Newmarket match. Priam retired to stud briefly in England before being sold to America for 3,500 guineas.

Perhaps like no other artist, John Ferneley could convey a feeling of a horse truly 'jumping out of his skin'. With the highlights glistening on his coat, despite the gloomy skies behind, Priam looks a picture of health. But it is hard to discern why John Kent and Lord George Bentinck, as well as Lord Chesterfield, variously described him as the best and most perfect racehorse they had ever seen. Indeed, it is possible to discern the rather leggy and light-ribbed look which 'The Druid' commented on. He has a lovely head, beautifully drawn by Ferneley, but again it seems exaggeratedly small. It is illuminating to see Ferneley's thoroughbred pictures hung alongside his painting *George Payne on a Hunter* in Lord Halifax's collection. With the hunter, fashion does not require such a disproportion of head, neck, and body, and Ferneley happily abandons the convention, thus emphasizing its effect in the racehorse pictures.

Ferneley, son of a Leicestershire wheelwright, is best known for his monumental hunting pictures such as *The Quorn at Quenby*. This picture was commissioned through a 5-guinea lottery among the members of the Quorn and was won by Sir Bellingham Graham. It is at the Graham family house at Norton Conyers in Yorkshire to this day.

Ferneley was a student of Ben Marshall's for three years, then travelled in England and Ireland before settling down at Melton Mowbray, which was to be his home for more than half a century; he made an annual trip to London to take in the exhibitions and renew artistic acquaintances. Ferneley painted entirely in oils, starting with detailed pencil sketches of the groupings. Then he would plan the backgrounds and make studies of the men and animals before embarking on the picture itself. Though hunting was his first concern he painted many racehorses, including Velocipede, Pussy, Defiance, The Cur, and Jupiter.

Rowton was described by his trainer, John Scott, as 'long and low, not fifteen hands, calf-kneed, straight hocks, no girth and a regular tickler'. Once more it seems Ferneley has flattered his subject, for Rowton, though small, certainly appears in oil less distressing than he is painted in words. But he was the apple of his owner's eye at least. For Rowton, without having run previously as a three-year-old, took the 1829 St Leger to give the Hon. Edward R. Petre his fourth win in the race and his third in succession, sufficient excuse for a further bout of the energetic carousing for which Mr Petre was renowned and which was shortly to bring about his ruin. Indeed, Rowton had been bought as a foal on a most bibulous occasion when his owner, Mr William Allen of Malton, was bid down during dinner 100 guineas as each new bottle of wine was opened. He finally changed hands at 200 guineas with his dam, Katherina, thrown in.

They were riotous days in Yorkshire. Before the stewards managed to get Rowton's Leger under way, there had been another entertainment on the course. About 700 'belt prickers, gaol birds, three-card tricksters, men with pea and thimble tables and general ruffians' had assembled after days of hooliganism in the town

John E. Ferneley: *George Payne (1803–78) of Sulby, Northants, Master of the Pytchley Hunt, on Clipper*. Oil on canvas, 84.6 × 109.5 cm. The Halifax Collection

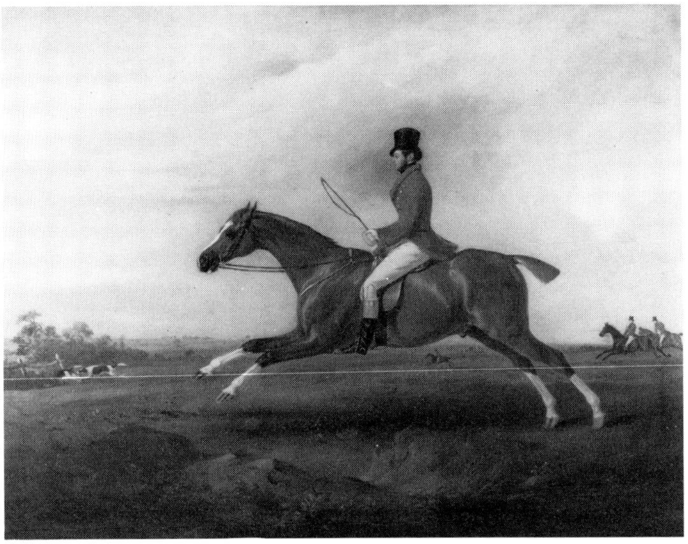

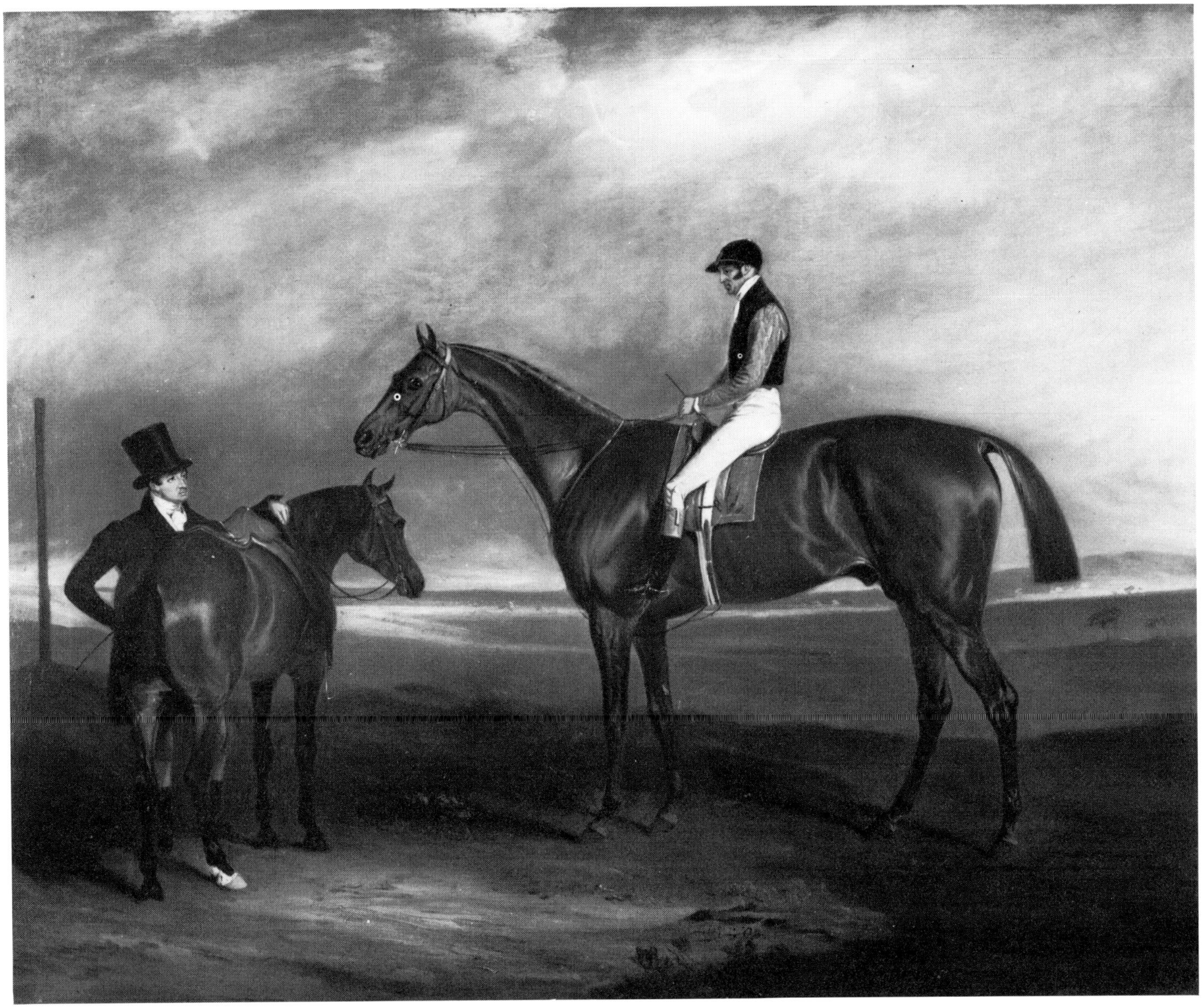

John E. Ferneley: *Rowton, with William Scott up*. 1829. Oil on canvas, 85.5 × 103.3 cm. The Halifax Collection

of Doncaster and the local authorities and gentry determined to deal with them. The police moved to the attack accompanied by 'a considerable number of Yorkshire sportsmen and their servants on horseback'. The annalist William Sheardown's account continues: 'Soon the three-card and thimblerig men found themselves being attacked on two sides. A hand to hand fight ensued before those who were not already maimed or prisoners fled across country. These were pursued by Lord Milton, his hunt staff, and many Yorkshire noblemen and gentlemen who each marked down a man and galloping over fences after him till he was dead beat, eventually cried "tally-ho" and captured their human fox.' With 150 prisoners dispatched to the borough jail, Rowton was able to get about his business of beating Lord Cleveland's colt Voltaire (subsequently the sire of Voltigeur) by a neck.

# *Edward Troye*

*1808–1874*

American Eclipse
Boston
Lexington

Edward Troye was scarcely older than his subject when he painted the great New York stallion American Eclipse. But already Troye had developed that sympathetic and unerring eye for the features of a fine horse in its declining years. The head is still alert, the tail high, but the ribs are showing, the back has slumped, and the muscled arch of the neck has ebbed away. In 1834, American Eclipse was already 20, but Troye still bestows on him a flaunting stance which belies the failing physique and recalls his triumphs as the champion of the North.

American Eclipse was at the centre of some of the legendary events of American racing. Yet he ran only eight times, and four of those encounters were when he was 8 and 9 years old. He was a grandson of Diomed, the first English Derby winner, and had the English Eclipse in his pedigree on the dam's side. He raced just once as a four-year-old at the old Newmarket turf track in New York, winning for his breeder, General Nathaniel Coles. The next year, for his new owner, Cornelius van Ranst, he ran two 4-mile races successfully and then was retired to stud as one of the most lightly raced sires in history.

But, after two years, his life of ease was interrupted in the cause of American enterprise. The New Yorkers had decided to build the world's first dirt track, the Union Course on Long Island, and American Eclipse was called upon to give the track a special lustre on its opening day in 1821. Already 7 years old, he was hauled out of the stud box and put into training to face the Southern mare Lady Lightfoot, who had already won thirty-one races. The contest was to be the best of three 4-mile heats. Pulling in a huge crowd for the delighted management, Eclipse trounced the mare in the first two runs. Twice as an eight-year-old he disposed of Southern horses, so stinging the esteem of the Carolina and Virginia horsemen that they laid down the, then, phenomenal sum of $20,000 if American Eclipse would take on the best horse the South could find.

Colonel William R. Johnson, the doyen of Southern racing, organized trials and finally came up with Sir Henry, owned by Lemuel Long, for the great day in the summer of 1823. The contest at the Union Course was three heats again, and Sir Henry ran away with the first one, but American Eclipse, with a new jockey, won the second and third to inaugurate the epic series of North v. South matches which so enthralled the American racing world in the first half of the nineteenth century.

American Eclipse was still within earshot of the Union Course, at John Snedeker's stud-farm, when Troye came to paint him. Troye's first American pictures had been exhibited only two years before at the Pennsylvania Academy. He had come to America from England at the age of 23, having 'commenced his profession as an animal painter in London after the style of Stubbs and

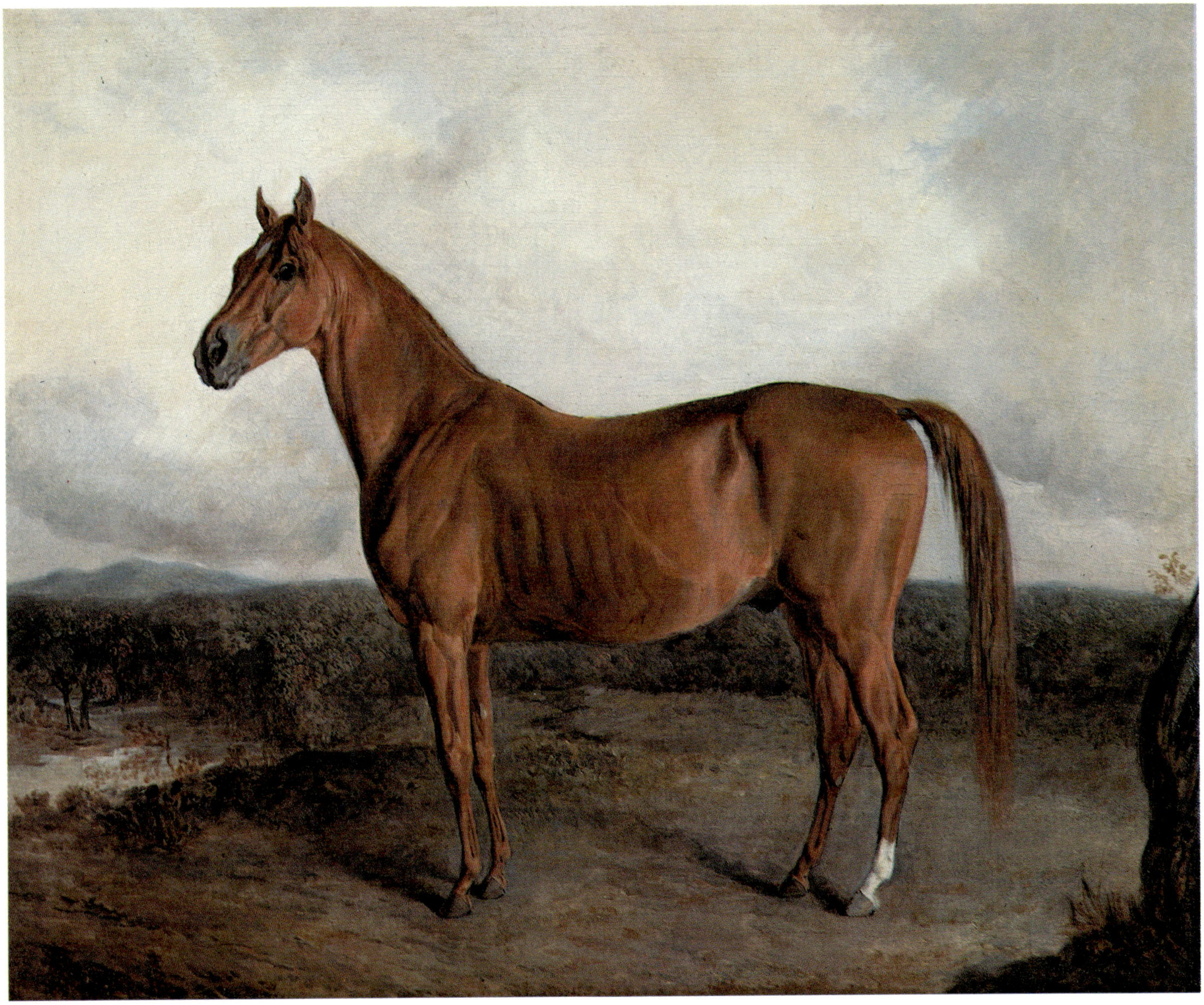

Edward Troye: *American Eclipse*. 1834. Oil on canvas, 60.9 × 73.6 cm. National Museum of Racing, Saratoga Springs, NY

Sartorius', though he had actually been born in Lausanne in Switzerland. The venture to the United States was to prove extraordinarily successful. For the best part of forty years, through some of the great eras of American racing, Troye was to find virtually no rivals as the painter of the American thoroughbred horse. Boston, Lexington, Pacific, and Glencoe were all recorded by Troye.

From the time when he was first taken up in Pennsylvania by John Charles Craig and introduced to many

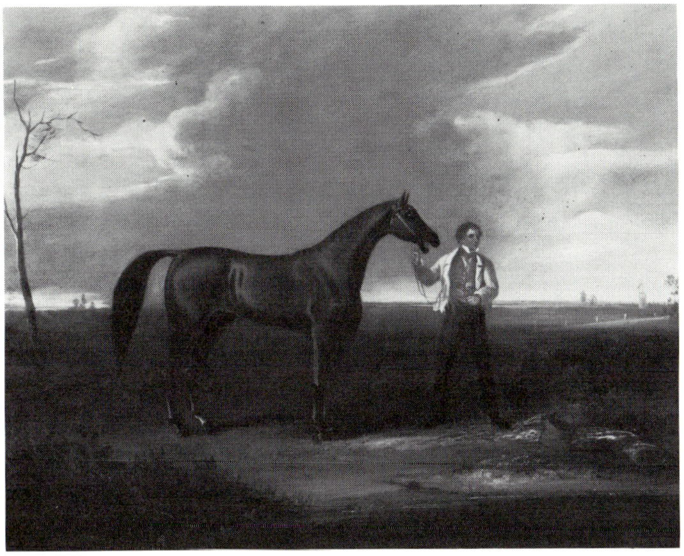

Alvan Fisher: *American Eclipse*. 1823. Oil on panel, 29.8 × 38.9 cm. Private collection

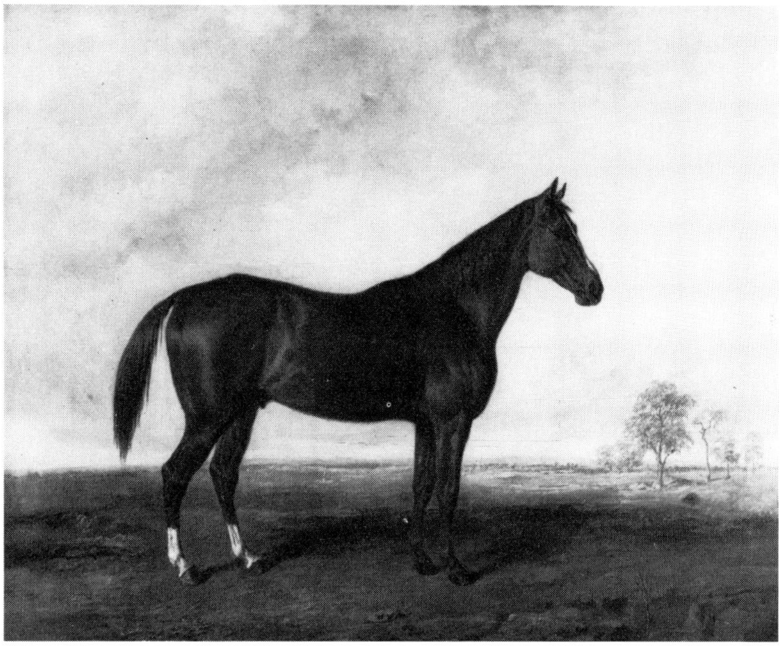

Edward Troye: *Boston*. After *c*.1840. Oil on canvas, 78.7 × 99cm. National Museum of Racing, Saratoga Springs, NY

Edward Troye: *Lexington*. *c*.1865. Oil on canvas, 76.2 × 101.6cm. National Museum of Racing, Saratoga Springs, NY

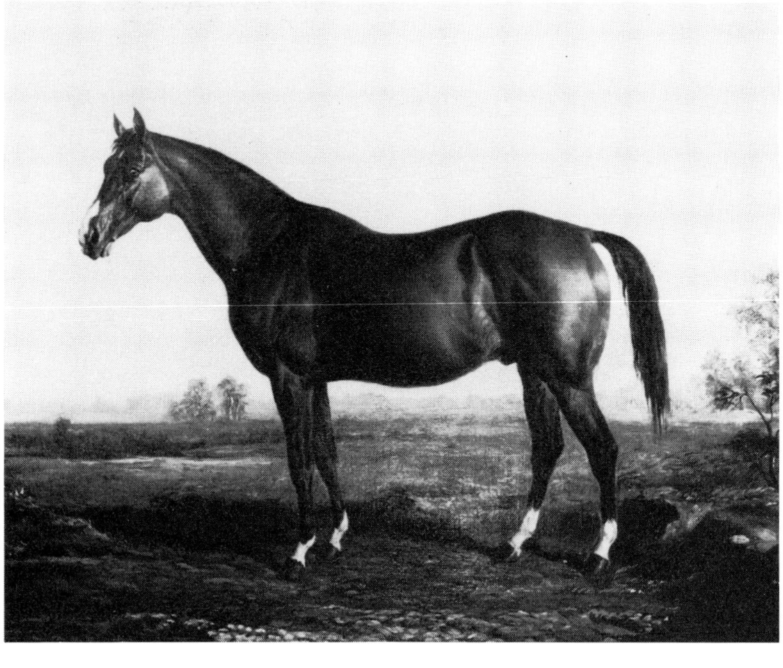

leading owners, Troye's work immediately appealed, not only for the personality which he drew from individual horses – the notorious evil temper evident in the portrait of Boston, the genuineness of Lexington – but also because of the precision of colour and conformation which he managed to record. Certainly, Troye was a fine judge of horse-flesh. In 1856, Keene Richards, from Kentucky, invited him along on an expedition to Syria and Palestine to buy horses from the bedouin sheikhs. This was in pursuit of an obsession which had gripped racing men on both sides of the Atlantic – the idea that a new infusion of Arab blood would have as inspiriting an effect on the thoroughbred as the Darley Arabian and the Godolphin Arabian had produced 150 years before.

All such hopes were to be disappointed and Richards's purchases had no discernible impact on the American stud-book. But they did have one legacy – a series of pictures by Troye which display a splendid freedom and vigour, showing horses with names like Massoud and Mohkladi, which have never had any impact on Turf history, but which are among Edward Troye's finest work. Troye finally stopped painting early in the 1870s, possessed of another mistaken obsession – that the advent of photography would put an end to the horse painter and his trade.

As Troye's picture manifestly shows, Boston was an ornery devil. A fine chestnut with white hind legs, he was won in a card-game by Nathaniel Rives. But when Rives tried to break him, it proved an uphill task. Boston would bolt, rear, and – his favourite trick – roll over, taking his rider with him. John Belcher, the trainer, cured him by lying in wait with a group of lads; when Boston rolled over, they sat on his head and gave him a mighty thrashing. Finally produced at the racecourse in the spring of 1836, the colt flew off in front, and then stopped stock-still in a sulk. The citizens of Richmond, Virginia, were entertained throughout the summer by a battle conducted over several months, often through their streets, between Boston, wild as ever, and his exercise-lad Ned, who finally got him to the races by the autumn, in a tractable-enough temper to win both his contests.

From his four-year-old season onwards, he lost only three races from forty-two starts. Track proprietors were known to pay $500 for him to stay away; the fans of those days being uninterested in great horses, it seems, only in close races. In 1841, he was matched against the Southern mare Fashion at the Union Course in New

York. The race, to be run in May 1842, monopolized the racing pages of newspapers throughout the winter. When the day came, forty US Senators and Congressmen abandoned the business of state in Washington and came up for the race. Eight thousand spectators paid out a princely $10 each for seats in the stand. The train service from New York broke down, with frenzied racegoers smashing up the ticket-office. Even so, 70,000 people managed to get to the course. The race itself was a flop. Boston was soundly trounced by Fashion in the first two heats.

Boston had been put to stud in between his exertions on the race-track, and he was leading sire for three seasons. When he was 14, he went blind, and also became so crippled and emaciated that he had to be hauled to his feet each morning and his legs massaged so that he could stand up. He died in 1850, but was posthumously leading sire in the three following years. From his very last crop came Lexington, proof beyond doubt that the wayward and stubborn Boston had been worth all the patience and care lavished on him throughout his life.

Lexington's story spans the history of Kentucky racing. His breeder, Elisha Warfield, had trekked west with his family in 1790. He qualified as a doctor at the first university west of the Alleghenies, and was a founder of the Lexington Jockey Club in 1809. He was already 72 when Lexington was ready to run, and in poor health, so he leased the horse to a former slave named Burbridge's Harry, who was a local trainer. Among the spectators for his second outing was Richard ten Broeck, an ex-Mississippi riverboat gambler. Ten Broeck determined to buy Lexington, who he envisaged would add great lustre to the Metairie track in New Orleans, in which he had an interest. Metairie was already planning for the Great State Post Stake of 1854, expected to be the richest horse-race ever.

Down in New Orleans, Lexington first disposed of a local heroine, the filly Sally Waters, and then, representing Kentucky, won the big race. Among those he beat was Lecomte, previously undefeated and representing Mississippi. Of course, there had to be a rematch. Lexington lost – for the only time in his life. Ten Broeck was beside himself and issued challenges to Lecomte's owner, General Wells, almost weekly for an entire year,

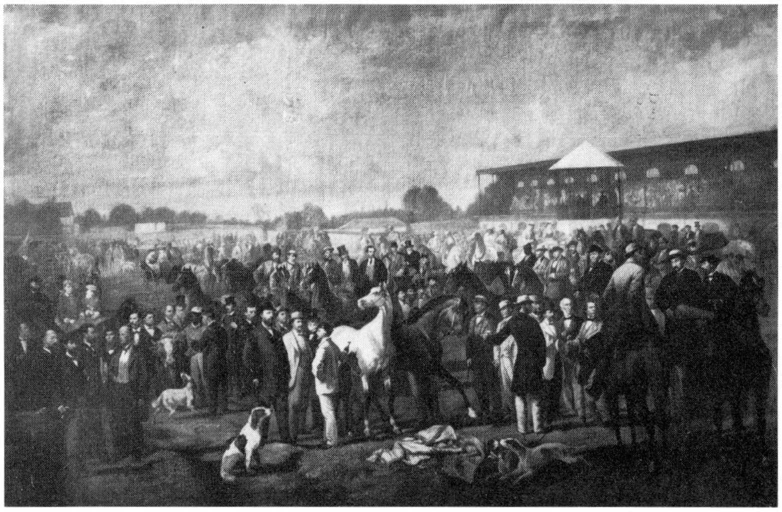

Victor Pierson and Theodore Moise: *Metairie Racecourse*. 1867. Oil on canvas, 137.1 × 214.5 cm. Fair Grounds Race Track, New Orleans

without tempting him to further combat. In the meantime Lexington won a huge bet for ten Broeck by lowering Lecomte's record for 4 miles by $6\frac{1}{2}$ seconds, though with the use of a flying start and two pacemakers. The two horses finally met in April 1855, but Lecomte was not fit and blew up in the first heat.

Richard ten Broeck sold Lexington to Robert Alexander to go to stud at Woodburn in Kentucky. The deal was made when the two men met on a trip to England. After selling Lexington, ten Broeck stayed overseas until his fortune became dissipated, when he returned to live in San Mateo, California, in relative penury. Lexington, as this late picture suggests, went blind. He was America's leading sire for sixteen years, largely through matings with mares by Glencoe, the 1834 English Two Thousand Guineas winner, who was exported to the United States in 1836. Alexander moved his horses north during the Civil War to Ohio and Canada, and they escaped the devastation which hit the South, and even officially neutral Kentucky. Sadly, though, as the great mansions of the South were burned and looted, many of Edward Troye's pictures were destroyed. With them went the pictorial record of many of the great racehorses of the early days of the American Turf.

# *H. B. Chalon*

*1771–1849*

The Colonel
Cardinal Beaufort

Henry Bernard Chalon was one of the most meticulous of the successors to Stubbs. From a family of Dutch extraction, Chalon was himself something of an anatomist and published in his *Studies of Nature* 'The horse's skeleton on a new system' and 'Explanation of the anatomical table of the horse's muscles'. He also had a formal training at the Royal Academy. Perhaps following Thomas Gooch's 'Life and Death of a Racehorse in Six Scenes', Chalon produced a series of seven, which were engraved, called 'The Passions of the Horse'. He was official animal painter first to the Duchess of York and later to King William IV.

Chalon painted at least two versions of The Colonel, who in 1828 was involved in the first dead heat in the Derby, being beaten by Cadland in the run-off. Cadland did not run in the St Leger, and The Colonel started favourite. He won the race by 3 lengths, though as usual there was a suspicion that some of the horses had been 'got at'. Colonel King's mare Bessy Bedlam was supposed to have been given a powerful purge by blacksmith-turned-punter Frank Richardson, and Velocipede was also thought to have been doped.

One rarity occurred, however. The field got away to an even start, at the first time of asking. In an era when false starts were a commonplace part of the general gamesmanship and villainy, this was a notable success, achieved by lining up the jockeys in the weighing-room before the race and threatening them with extreme measures. The starter, Mr Lockwood, told them: 'I shall require you all to draw up about forty or fifty yards behind the post, walk gently up to it, and when I remove my hat from my head and say 'go' it will be a start.'

The Colonel was owned by the Hon. Edward R. Petre, who had won the race the previous year and was to win it again the following year. The Colonel was later sold for £4,000 to King George IV, with the specific intention of winning the Ascot Gold Cup, but he was beaten by Zinganee (see pp. 85–6). He was eventually bought by Richard Tattersall and went to his Dawley stud.

Lord Egremont's Cardinal Beaufort came from nowhere and disappeared in the same direction. A bay son of Gohanna, he had never been on a racecourse before he won the Derby of 1805. His Lordship sold him on after two defeats; he was eventually passed through the hands of seven owners, winning races for every one of them. After a last victory for General Gower, at Newmarket in 1808, nothing more is heard of him.

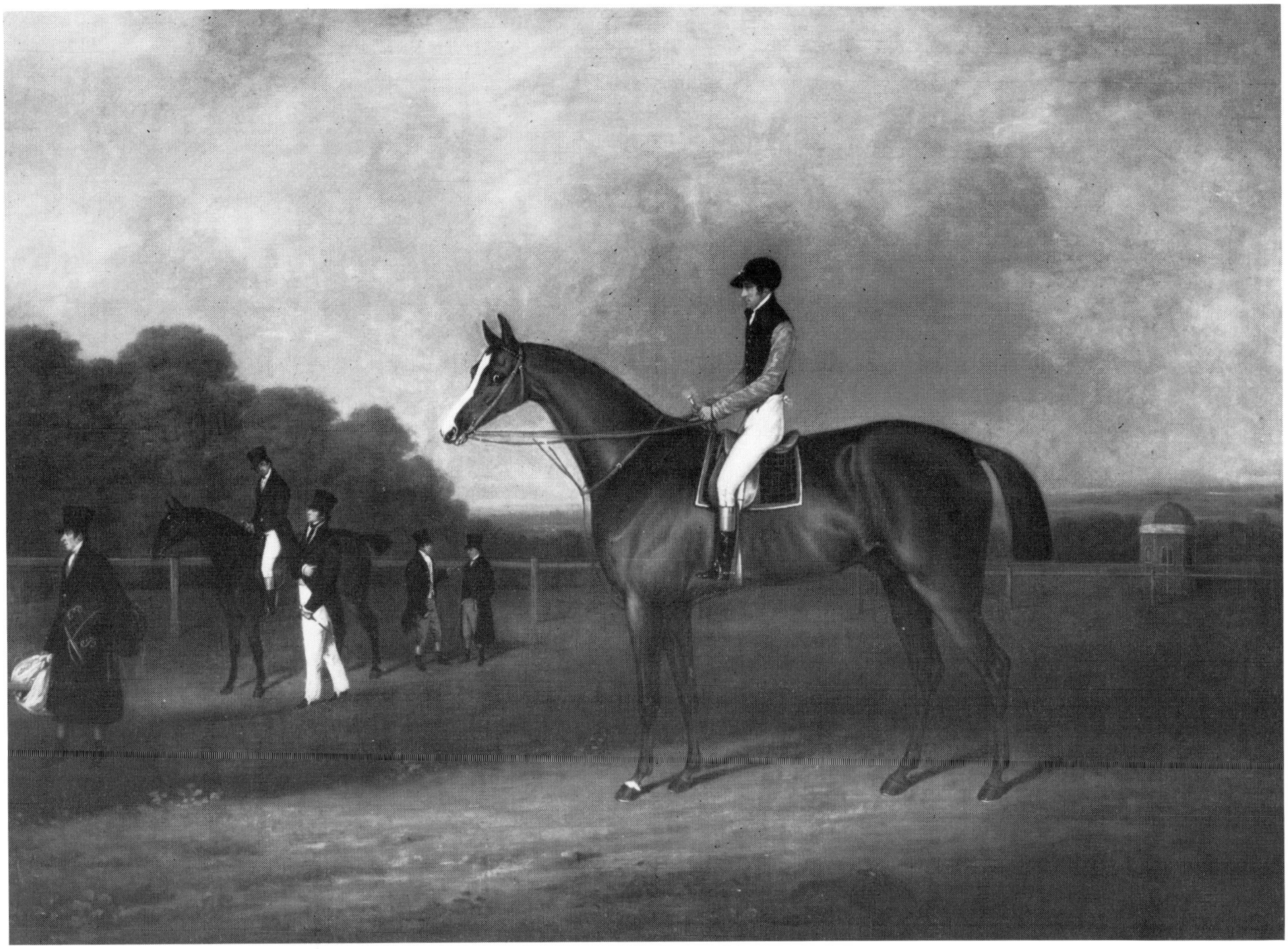

H. B. Chalon: *The Colonel, with William Scott up*. 1829. Oil on canvas, 73.7 × 102.2 cm. Private collection

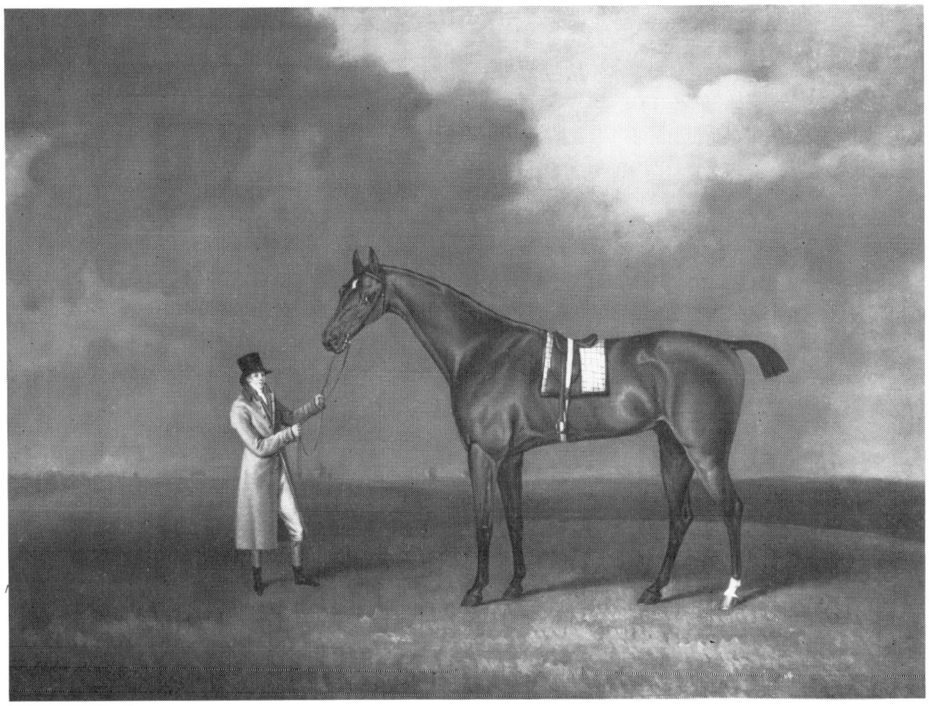

H. B. Chalon: *Cardinal Beaufort*. 1807. Oil on canvas, 69.9 × 90.2 cm. Private collection

# *J. F. Herring*

*1795–1865*

Blacklock
Jerry
Memnon
Plenipotentiary
Touchstone
Lottery

Poor Blacklock was one of the most maligned creatures in the story of the English thoroughbred. Herring's picture leaves little doubt that he thought Blacklock as ugly a beast as you might find, an opinion that was shared even by the Yorkshiremen who supported him on the racecourse. The great bloodstock authority of the day, Dr Shorthouse of the '*Pink 'un*', always referred to the 'accursed Blacklock blood'. When he was a foal he was turned down by Mr Sylvester Reed with the opinion that 'he neither liked his forelegs nor the remembrance of his dam when he saw her crawling past his window to Mr Moss's through the streets of York after she had been purchased for £3'. His fetlocks and pasterns were regarded as hopelessly straight and even his owner Richard Watt apparently thought there was a yellow streak in him which was bound to come out in his stock. Yet his line produced the most notable racehorses of the nineteenth century, down through Voltigeur to Galopin and St Simon.

Blacklock was a good performer on the racecourse as well. He was bought initially by the extraordinary York bloodstock dealer Mr Joseph Kirby, who carried on an international trade in racehorses, travelling as far afield as Russia to sell his wares. Kirby won two races with Blacklock as a two-year-old, and then sold him on to Richard Watt for £40. Watt was the squire of Bishop Burton in east Yorkshire (see pp. 80–3), who raced in the harlequin colours and owned Manuella, Altisidora, and Mandane. Blacklock was trained for the St Leger of 1817, for which he arrived at Doncaster attired completely in oilskins and processed down the High Street through huge crowds, as though it were a royal progress.

He was an odds-on favourite, and there seems little doubt that he would have won but for the behaviour of his trainer, Tommy Sykes. According to Henry Dixon's memoirs of the time: 'His orders to Jackson the jockey were "to look oot for me at the distance, and I'll tell you what to do". Amid the clatter of eighteen horses and the many-headed multitude all "Blacklocking", it was a wonder that he could make himself heard by Jackson, but he unfortunately did, and "Pull till em John, pull till em; thoo hast it all thee own way," were his words which unfortunately fell on Bob Johnson's ear as well. Bob was not usually very leery, but he immediately pulled Ebor quite wide, in order that Jackson who was watching Ben Smith on Restless, next the rails, might not see him so readily, and then snapped him on the post.' The tradition of the hard luck story is as old as racing. Ebor, who won the race, ridden by Bob Johnson, was a 25–1 outsider.

Blacklock was brought out two days later to win the Gascoigne Stakes over the St Leger course and then again the following day for the Doncaster Club Stakes over 2 miles. There was no mollycoddling in those days. He

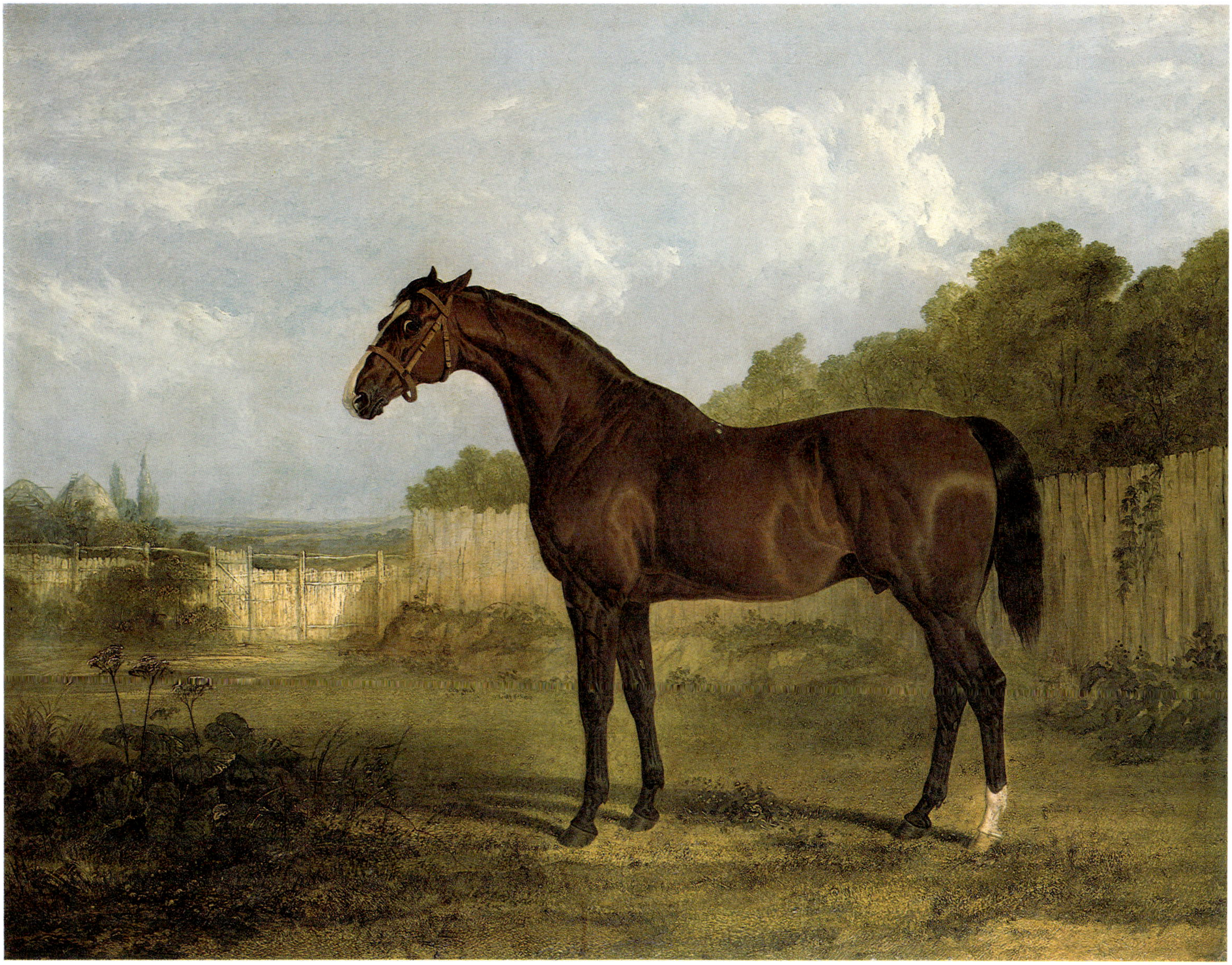

J. F. Herring: *Blacklock*. 1826. Oil on canvas, 69.2 × 89.5 cm. Private collection

won the Gold Cup at York the following year and nine other races around the North. When he went to stud he led a peripatetic life, being found at various locations in Yorkshire, from Leeds to Beverley in the East Riding, and even getting as far as Bildeston in Suffolk. He sired Velocipede, Voltaire, and Brutandorf.

When he died after serving a mare at Bishop Burton in 1831, he was still allowed no respite. Buried briefly under a tree in the grounds, he was then bizarrely exhumed, his bones put together by an anatomist, and the construction surmounted by the skeleton of a rider for which Richard Watt paid £10 and whose teeth would chatter at the pull of a string. The ghoulish gallopers were then taken for exhibition at the Beverley agricultural show, and for the next century they stood on display at Bishop Burton Hall. But then Richard Watt had never really liked Blacklock.

There is no mistaking that Herring has given Jerry's jockey, Ben Smith, a look of petrified fright in this picture – and well he might! Jerry was as black as jet, yet the plots against him for the 1824 St Leger were even darker.

The horse had come out and won the York St Leger and then improved in condition so that he was thought a certainty for the Doncaster race. As August passed, however, Jerry went out further and further in the betting. Mr R. O. Gascoigne, his owner, and Croft, the trainer, drew the obvious conclusion: the horse was to

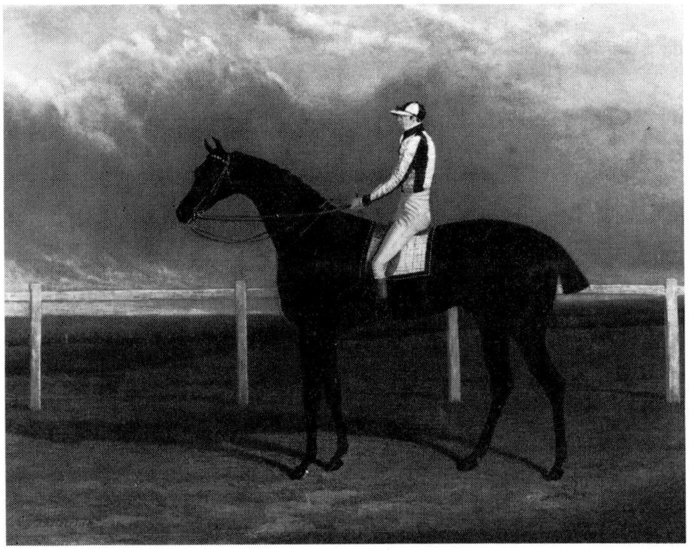

J. F. Herring: *Jerry, with Ben Smith up*. After 1824. Oil on canvas, 36.8 × 48.3 cm. Woodward Collection, The Baltimore Museum of Art

be nobbled. So they took every precaution, including a huge and ferocious dog who was tied to the door of the horse's box all night. When it was time to set out for Doncaster, Jerry still seemed in the pink of fitness. Croft was as puzzled and suspicious as ever, when fickle fate delivered the solution into his hands.

Croft, so the story goes, was staying at an inn on the way, when up rode the evil Robert Ridsdale, organizer of many a blackguard betting coup, and in his company was none other than Jerry's intended jockey, one-eyed Harry Edwards. Or perhaps the incident happened at a toll-gate. But it was enough for Croft, who made haste through the night to warn Mr Gascoigne. On the morning of the race they found Ben Smith, who had already won five Legers, without a ride. He was engaged, and sworn to say nothing. Only as Edwards was going to scale did Croft inform him that he would not have the ride. 'An what's mair,' said Croft, 'there's a couple o' men at the weighing room door ti see that you don't go out to have any conversation wi' that friend o' yours.'

Jerry won comfortably by 2 lengths having started at 9–1. George Payne, one of the Turf's great 'plungers', recalled this early catastrophe of his youth: 'The effect was immense on the party who had plotted against Jerry. Gully lost a big stake and said to me, "Well Mr Payne, we are done and the money is gone; but if it's any use to you, I can tell you that Memnon will win next year's Leger." Which he did. I was not quite twenty-one, and my losses over Jerry's Leger were £26,000.'

Jerry was by Smolensko – the first horse that Herring is recorded as having painted – out of Louisa by Orville. He won some good races in the following years, including a defeat of Tarrare at the August York meeting of 1827. However, by the following year he was being offered for 10 guineas per service from the Grantham Arms at Boroughbridge in Yorkshire.

The portrait of Memnon at Doncaster recently fetched the highest price for a Herring picture at public auction, and it is not hard to see why. Set against a darkening sky, the gleaming bay with his dark legs is a supreme example of Herring's ability to give a lustrous depth of quality and well-being to a thoroughbred's coat. The gay harlequin colours of Richard Watt give a lightness, and a lightheartedness, to the foreground. But the picture is also carefully composed with the lad on the cantering pony leading the eye towards the Doncaster stand and the coaches and teams arriving to take the gentry home. Memnon looks perfectly at ease in this picture marking his victory in the 1825 St Leger. But it had been a rough race.

A son of Whisker out of Manuella, Memnon was Richard Watt's third success in the St Leger. The horse's abilities had been noted as a two-year-old by John Gully, who announced after the Champagne Stakes, in which Memnon beat The Alderman, 'There go the first two in the St Leger.' Gully then proceeded to take all sorts of

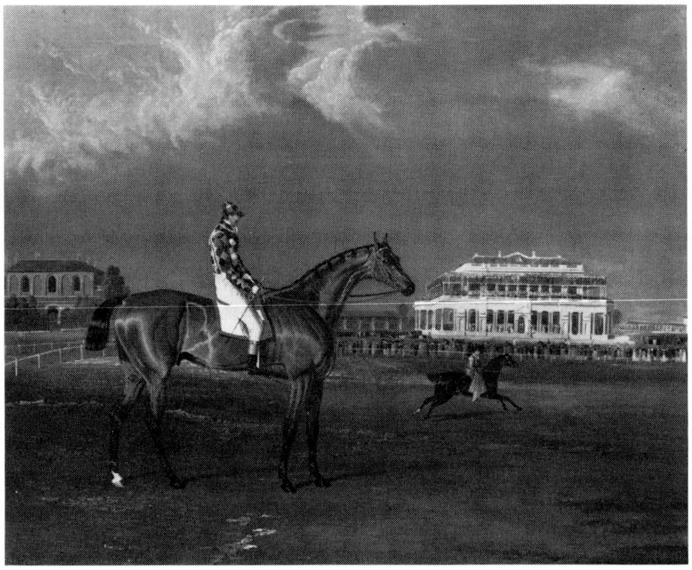

J. F. Herring: *Memnon, with William Scott up, at Doncaster*. 1825. Oil on canvas, 70 × 86.4 cm. Private collection

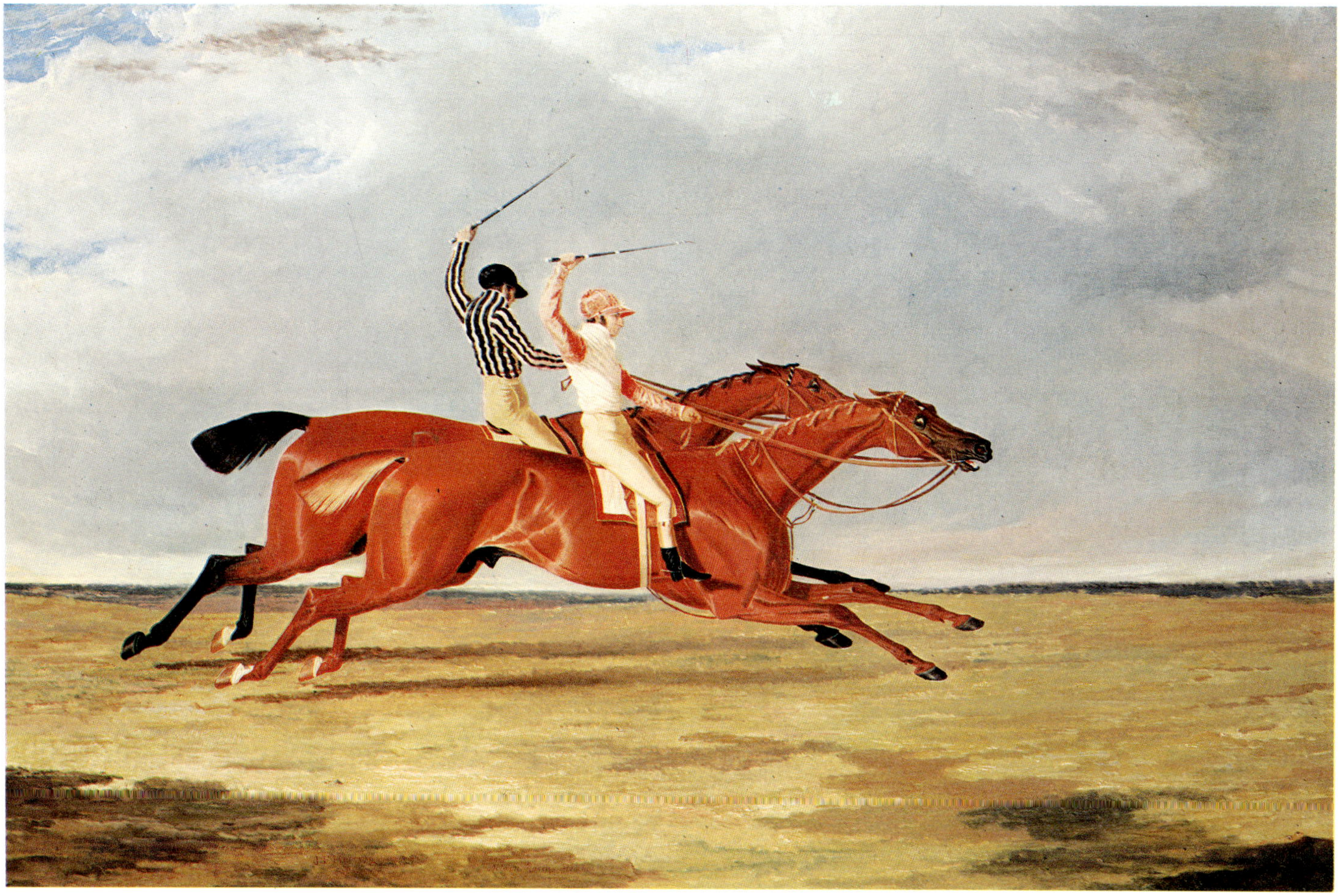

J. F. Herring: *Actaeon beating Memnon*. 1826. Oil on canvas, 61 × 91.4cm. Private collection

odds about them: 1,000–25 that his prediction was right; another 1,000–20; and a third that he would beat The Alderman. The public followed Gully's loudly proclaimed line. So it was not surprising that attempts were made to persuade Richard Watt to sell the horse before the race. He declined with the famous words, 'Until the St Leger has been run, Memnon belongs to the public and money wouldn't buy him.'

The bookmakers were reduced to other methods and so, perhaps, were those who stood to win on Memnon. As usual there was a false start. There was one very fast but unbacked filly in the race, Fleur-de-Lis, who stood a chance of taking the prize as 'bookmaker's friend'. As the horses entered the straight she was ridden into, according to one account, and knocked over. Certainly she fell. Sam Chifney, riding The Alderman, managed to negotiate the mêlée, which also brought down Zirza. Memnon came on the outside and won easily by 3 lengths, The Alderman was second, and John Gully was rich. The result of the race was so eagerly awaited in the country that dogs had been specially trained to follow a trail and take the news to Manchester; carrier pigeons were the messengers to London.

Memnon was sold after the St Leger to Lord Darlington, who had a penchant for paying fancy prices for proven horses. The rumour was that Memnon cost him 3,000 guineas. Memnon took some fearful punishment in his career. He was whipped unmercifully by Bill Scott when he won the Champagne Stakes from The Alderman. Under Lord Darlington's ownership he narrowly lost a match at York on the Knavesmire against Actaeon in which, according to the *Sporting Magazine*, Sam Chifney gave him 'a stroke of the whalebone which might have been heard to Bishopthorpe'. In 1827 he had two punishing races at Doncaster against Fleur-de-Lis, beating her narrowly the first time and then dead-heating with her. Not surprisingly, at the Craven meeting of 1828 he simply seems to have 'turned it in' and was retired. Eventually, Lord Darlington sold him to America, where he made no great mark.

Great horses and low cunning combined to make the 1834 season in England one of the most dramatic on record. As Derby Day drew near, three leading contenders had come to the fore.

The Two Thousand Guineas at Newmarket had been won by Glencoe, who was to become responsible for one of the best American sire lines, including Hindoo and Hanover. But he had previously been defeated by Plenipotentiary, owned by a senior member of the Jockey Club, Mr Stanlake Batson. Meanwhile the Chifney brothers were nurturing their Derby hope, an unraced colt called Shilelagh. Unfortunately, they tried him in front of unreliable witnesses and the story of his prowess reached the bookmakers, whose intelligence service a century and a half ago was as impressive as it is today. The Chifneys could not get their money on. The family who had 'hooked up' one Derby favourite, Manuella, thereby ruining the owner, could be relied on not to surrender without a fight. They found a 'ringer' for Shilelagh, blistered him and bandaged him, and sent him out for exercise two days before the race. The stratagem worked and the Chifneys were able to place their wagers. 'Plenipo', meanwhile, had not run since the Craven Stakes, but that did not stop him becoming favourite.

After five false starts the Derby field were away before a huge crowd and in the most perfect conditions. Glencoe was ahead coming out of Tattenham Corner, but 'Plenipo' got up smoothly to win by 2 lengths with

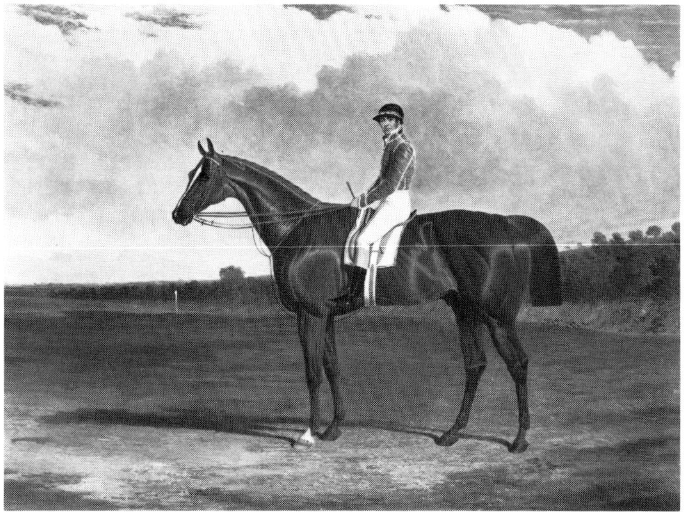

J. F. Herring: *Plenipotentiary, with Patrick Conolly up*. 1834. Oil on canvas, 55.9 × 76.2 cm. Private collection

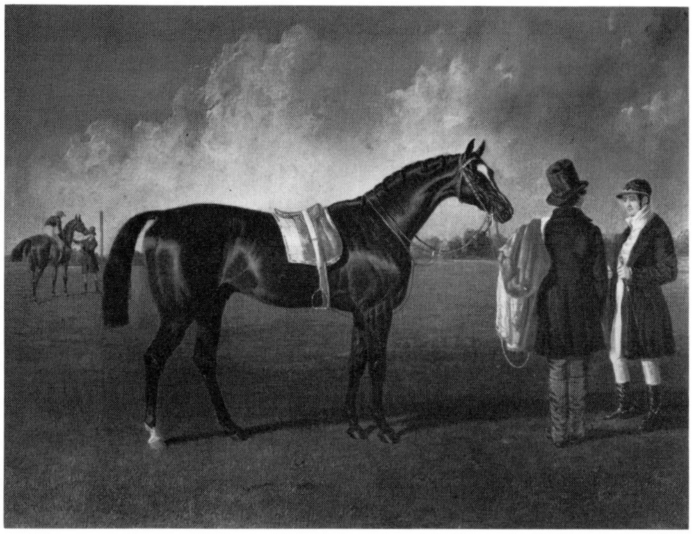

J. F. Herring: *Touchstone, with his jockey G. Calloway*. 1834. Oil on wood, 22.2 × 29.8 cm. Jockey Club, Newmarket

Shilelagh displacing Glencoe for second place. There was the warmest reception from a crowd who knew they had seen three outstanding racehorses. And so to Doncaster for the St Leger.

'Plenipo' and Shilelagh were the favourites, with Glencoe not competing. 'Nimrod' described the tone of the ensuing contest in his memoir of the Turf: 'That the Doncaster St Leger race of 1834 was a robbery, there is not to be found a man in all His Majesty's dominions, unconnected with the fraud, to deny. But by what means the best horse that England has seen since the days of Eclipse – a horse allowed to have been, as Plenipotentiary was allowed to have been, a better horse than Priam was – was made the worst horse in the race (so bad indeed as to have been beaten before he got a quarter of the distance he had to run) will perhaps never be known, except to those who made him so. Mr Batson, his owner, like Aemilius Scaurus the Consul, stood on his character and made no defence; but as a St Leger horse is the property of the public, we think the public had a right to some kind of explanation under Mr Batson's hand.'

As this expostulation suggests, Plenipotentiary was obliterated, the race being won by the Marquis of Westminster's Touchstone, about whom any odds from 40–1 upwards might have been had on Town Moor. Shilelagh came third. There seems no doubt that 'Plenipo' had been 'got at'. On his death-bed, Mynott, his lad, confessed that he had been bribed to hand over the key to his horse's box at the Doncaster Hotel. It was said that

'Plenipo', normally a fearsome horse to saddle and mount, had to be kicked in the ribs to persuade him to get up on Leger morning, and that Patrick Conolly, his jockey, remarked to John Scott as he went down, 'My horse is as dead as a stone.' As it emerged, however, the victor Touchstone was himself a remarkable animal.

Lord Westminster's trainer, John Scott, had never seen Touchstone, a son of Camel, until the Liverpool St Leger, in which he made all the running, though losing at the end. Scott immediately remarked to Lord Derby and Lord Wilton that the horse would win at Doncaster. It was arranged that he would go to Scott's stable at Malton in Yorkshire. This meant walking the horse into Yorkshire. There were, it seems, too many alehouses on the way and the groom emerged from one especially hospitable resort on the Pennines to find Touchstone gone. He was later recaptured by a seaman who took him to Sheffield.

Eventually, fit – it seemed – only for the knacker, Touchstone arrived in Malton. He was still so backward on the eve of St Leger day that William Scott elected to ride Lady de Gros. G. Calloway, who got the ride, was apparently so astonished to find himself in front that he kept looking all about him as though begging the rest of the field to come back from the abyss to which Touchstone's speed had consigned them.

In fact, Touchstone turned out to be a really good racehorse, winning the Ascot Cup twice and the Doncaster Cup. But it was as a sire that he truly made his mark, producing Surplice, Orlando, and Cotherstone who all won the Derby among other Classics, Mendicant who won both the One Thousand Guineas and the Oaks, Blue Bonnet and Newminster who won the St Leger, and Flatcatcher, Nunnykirk, and Lord of the Isles who won the Guineas. Touchstone was 31 when he died, having sired 343 winners. Poor 'Plenipo', though, ended up serving half-bred mares for £5.

Just as Stubbs's vision of the rearing Whistlejacket has a power which would have been diminished if the intended background had been included, equally some of Herring's unadorned studies have a special impact. There are some fine examples in the possession of Messrs Tattersall, and the portrait of Jem Mason on Lottery, too, is extraordinarily effective. The jockey is entirely relaxed, hand on thigh, foot loosely in the stirrup. The horse, turning away in a most unusual pose, has had his attention attracted by something in the distance. It is a most revealing and appealing painting. Yet it was only

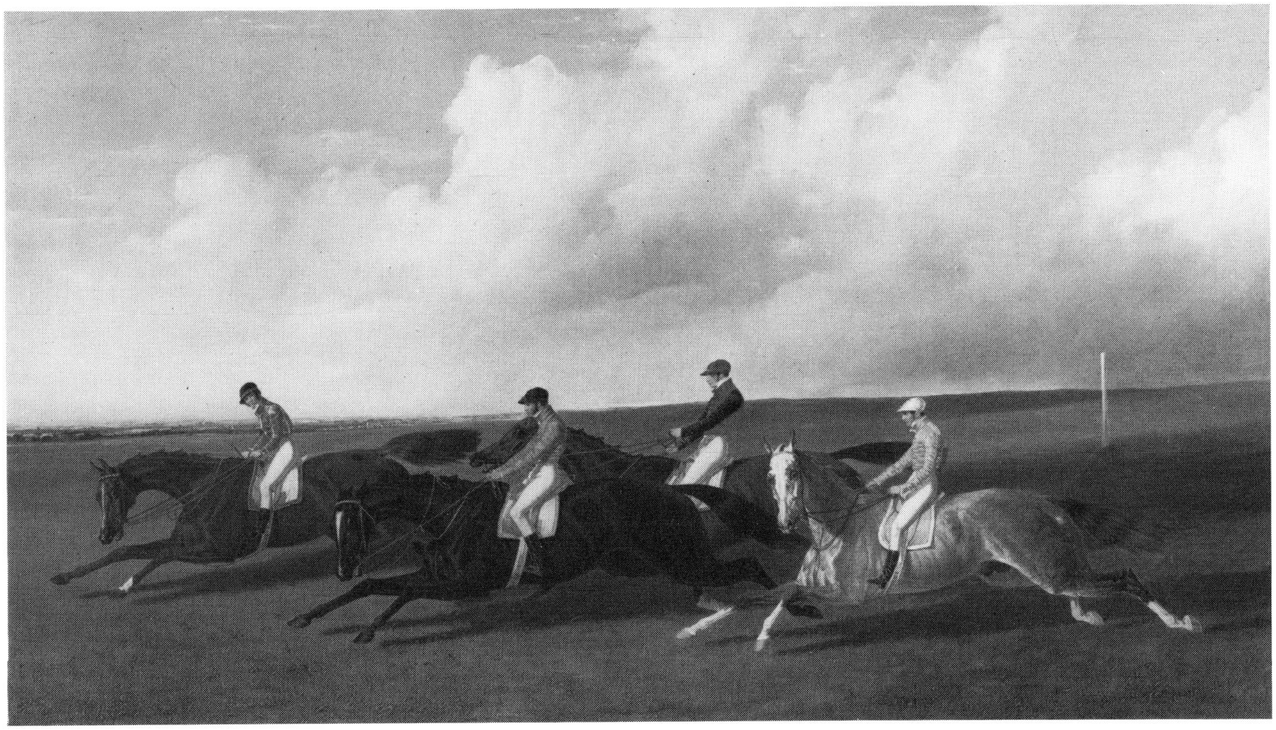

J. F. Herring: *Plenipotentiary leading Touchstone, Priam, and Grey Momus.* 1841. Oil on canvas, 61 × 106.7 cm. Private collection

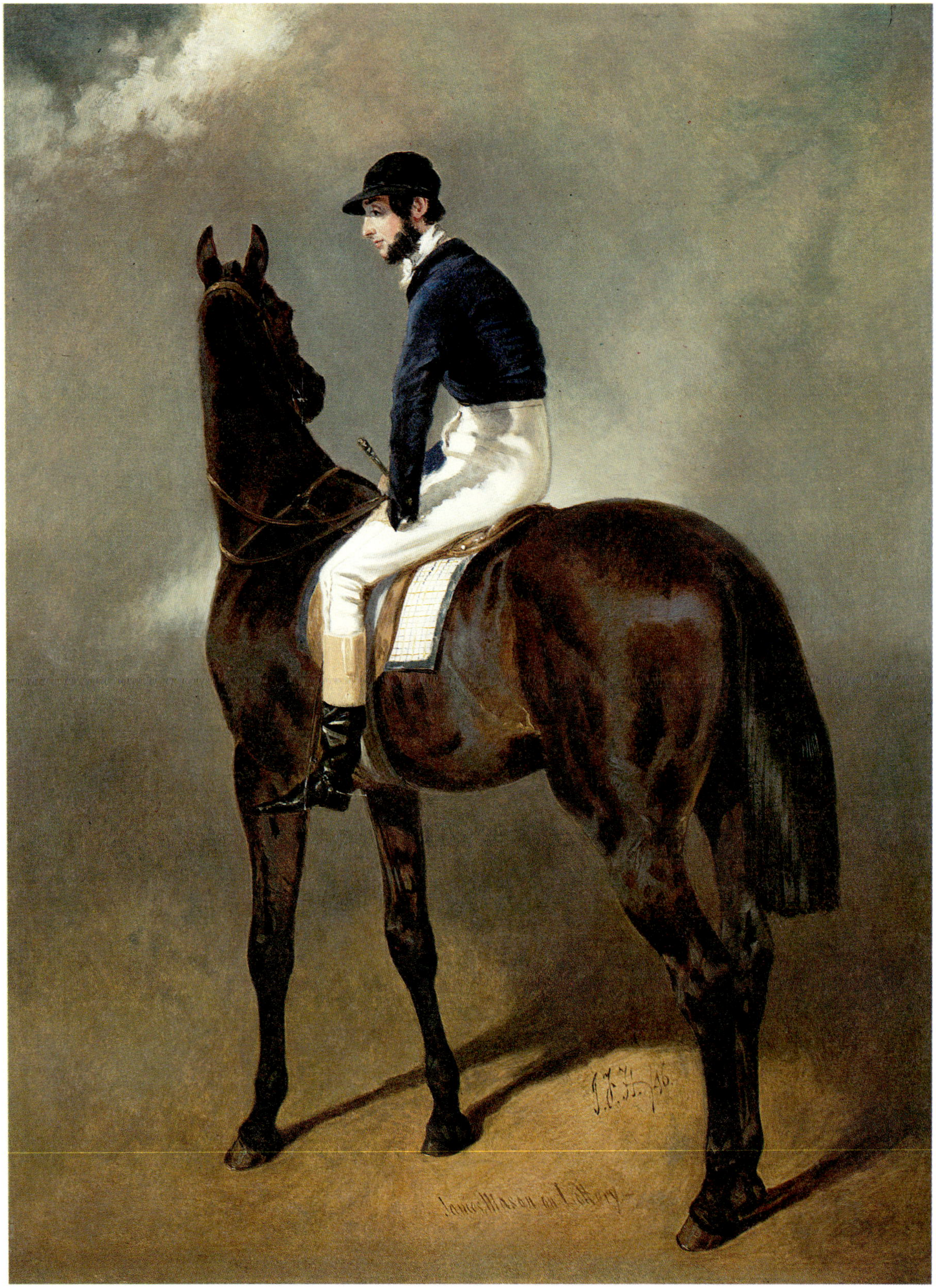

J. F. Herring: *Jem Mason on Lottery*. 1846. Oil on canvas, 61 × 45.7 cm. Private collection

part of the infinite pains involved in building up the great picture of 1846 by which Herring commemorated the new sport of steeplechasing, which in sixteen years had taken such a hold in England as to rival Flat racing.

We still have the study of Jem Mason alone, which was an early stage. Then in the Mellon collection there is the study of three steeplechase 'cracks' together, with Allen McDonough (on the left) on Brunette and Tom Oliver on Discount. The final painting is an action picture of twelve horses taking a jump.

Lottery won the first Grand National steeplechase at Liverpool in 1839. Huge crowds turned out to see the seventeen runners, who faced a course of more than 4 miles, with twenty-nine jumps. The fences were formidable. The brook, which was to be baptized by Captain Becher that day when he fell into it from Conrad, required a 23-ft jump, and the take-off was from ploughed land. There was a solid 5-ft stone wall in front of the newly erected stands, and also what was called the 'Table Jump', where the horses landed in a field which was 4 ft higher than their take-off. One horse, Dictator, was killed in the race, setting a melancholy pattern for the future, and only four finishers are recorded. But Lottery won easily. The next year he crashed through the stone wall and was put out of the race, which was won by

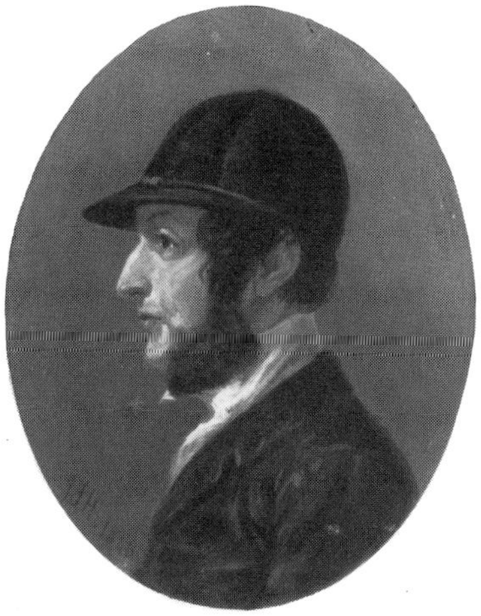

J. F. Herring: *Jem Mason*. 1846. Oil on board, 13.3 × 10.8 cm. Clarence House, London

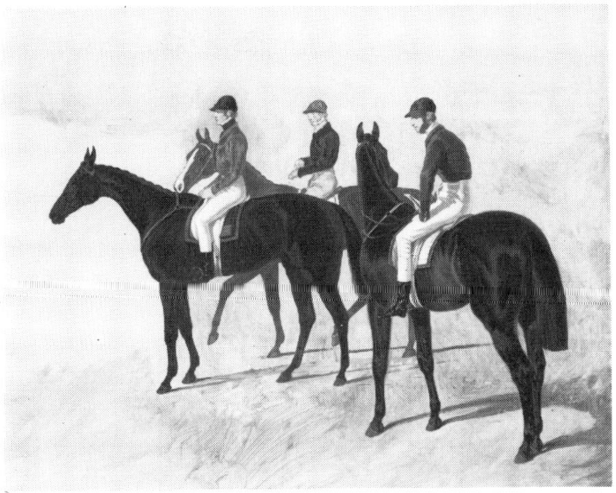

J. F. Herring: *Study of Three Steeplechase Cracks: (l. to r.) Allen McDonough on Brunette, Tom Oliver on Discount, and Jem Mason on Lottery*. 1846. Oil on canvas, 71.1 × 91.4 cm. Paul Mellon Collection, Upperville, Virginia

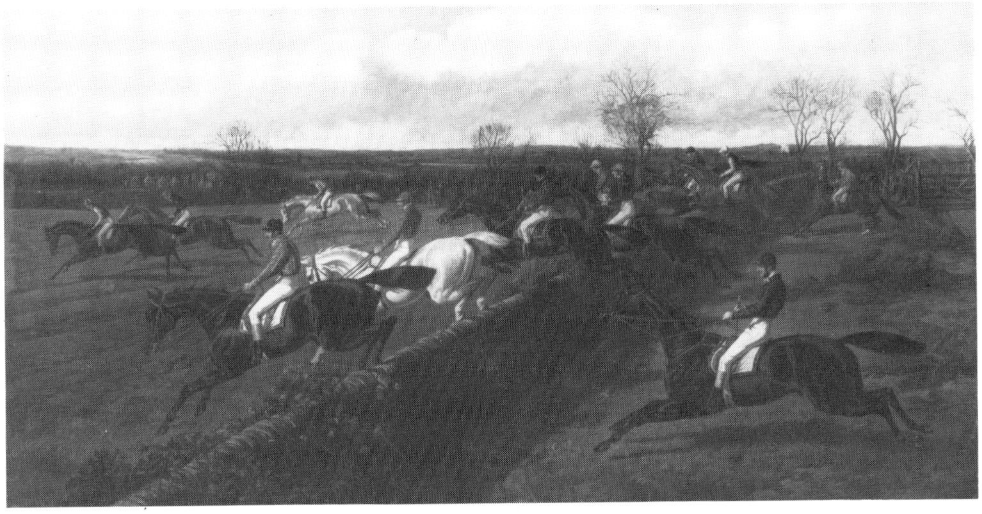

J. F. Herring: *Steeplechase Cracks*. 1846. Oil on canvas, 53.3 × 105.4 cm. Clarence House, London

Jerry (not, of course, the winner of the 1824 St Leger).

The 1840 Grand National was one of Lottery's few failures; he became so all-conquering on the racecourse that he was required to shoulder weights of over 13 stone. One clerk of the course framed a race as, 'Open to all horses except Mr Elmore's Lottery.' Lottery had been bought by Mr John Elmore for £120 at Horncastle horse fair in Lincolnshire. His sire was also called Lottery and came, almost certainly, from the line of Tramp and Dick Andrews. He was 16 hands, with a deep girth and short quarters. Although he had won a couple of races on the Flat at 4 years old, he was turned away to mature near London, passing his days in rural Finchley and Harrow, and seeing his first competitive jumps at the Notting Hill Hippodrome.

But his days of rest were soon over. He turned out at St Albans in a steeplechase in 1837, had a further season's rest, and thereafter was worked immensely hard. He ran six times in just over a month in 1840, in places as far apart as Liverpool, Fakenham, and Cheltenham. He retired after winning his sixteenth steeplechase at Windsor in 1844. After being used as his trainer George Dockeray's hack at Epsom, he ended up in leafy Neasden near London, put to the plough by a Mr Hall. Indeed, he is said to have died in the plough chains.

His rider, Jem Mason, was a great dandy. Son-in-law of Mr Elmore, he had his boots made in separate parts, the foot by one St James's bootmaker and the shank by another. Faced with a jump overhung by thorn bushes while riding Lottery one day, he preferred to take him over a locked five-foot-six gate with the words: 'I'll be hanged if I am going to scratch my face, for I am going to the opera tonight.' Lottery was none too fond of Mason's style of riding, and the jockey was often obliged to mount him wearing his greatcoat to disguise the fact that he was in racing silks.

John Frederick Herring was a most prolific artist. Apart from twenty-three Derby winners and thirty-four St Leger winners, he painted a host of animal, farmyard, and hunting pictures which maintained him in some affluence to the end of his days. Even when he had left London in his later years, and rented a house at Meopham in Kent, he was able to claim that he only had to send a note or two up to town saying he had some work to show and 'down would come the dealers and clear the deck'. An enormous number of his pictures were engraved and published throughout his life: 7*s*. 6*d*. plain and 15*s*. colour was the price from Fuller's for his early St Leger prints. More than forty years after his death, Sir Walter Gilbey had no hesitation in describing Herring's abilities as genius, 'for genius it deserves to be called'.

By the 1920s, however, when Walter Shaw Sparrow was resuscitating the reputations of many English sporting artists, Herring met with less unqualified approval. Shaw Sparrow clearly did not like what he knew of Herring personally. He described him as hypersensitive to criticism, lacking humour, and in constant expectation of overpraise. 'The truth is that honours came upon him too rapidly, he could not grow into them at his ease.' Overpraise was certainly in short supply from Shaw Sparrow: 'Herring's landscapes, painted coolly and precisely, are uninspired, mapped and pretty. His horsemen too have little variety of character, they are brothers or first cousins. There is fun in Alken, a great fondness for life and adventure, while Herring's vogue through about eighty years has owed nothing at all to humour and to the dramatic sense that generally accompanies humour.'

'Herring's vogue' did indeed go into decline, despite the fact that he was still much admired by Sir Alfred Munnings and the sporting artists of the first half of the twentieth century. After the Second World War, his paintings sold for less than £100. In recent years, however, helped by Oliver Beckett's informative and illuminating researches, Herring has grown in reputation so that he now stands second only to Stubbs in the estimation of the sale-room connoisseurs.

Herring was of Dutch extraction, the son of an upholsterer and fringe-maker, who had a shop in Newgate near the Old Bailey in London. His early life makes a wonderful tale – and is mostly true! A romantic teenage marriage, against his parents' wishes, to young Anne Harris. On the whim of seeing the magic word 'Doncaster' on the Royal Leeds Union coach in London, he boards it at the coachman's side and arrives in the North just in time to see the St Leger and make his appointment with destiny. It is 1814. Next, we discover him wandering the streets of Doncaster until he comes upon a coachmaker attempting to copy on to the footboard one of Alken's prints of the Duke of Wellington riding Copenhagen. He gives him a hand and the proprietor admires his work. Our hero asks for a trial as a coachman, is successful, and wins the driver's seat on the Wakefield to Lincoln coach. For two years, in this brief heyday of 'The Road', he holds the reins on the 'Nelson' coach. He paints inn signs and decorates coaches. Then he is transferred to the Doncaster–Halifax run and has another fateful meeting.

Charles Spencer-Stanhope, who was to become a lifelong friend and patron of Herring, lived at Cannon Hall, Barnsley, in Yorkshire. Oliver Beckett retails the story of their first encounter, as set down by Spencer-Stanhope's niece. The coach was passing a field of cattle: 'My uncle remarked to the coachman, "Well, those cows belong to the lean kine." "Oh, sir," said the coachman, "but they are so picturesque." "Picturesque," said my uncle, "that is an odd word for you to use. What do you know about the picturesque?" "Well something, sir," answered the coachman, "I'm very fond of it, and I wish when you come to Doncaster, that you would come and see me, and I would show you some of my drawings."' There was undoubtedly some residue of Dutch caution or, perhaps, just a love of the road in Herring, for he did not immediately quit his job, despite the offer of a year's worth of commissions. Indeed, he became coachman on the most celebrated equipage of them all, the York to London 'Highflyer'.

By 1821, however, he was painting full-time in Yorkshire, executing commissions for the Dukes of Portland and Newcastle, producing an equestrian portrait of the commandant of the Huddersfield Yeomanry, and depicting the St Leger winners, of whom he had retained sketches going back to Filho da Puta in 1815. In Memnon's year, 1825, the *Doncaster Gazette* arranged with him to publish a series of St Leger winners as prints. There were eleven to begin with, and the project, under the patronage of the Duke of York, was to continue in future years.

In 1830 Herring, now with six children, moved to Newmarket, which was in one of its periods of decline. Three years later he returned to London, where among his friends was Ben Marshall. It was Marshall who, asked once if he had ever seen Herring sketch, replied, 'No. But I once saw him put a pencil to paper and a horse's head ran out of the end of it.' But elsewhere there are hints of professional jealousy, with artists complaining that they were made to sit around at the racecourse waiting for Herring to complete his sketches.

Despite a recurring fear, evident in his correspondence, that such carping and criticism might chip away at his reputation, Herring was on good terms with many of his fellow artists. There can be few more generous relics left by any painter than the notes and drawings he sent to William Frith to help him with depicting the horses for his *Derby Day*.

Herring visited Paris in 1840–1, invited by the Duke d'Orléans, the heir to the throne, to paint five of his horses. He was also enjoying royal patronage at home. In 1845, he was officially appointed animal painter to Queen Victoria's mother, the Duchess of Kent. The Queen herself commissioned him to produce a portrait of her favourite hack as a birthday present for her beloved Prince Albert. The Queen's appreciation remained with him to the end. When he was elderly and infirm, she had her horses sent down to his home in Kent to be painted, rather than lay the burden of a journey to Windsor on him.

J. F. Herring's brother Benjamin was also a painter, as were his sons: Charles, the most able, who died young; J.F. junior, who was a prolific artist; and Benjamin.

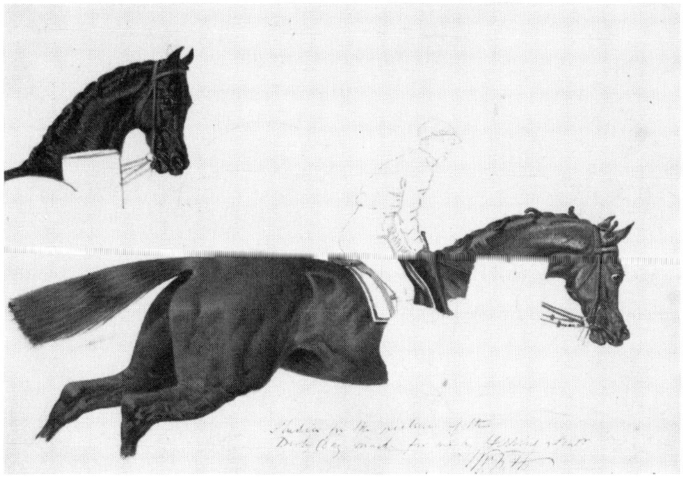

J. F. Herring: *Study for W. P. Frith's 'Derby Day'*. 1857. Pencil and gouache, r.h. part of sheet measuring 19 × 45.5 cm. The British Museum, London

William Powell Frith: *Derby Day* (detail). See p. 32

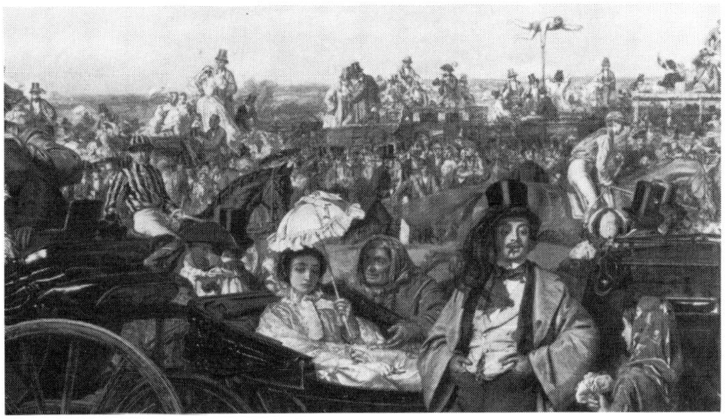

# *Abraham Cooper*

*1787–1868*

Elis
Surplice
West Australian

Lord George Bentinck, Jockey Club reformer and pillar of the English Turf, owned Elis. But Elis's victory in the St Leger of 1836 was the result of practice sufficiently honed as almost to be described as sharp. Elis was, as Abraham Cooper's picture shows, a big tough-looking colt. But, in fact, he had rather weak joints in his fore-legs, and Lord George was afraid that, in those pre-railway days, the 200-mile walk from Goodwood to Doncaster for the race would be too much for him. So His Lordship devised a secret plan which would both get Elis up to the course and allow his owner to skin the bookmaking fraternity in the most decisive fashion.

Elis was kept very visibly at home with his trainer for a full week after the last date on which he could possibly have left in the normal way and reached Doncaster in time. The betting men, as well informed as ever, allowed Elis's odds to drift out to 12–1, and even longer as the days went by. Then just four days before Elis was due at the course, Lord George produced his secret weapon – a horse-box. There are earlier records of a horse-box being used. As far back as 1816, a Worcestershire gentle-man, Mr A. W. Terrett, who had been employing a caravan to save his bullocks having to walk to the Smith-field Show and thus lose condition, thought the idea might work with his horses and had his colt Sovereign boxed for the trip to Newmarket for the Two Thousand Guineas. But, compared with this prototype, Lord George's version – a completely enclosed wagon drawn by six post-horses – was as Concorde to a Sopwith Camel.

Elis and his companion, The Drummer, were loaded up and dispatched northwards at the frenetic speed of 80 miles a day. Lord George's trainer John Kent records in his memoirs the astonishment in every town and village through which the party passed: 'Some asserted that a wild beast of extraordinary ferocity was locked up inside, others that a notorious criminal was being sent to be tried at the assizes. Pedestrians eyed it with amazement. Coachmen and passengers were astounded at seeing six post-horses attached to such a strange-looking machine.' However, Elis duly arrived, survived a mere three false starts, took the lead at the Red House, and won the Leger with considerable ease.

Lord George, though, had a fright before he collected his betting money. He had unwisely delayed taking the 12–1 on offer, no doubt imagining that the price might lengthen even further. By the time he tried to strike his bets, the stratagem of the van had been revealed, and the price had tumbled to 3–1. Lord George, in peculiarly ruthless fashion, announced that he would scratch Elis unless the betting public surrendered to him some of the bets they had taken at the longer prices. Presented thus with Hobson's choice, sufficient of the punters gave way to allow Lord George the killing he felt was his due.

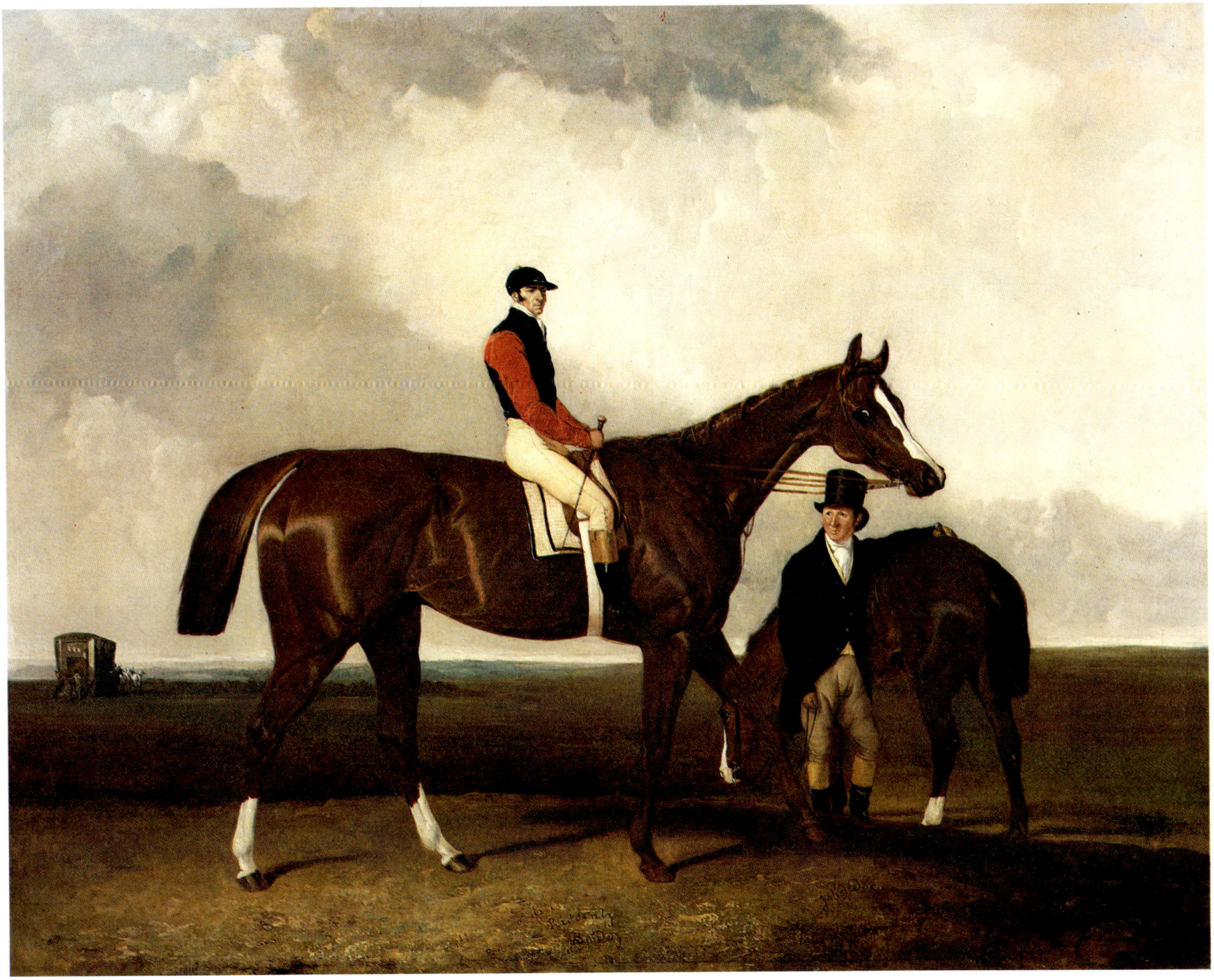

Abraham Cooper: *Elis at Doncaster, with 'Old' John Day up, and his Van in the Background.* 1836–7. Oil on canvas, 89 × 109.2 cm. Paul Mellon Collection, Yale Center for British Art, New Haven, Conn.

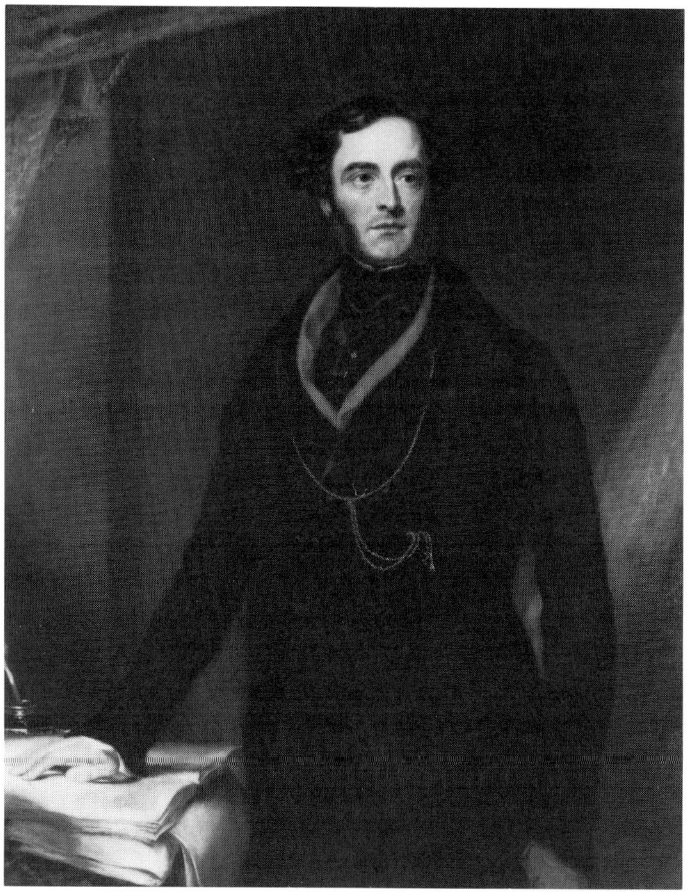

Samuel Lane: *Lord George Bentinck*. 1836. Oil on canvas, 128.3 × 101.6 cm. National Portrait Gallery, London

Elis's own virtues were rather obscured in the dramas surrounding his transportation. But two very good horses, Scroggins by Tramp and Beeswing by Dr Syntax, were behind him in the St Leger and he went on to beat another good animal, Slane, at a private match on Newmarket Heath the following year. Elis was by Langar out of Olympia; he made little impression on the studbook.

Lord George was somewhat fortunate to have survived to collect his winnings on Elis, for earlier that year he had nearly been killed in a duel. He and other 'aristocratic monopolists' were suspected by the famous Squire George Osbaldeston of weighting the handicaps at the old Heaton Park course near Manchester to their own advantage. The Squire therefore sought and eventually found an unknown horse, called Rush, with which he could upset their calculations. Among those who lost bets when the Squire and Rush won their race was Lord George Bentinck. Bentinck refused to pay on the grounds that the race was a robbery and the Squire called him out.

The Squire was a dead shot who had recently killed 98 birds out of 100 on the wing in one day. Bentinck was lucky to have as second a certain Colonel Anson, who seems to have effectively saved his life. The Colonel made Bentinck appear on the duelling-ground dressed entirely in black, without a single white spot to help his opponent's aim. Ordering both men to fire instantly on the count of three, he began, 'Gentlemen, are you ready? One,' then the Colonel left a seemingly endless pause, followed suddenly by, 'two, three,' as though in one breath. It was enough to throw the Squire's normally unerring aim. Even so, the shot went through Lord George's hat and was thus within a hair's breadth of depriving him of his first Classic win, let alone the six others which were to follow before His Lordship retired from racing to concentrate on politics.

Abraham Cooper was, in his own day, the most popular of painters. He was elected early on in his career to the Royal Academy, where he had the extraordinary record of exhibiting for fifty-eight consecutive years. He was also the most prolific contributor to the old *Sporting Magazine*. As a boy of 13 he had helped his uncle, the manager of Astley's Circus, which put on equestrian dramas and awe-inspiring trick riding for the London public. Later, he became a pupil of Ben Marshall, and before long his rival. Throughout a long career Cooper seems to have remained prosperous, and in his turn became tutor in painting to William Barraud and Harry Hall.

Battle scenes were among his favourite subjects, especially the dramas of the English Civil War: Prince Rupert and Cromwell at the Battle of Marston Moor, the Retreat from Naseby, the Siege of Newark. But he was not averse to treading on the margins of journalism with contemporary pictures of the Crimean War. Critics noted with affectionate amusement a white charger who appeared with endearing regularity in battles centuries apart. In his sporting paintings he was flattering to the rider and his mount equally, and there are some imposing pictures of masters of hounds cast to cut a handsome figure on a fine horse. Cooper painted many famous racehorses, including Plenipotentiary, Phosphorous, Camel, Mango, Amato, and Pussy.

Among Cooper's patrons were the Day family of Danebury, and he painted a charming picture of them in which he was able to display his portrait and animal painting skills together, for once, in a racing setting.

Sam and William are on the racehorses Venison and Chapeau d'Espagne. Old John Day is on hand with the two ladies, Mrs Anne Day and the young Mrs John Day, in an unpretentious mule wagon. John, with his back to us, is leaning on its shaft. It is a beguiling vision of a contented family, united in their skill and dedication to the thoroughbred horse. Indeed, life was good for them when this picture was painted in 1838. Lord George Bentinck had just financed the laying-out of the famous gallops at Danebury, Chapeau d'Espagne had won the One Thousand Guineas the year before, and Venison was an old favourite who, though beaten in Bay Middleton's Derby, had won twelve lesser races as a three-year-old and was the trial horse for Elis.

Within three years, Lord George and the Days had quarrelled (see p. 115) and the family were drifting into their disreputable association with John Gully, Henry Padwick, and the money-lending fraternity. In one of racing's most unruly eras the Days gave best to few in

Abraham Cooper: *The Day Family* (see text for detailed identification of subjects). 1838. Oil on canvas, 96.8 × 127.3 cm. The Tate Gallery, London

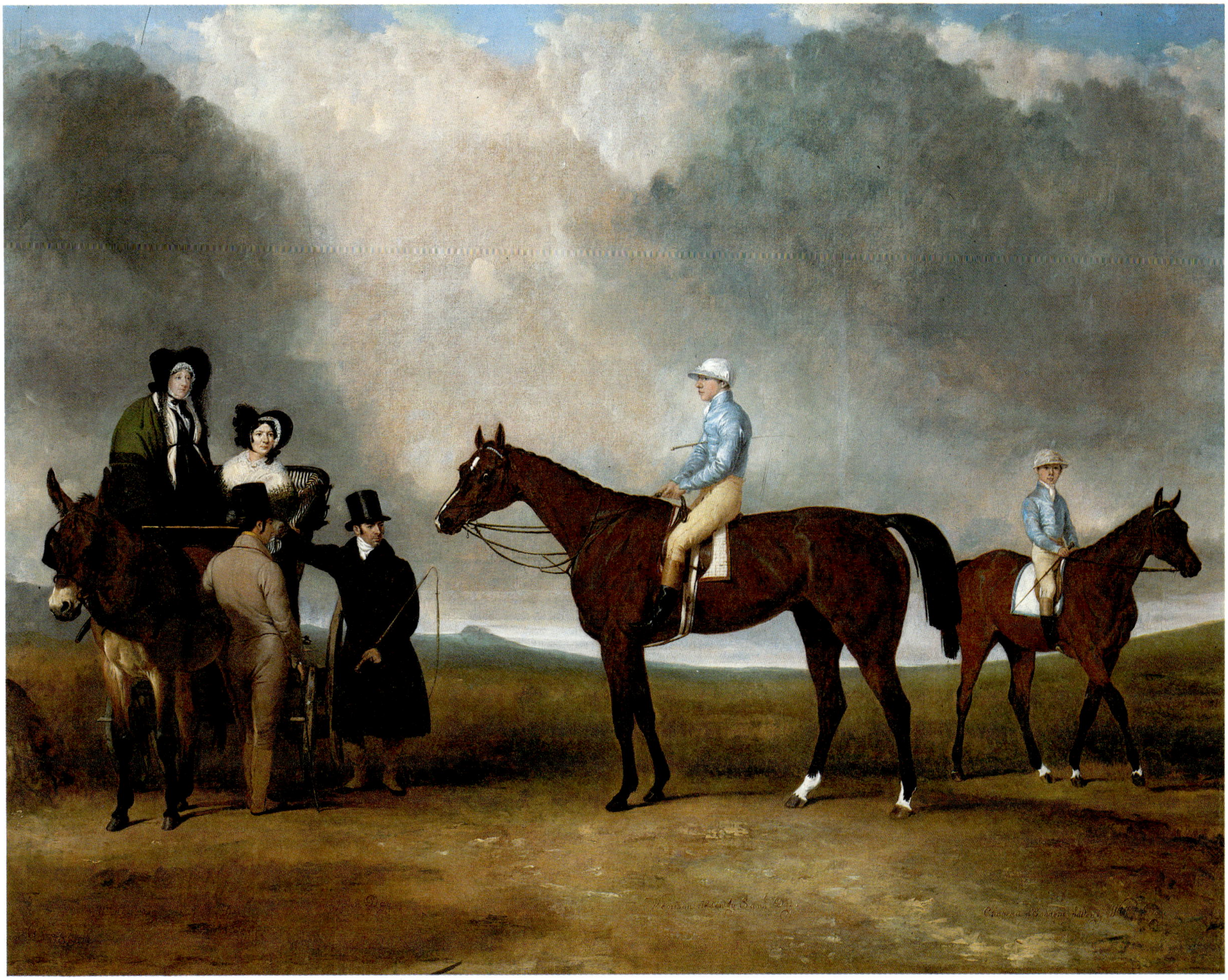

the tricks, stratagems, and downright sharp practice of the time. In the end the family broke up. William was warned off the Turf and the two Johns parted after a quarrel, with the elder John reduced to dependence on William after a ruinous ploy in the Two Thousand Guineas.

Surplice was a colt out of Crucifix who won the Derby of 1848, having been sold with the rest of Lord George Bentinck's stud two years before (see p. 115). In this picture he looks as though he has been very heavily sweated and worked, with every muscle and line depicted by Cooper to the point of exaggeration.

John Kent had been released from the difficulties of training for the choleric Lord George only to find himself with two silly sprigs, Edward Mostyn (later Lord Mostyn), Surplice's owner, and his racing manager Francis Villiers. Villiers was convinced that their other horse Loadstone would win, and backed him heavily. Few of the public seem to have followed him and Surplice started at evens. He won only by a neck from Springy Jack. Surplice also won the St Leger, thereby becoming the first Epsom winner to take the Doncaster Classic since Champion in 1800, though the feat was then repeated in the following two years by The Flying Dutchman and Voltigeur, suggesting, as may be the case today, that the barrier is more in the mind than in reality. West Australian, two years further on, achieved not only the double but the Triple Crown, the first member of an extremely exclusive club.

Abraham Cooper: *Surplice*. 1848. Oil on canvas, 61 × 75 cm.
Tattersalls, Newmarket

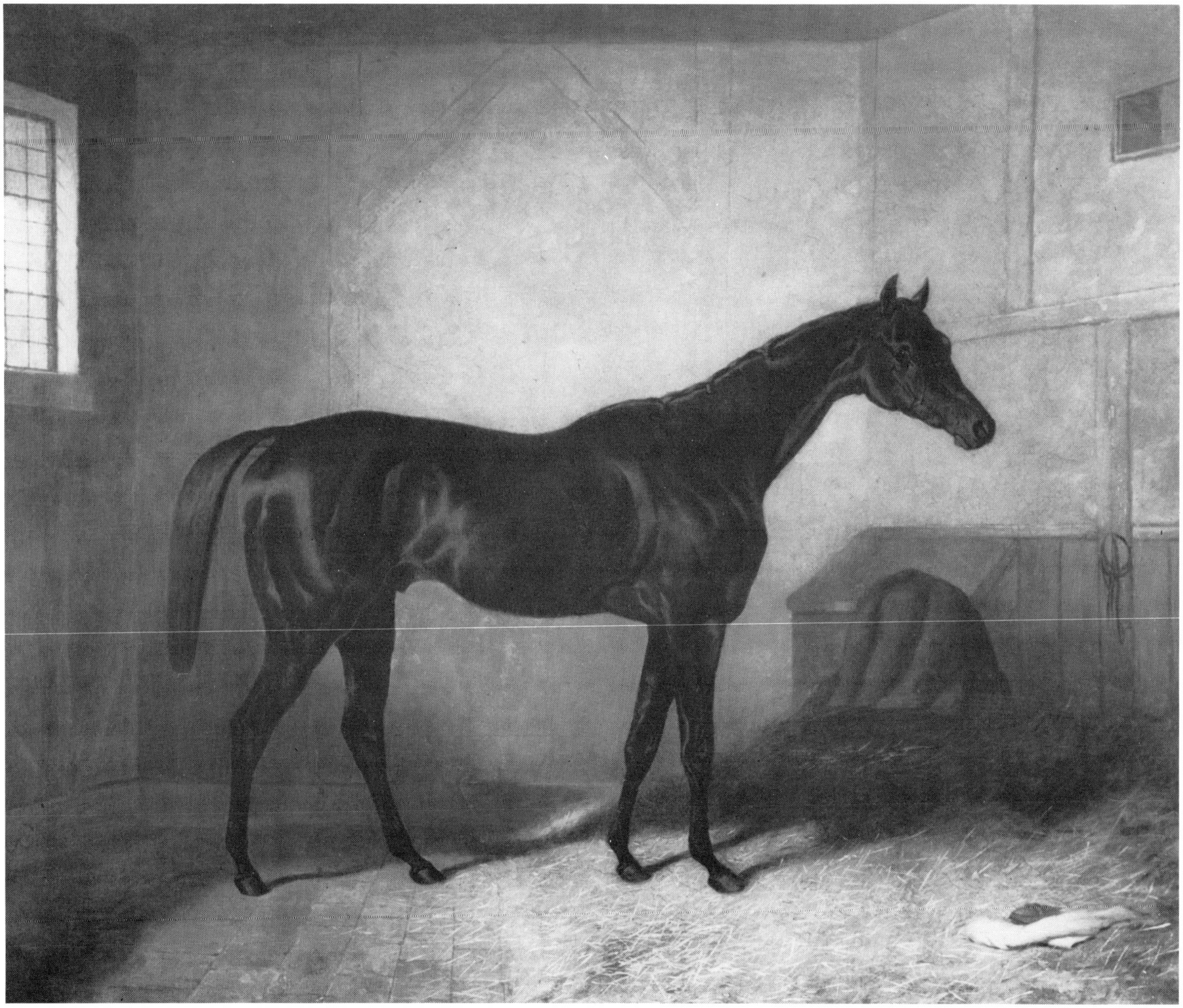

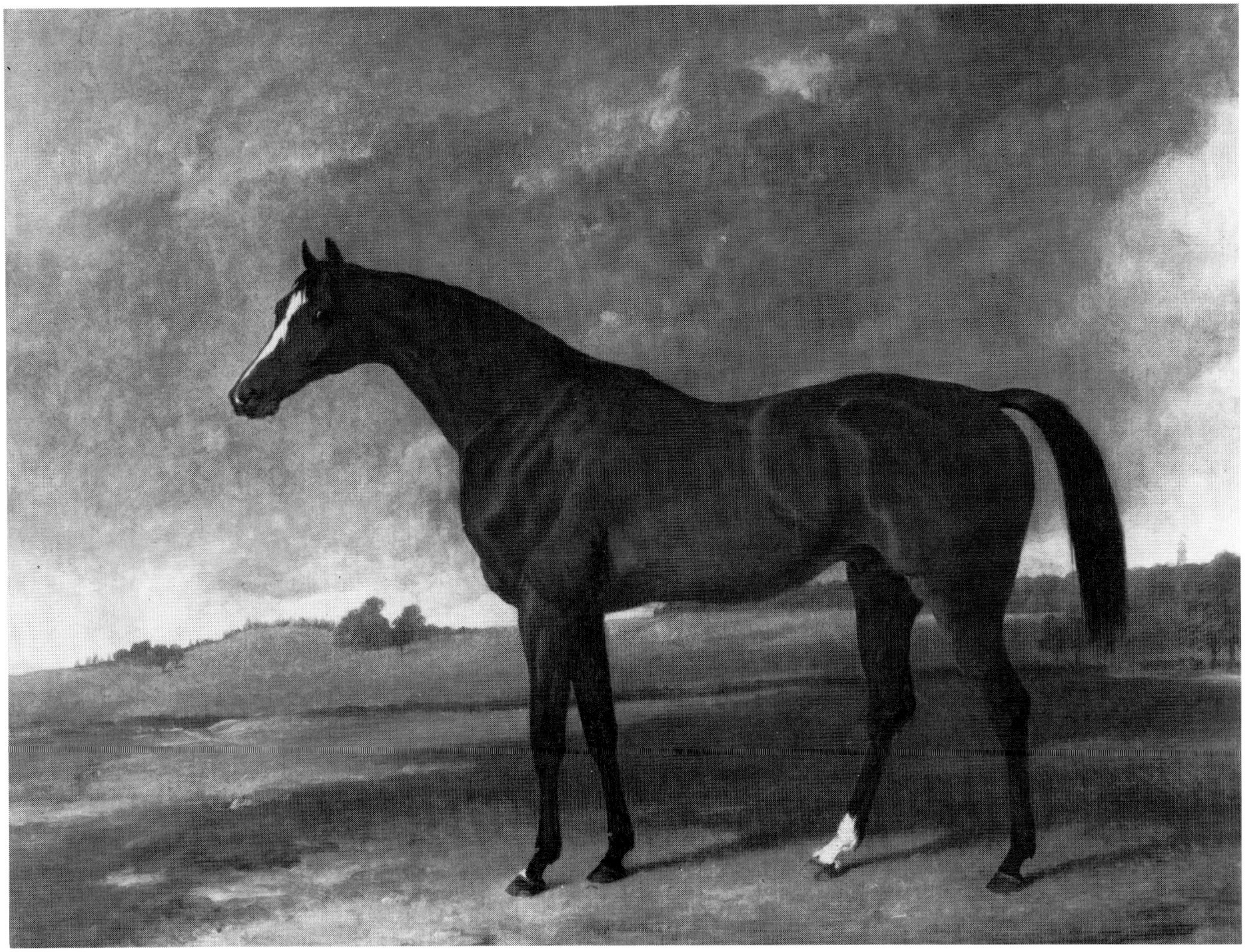

Abraham Cooper: *West Australian*. 1855. Oil on canvas, 44.4 × 59.6 cm. Private collection

Mr John Bowes owned and bred West Australian, his fourth Derby winner. Having tried the colt heavily as a two-year-old, he had taken the train down from John Scott's Yorkshire stables and backed him to win £30,000 in the following year's Derby. In the wake of Epsom, with victories secured in two of the three Classics, John Scott was prepared for every ruse and stratagem to prevent him getting West Australian to the St Leger start. The 'nobbling doctor' Frederick Whitbourne and his confederate Harry Hill were known to be over-extended on West Australian's account. The horse himself being well, suspicion fell on Frank Butler, his jockey. The stewards summoned him and, according to John Corlett, a friend of Scott's, 'Lord Derby alluded to the unsatisfactory nature of the betting and stated that John Scott considered the horse to be so thoroughly well that, if beaten, he would be tried again publicly directly after the race. One of his familiar grunts was all Butler ventured to reply, but the effect in the ring was magical, and West Australian's restoration to favour so startling that everybody was prepared for the hollow way in which he won.'

Butler reported to Lord Derby after the race, in the most injured fashion, that Scythian's jockey had tried three times to knock West Australian over: 'so I hups with my whip and I says, "You dam young davvle, if you comes hat me again I'll knock your dam heye hout."' West Australian went on to win the Ascot Gold Cup and it was his progeny who were largely responsible for restoring the blood of the Godolphin Arabian to prominence, via Hurry On to Airborne and Santa Claus in our own time.

# *F. C. Turner*

*1782?–1846*

Crucifix
Little Wonder

The index to *The Racing Life of Lord George Bentinck* is unequivocal about his filly Crucifix:

> Crucifix:
> offer for, p. 253
> foul designs to defeat, p. 308
> ruin of, in a false start, p. 309

Lord George bought Crucifix with her dam, Octaviana, for £60 from Lord Chesterfield. There was general agreement that she was one of the scraggiest and most unpromising foals ever seen. But Lord George was a fervent admirer of her sire, Priam. So she came to Danebury to be trained by the Day family, and in the fullness of time to be the cause of the great quarrel between Lord George and the Days which enlivened the popular press of 1841.

Crucifix was unbeaten in eight races as a two-year-old. The Days always tried their horses very thoroughly at home and they knew early on that their ugly duckling would turn out a swan. From her first outing on a racecourse Lord George backed her in a series of what would now be called 'long-range doubles', coupling each race with the next year's Oaks. By the time the Classic season of 1840 came round, there were a great number of people in the betting ring with good reason to wish the filly the worst of health. As Lord George's subsequent trainer, John Kent, put it, 'the usual agency of countless false starts' was used in an attempt to defeat her. But she won both the One Thousand Guineas and the Two Thousand Guineas in the space of three days – starting in the One Thousand Guineas at 10–1 on – and

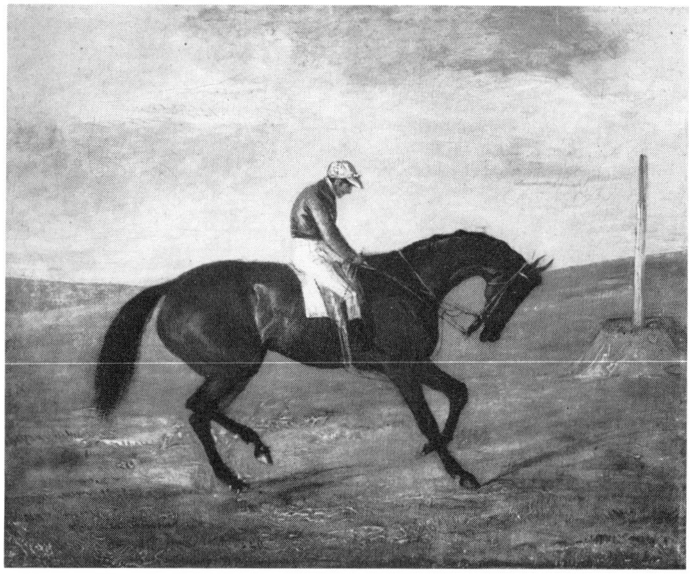

F. C. Turner: *Crucifix*. 1840. Oil on wood, 19.7 × 24.7cm. Jockey Club, Newmarket

she arrived at Epsom as favourite for the Oaks at odds of 3–1 on.

Lord George in his role as Turf reformer was responsible for many improvements, for example the saddling enclosure and the system of numbering on the racecard and number-boards, but above all he was concerned about the chicanery of starting, and he introduced flag starts and fines for jockeys who failed to get away properly. The start of the 1840 Oaks must have put iron into his resolution. There were only fifteen runners, but it took more than an hour from the time the fillies arrived at the post for the starter to get them away. There were mêlées and false starts and innumerable cries of 'Not yet, sir!' In the course of this fractious hour Crucifix hit her leg or was kicked, an injury which was to end her career, though not before she had finally been got away by the starter and won the race. 'She was beyond all question a victim to the rascally policy pursued by her envious and unscrupulous opponents,' said John Kent.

Lord George seems to have made a nice distinction between his disinterested pursuit of fairness on the racecourse and the inveterate indulgence in sharp practice on his own behalf in the betting ring. Soon after she came home from Epsom, it was realized that Crucifix was unsound. Not content, however, with the £100,000 or so he had already won with her, Lord George decided there was one last coup to be pulled. He left her engaged in the St Leger, for which she was, naturally, favourite. His Lordship then proceeded, through every means and third party he could find, to lay against Crucifix, while, at the same time, accepting bets on her though knowing she would never run.

Old John Day, Crucifix's trainer, seems to have declined to go along with all the subterfuges that were necessary to keep the ploy going, such as changing the horse's clothing as though she had galloped, while his son John was getting into the betting market himself, behind Lord George's back.

When His Lordship found out, there was a very public parting of the ways and Crucifix went off with the rest of the Bentinck string to Goodwood. The Days had the last laugh. In 1846 they ran a horse at Goodwood, named Mathematician, which ruined a huge gamble of Lord George's. He was so furious that he immediately offered to sell his entire stud for £10,000. Edward Mostyn took him up, and Bentinck was out of racing

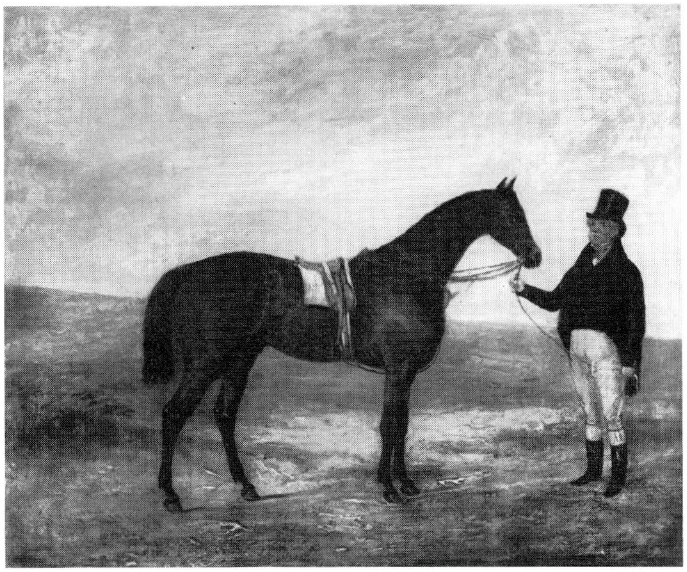

F. C. Turner: *Little Wonder*. 1840. Oil on canvas, 19.7 × 24.7 cm. Jockey Club, Newmarket

for ever. Included in the deal was Crucifix, for whom there was an immediate, unaccepted offer of £7,000, and a foal of hers called Surplice. Two years later Surplice won the Derby, thereby eliciting from Lord George the famous 'superb groan'.

Little Wonder won the Derby in the same year as Crucifix won the Oaks. He was an obscure pony-sized creature who was allowed to start at 50–1, and yet another of the horses who is suspected of having been a four-year-old when he won the three-year-olds' Classic. But even his owner, Mr David Robertson from Berwick-on-Tweed, probably did not know. The trainer William Forth, however, was rumoured to have won £18,000. This was the race in which the boy jockey on Little Wonder, W. Macdonald, coming with a late run, received the famous offer from Bill Scott on Launcelot, the favourite: 'A thousand pounds for a pull.' 'Too late, Mr Scott,' the lad replied, 'too late.'

F. C. Turner has been identified by Judy Egerton as Francis Calcraft Turner, of Lambeth in London, who died aged 64 in 1846. He was, by his own assertion, the keenest of hunting men, following hounds in Kent and Essex. Most of his surviving works are scenes of hunting, but he painted a number of other thoroughbred pictures, including the 1837 Oaks winner, Miss Letty.

# *Sir Edwin Landseer*

*1803–1873*

## Voltigeur

It is now more than 130 years since the Earl of Zetland sent out Voltigeur to face The Flying Dutchman at York in the most famous match in the annals of racing. Five generations have passed, the earldom has become a marquisate, and a scion of the house is a pop star. But Aske Hall, trimmed and reshaped since those days, remains a shrine to the champion of 1850. For to own a great racehorse illuminates a family enduringly, almost like a vice-royalty of India or a title earned in battle. There is a bronze of Voltigeur facing the main door at Aske. There is a bone from a foreleg, wisps of his hair, prints by Herring and Hall, and, above all, Landseer's vast picture, the only portrait of a racehorse he ever painted.

Lord Zetland needed some persuading to buy Voltigeur after he had failed to make his reserve of £300 at Doncaster sales. The brown colt, by Voltaire out of a Mulatto mare, was already in his second year when he came into the hands of Robert Hill, the Zetland trainer. Hill had some extreme notions about training racehorses, even by the standards of those tougher times. He worked Voltigeur throughout his career, summers included, in two hoods, in a vain attempt to slim his neck to some imagined paradigm of fitness. But he was enough of a horseman to recognize a 'crack'. One trial and one minor two-year-old race at Richmond in North Yorkshire and the astounded connections hastily took Voltigeur out of circulation until the time came for him to complete the formality of winning the Derby.

The news, if it ever reached London, was discounted and Voltigeur was allowed to start at 16–1, thus enriching a goodly proportion of the population of Yorkshire. The race was won comfortably enough from Pitsford; the worst moments for his backers came when Lord Zetland, in dudgeon, threatened to withdraw his horse, after discovering that forfeits due from his previous owner had not been paid. Hill then took Voltigeur home to prepare another coup. The horse would run not only in the St Leger, but also in the Doncaster Cup two days later, where he would take on the unbeaten Derby winner of the previous year, The Flying Dutchman. Voltigeur must have been a prodigiously tough horse, for the three days at Doncaster, that autumn of 1850, proved an unexampled challenge.

In the St Leger, Job Marson got into all sorts of trouble

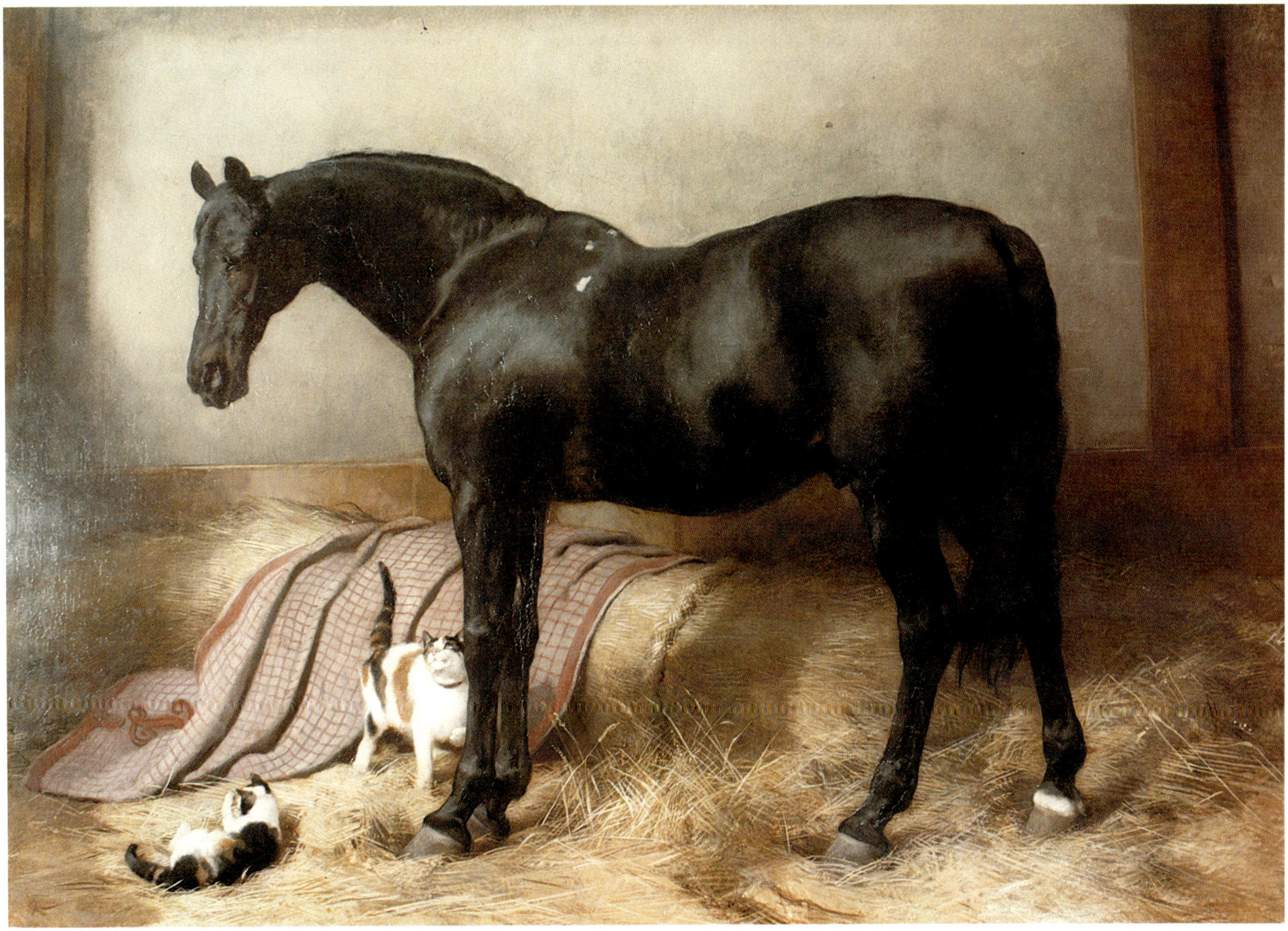

Sir Edwin Landseer: *Voltigeur*. 1870. Oil on canvas, 233.7 × 330.2 cm. Aske, Richmond, Yorkshire

J. F. Herring: *Charles Marlow on The Flying Dutchman beating Nat Flatman on Voltigeur at York*. 1851. Oil on canvas, 67.3 × 100.3 cm. Jockey Club, Newmarket

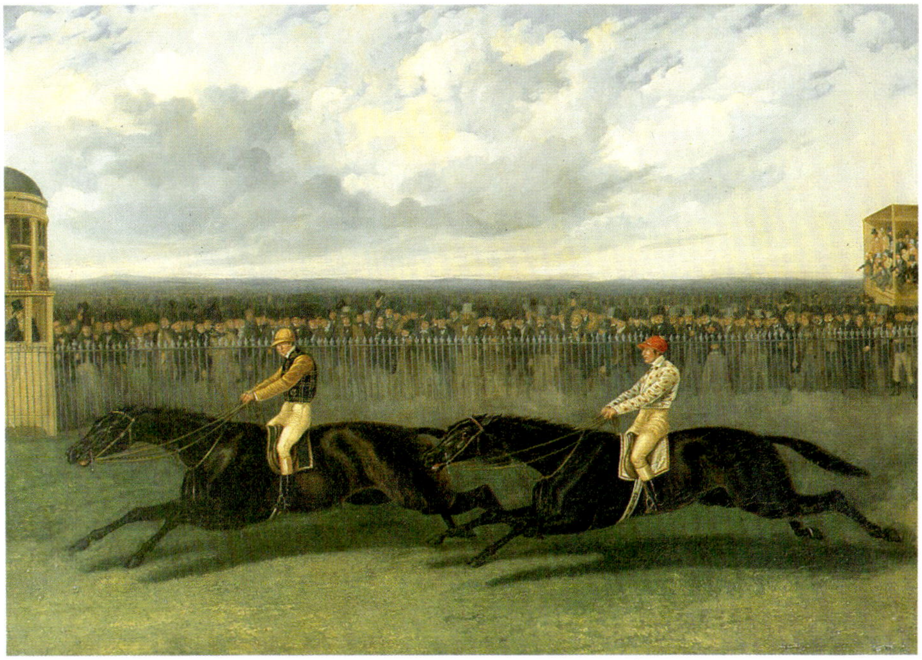

on Voltigeur, being consistently impeded by a horse called Chatterbox, and only just held on to dead-heat with Russborough. As was the ruthless custom of the day, there was a run-off. Again, Russborough gave him a hard race, but Voltigeur won by a length. Marson was a strong jockey who loved a mêlée and a tight finish. According to 'The Druid' he had no trouble making 8 stone, so it has to be assumed that his employers were none too pleased with his St Leger performance, for he was 'jocked off' and replaced by Elnathan (Nat) Flatman for the Cup.

The Flying Dutchman's trainer, Jo Fobert, had got wind of the plans for Voltigeur and had worked his horse twice at a gallop in the last few days before the race, overdoing it perhaps, but nothing to compare with Voltigeur's ordeal in the St Leger. Only the two Derby winners started for the Cup and the ecstatic and incredulous Doncaster crowd saw Voltigeur get up by half a length. There was no other topic among Northern racing men that winter, and eventually Lord Zetland and Lord Eglinton, the Dutchman's owner, agreed to a rematch at York, to be run on 13 May, 1,000 sovereigns at stake.

Harry Hall's picture of the start conjures up the atmosphere of that day on the Knavesmire. The stands crowded in the distance; the two horses like duellists, back to back; the Dutchman, with a posse of 'seconds' busying themselves around him, glancing apprehensively back at his rival; Voltigeur, apparently calm and prepared, with Flatman already mounted and touching his cap to the solitary figure of Lord Zetland. There were those in the paddock who felt that Hill's rigours had finally broken the strength of Voltigeur, but his supporters were still confident. The betting was even. Crowds of men had walked down from Richmond and Teeside to York, taking two or three days, just to be present. The race was 2 miles, the Dutchman carrying $8\frac{1}{2}$ lb. extra for his age.

Voltigeur made the running all the way until the last 100 yards. By then, Charles Marlow was giving the

John Dalby: *The St Leger of 1850: Voltigeur, with Job Marson up (in the spotted colours), dead-heating with Russborough, ahead of Bolingbroke.* Oil on canvas, 59.6 × 89.5 cm. Private collection

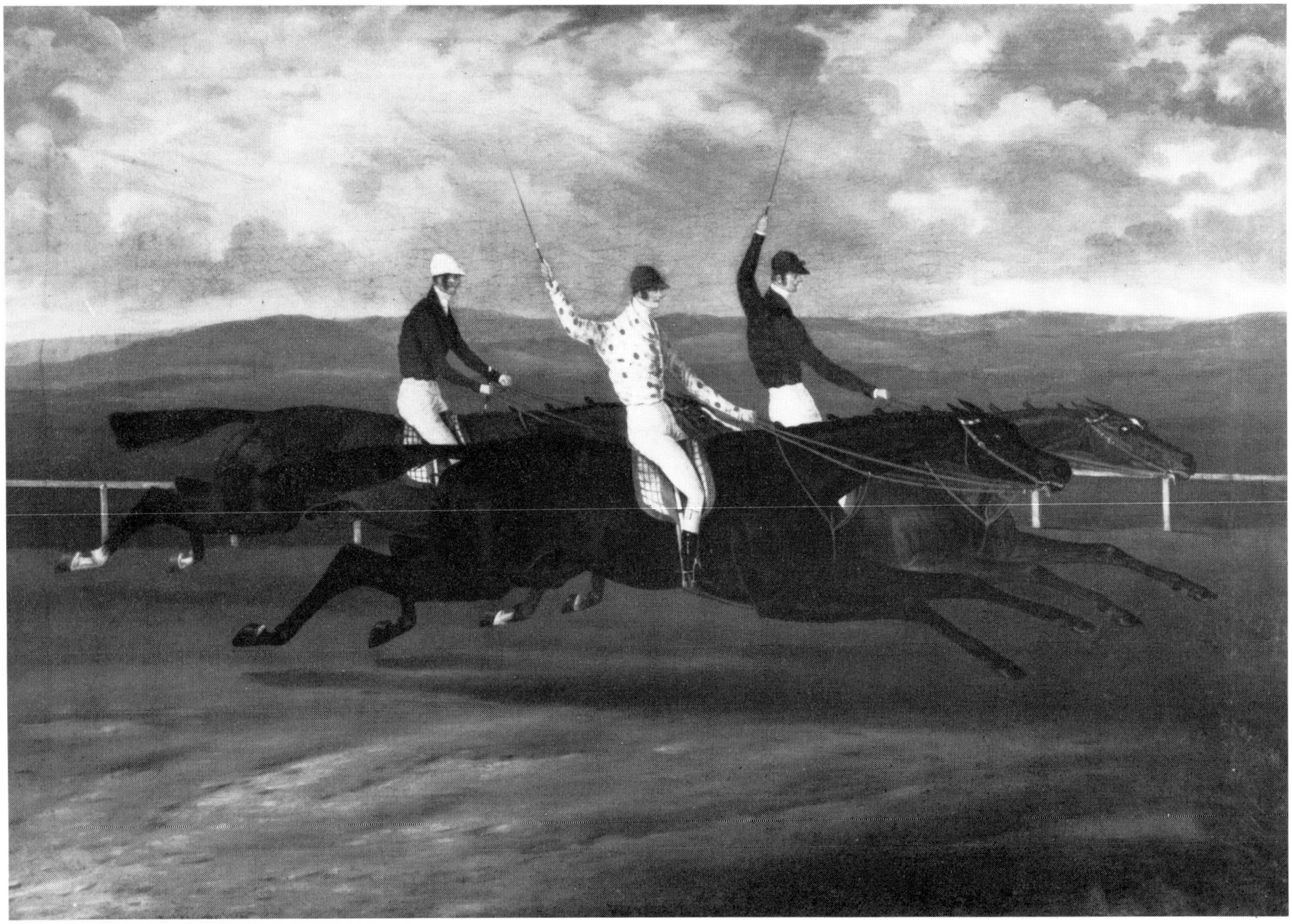

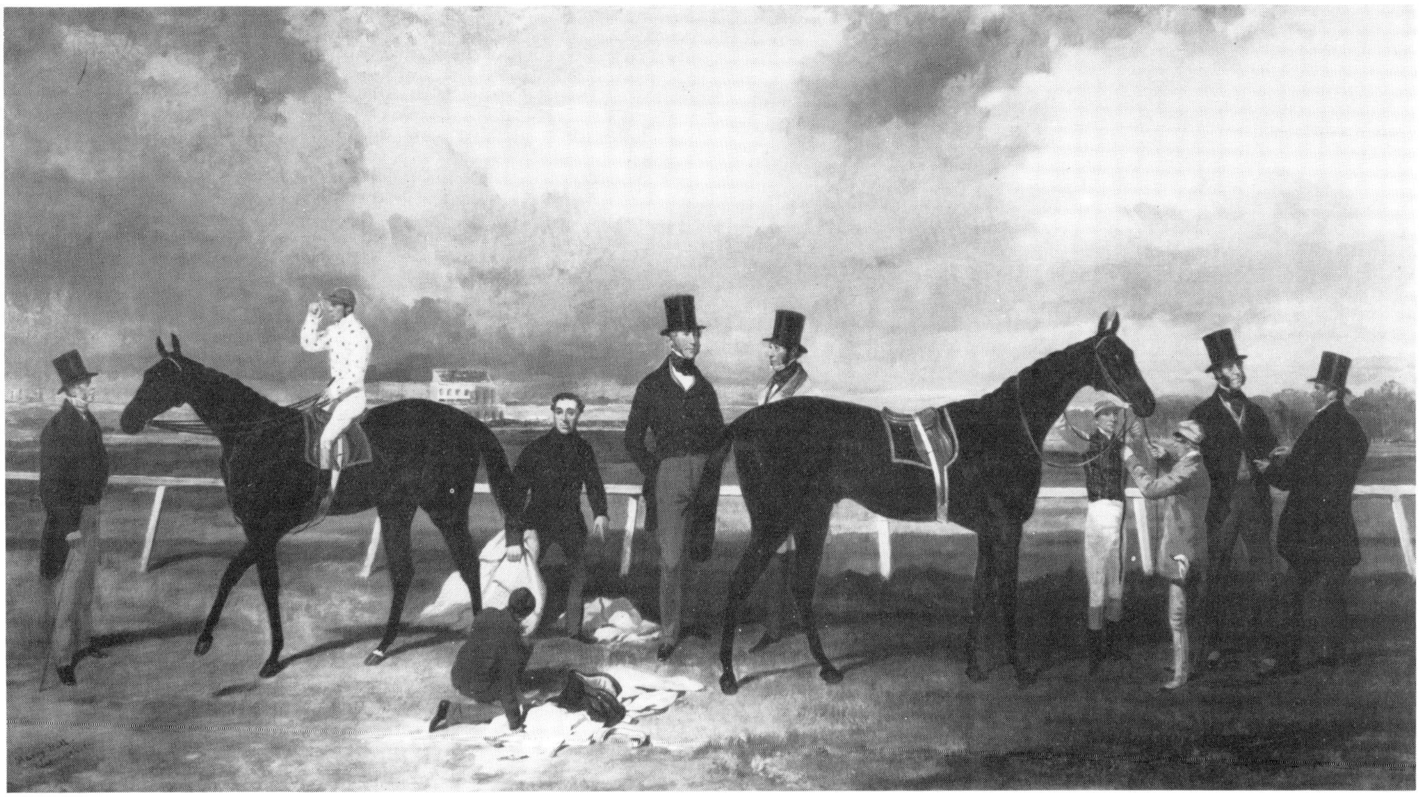

Harry Hall: *Voltigeur (l.), with Nat Flatman up, watched by his owner Lord Zetland, and The Flying Dutchman, with Charles Marlow about to mount, before the Start at York.* *c.*1851. Oil on canvas, 72.4 × 139.7 cm. Aske, Richmond, Yorkshire

Dutchman some terrible punishment with whip and spur, but he got him home by something under a length. The symmetry of these two great contests is with us to this day. For Voltigeur sired Vedette and The Flying Dutchman the mare The Flying Duchess, the parents of Galopin, sire of the incomparable St Simon.

Sir Edwin Landseer, Queen Victoria's favourite painter, was a child prodigy whose genius for animal painting found its fullest expression in his pictures set in the Highlands of Scotland. There is a violence in some of his work which can repel, and he was long out of fashion. But recent exhibitions in London and Philadelphia have restored him to the forefront of public appreciation and shown the full range of his talent.

Lord Zetland was a friend of Landseer and it was thus that the great Victorian painter was persuaded to undertake this portrait. The poor Earl had a difficult time with the temperamental artist. In 1861 he was offering to have Voltigeur brought down to London for the picture. Two years later there is another letter offering to send the horse to London in July, but asking Landseer to name a date, 'as I should wish him not to be in town longer than is really necessary'. Finally, just three years before his death, the Earl saw the finished picture in the spring of 1870, and asked Landseer to submit his account, 'as I should be glad to avoid this part of the transaction failing to be settled by my executors'.

The Earl expressed himself well pleased and it is still possible to see in the huge picture the legendary characteristics of the great horse: the depth from shoulder to withers and the heavy, almost fleshy look Hill strove so hard to reduce. But he has rather a doleful air, induced perhaps by weariness of the artist's working methods. He stands oddly, perhaps over a bit on the forehand, and the background is not fully finished. Indeed Landseer seems more interested in the tortoiseshell cats, one of whom was Voltigeur's inseparable companion and slept for hours on his back – no doubt the one looking impishly up at him from his feet.

The picture deteriorated over the years at Aske, but it has fortunately been restored by Paul Ackroyd at Gateshead, and is now back in its rightful place at the Zetland house.

# *Frederick Woodhouse senior*

*1820–1909*

## Archer

The first settlers had themselves scarcely reached Botany Bay, when a consignment of racehorses was dispatched after them. There are records of racing in Australia at Parramatta at the very beginning of the nineteenth century. The privations of the 12,000-mile journey from England in those days must surely have taken its toll, but it is a tribute to the toughness of the blood horse that the animals not only survived, but quickly adapted to Australian conditions. By 1838, the Melbourne Racing Club was established. In 1851, the start of the Victoria gold rush brought sudden and huge wealth, and in its wake the foundation of Victoria's Turf Club and Jockey Club to indulge the competitive instincts of the diggers and the land speculators.

The colonial government was already operating a scheme to assist migrants, and one of the Englishmen who took advantage of the cheap passage was Frederick Woodhouse, a London artist, already 38 and with four sons. He arrived in Melbourne neatly in time to record the start of the great era of Australian racing. The first Champion Stakes and the first Australian St Leger were run in 1859, the year after he arrived, and the first Melbourne Cup in 1861. Woodhouse was to portray the Australian thoroughbred champions for the next fifty years and leave behind an abundant record of the golden age of the Australian Turf.

Woodhouse's paintings, bright and full of light, with a constant eye for the singularities of the Australian landscape, are quite distinctive. His cloudscapes spiral dramatically away from the centre of his canvases in whirlpools of blue and white, giving an inspirational effect to his outdoor pictures. Dr Colin Laverty, in his affectionate and informative study of the Woodhouse family, says that Frederick trained under Herring before he left England, and there is no doubt that he contrived to absorb some of Herring's skills at portraying the thoroughbred horse. The grey at the front of his painting *The Inaugural Meeting of the Victoria Amateur Turf Club* is not an unworthy tribute to Woodhouse's tutor. But, clearly, Woodhouse found a special lodestone in the southern hemisphere and his pictures are full of a verve and delight, indeed an optimism, about his surroundings which was rare in the Europe he left behind.

Woodhouse's picture of the winners of the first twelve Melbourne Cups shows how the two outstanding owners of the time, John Tait and Etienne de Mestre, dominated an event which, almost from the beginning, captured the imagination of the Australian public. De Mestre owned Archer, in the centre of the painting, who won the first two Cups carrying the all-black silks. Five years later, de Mestre won again with Tom Whiffler, shown standing behind Archer. John Tait, from Sydney, owned and trained three winners: Glencoe, 1868, rearing up in the centre with the yellow jacket and black cap; the

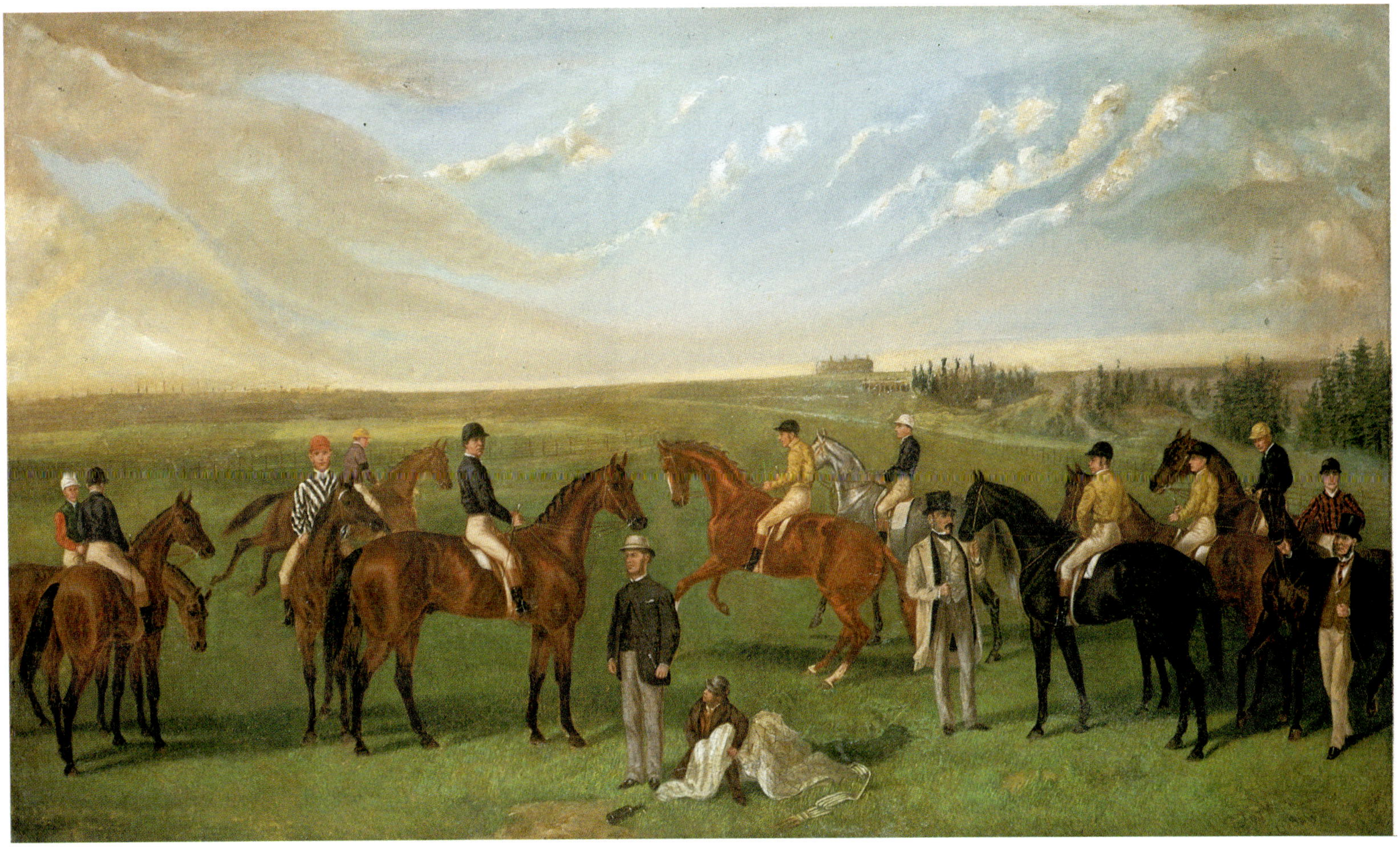

Frederick Woodhouse senior: *Archer and the Winners of the First Twelve Melbourne Cups* (see text for detailed identification of subjects). 1889.
Oil on canvas, 74 × 125 cm. Victoria Racing Club, Melbourne

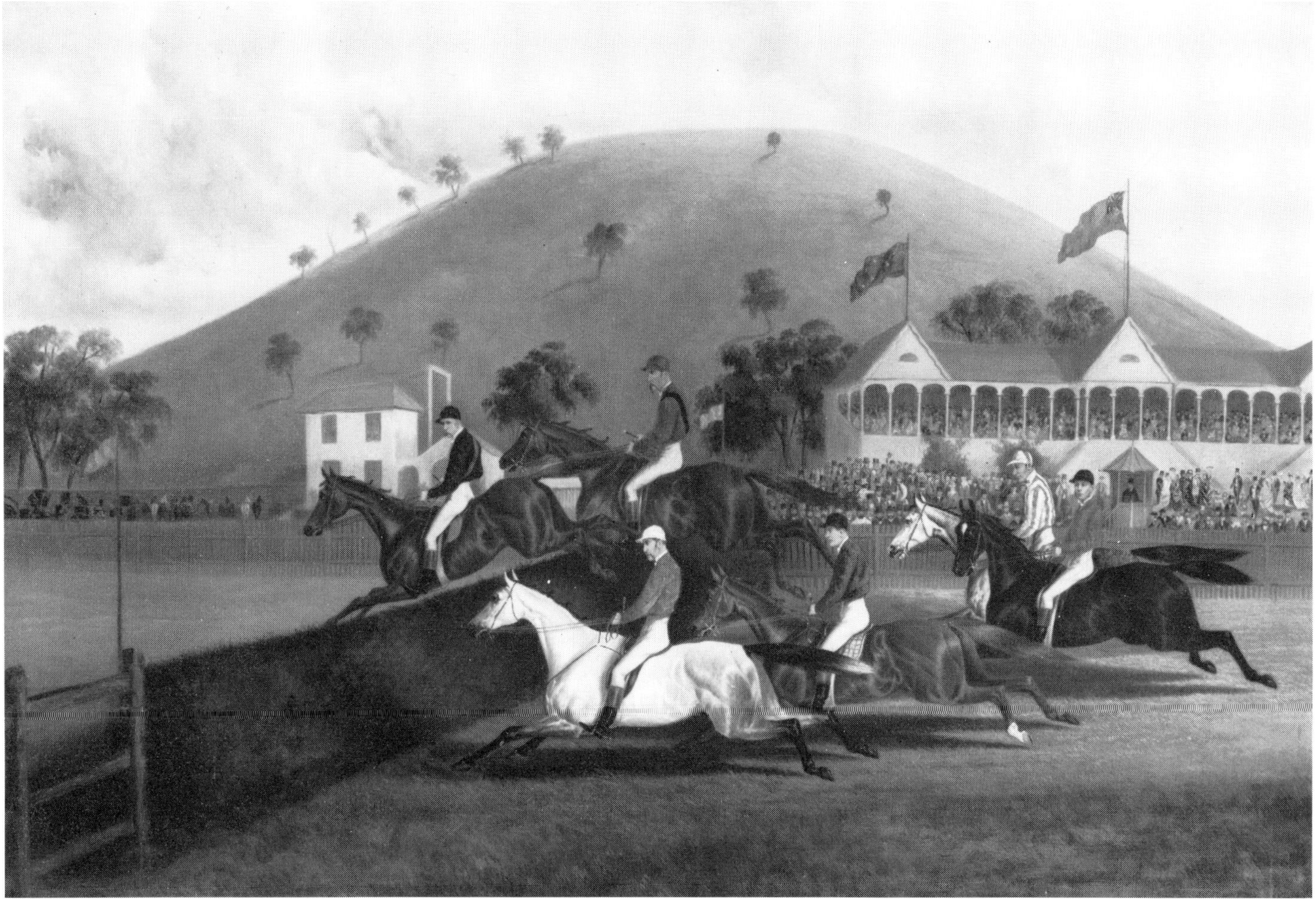

Frederick Woodhouse senior: *The Inaugural Meeting of the Victoria Amateur Turf Club: (l. to r.) Canary, Dutchman, Sheet Anchor, Sailor (placed first), Graystanes (third), and Nimbook (second).* After 1876. Oil on canvas, 87 × 128 cm. Victoria Amateur Turf Club, Caulfield, Victoria

Frederick Woodhouse senior: *The Start of the Second Melbourne Cup.* 1863. Oil on canvas, 86.5 × 178.5 cm. Victoria Racing Club, Melbourne

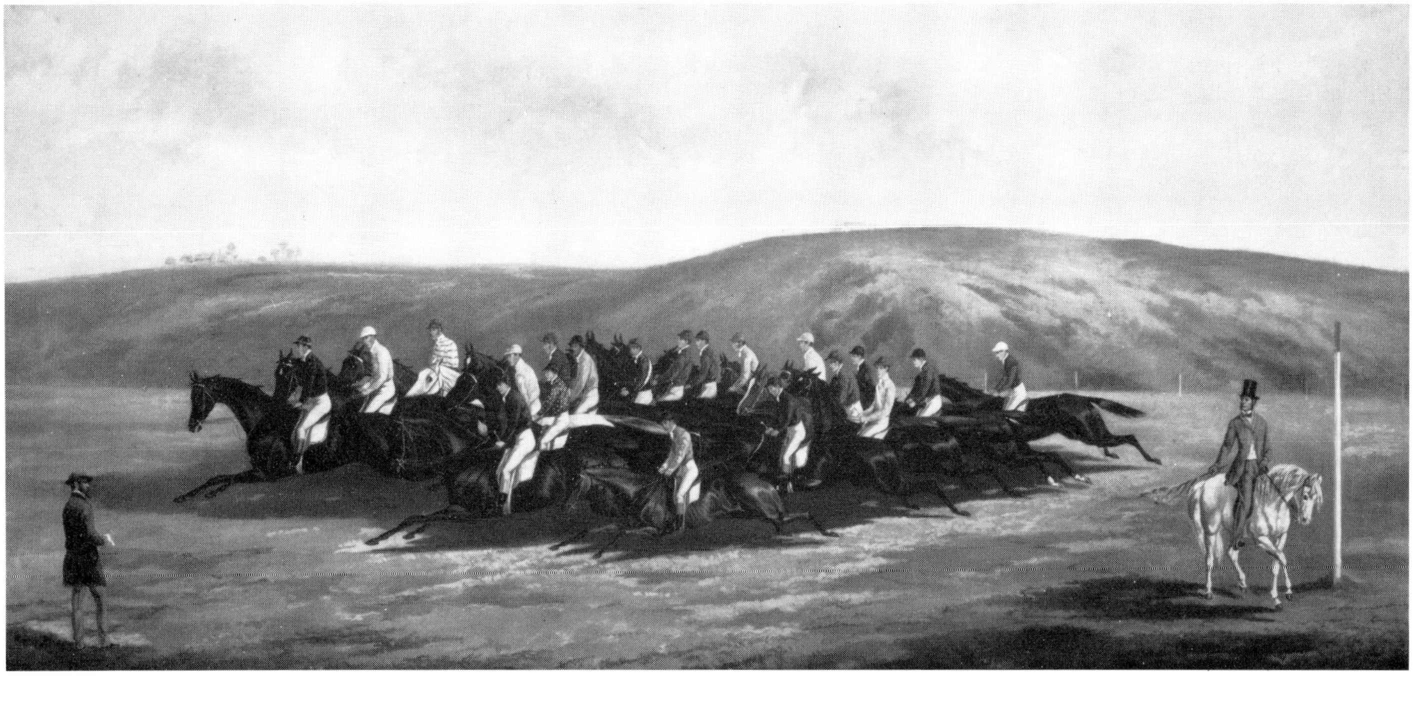

brown horse, The Barb, 1866; and the bay, The Quack, 1872. Tait also trained The Pearl to win in 1871, shown with the black jacket and yellow cap.

Archer won the second Melbourne Cup by 6 or 8 lengths, having effectively routed the opposition a full half-mile from home. In Woodhouse's picture of the start, Archer is shown getting away well on the inside in a field of twenty, the starter George Watson, on the grey pony, having obviously achieved an unusual, or perhaps artistically licensed, discipline. By 1880, the Melbourne Cup had become a national event, drawing a crowd of 100,000 from all over Australia.

There is no doubt that action and drama appealed to Woodhouse. The year after he arrived, there was a famous shipwreck when the steamship Admella, bringing horses from Adelaide to compete in the new Champion Stakes, was lost off Mount Gambier. Woodhouse painted a celebrated canvas of the event. There are also some lively driving scenes, with horses and dogs zipping along. His straightforward horse portraits are, however, more cursory. The picture of Briseis is a rather offhand tribute to a distinguished filly who not only won the Melbourne Cup of 1876, ridden by a teenage jockey, Peter Bowden (shown standing on the left), but also won both the Derby and the Oaks at the Victoria Racing Club, ridden by Tom Hales, who is in the saddle here.

The younger Frederick Woodhouse, who was 10 years old when the family arrived in Australia, had a softer style and a less elated view of his new country. But he was a careful painter of portraits, with appealing studies of horses such as Chicago, Mentor, and Emmalea. He died in 1927. His three brothers, Herbert, Edwin, and Clarence, were also painters in a dynasty which recorded Australian country life and the heroes of the Turf for seventy years.

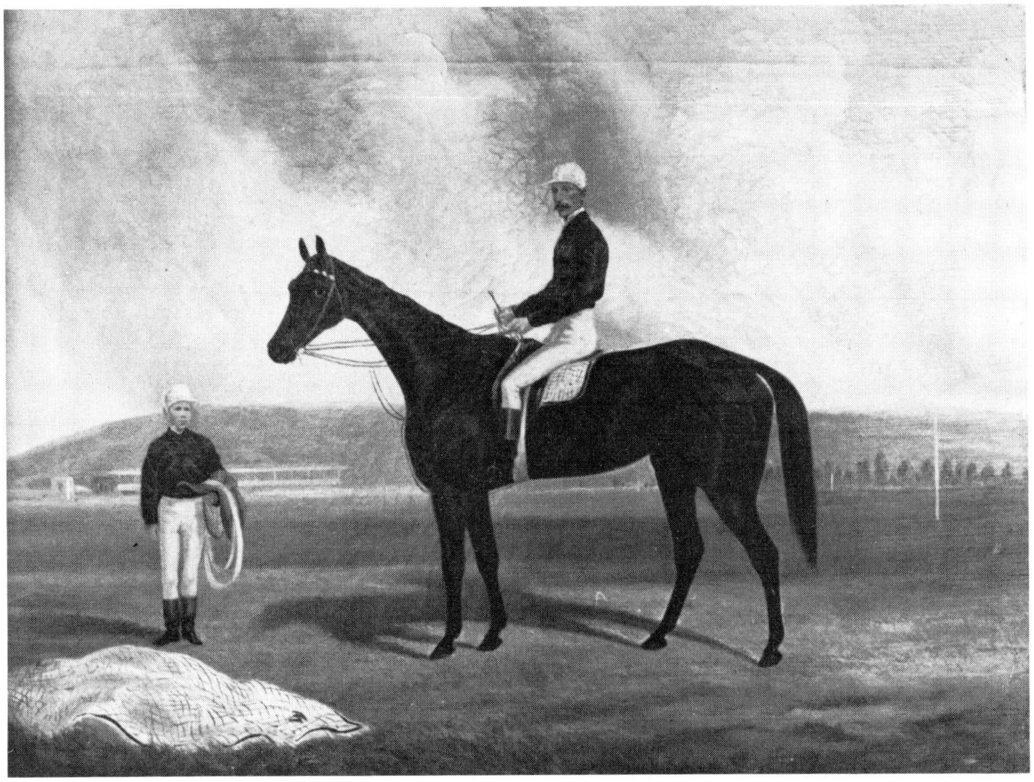

Frederick Woodhouse senior: *Briseis, with Tom Hales up, and the jockey Peter Bowden.*
After 1876. Oil on canvas, 50 × 67 cm. Geelong Racing Club, Victoria

# *Henri Delamarre*

*1829–1913*

## Potocki

This splendid and naïve painting of a bold but ugly dark bay horse, ears set back, stepping out in a fenced paddock, with another animal rearing in the background as its jockey tries to mount, has a piquant place in the history of French racing. The horse is Potocki who won the Prix du Jockey Club in 1857, the year that the great racecourse at Longchamp was opened in the Bois de Boulogne, after prolonged negotiations between the city of Paris and the Société d'Encouragement. His owner was Auguste Lupin, one of the Société's founding enthusiasts.

Potocki was a tough horse who went on to win the Prix du Cadran as a four-year-old to confirm his French Derby form. He was probably by The Baron (though Nunnykirk, an English Two Thousand Guineas winner, was given the credit by some), which would relate him sufficiently to Blacklock to account for his looks. The dam was a mare called Myszka. Potocki's Prix du Jockey Club was only one of six which saw Lupin's famous colours come home to victory.

Henri Delamarre, a friend of Lupin's and a fellow racehorse owner of great distinction, was no more than a gifted amateur as a painter. Yet Lupin was happy to give Delamarre the task of recording the figure of his French Derby winner. To this day the French, who have equalled and surpassed the rest of the racing world in every other obeisance to the thoroughbred horse, have been curiously indifferent to that urge which happily possesses proud owners elsewhere, the desire to see their champions immortalized in art.

However, some of France's finest artists have been fascinated by the racing scene. Delacroix is unsurpassed as a painter of horses. Degas's pictures of racing in Paris and Normandy, as evocative as any of his ballet scenes, are in galleries all over the world. Toulouse-Lautrec was a devotee of the race-track and Dufy's paintings of Epsom and Ascot are famous. But the rich and wealthy patrons, who put such resources and such energy into developing fine bloodstock and laying out perhaps the most beautiful racecourses in the world, patronized only spasmodically the artists of the day. The portraits of the great French champions are generally of indifferent quality and have been made worse by neglect.

At least this picture of Potocki has a fine vigour.

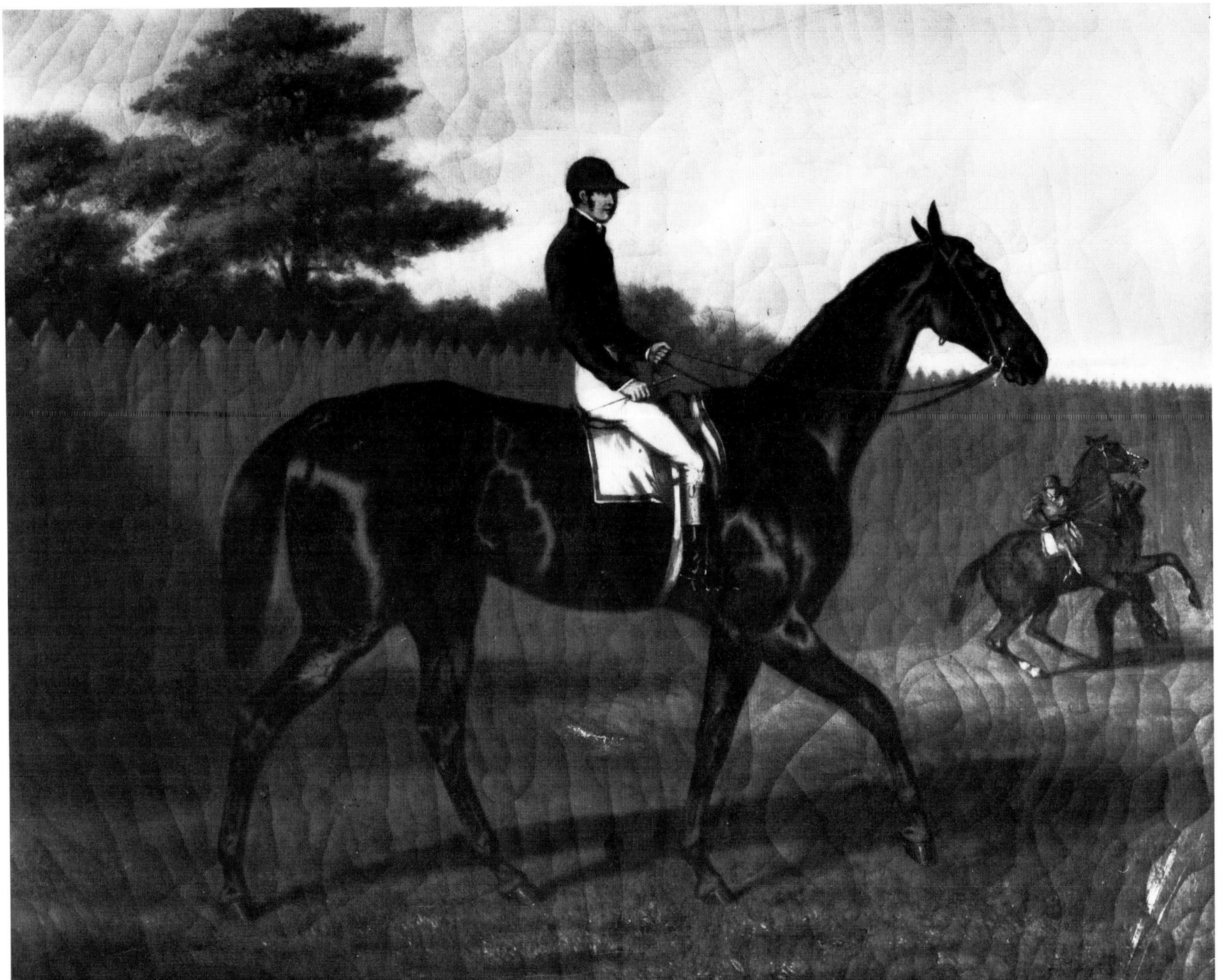

Henri Delamarre: *Potocki*. 1893. Oil on canvas, 53 × 63 cm. Société d'Encouragement, Paris

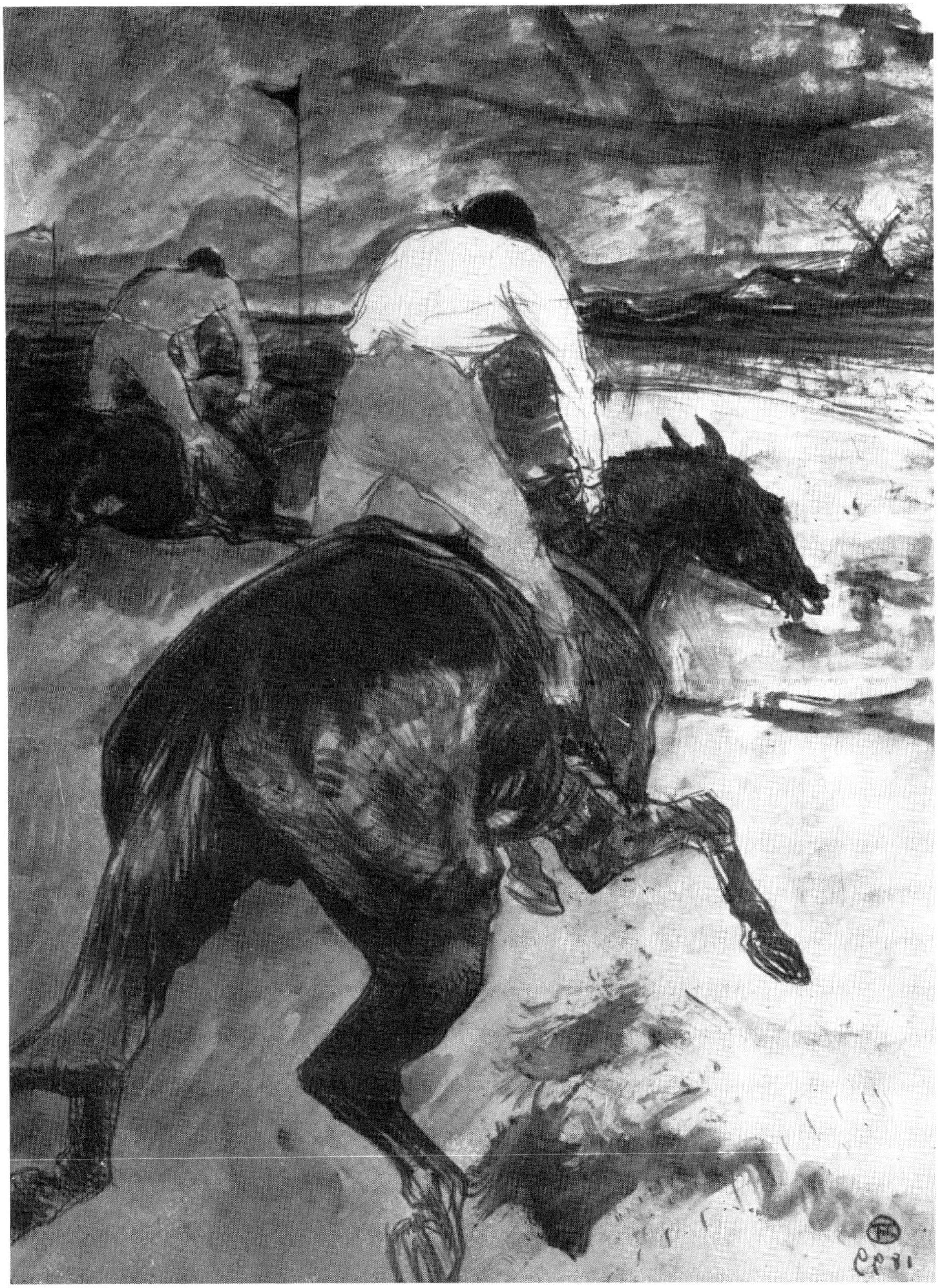

Henri de Toulouse-Lautrec: *The Jockey*. Lithograph, 1899, 51 × 37 cm. Cabinet des Dessins, Musée du Louvre, Paris

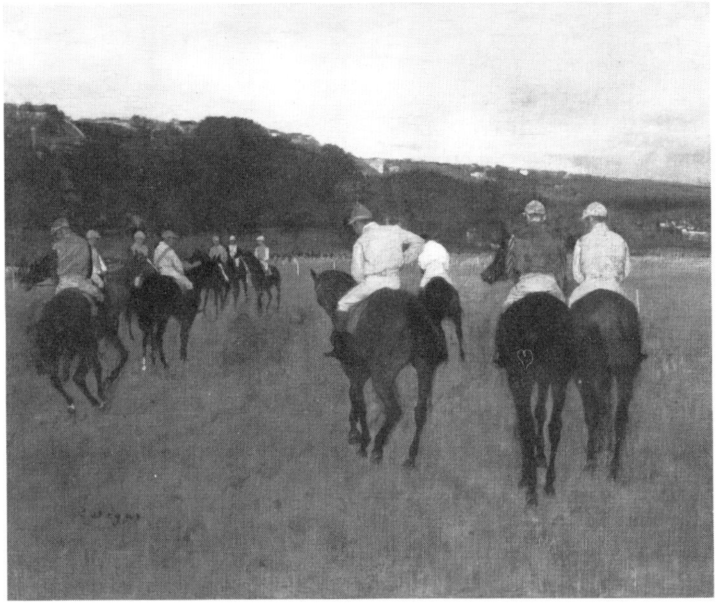

Edgar Degas: *Horses on the Course at Longchamp*. c.1873–5. Oil on canvas, 30.5 × 40 cm. Museum of Fine Arts, Boston

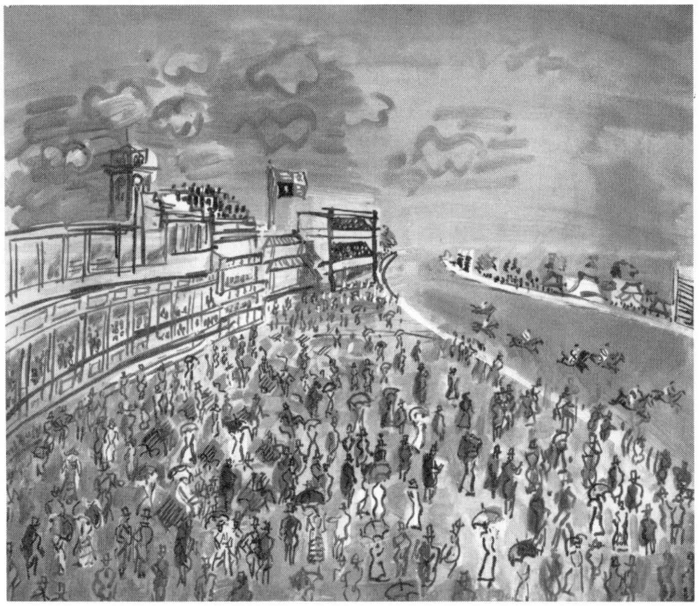

Raoul Dufy: *Ascot Races*. 1931. Watercolour, 54 × 65 cm. Private collection

Clearly, Delamarre had a taste for action painting; he made a celebrated rendering of the start of the Grand Prix of 1864. That race was won by Delamarre's colt Vermout, from the English Derby winner Blair Athol. Even the Emperor, Napoleon III, raised his hat that day. Delamarre was the owner also of Boiard, a backward, thin, and poor-looking two-year-old, whom everyone advised him to sell. Happily, M. Delamarre's loyalty to Boiard was rewarded when he not only won the Prix du Jockey Club, but went on to beat the English Derby winner Doncaster in the Grand Prix and then take the Ascot Gold Cup the following year. Delamarre died in 1913 at the age of 84.

The owner of Potocki, Auguste Lupin, honoured to this day in the Prix Lupin, was also testimony to the health-giving properties of the Sport of Kings. He lived to be 89, and died in 1895, thus seeing sixty years of French racing from that first recorded contest in the Bois de Boulogne (in which he rode his horse Piccadilly to beat the Prince de Moscowa), through the foundation of the Société d'Encouragement, to the era of the great French grey Le Sancy, who electrified French crowds in the 1890s. Lupin bred Dollar, the best son of The Flying Dutchman, whom he sent over to win the Goodwood Cup in 1864, the start of two formidable years for French horses in England.

# *Harry Hall*

*c.1813–1882*

Gladiateur
Sir Tatton Sykes
Irish Birdcatcher
Iroquois

The relics and memorials of Gladiateur, supreme icon of the French Turf, are venerated to this day in the shrines of the European thoroughbred. His skin and his hoof, beneath Harry Hall's portrait, command the council chamber of the Société d'Encouragement in Paris. His tail adorns the card-room of the English Jockey Club in Newmarket. His effigy holds pride of place at Longchamp. For Gladiateur, winner of the English Two Thousand Guineas, the English Derby, the Grand Prix de Paris, and the English St Leger – all in the *annus mirabilis* of 1865 – was the messiah for which a remarkable group of men had hoped and planned.

Thirty-two years previously, the Paris of Louis Philippe was in a ferment of vigour and creativity. Victor Hugo and Alexandre Dumas dominated the salons. Alfred de Musset was admitting his passion for George Sand. Berlioz, after wandering the streets of the city, hopelessly in love with the English actress Harriet Smithson, eventually staggered home full of inspiration 'for my greatest symphony'. And at the other end of town, the young bloods of the age worshipped style in manners, clothes and, above all, horse-flesh. The cut and gait of the riding horses were as minutely observed as the accoutrements of the coaches in Rotten Row, across the Channel. Every day the paths through the Bois de Boulogne were the scene of races and contests, hazardous to the riders as much as to passers-by.

But these chevaliers had no first-rate horses – at least nothing to compare with the English thoroughbred. So in 1833, thirteen of them, led by the Duke d'Orléans, formed the Société d'Encouragement with the declared aim of founding studs and encouraging racing to match and surpass the standards of the English. It took little more than a generation not only to establish the courses at Chantilly and Longchamp, but also to produce, in Gladiateur, a horse owned and bred in France who could defeat the best in England.

Gladiateur was a big bay, with not a white hair anywhere. He was prodigiously muscled, as Harry Hall's portrait shows, with a very long shoulder. He was by Monarque out of Miss Gladiator and came from the curious Massey's Barb Mare family, which only came into its own in the middle years of the nineteenth century with Gladiateur, Hermit, and Doncaster, then later Minoru and Ard Patrick among other Classic winners. Gladiateur was owned and bred by Count Frédéric de Lagrange, an aloof but extraordinarily successful man in business and politics as well as on the Turf. He owned the first French-bred horse to win an English Classic, Fille de l'Air, winner of the Oaks in 1864.

Gladiateur came to the Two Thousand Guineas of 1865 hardly looking a fit champion of Gallic pretensions. He had a lump on the foreleg from being trodden on while a foal. He had been lame throughout the winter,

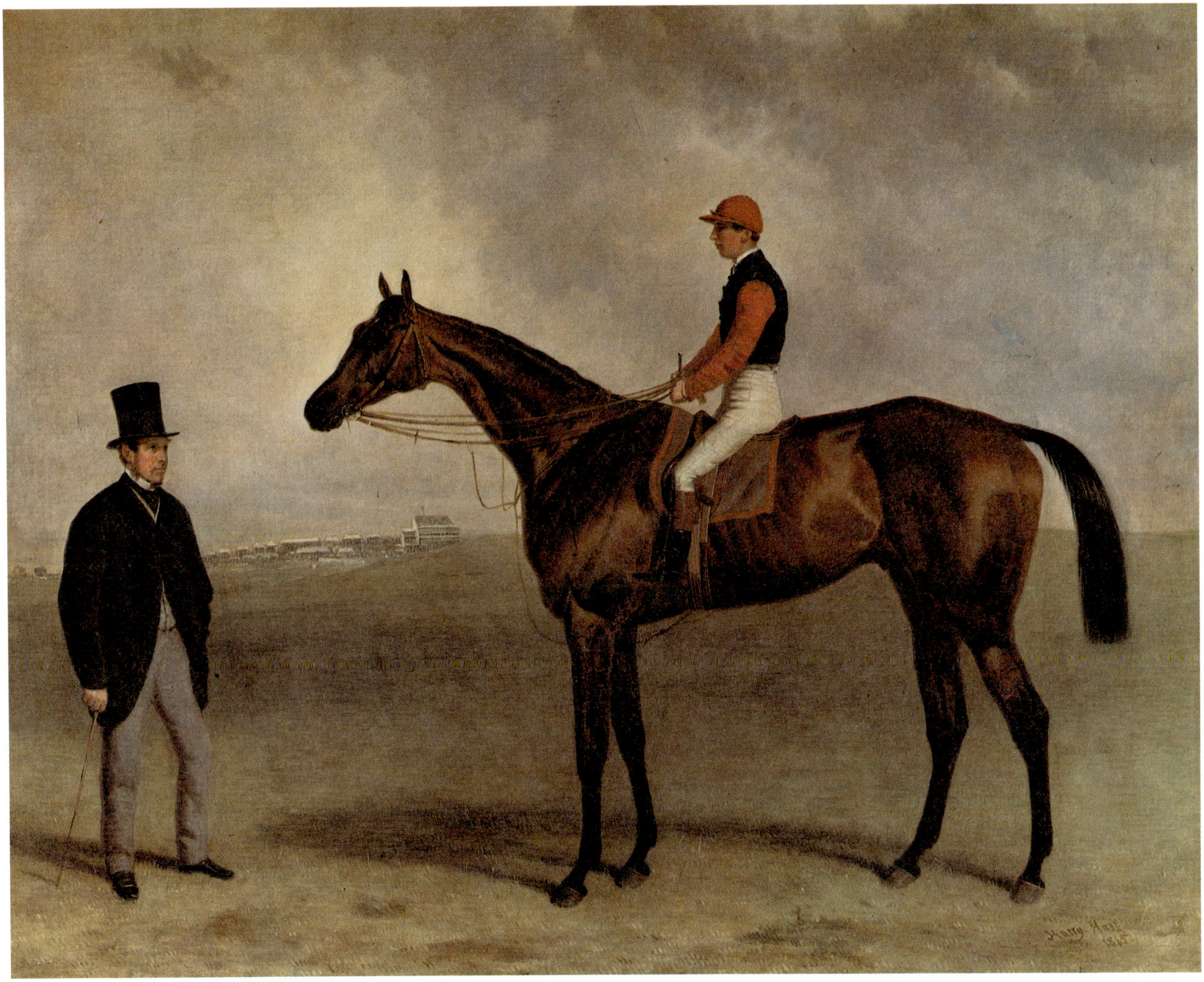

Harry Hall: *Gladiateur, with Harry Grimshaw up, and his owner Count Frédéric de Lagrange*. 1865. Oil on canvas, 100 × 125 cm. Société d'Encouragement, Paris

and his legs had been blistered. It was said that from Christmas to March he could scarcely walk, and in the paddock at Newmarket he was dismissed as backward. But he duly won at 7–1. He started favourite for the Derby and for days before was protected by a gang of hired toughs; such was the nationalistic fervour, on both sides, that the French were convinced that either the horse or the jockey, young Harry Grimshaw from Middleham, would be 'got at'.

On Derby Day itself, the horse came through effortlessly to win by a couple of lengths. The English crowd were generous enough, and a dinner was given by the Jockey Club for distinguished Frenchmen who had been present. But French delirium knew no bounds. Gladiateur was lionized in imperial fashion by the French press; indeed the enthusiasm of the mass of the French public for racing seems to have originated with Gladiateur. And when he came home to Longchamp to carry off the Grand Prix, there were celebrations in the streets throughout Paris. Lagrange's blue and red colours were everywhere. A crowd of 150,000 turned up to see the race and there was a motion of congratulation from the legislature. 'We had two Bastille Days that year,' wrote one observer. Gladiateur returned to England to win the St Leger from the filly Regalia, whom he also trounced by more than 40 lengths in the following year's Ascot Gold Cup.

Gladiateur's Epsom victory is the subject of two of Henry Alken junior's splendid action pictures. First, the scene at Tattenham Corner with the winner lying tucked well in on the rails; the picture has tremendous detail and perspective and a wonderful sense of tension as the decisive action unfolds. Then, the winning-post study with the French horse comfortably clear, the crowd surging behind the runners, the policemen rigidly at attention near the finish while their colleagues further down the course dash frantically across the track to try and cut off the advancing spectators.

Sadly, after three years of triumph, a malign cloud seemed to touch all the connections of Gladiateur. The horse himself was a failure at stud and was sold off to an Englishman for 7,000 guineas. His jockey, Harry Grimshaw, was killed in a coaching accident while leaving Northampton races. His English trainer, Tom Jennings, had a series of financial disasters. His French trainer, Frank Carter, was found dead in the River Seine. And Count de Lagrange was broken by the Franco-Prussian War of 1870. An English acquaintance, John Corlett, wrote in his *Racing Recollections*: 'He was generally regarded as an Adonis. When we next saw him, two years later, he was an old man, his hair was grey, he had a frizzled moustache and his figure was shrivelled.' He died of gout in 1883.

Harry Hall, selected by the Count to paint Gladiateur, was one of the most prolific equine artists of all time. He lived and worked for more than forty years at Newmarket. Over a hundred of his portraits were reproduced in the old *Sporting Magazine*. Inevitably there is a sameness about his work, and he was dismissed by Shaw Sparrow as 'Herring's echo', but he was valued by owners as an artist who could produce careful and accurate studies of their favourite horses. There can be no doubt that this picture of an extremely fit-looking animal, with Grimshaw up and the Count looking on, is a good representation of a great racehorse.

Sir Tatton Sykes, the racehorse, was named after the first baronet of that name, to commemorate a famous if turbulent friendship. The horse was owned by William Scott, the jockey, who won nine St Legers. He and his brother John, the 'Wizard of the North' who trained at Malton, were both long-standing friends of Sir Tatton Sykes of Sledmere in east Yorkshire, owner of the famous stud. Indeed, it was Sir Tatton's dying wish that he should once more be taken over to see the Scotts at Whitewall. Early in 1846, William Scott asked Sir Tatton if he would allow the horse Tibthorpe, 'the winner-to-be of this year's St Leger' according to Scott, to be named after him. The newly dubbed Sir Tatton Sykes

Henry Alken junior: *Tattenham Corner, Derby of 1865*. Oil on canvas, 55 × 80 cm. Société d'Encouragement, Paris

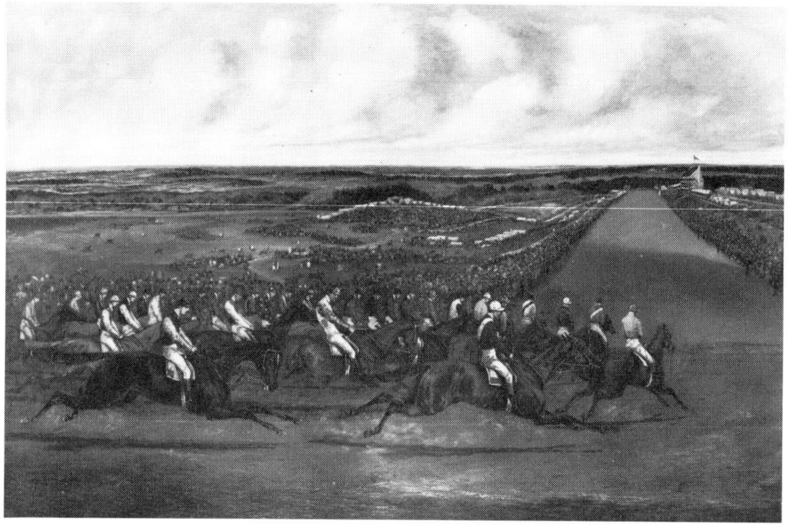

Henry Alken junior: *The Winning-post, Derby of 1865*. Oil on canvas, 55 × 80 cm. Société d'Encouragement, Paris

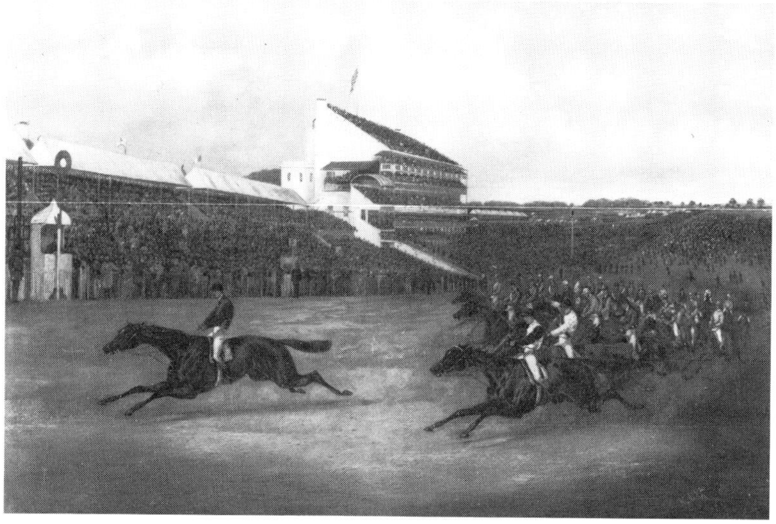

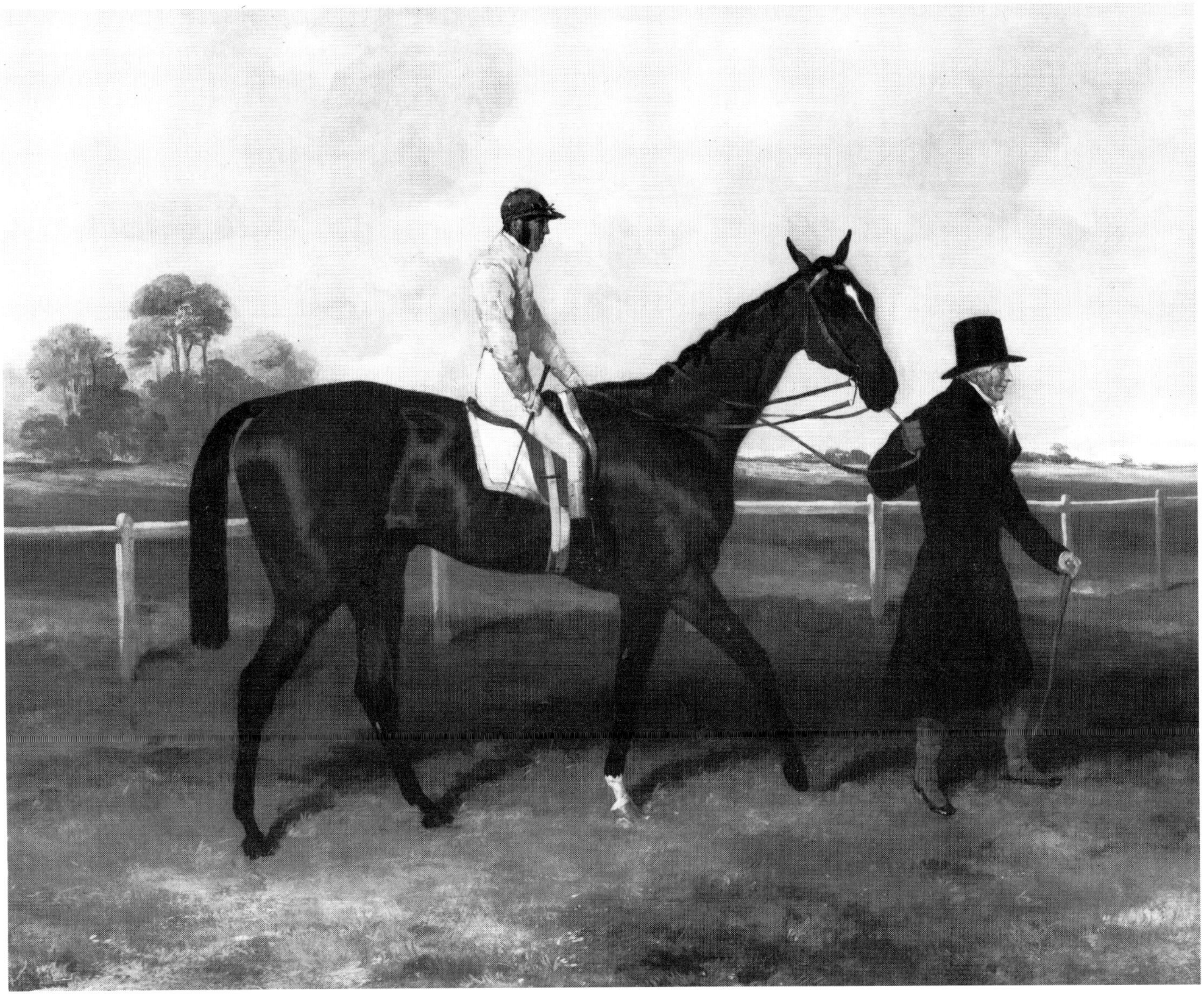

Harry Hall: *Sir Tatton Sykes leading in his namesake Sir Tatton Sykes, with William Scott up.* 1846. Oil on canvas, 71 × 91.5 cm. Paul Mellon Collection, Yale Center for British Art, New Haven, Conn.

won the Two Thousand Guineas and looked set to win the Derby.

Unfortunately, William Scott fortified himself even more than was his custom before the race. At the start he devoted his prime energies to damning the starter in sufficiently intemperate terms to earn him a £5 fine. The starter had his revenge and Scott was left many lengths when the flag fell. For all that, he made up ground and was in the lead in the straight. But then Scott seems to have lost control and the horse veered all over the track, as though he too had partaken of the hard stuff. He managed only second. Before the St Leger, the Baronet foolishly sent over a barrel of the notorious Sledmere ale to the Scotts. A delegation had to be sent to summon Sir Tatton, the man, to supervise both horse and jockey night and day until the Doncaster race was won.

The beneficiary of the Derby fiasco was the famous prize-fighter John Gully, whose self-satisfied portrait was recorded by Harry Hall. He owned Pyrrhus the First, the winner, trained by John Day. Gully, a publican's son from Bristol, was sprung from a debtors' prison in order to fight Henry Pierce, the 'Game Chicken', in the prize-ring. After two more matches he had the foundations of a fortune which took him into Parliament as MP for Wakefield and Pontefract, and into the landed gentry as the owner of Ackworth Park.

Harry Hall: *Irish Birdcatcher*. After 1836. Oil on canvas, 70 × 91.4 cm. Woodward Collection, The Baltimore Museum of Art

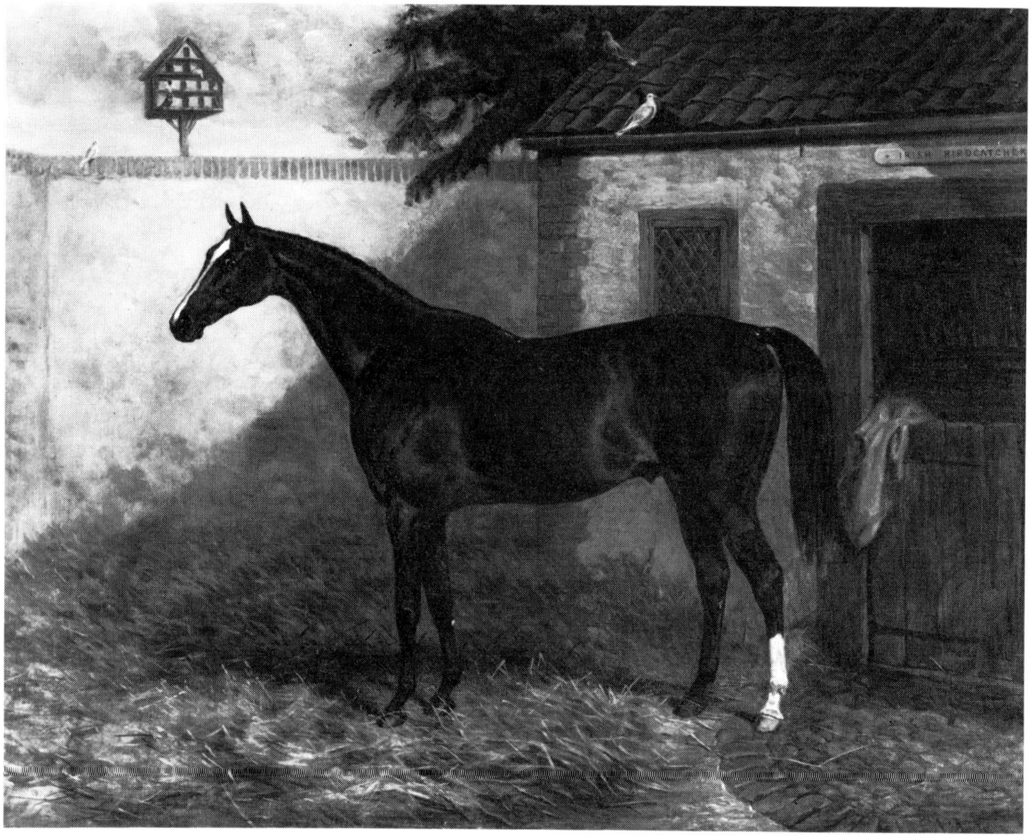

Harry Hall: *Iroquois*. *c*.1881–2. Oil on canvas, 42.5 × 52 cm. Private collection

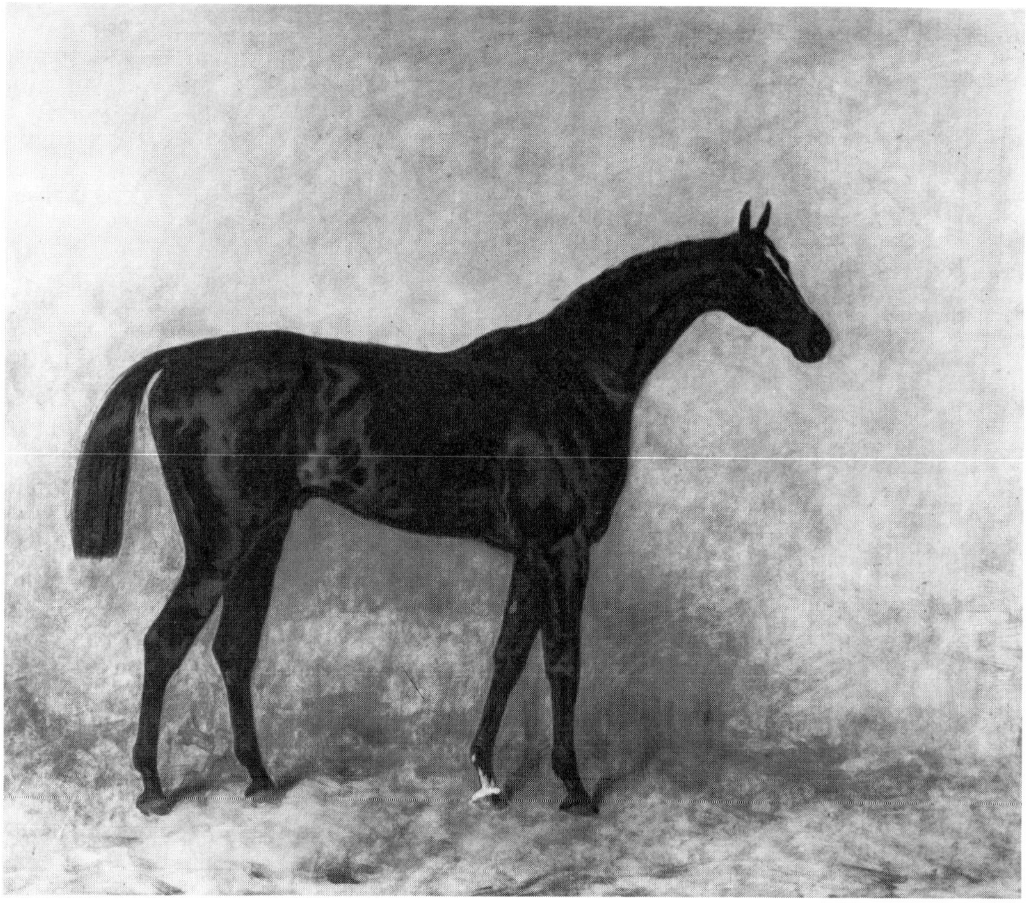

*Pierre Lorillard*. Keeneland Library, Lexington

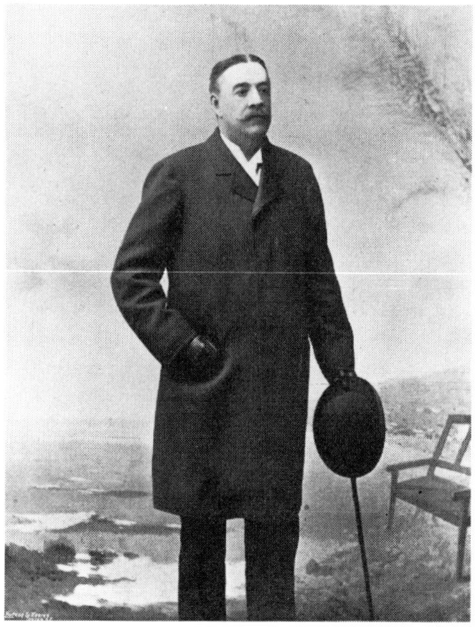

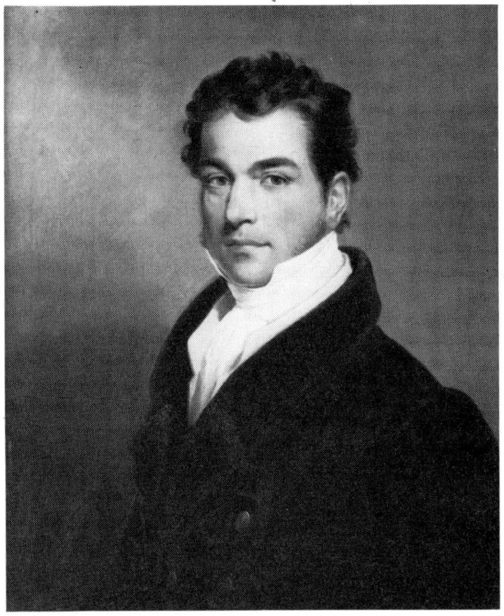

Harry Hall: *John Gully (1783–1863)*. Oil on canvas, 74.9 × 62.2 cm. Private collection

Gully was the leading light in the 'Danebury Confederacy', which centred round the Day family's stables in Hampshire (see pp. 110–12), but extended to shadowy animals of doubtful ownership in many different establishments. Gully and his associates Robert Ridsdale and Harry Hill constructed elaborate betting conspiracies woven around suborned jockeys, unfit or incapable horses, and hidden ownership. But he was sinned against with equal vigour. William Day, his trainer's son, was 'warned off' for a plot against Gully's 1845 Derby hope, Old England. Indeed, the incident was the beginning of the end for Danebury. William Day in his acerbic memoirs characterized Gully as 'tyrannical and overbearing in disposition, extremely avaricious, and, like men of his class, not over-scrupulously nice in the acquirement of wealth'. Unfortunately, unlike some of the other victims of Day's vitriol, Gully seems to have found no friend to testify more kindly to better qualities. He lived, however, to be over 80, still in possession of at least a portion of his gains.

Irish Birdcatcher was the first great thoroughbred to be bred and raced in Ireland. Wit is not the first quality associated with Harry Hall's painting, but the doves and the dovecot can presumably be taken as a pun on the horse's name. The white blaze and the white sock half-way up his leg, for which he and his stock were known, are clear enough. But he seems darker than the contemporary description in the *Sporting Magazine* would have it: 'chestnut, flanks ticked with grey hairs, a bunch of white hairs at the butt of his tail'. Nor is there much sign of the 'Birdcatcher spots', a term still current among racing men.

Birdcatcher was quite a performer on the racecourse in Ireland. In the 1836 Peel Cup, as a three-year-old, he was recorded as having passed the winning-post 500 yards ahead of his nearest rival. Unfortunately, he then careered on beyond the course and hurtled down a steep and stony road. He was never the same again. But, with his great element of Byerley Turk blood, he produced one of the most consistently potent lines in English racing, stretching down through Stockwell, Doncaster, Bend Or, Ormonde, and via Oxford to Isonomy and Isinglass.

Iroquois was the horse who stopped all business on the New York Stock Exchange on the first day of June in 1881. He was the first American-bred to win the English Derby and the celebrations were appropriate when the news came across the transatlantic cable. His shoes were reputedly made at Tiffany's from new-fangled aluminium and his work was conducted against a stop-watch by his American trainer Jacob Pincus.

Iroquois was one of a batch of yearlings brought over to England in 1879 by Pierre Lorillard, one of two American brothers, snuff and tobacco millionaires, who dominated the racing of their day in the United States. Based at the Rancocas stud in Jobstown, New Jersey, Pierre Lorillard established an enormous racing empire. In 1880 he had the hitherto unheard-of total of eighteen yearlings nominated for the breeders' stakes. But he was determined to make his name in racing in Europe as well, hence his raid not only on England, but on France too.

Iroquois won only four of his twelve races as a two-year-old – Pincus and Lorillard believed in working their horses hard – but he was spotted by the celebrated jockey Fred Archer, then at the height of his powers, who asked for the ride at Epsom. It was a copy-book race from Archer. He tracked the favourite Peregrine on the rails, and then, when the leader veered out for a moment, Archer was through to land the race by a neck.

Iroquois won his St Leger and then returned to race and go to stud in America. But Lorillard remained attached to England and went into partnership with Lord William Beresford. They had the 1899 One Thousand Guineas winner, Sibola. In the same year, Iroquois died at stud in Tennessee.

# *Henry Alken junior*

*1810–1892*

## Sefton

Henry Alken junior has suffered by comparison with his father, particularly as he did not care to limit the commercial advantage of signing the same name as the man whose prints were in nigh on every house and cottage in England. None of Henry junior's work shows the humour and fondness for the absurdity of jumping horses found in Henry senior's scenes of steeplechasing. But Henry junior was possessed not only of a respectable technique, but also of a fine sense of the drama and excitement of the racecourse which may exceed those qualities in his father. The two pictures of the Derby of 1865 (illustrated with Harry Hall's picture of the winner, Gladiateur; see p. 130) are quite the peer of his father's work in the 1819 Newmarket pictures shown here.

The appeal of both Alkens for the huge public which they commanded was the fun, frolics, and disasters of the hunting field and the chase – their pictures of which were reproduced by the thousand. They also found a ready market for general racing scenes, but they were not much inclined to spend their time on individual racehorse portraits, although Henry Alken senior did paint Cotherstone, the 1843 Derby winner, and Poison, winner of the Oaks in that year. Other horses appear spasmodically through his work, but they were never a major part of the output of the man who painted and wrote for so long under the endearing pseudonym 'Ben Tally Ho'.

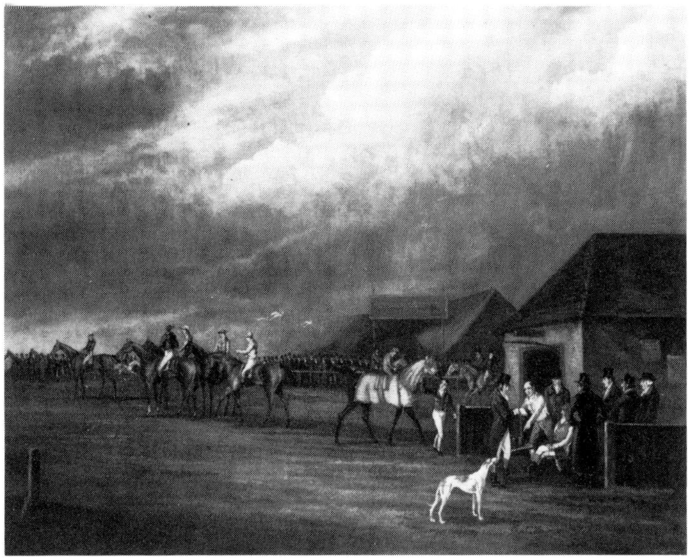

Henry Alken senior: *Weighing in at Newmarket*. 1819. Oil on canvas, 96.5 × 124.5 cm. Private collection

Henry Alken junior found towards the end of his life that it was necessary to produce whatever was commissioned. When he painted Sefton he was already in straitened circumstances, and he died in penury in 1892. Sefton belonged to a noted Scottish owner, W. Stirling Crawfurd, who had winners of the Oaks, the St Leger,

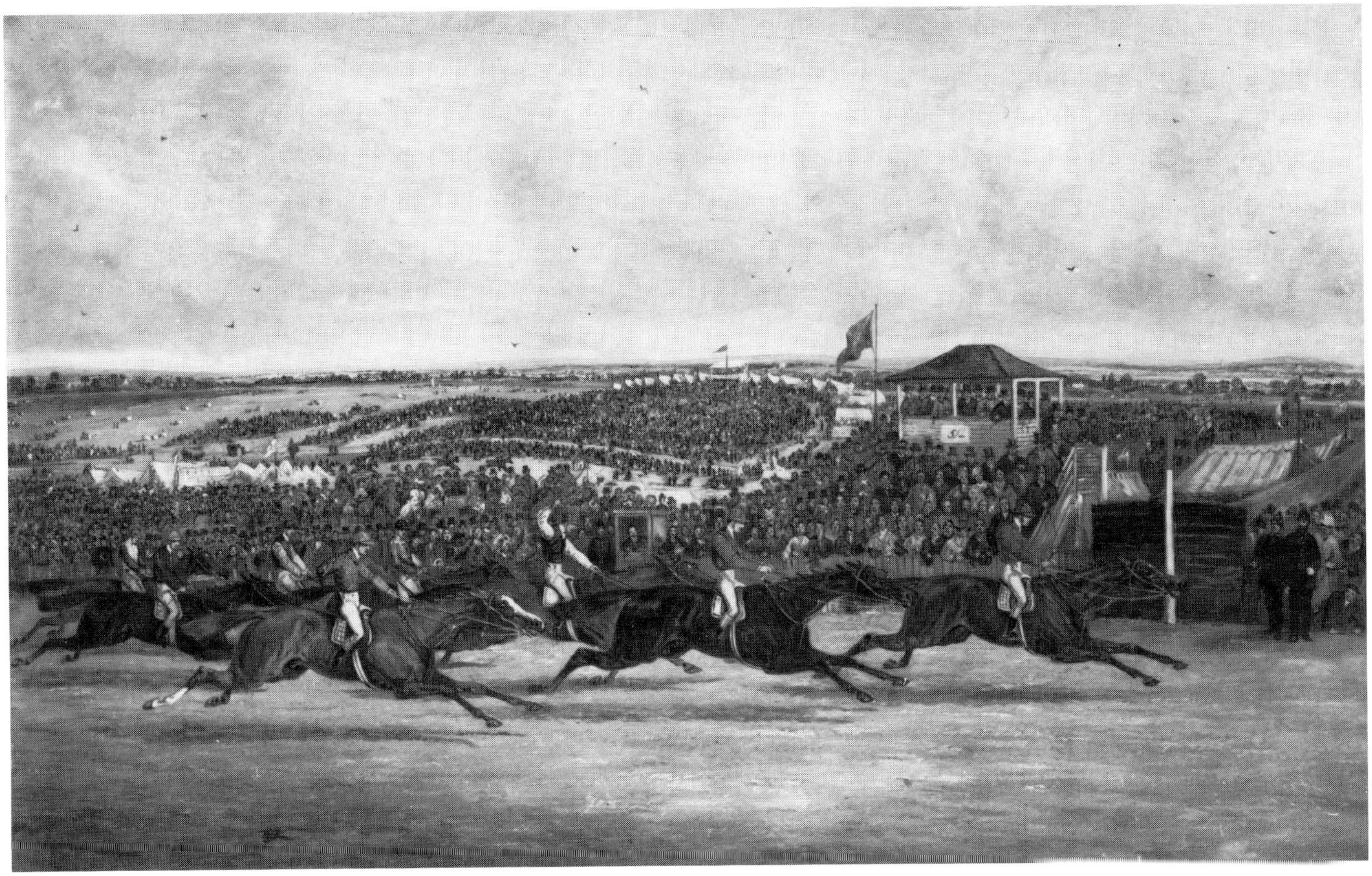

Henry Alken junior: *Sefton, with Harry Constable up, winning the 1878 Derby from Insulaire and Childeric*. Oil on canvas, 43.2 × 73.7 cm. Private collection

and both Guineas. Sefton was his only Derby winner. A long-looking bay, he had cost 1,000 guineas as a yearling. Although unsuccessful as a two-year-old, he picked up the City and Suburban Handicap on his second outing at three.

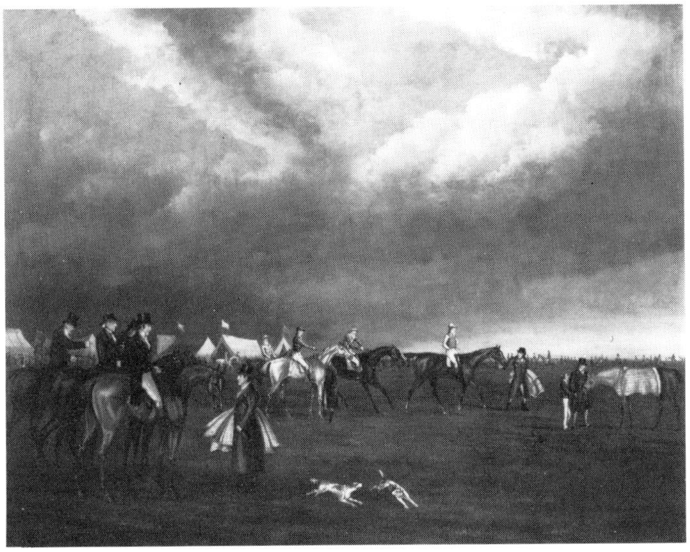

Henry Alken senior: *Before the Start at Newmarket*. 1819. Oil on canvas, 96.5 × 124.5 cm. Private collection

In the 1878 Derby, Sefton was faced with the French Derby winner Insulaire. The chances are that the French colt would have given Count de Lagrange his second Derby win, and thus revived his spirits after the depredations of the Franco-Prussian War and the torments of gout. Insulaire was coming with a late rush when Fred Archer on Childeric shouted a warning to Harry Constable, Sefton's jockey. Sefton was spurred on and won by half a length in the heavy ground.

Sefton won at odds of 100–12, and delivered a last coup to George Payne, the very same man who as a young punter had lost £26,000 on Jerry's St Leger, all of fifty-four years before (see p. 100). Payne died, apparently of sunstroke, on Lewes racecourse later that year. It may perhaps be taken as encouraging that after half a century of cards, hunting, and 'plunging' there was still sufficient coin left in the old man's pocket to back his fancy. Few of the other great gamblers in English racing managed to last out a decade.

# *Lynwood Palmer*

*1868–1941*

## St Simon

Lynwood Palmer's romantic and fiery painting of St Simon hangs somewhat obscurely in one of the darker corridors of the Jockey Club at Newmarket. Yet it is arguable that this is the greatest horse ever to compete on the English Turf.

St Simon was never beaten and, though he was not entered for any of the Classics, he won every race he contested with such consummate ease that he appears never to have been fully extended on the racecourse. Indeed, the only man who may have known how fast St Simon really could go was Fred Archer, who unwisely touched him with the spurs during morning work on Newmarket Heath. To quote his owner, the Duke of Portland: 'We saw him shoot out, pass his own stable companions, dash through another trainer's lot of horses galloping in front, scatter them like pigeons before a fox, and disappear from view.' When Fred Archer was eventually discovered on foot and leading the colt at the entrance to Newmarket Town, he said, 'I will never again touch that animal with a spur; he's not a horse, he's a steam engine.'

The Duke of Portland was only in his early 20s when St Simon, almost literally, fell into his hands. The young Duke was walking to the Jockey Club luncheon room on Newmarket racecourse when St Simon's breeder, Prince Batthyany, who was just in front of him, fell back into his arms, dead, apparently from over-excitement at the prospect of seeing Galliard win the Two Thousand Guineas. At the consequent sale of Batthyany's horses, the Duke bought St Simon, for 1,600 guineas, only because a colt called Fulmen, his first choice, went past the ducal limit of 4,500 guineas. St Simon had not been entered for any of the Classics apparently because his dam, St Angela, already 17 or 18 years old, had bred nothing of note, and it had therefore seemed to the Prince hardly worth investing in the entry fee. His sire, Galopin, had won the Derby for the Prince in 1875.

St Simon won all his two-year-old races easily, including giving a stone to his rivals in the 1887 Prince of Wales Nursery at Doncaster, but it was as a three-year-old that he proved himself, in the words of bloodstock authority Charles Richardson, 'an absolute phenomenon'. Among his opponents for the Ascot Gold Cup was Tristan, who had already beaten the Derby winner Iroquois and the St Leger winner Dutch Oven, and subsequently beat another Derby winner, Harvester. Yet St Simon slaughtered him and the rest of the field by 20 lengths. Again in the Goodwood Cup, his last race, he won by 20 lengths from Ossian. When he won the Ascot Gold Cup it took the jockey almost a mile past the post to pull him up, and the same at Goodwood, when he was nearly at the top of Trundle Hill before he could be stopped.

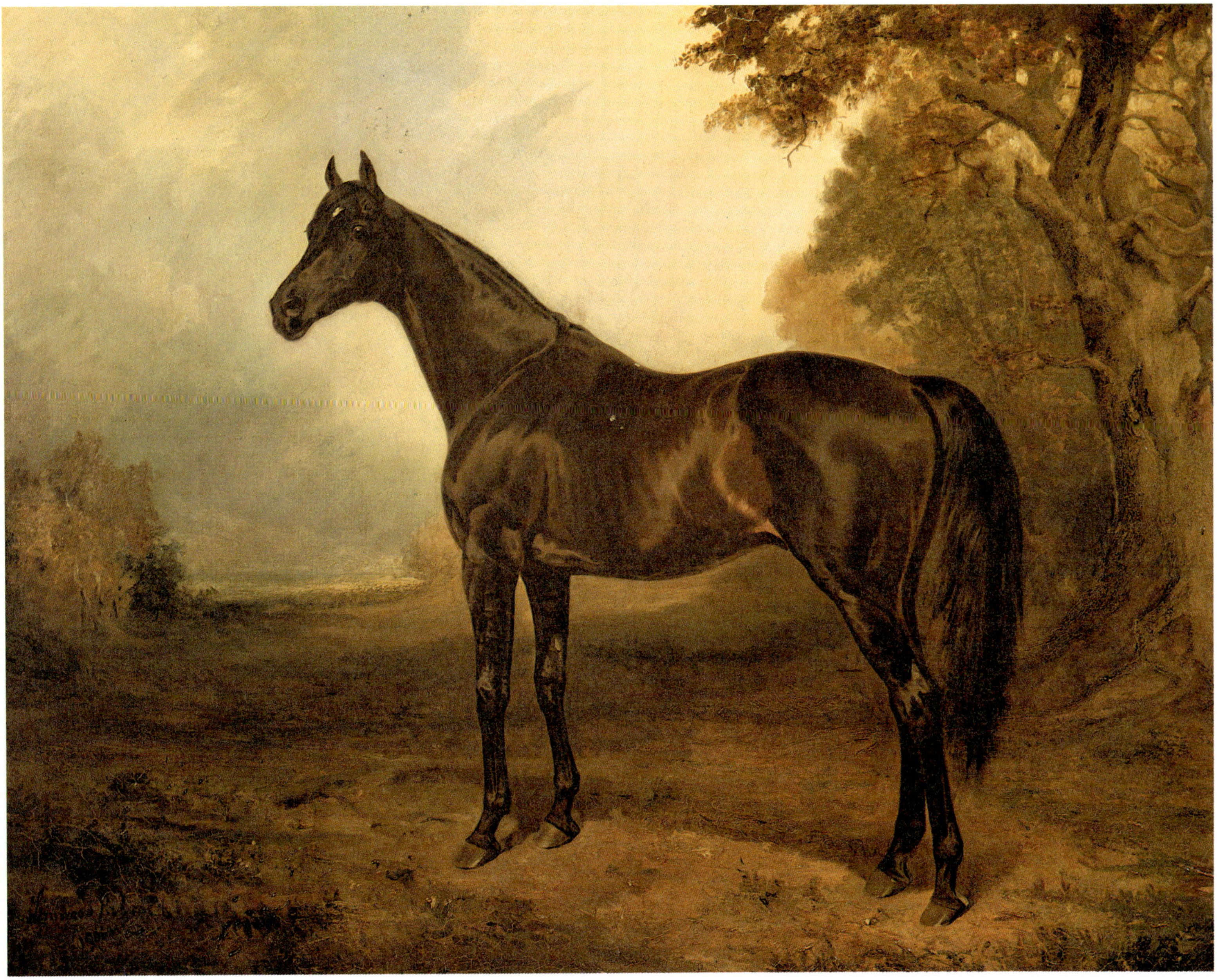

Lynwood Palmer: *St Simon.* 1906. Oil on canvas, 107.9 × 138.7 cm. Jockey Club, Newmarket

Mat Dawson, his trainer, believed St Simon the best horse who ever lived, and he noted in him that quality of 'electricity', a characteristic discerned by other great horsemen, such as Federico Tesio, breeder of Ribot, in truly outstanding horses. Indeed, it was in order to conserve that 'electric' quality that Mat Dawson advised that St Simon should be retired to stud when he was only 3 years old. He was vindicated in the most overwhelming fashion. St Simon sired ten different winners of seventeen English Classic races, including the full brothers Persimmon and Diamond Jubilee, as well as La Flèche, Semolina, and St Frusquin. He was the leading sire for nine years and died in 1908 having sired the winners of more than £$\frac{1}{2}$ million. His skeleton went to the Natural History Museum in London.

Lynwood Palmer was a romantic painter to the point of sentimentality, and there is no mistaking the pride and arrogance of the great stallion as he bestrides an idealized landscape in this portrait. But it is hard to recognize the other qualities for which St Simon was known. He was a big brown horse like all the best of the Blacklock line, undoubtedly much bigger than his sire, with a girth of fully 6$\frac{1}{2}$ ft and a lot of bone below the knee. His action was anything but classic. When the Duke first saw him work, 'he appeared to move more like a rabbit than a horse and could not apparently stride over a straw'. When fully extended, wrote the Duke, 'he went nearly flat on the ground, resembling a greyhound more than a horse'. St Simon certainly had an evil temper and his lad more than once had to be rescued

A. C. Havell: *St Simon*. After 1888. Oil on canvas, 35.5 × 60.9 cm. Tattersalls, Newmarket

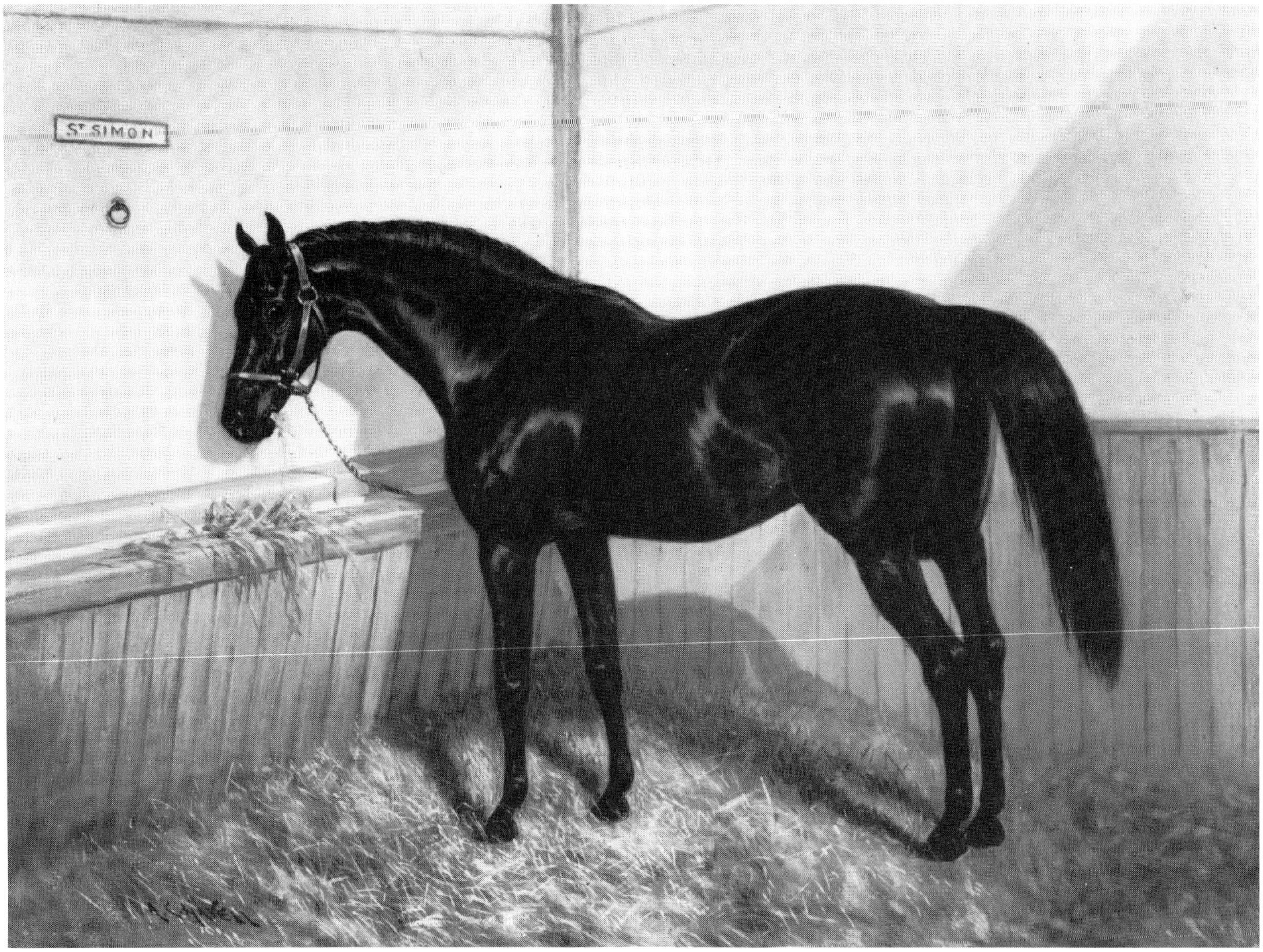

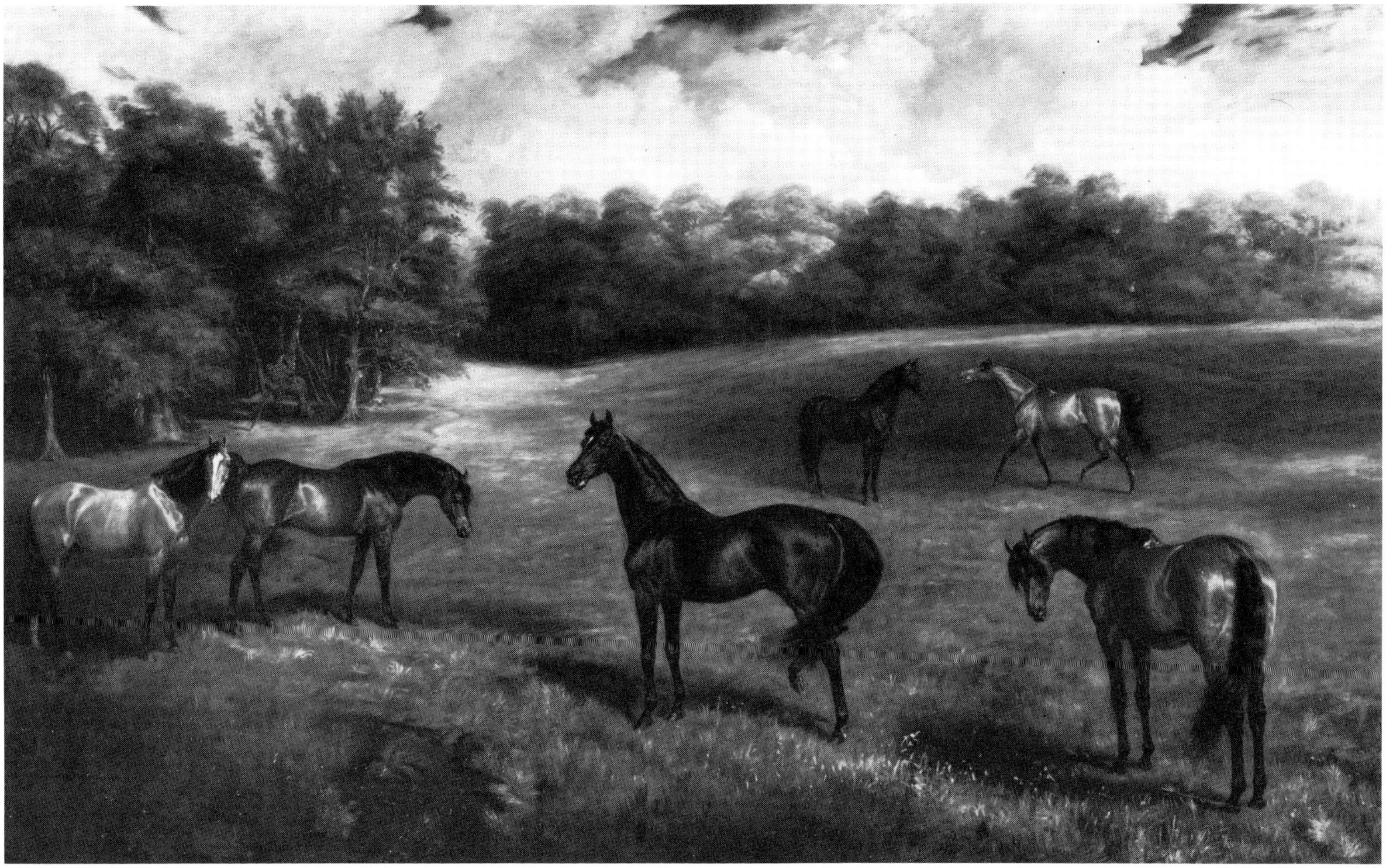

Lynwood Palmer: *The Duke of Portland's Six Stallions* (see text for detailed identification of subjects). 1900. Oil on canvas, 167.6 × 274.3 cm. Private collection

from a savaging in his box. It is interesting that in Palmer's picture, St Simon's tail hangs well below his hocks, for it was notorious that to the end of his days the horse objected violently to having it cut.

There are a number of other studies of St Simon, including a pleasing portrait set in the stables at Welbeck by R. Alexander, again with his tail almost to the ground, and a fine study by A. C. Havell at Tattersalls.

Lynwood Palmer was a vicar's son from Lincolnshire who emigrated to Canada where he worked on a ranch, later moving south to New York. It was more than a decade before he returned to England. He became one of the most prolific painters and book illustrators in the early decades of the twentieth century and for many years was considered a peer of Munnings, owners particularly valuing his rather sweet style. But he has in more recent times been eclipsed, as the innovative power of Munnings has become fully appreciated.

The scene of the Duke of Portland's six celebrated stallions all together in a field rather stretches credulity, but it is a graphic reminder of how the Duke dominated the bloodstock world at the close of the nineteenth century. The two horses in the background are St Serf (on the left) and Raeburn, with (from left to right) Carbine, Ayrshire, St Simon, and Donovan in the foreground. 'It was a fine sight to see them all at exercise,' wrote the Duke. 'On the occasion of the Welbeck Tenants' Agricultural Show, the tenants and others attending the show were always taken to see the stallions and yearlings. Sometimes as many as 12,000 to 15,000 people turned up.' And the trainer Mat Dawson wrote in 1895: 'His Grace has now three of the four best horses in the world, which I presume to be St Simon, Ormonde, Donovan and Carbine.'

# A. C. Havell

*1855–1928*

Carbine
Lemberg

Carbine was the first and perhaps the greatest of the stars from the antipodean firmament which have descended from time to time to astonish the racegoers of Europe and America. In 1977, Balmerino came straight from a racing season in the southern hemisphere to beat all Europe's best, save Alleged, in the Prix de l'Arc de Triomphe in Paris. In 1904, his New Zealand predecessor Moifaa survived a shipwreck to swim ashore and win the English Grand National.

In 1932, the Californians greeted askance the arrival of another New Zealander, Phar Lap. Tom Woodcock, his trainer, did not bother to work him, but just hacked him about the sand-dunes around the Caliente track. He refused to practise him through the starting-gate, and put up the jockey an hour before the off, to wander around the inner track in the heat of the day. Once the $1\frac{1}{4}$-mile race had started, Phar Lap loitered about fifty yards at the rear, apparently inspecting the racecourse fixtures and fittings, then decided to race. He took the 'hundred thousand' Caliente prize in record time. Two weeks later he was dead, poisoned by some bad food. His carcass was stuffed and put on display at the Belmont track and then sent back to Australia, where he had won the Melbourne Cup and thirty-six other races.

Australian and New Zealand horses have never been dull emissaries, though they have often been cheap. The progeny of bargain Australian-breds, such as Pago Pago and Sky High, have won around $50 million in the United States since the war. But none has matched the record of the great Carbine, whose son Spearmint, grandson Spion Kop, and great grandson Felstead all won the Derby. Carbine was raised near Auckland in New Zealand, at the Sylvia Park Club. He was a tremendously tough racehorse who won five big races in eight days at Randwick in Australia in 1890. The same year he won one of the legendary Melbourne Cups. He was carrying 10 st. 5 lb. in a field of thirty-nine. Yet he finished in record time, $2\frac{1}{2}$ lengths in front of Highborn, who was carrying nearly 4 st. less. Carbine had run forty-three races when he was retired to stud by his owner Donald Wallace. He was at stud only four years in Australia, but more than half of the Melbourne Cup winners of the past eighty years have been directly descended from him. His stay in Australia was curtailed by an astute bit of aristocratic business acumen by the Duke of Portland in 1895.

The Duke already owned a clutch of outstanding stallions: Ayrshire, Donovan, St Serf, Raeburn, and, above all, the nonpareil St Simon. He determined, however, to acquire a stallion who was not related to his champions. Hearing from an Australian intermediary in London, Mr Charles Hart, that Carbine might be for sale, he commenced negotiations by means of the electric telegraph with Donald Wallace. Eventually, a price

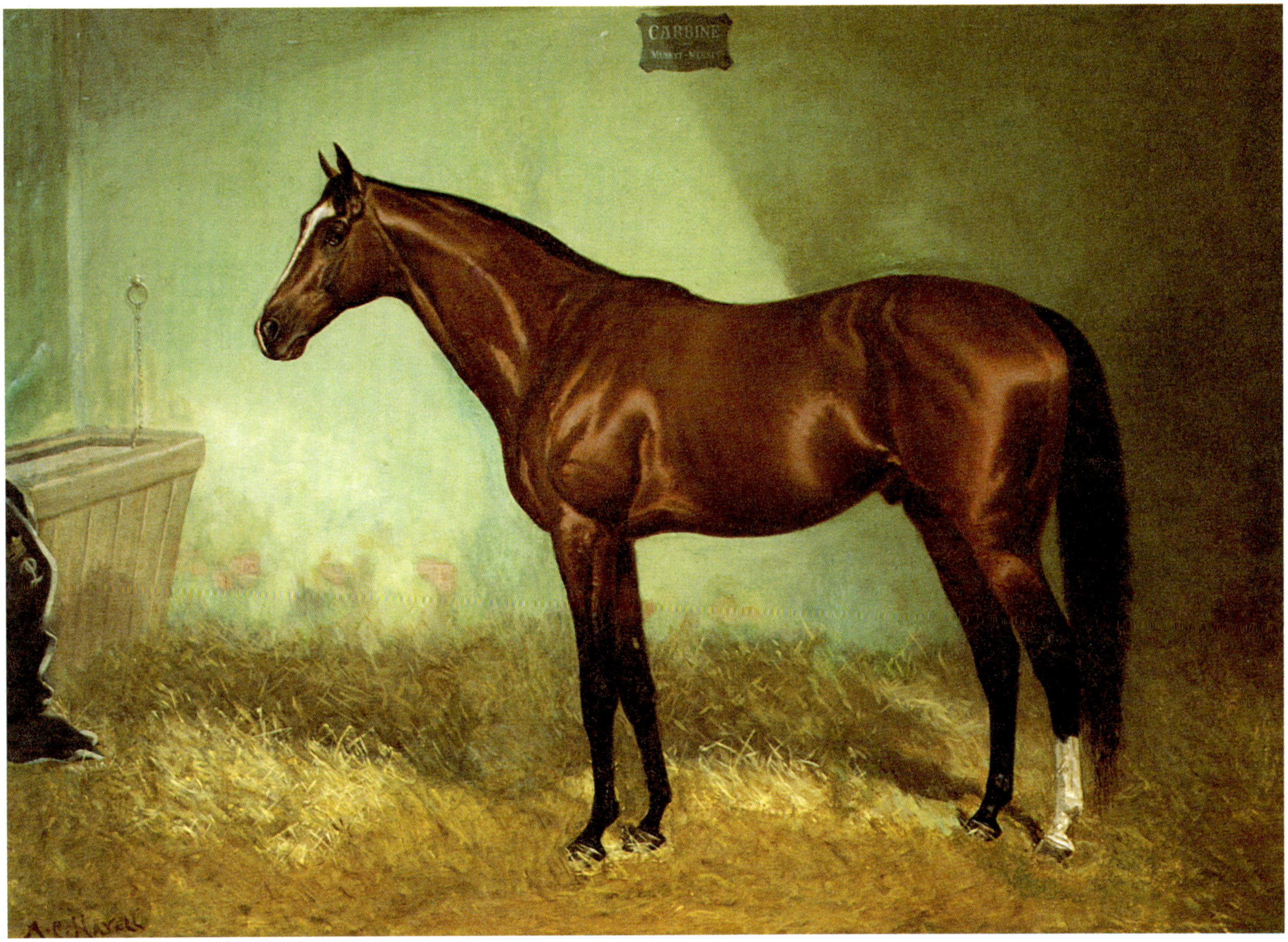


A. C. Havell: *Carbine*. After 1895. Oil on canvas, 33 × 43 cm. Australian Jockey Club, Randwick

of £13,000 was agreed, a daring venture for a horse that the Duke had never seen and about whom he could obtain no assurances concerning the soundness of his wind. 'We never examine horses for their wind,' Charles Hart assured His Grace airily. Carbine arrived safely in England to find that he had three years' work at stud, at 200 guineas per service, already organized for him. The Duke was in pocket from the outset.

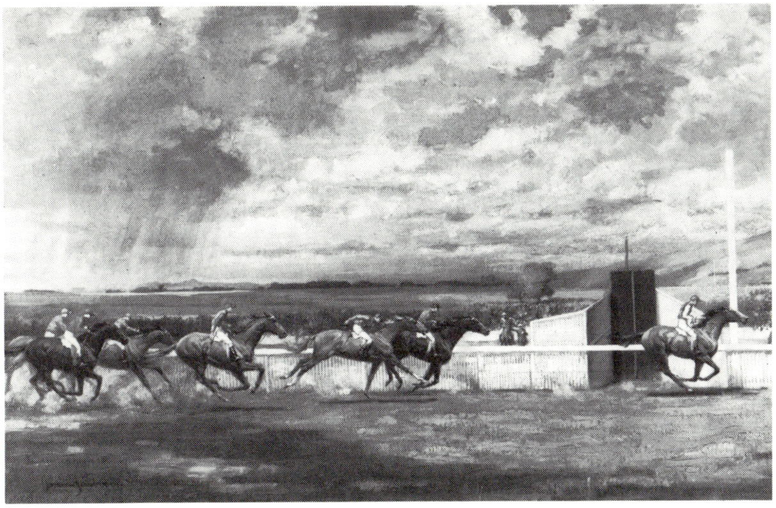

Martin Stainforth: *Carbine winning the 1890 Melbourne Cup from Highborn*. Oil on canvas, 63.5 × 104.1 cm. Private collection

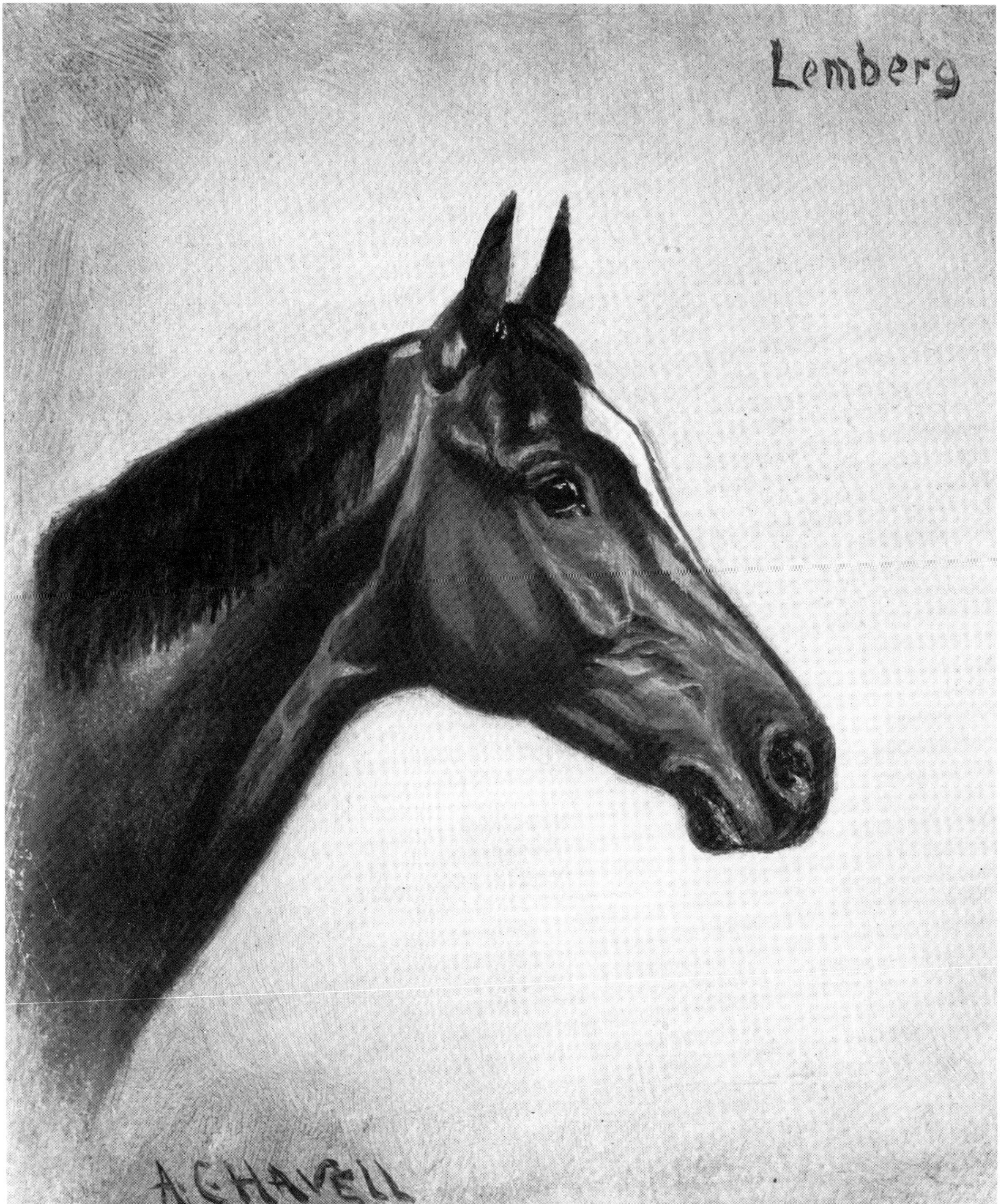
Lemberg
A.C. HAVELL

The first day Carbine saw snow at Welbeck, he pawed the ground, smelt the stuff, and absolutely refused to leave his box. The next day, he decided to try a taste, liked it, and immediately hurtled out into the yard and rolled about. Carbine was not without his foibles. The Duke wrote: 'He could not bear to get his ears wet, and once, when he was being saddled and bridled for the Melbourne Cup, it began to rain. For some time he refused to go out of his box; so, in desperation, his trainer Higginbotham put up an umbrella and walked to the starting post carrying this over the horse's head. When he was at the starting post with the other horses, he paid no further attention to the wet – and he won the race. In consequence of this idiosyncrasy, Higginbotham had a leather protector made like a small umbrella, which he attached to the bridle, so that rain could not fall on Carbine's ears; and this contraption was sent to Welbeck with him. He did not mind rain on his body, but could not bear it on his ears.'

Carbine came from the Camel–Touchstone line. He was 27 years old when the Duke found him bleeding from a brain haemorrhage in his box and had him put down with chloroform. His skin was sent back to Auckland and his skeleton to a Melbourne museum. The Duke of Portland had a theory that stallions were at their most potent in their first season, but Carbine proved him wrong. It was eight years after his arrival in England that he got his best son Spearmint, who won the Derby of 1906 and then, only eleven days later in Paris, won the Grand Prix. When the Duke died in 1943, with thirteen Classic winners to his name, Carbine had been dead nearly thirty years. Yet the Duke still could not know that, through Nearco on the dam's side, the blood he had imported with such deliberation from Australia half a century before was to match even the great St Simon in its ultimate influence.

Alfred Charles Havell was literally the house artist for Messrs Fores, the London art and print dealers. He was installed in a room above the gallery in Piccadilly, from where, enveloped in a fug of tobacco smoke, he turned out a stream of work for Fores to publish. He was a member of the extensive Havell family, who were a feature of nineteenth-century sporting art in England. Though Alfred's reputation has proved as evanescent as his cigar smoke, he was in fact a superb craftsman, and some of his paintings, such as that of Carbine and the Tattersalls version of St Simon (see p. 138), are of a quality which bears comparison with all but the best of his contemporaries. Across the turn of the century, he painted some wonderfully luminous studies of champions who had notable Australian connections, though it is not clear whether he ever visited Australia. The Carbine picture hangs in the Australian Jockey Club, but it is the English Jockey Club which houses his fine portrait of Lemberg.

Lemberg belonged to Alfred W. Cox, the Australian mine owner from Broken Hill. Cox, a cigar eternally clamped between his teeth, raced under the pseudonym 'Mr Fairie'. He was not, however, a shrinking violet and the 1910 season was enlivened by a bidding duel between Cox and Lord Rosebery for the services of the jockey Danny Maher. Maher had been riding for His Lordship for a number of years, but in the 1909 season he had some brilliant wins on Cox's horse Bayardo. Cox became convinced that Maher would make all the difference to Lemberg's chances. Indeed, Lemberg went down to Lord Rosebery's horse Neil Gow in the Two Thousand Guineas, solely, most spectators thought, because of Maher's superior jockeyship on the winner. This heightened Cox's determination to secure his services. Maher remained loyal to Rosebery, but in the process extracted an estimated £8,000 in retainers alone.

The Australian had the last laugh. Neil Gow, ridden by Maher, could only manage fourth in the Derby. Lemberg ridden by Bernard Dillon survived fifteen minutes of delay at the start to win by a neck from a very good field which included Greenback and Swynford, Lord Derby's colt.

A. C. Havell: *Lemberg*. After 1910. Oil on wood, 10.8 × 9.5 cm. Jockey Club, Newmarket

# *Henry Stull*

*1851–1913*

Domino
Hanover
Miss Woodford

Henry Stull's pictures are always an immediate delight. They were painted to make an instant impact in periodicals like *Leslie's Weekly*, to which he was an indefatigable contributor. The paintings have the quality of caricature, with the jockeys bow-backed as they urge their charges along, and the horses extended like dragons so that it is almost surprising fire is not emerging from their nostrils.

Harry Stull, a Canadian from Hamilton, Ontario, was always in the thick of American racing during its halcyon years at the end of the nineteenth century. He was a friend of Samuel Riddle, the textile tycoon, who later owned Man o' War. Swarthmore, one of Riddle's best horses, ran in Stull's colours. For twenty years up till 1910, there was hardly a decent thoroughbred who escaped a portrait session with Stull.

Domino, the 'Black Whirlwind', held the two-year-old money-winning record for thirty-eight years. He was an out-and-out sprinter who was, nevertheless, subjected to some cruel races at longer distances. On his gravestone are the words: 'Here lies the fleetest runner the American Turf has ever known, and one of the gamest and most generous horses.' Domino, a son of another fast horse, Himyar, was bought by the Keenes at Tattersalls sales in New York and won all nine of his two-year-old races. He became embroiled in a series of punishing match races, caused by his owner James R. Keene's inability to resist the taunts of fellow owners about the horse's stamina. Domino ran a dead heat with Richard Croker's Dobbins at 2 years old. The following year, Byron McClelland provoked Keene into two matches with Henry of Navarre, at distances a furlong beyond the mile which was really Domino's limit.

The race was staged at Gravesend in September 1894, before a vast crowd which included two of America's legendary punters, Riley Grannon and 'Pittsburgh Phil'. Grannon is supposed to have challenged 'Phil': 'I've got 100,000 dollars says Henry of Navarre will win.' 'Phil', otherwise known as George Smith, accepted. The match was a see-saw affair with both horses on level terms at the furlong pole. Henry of Navarre got up for a few lengths and then Domino fought back. At the line, the judges could not separate them. A dead heat was declared.

Three weeks later they met again at Morris Park over

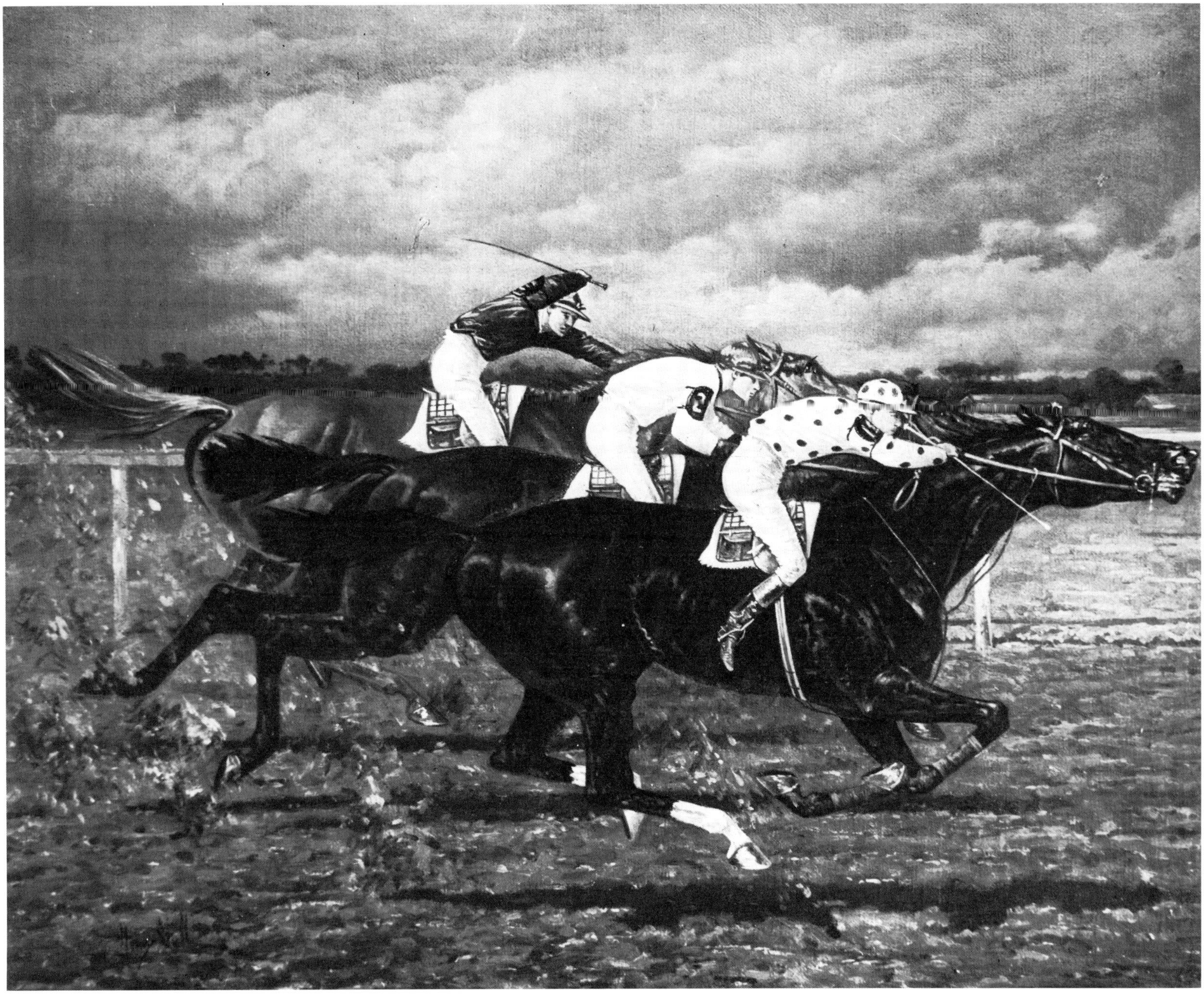

Henry Stull: *Domino's Futurity*. After 1893. Oil on canvas, 40.6 × 50.8 cm. National Museum of Racing, Saratoga Springs, NY

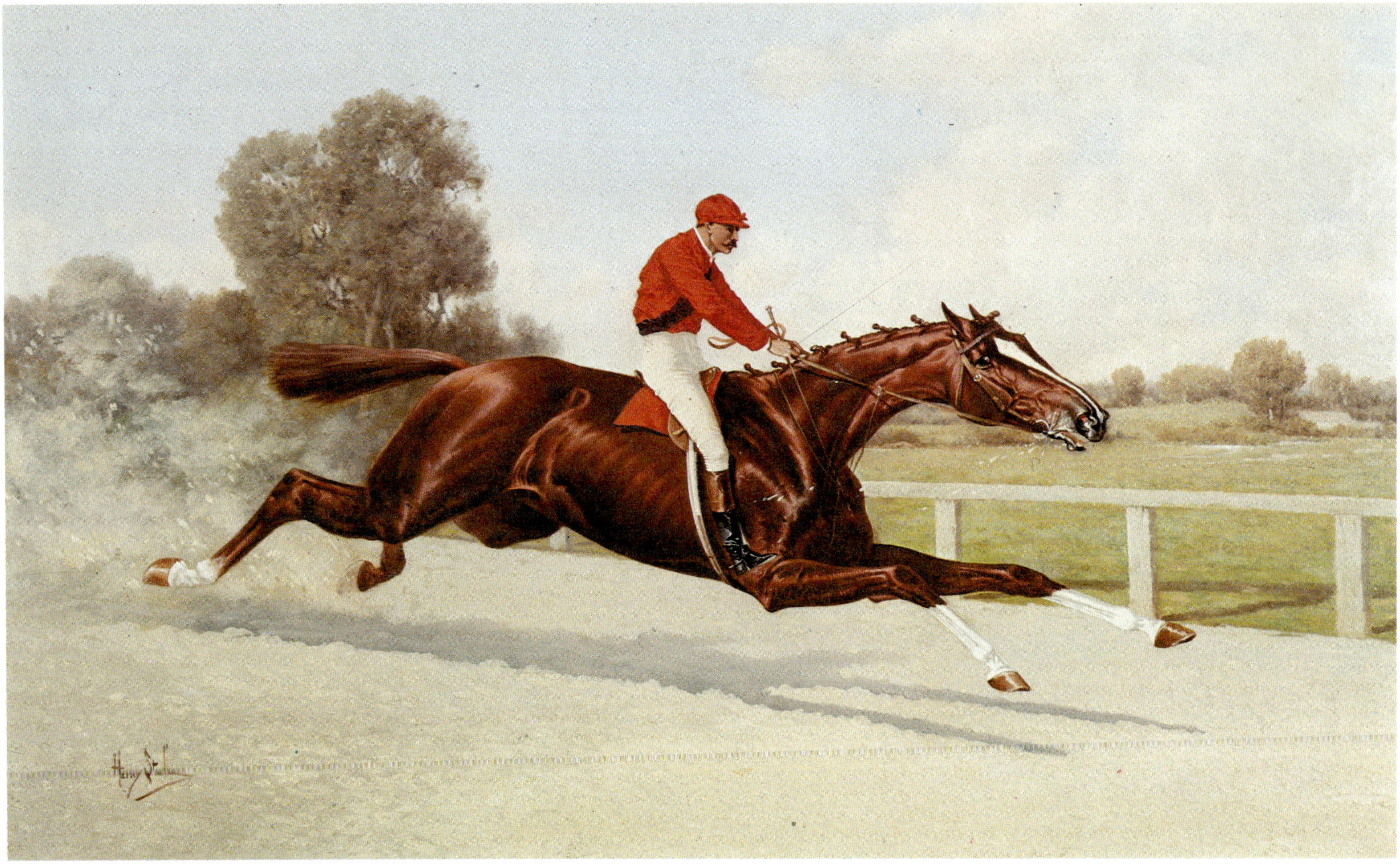

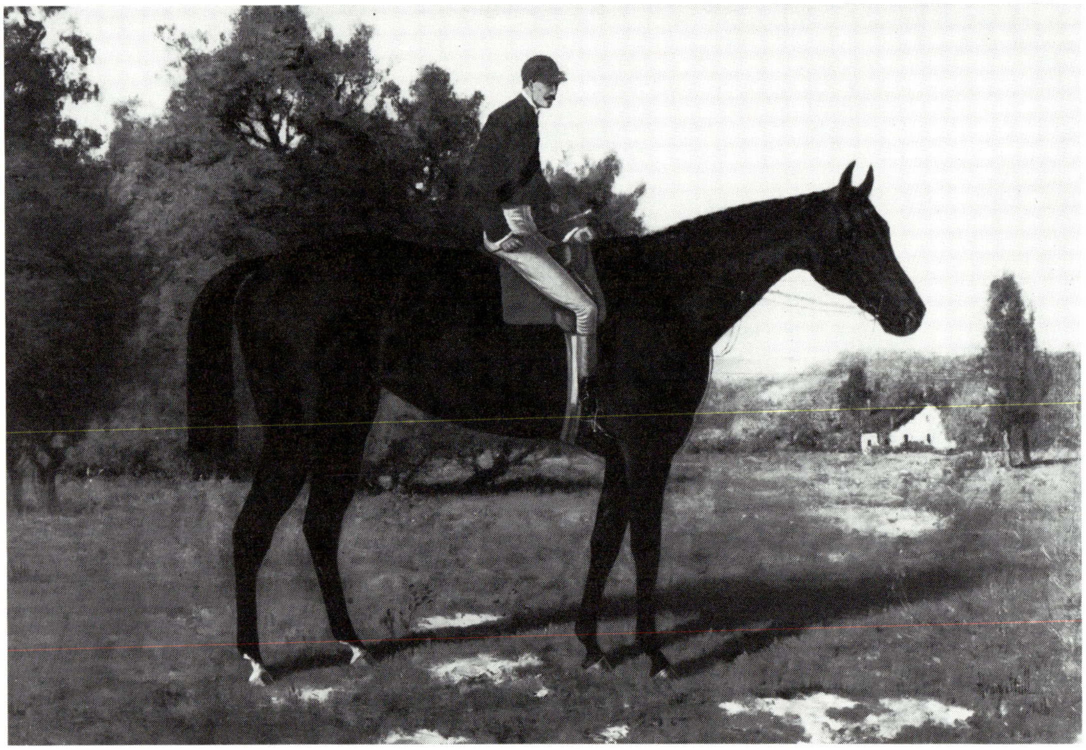

Henry Stull: *Hanover*. 1887. Oil on canvas, 60.3 × 99 cm. National Museum of Racing, Saratoga Springs, NY

Henry Stull: *Miss Woodford*. 1886. Oil on canvas, 45.7 × 70.5 cm. National Museum of Racing, Saratoga Springs, NY

the same distance, and Henry of Navarre won comfortably. Domino clearly was not at his best beyond a mile. He won eighteen races out of nineteen up to a mile, and only one out of six at longer distances. He died just two years after going to stud, leaving only four entire sons. Among these, however, was Commando, who established one of America's leading sire lines, including Colin, Blue Larkspur, and Equipoise.

Stull's amusing picture of Hanover, hurtling along like a steam train, commemorates a horse who had one of the hardest and most successful campaigns on record. As a three-year-old, in 1887, he raced twenty-seven times and won twenty, collecting $87,000. In the month of July, he won five stakes races off the reel. Hanover was one of the trio of tremendous colts from the 1884 crop owned by Phil and Mike Dwyer, the 'Brooklyn butcher boys'. Tremont was the star of the 1886 season and Kingston was bought by them the same year, as they themselves admitted, 'to get him out of Hanover's way'. Kingston went on to race for nine consecutive years, winning 89 races out of 138 contests. Nothing daunted, he then retired to stud and became a noted sire.

The Dwyers also owned Miss Woodford, by Billet, a son of Voltigeur. She was the first American-bred to win $100,000. She notched up one string of sixteen consecutive victories, including a win in the Pimlico Stakes when Iroquois, the English Derby winner, was among those beaten.

# Adrian Jones

*1845–1938*

## Persimmon

The larger-than-life-size statue of Persimmon – the Prince of Wales's great Derby winner of 1896 – which stands before the royal palace of Sandringham in Norfolk, is by a hand now almost forgotten. Yet this same sculptor's work is seen, and, it might be ventured, appreciated, by more people each day than perhaps any other in the world. For his is the great four-horsed Quadriga of Peace which, floodlit at night, gallops across the sky above Hyde Park Corner in London; his, too, the Cavalry Memorial in Hyde Park, and the monument to the Duke of Cambridge which is an ever-present hazard to motorists in Whitehall, London.

When, in 1933, Captain Adrian Jones, MVO, MRCVS, FRBS, set down his memoirs of a turbulent life, he was almost 90 years old and secure enough to recall his battles with 'Sir Frederick Leighton, Sir John Millais, Alma-Tadema, G. F. Leslie and others whose names are hardly remembered today outside their family circle'. Fifty years have had their revenge and Captain Jones's very success has ensured that his work is locked away in the trophy cabinets of the cavalry regiments and consigned to the shadows of the Royal Collection. When his paintings and sculptures do come to the sale-room they are largely ignored. Jones is not a name to conjure with in equestrian art. Yet there is a combination of anatomical precision and dynamism of line in his work which reflects a considerable talent.

Adrian Jones did not take up professional work as an artist until he was past 40. But he was well prepared. A Shropshire man from Ludlow, he had trained as a vet and then joined the army. He had ridden races against the Aga Khan's horses in India in the 1860s, seen the mystic King Theodore emerge on a white pony from the gates of Magdala to face his doom in the Abyssinian War, learnt steeplechasing with the Queen's Bays in Ireland, seen Lord Charles Beresford's armoured boat sail vainly down the Nile to relieve Gordon at Khartoum, and marched with the Inniskilling Dragoons to Pietermaritzburg in the first Boer War of 1881. In all his

Adrian Jones: *Persimmon*. 1905. Bronze, height 293 cm, length 396 cm (not including plinth). Sandringham House, Norfolk

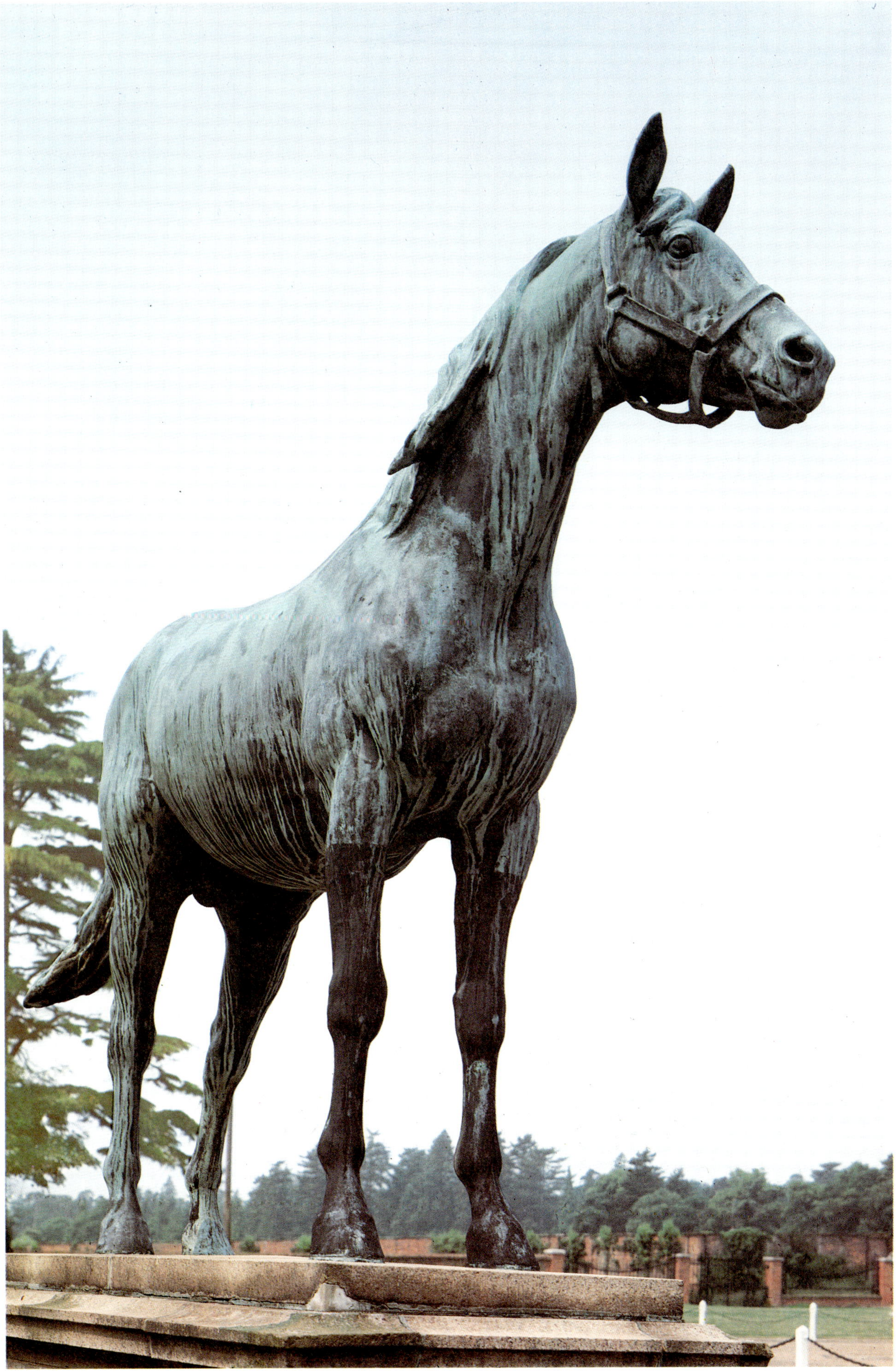

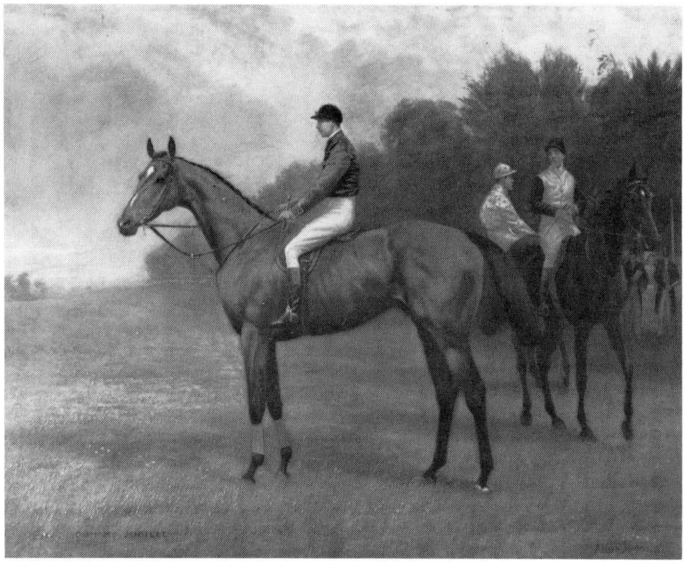

Adrian Jones: *Diamond Jubilee*. 1900. Oil on canvas, 69.8 × 88.9 cm. Royal Collection

work there is the sure mark of a man who has seen horses in all sorts of action and knows their every muscle.

Captain Jones, artist, was soon favoured by the Prince of Wales, who saw his work at a Royal Academy exhibition and commissioned him to paint the 1900 Grand National winner, Ambush II, as well as Diamond Jubilee – who twice put his hind legs through Jones's canvas – and a number of Princess Alexandra's horses. This social success by an untrained artist had aroused enough jealousy at the Royal Academy to land Jones at the centre of a notable scandal in 1893. An inspired article in the *Magazine of Art* accused him of using 'ghosts' more talented than himself to fashion his sculptures; an unjustified but wounding insinuation which he defeated only with the personal assistance of the Prince of Wales, himself just emerged from the imbroglio of the Tranby Croft card-cheating scandal.

The statue of Persimmon was commissioned by the Jockey Club, to be presented to the Prince. Jones had already painted the horse, with Jack Watts up, from sketches made at Newmarket and Epsom, and had then executed a statuette for Princess Alexandra. But the great statue has a special virility, which testifies to the qualities of St Simon's most famous offspring. Persimmon was considered by contemporaries to be almost perfectly made for a racehorse: straight from shoulder to elbow, great depth from the withers, lightish head and neck and not too broad a front, but good loins and quarters. He did not look such a picture as a two-year-old, being still rather ungainly. But that did not stop him giving 35 lb. and a beating to a horse called Rags in his first trial. In his third race as a two-year-old he came up against another St Simon colt, St Frusquin, and was beaten.

Persimmon wintered badly while St Frusquin flourished. The Two Thousand Guineas went to St Frusquin while the royal trainer, Richard Marsh, was hard put to get a gallop into Persimmon. Suddenly, in the last couple of weeks before the Derby, Persimmon started to come to himself. But Marsh's troubles were not over. The royal colt flatly refused to board the train that had been booked to take him to Epsom, lashing out in all directions. Marsh finally called out in despair: 'I'll give a sovereign apiece to those who help get him in.' Half Newmarket appeared in a trice and the horse was literally swept off his feet and carried bodily into the box. Then on Derby morning, Persimmon sweated up alarmingly as he worked on the Downs, and Marsh again thought his chance was gone.

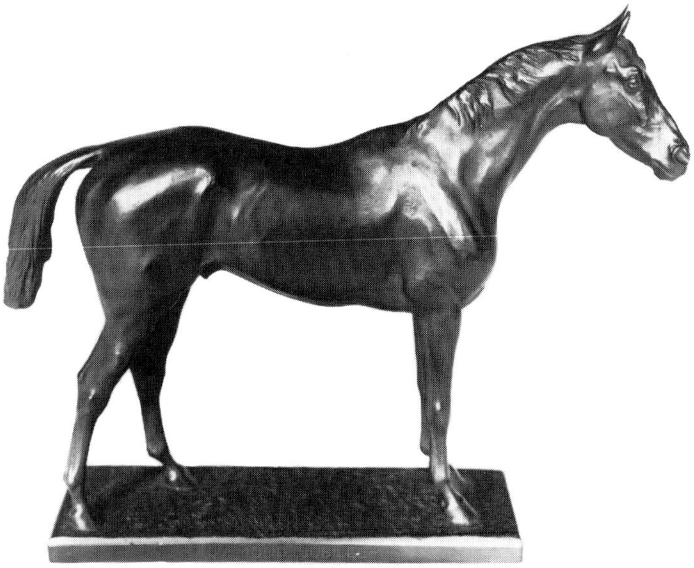

Adrian Jones: *Diamond Jubilee*. 1904. Bronze, height 45.7 cm, length 53.3 cm. Sandringham House, Norfolk

The race itself was a desperate affair. A quarter of a mile out, Watts found himself behind St Frusquin on the rails, with his horse apparently faltering. But Watts picked Persimmon up and half a furlong out the two St Simon colts were abreast. From then on they were locked together with Persimmon finally getting up by a neck. The Prince of Wales came on to the course to lead in his winner to the most tumultuous cheering.

Persimmon never looked back. He won the St Leger and the Jockey Club Stakes and then, as a four-year-old, the Eclipse and the Ascot Gold Cup. In his first season as a sire he produced the incredible filly Sceptre, who won both Guineas races, the Oaks, and the St Leger. She was fourth in the Derby; indeed, Persimmon never did get a Derby winner. He was 16 when he died of a broken pelvis.

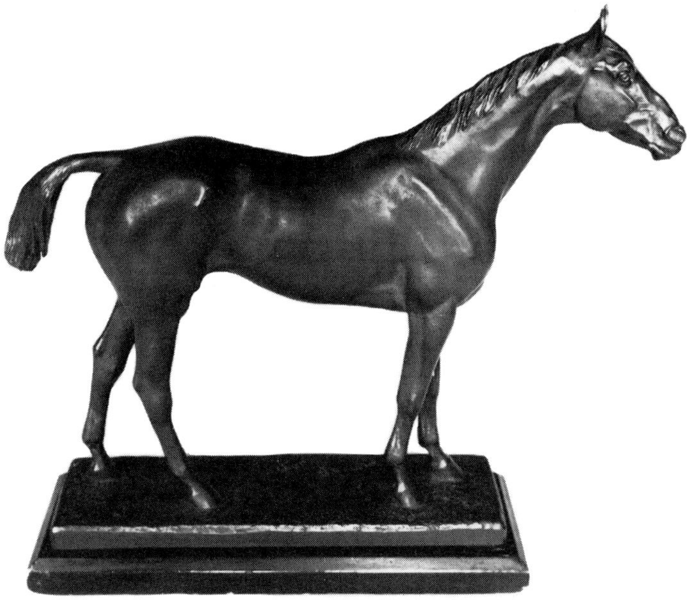

Adrian Jones: *Ambush II*. After 1900. Bronze, height 47 cm, length 53.3 cm. Sandringham House, Norfolk

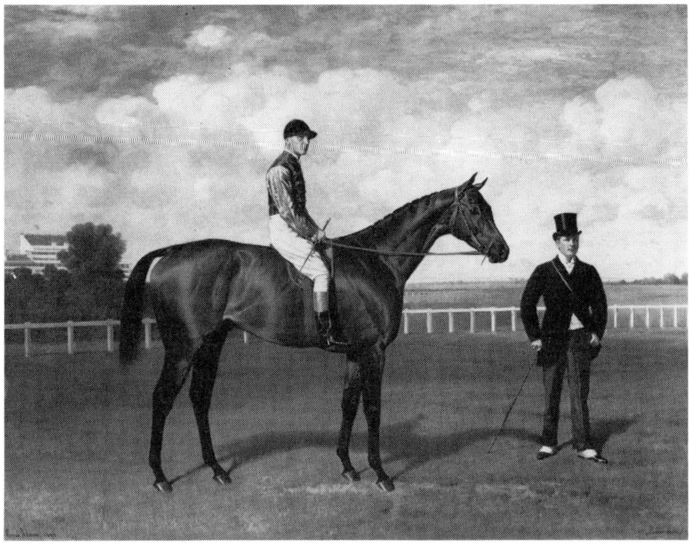

Emil Adam: *Persimmon, with Jack Watts up, and his trainer Richard Marsh*. 1896. Oil on canvas, 104 × 137.1 cm. Jockey Club, Newmarket

# Emil Adam

*1843–1924*

Diamond Jubilee
La Flèche
Ormonde

Diamond Jubilee, named by the Prince of Wales to celebrate Queen Victoria's Jubilee of 1897, was the occasion of more royal festivities than any horse before or since. A dismal failure as a two-year-old, winning only once from six starts, he went on to win the Triple Crown in 1900, taking the Two Thousand Guineas easily, and then the Derby by three-quarters of a length. By the time of the St Leger at Doncaster in the autumn, he was one of the hottest favourites ever, at 7–2 on. He won by a length.

The painting shows Diamond Jubilee in the royal colours with jockey Herbert Jones up. Jones is very definitely still following the old-fashioned riding style, with long stirrup-leathers, despite the fact that the American jockey Tod Sloan had already arrived in England using the crouched, bottom-in-the-air style, which was soon to be universally adopted. Clearly, it was not an instantaneous revolution. Indeed, Sloan was one of those beaten by Herbert Jones in the St Leger; he was third, 3 lengths away, on a horse called Courlan. Jones was given £1,000 by his grateful royal patron, but with the proviso that he should receive only the interest for some years, lest he should spend it all profligately. This helped to keep him in sufficient trim to ride King Edward's third and last Derby winner, Minoru, in 1909.

In 1901, with the Queen dead and the country in mourning, Diamond Jubilee went into a decline. Carrying, as was the custom, the Duke of Devonshire's colours, he could not win any of his four-year-old races and was eventually sold off to Argentina for £30,000.

It is easy to see from Emil Adam's picture why Diamond Jubilee was widely acknowledged to be one of the most perfect horses in conformation, with his strong assertive head, powerful front, and full quarters.

G. D. Giles: *Tommy and Toddy (Tommy Loates and Tod Sloan at Newmarket, 1898)*

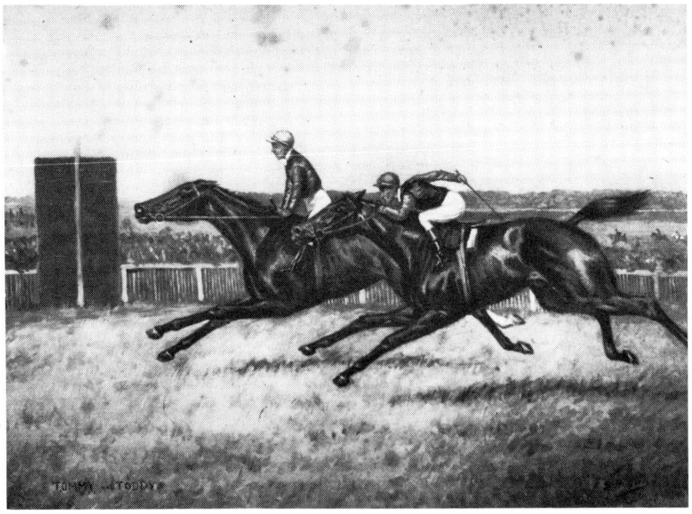

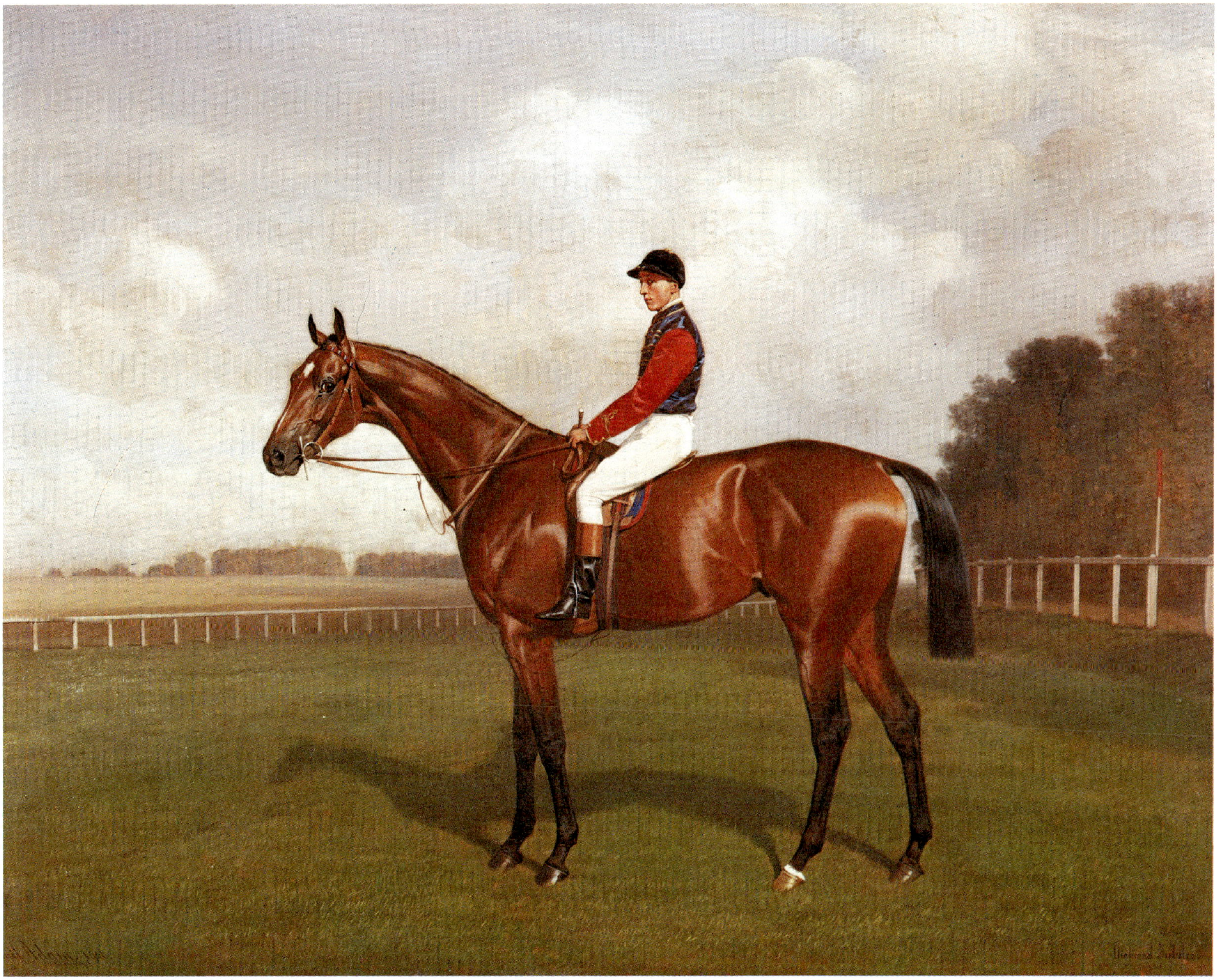

Emil Adam: *Diamond Jubilee, with Herbert Jones up.* 1900. Oil on canvas, 104 × 137.1 cm. Jockey Club, Newmarket

He was the third extraordinary product of the Prince of Wales's policy of sending his mare Perdita II repeatedly back to the stallion St Simon. This produced an Ascot and Goodwood Cup winner in Florizel II, Persimmon, who was the Prince's first Derby and St Leger winner, then Diamond Jubilee.

Emil Adam's grandfather had been court painter to Napoleon's viceroy in Italy, and his father too was an equestrian painter. Emil, born in Munich, lived mainly in Nymphenburgh after his marriage and was patronized throughout the Continent, particularly by the aristocratic families of the Austro-Hungarian Empire. By 1880 he had been attracted to the flourishing racing scene in England, and was already well established when he painted Diamond Jubilee. His patrons appreciated not only his great facility at representing faithfully their favourite horses, but also the care with which his backgrounds, landscapes, and skies were studied. The Duke of Westminster, for whom he had painted the 1886 Derby winner, Ormonde, said: 'Emil Adam is the only artist I know who can really conceive and put on canvas a thoroughbred as it really is.'

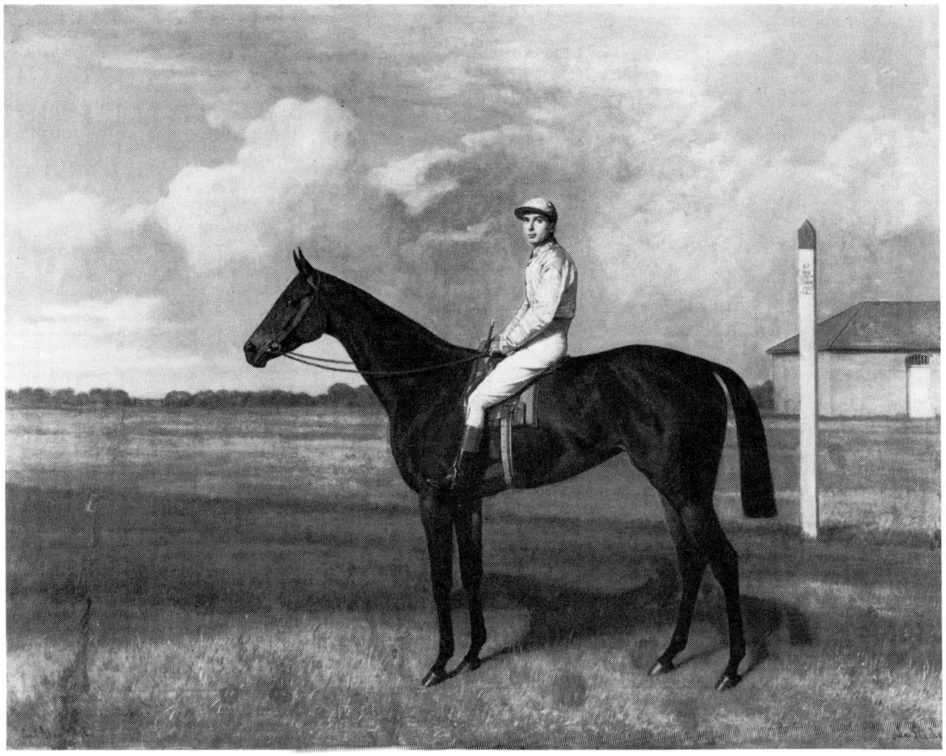

Emil Adam: *La Flèche, with Jack Watts up, at the Cambridgeshire Start, Newmarket*. 1892. Oil on canvas, 104 × 137.1 cm. Jockey Club, Newmarket

The Jockey Club's splendid dining-room in Newmarket is almost entirely an Emil Adam gallery, and his triumphal style, remote, dignified, and luxurious, makes an appropriate background for the members' prandial ruminations. The most affectionate study is of La Flèche at the Cambridgeshire start at Newmarket, a race she won carrying 8 st. 10 lb. Adam has not disguised the high quarters and odd rump of the filly, who was St Simon's best daughter.

La Flèche was a wonderfully fast and tough bay. She had been bred by Queen Victoria, and was sold as a yearling for a purple price, 6,000 guineas. Thereafter, she had more than her share of the vicissitudes of life. She won all her races as a two-year-old, and then took the One Thousand Guineas in easy style. She was a hot favourite for the Derby in 1892, starting at odds-on. The punters in the Epsom stands were astounded to see her thoroughly beaten by Lord Bradford's chestnut, Sir Hugo. Thirty years later, the writer Alexander Scott was still confessing to puzzlement at the outcome.

The explanation seems to lie in the reports, brought back from the far side of the course, of La Flèche's jockey, George Barrett, shouting and waving his arms and berating the other riders all the way to the top turn. La Flèche was almost distanced at Tattenham Corner. Then Barrett got down to his task and brought the filly with a strong but hopeless run, which deceived the great mass of spectators. Barrett was later to suffer from prolonged bouts of insanity. La Flèche was brought out two days later for the Oaks and, patently tired, managed to hang on to win by a short head. In the hands of Jack Watts, she won the St Leger quite easily from Sir Hugo. At 5 years old she was still good enough to win the Champion Stakes and the Ascot Gold Cup.

The following year La Flèche came up for sale at Newmarket, and found herself involved in the shenanigans of the famous Lady 'Satin Tights', the uproarious young wife of Sir Tatton Sykes (the second baronet of that name). Lady Sykes persuaded her friend Lord Marcus Beresford to bid for the mare. The price spiralled rapidly up to the astounding figure of 12,500 guineas and the horse was duly knocked down to Lord Marcus. The animal was then dispatched on the railway up to Yorkshire, simultaneously with a blithe telegram advising Sir Tatton of the consideration required for this new addition to his stud. For a full fortnight, poor La Flèche

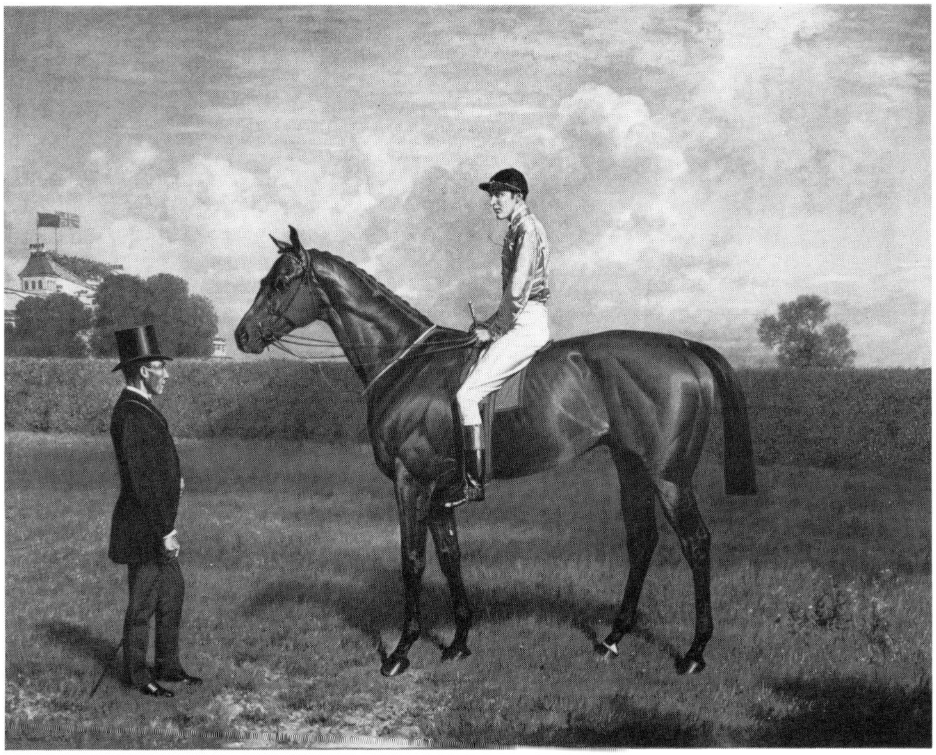

Emil Adam: *Ormonde, with Fred Archer up, and his trainer John Porter.* 1887. Oil on canvas, 101.6 × 127cm. Jockey Club, Newmarket

remained a prisoner in her railway box at Sledmere while the wrathful Sir Tatton swore he would not accept her. The station-master fed her from his own allotment while the marital tussle continued. Finally, she was accepted into Sledmere where she remained until her death in 1916.

But there must have been a dark fury in La Flèche's family. She bred only two good horses: John o' Gaunt, who lost the Derby to St Amant in a thunderstorm, and Craganour, whose luck was pitiful. He lost the Derby on a disqualification in 1913 (see p. 160).

Ormonde, the other great horse who graces the walls of the Jockey Club dining-room, won the Triple Crown in 1886. He was considered in his day the very model of a racehorse, and Emil Adam's picture, renowned for its exactness, emphasizes all those virtues which contemporaries discerned: a long and upright humerus, a short back, wonderful quarters, a deep barrel chest, straight hind legs. For all that, as the picture shows, Ormonde had a plain enough head and a rather short neck.

He was owned by the Duke of Westminster who believed in making full use of his property. Soon after the St Leger, the Duke went down to the stables at Kingsclere and insisted, to his trainer's horror, on taking Ormonde out. 'I want to ride, Mr Porter,' he announced, 'and I am accustomed to having my own way.' The Duke later confided: 'It was the most disagreeable experience I ever went through. When he started in his gallop he put his head down between his knees and I thought I was going to be shot over his head with every stride.' The following year the Duke decided to invite Ormonde to a garden party he was holding in London for the Royal Jubilee. The horse was brought up on the train to Waterloo, then walked across Westminster Bridge and through St James's and Green Park to Grosvenor House, where he was the star attraction, nibbling orchids offered by the ladies.

Ormonde turned out to be a 'roarer' (a horse who is wrong in his wind) and was sold off to Argentina and subsequently to a Californian breeder, William O'Brien Macdonough, for a record $150,000. From Argentina, Macdonough shipped Ormonde back to England to serve some mares he had there, and then onwards to California. The travel-weary animal finally arrived at Macdonough's farm – which was named Ormondale in his honour – virtually sterile. But he did sire the Futurity winner named after the farm. Ormonde died in 1904.

# *Frederick Lutyens*

*1863–1924*

## Minoru

In the subdued splendour of Lutyens's picture, King Edward VII's last great horse adorns a wall of the Jockey Club at Newmarket – a portrait as rich and idolatrous as any in that pantheon of the thoroughbred. Minoru's story is resonant with the melancholy of an age. It is racing's own small memorial of the sadness of things past, of the world that was swept away in the August of 1914. The day Minoru won the Derby is as vivid in the history of England's Golden Age as the relief of Mafeking and the Diamond Jubilee. By the time of his death, Epsom was a barracks and The Curragh a byword for mutiny.

The King had enjoyed little luck on the racecourse in the eight years he had been on the throne, but the arrival of Minoru, leased from Colonel William Hall-Walker of the Tully stud in County Kildare, had sent the royal pulse quickening once again. The King's racing manager was commanded to telegraph daily with the latest details of the colt's progress. The year of 1909 was a good one for the colts. Though Minoru duly won the Two Thousand Guineas, there were at least four others in the Derby, Louviers, Bayardo, Sir Martin, and Valens, who were horses of high quality. Indeed, Sir Martin started favourite. And Bayardo went on to win the St Leger and more than twenty other races, including the Ascot Gold Cup. But on that Wednesday at the end of May, all sentiment was with the royal colt. Minoru was a handsome dark bay, slightly built, and with an easy temperament. He looked very fit, though he had done little work.

The runners broke evenly, but coming down the hill Sir Martin seems to have crossed his legs. There ensued one of those frightening mêlées with which the Derby story is studded. Sir Martin went down. Bayardo had to be snatched up and almost followed him. Louviers and Minoru were left clear, with Louviers having the advantage. But Minoru was being ridden by Herbert Jones, 'that man of iron nerve' as the Duke of Portland called him. A gap opened and Jones forced Minoru through. Louviers was not done with. Twice the lead seemed to change and after they crossed the line locked together there was a great silence as Epsom held its breath. Minoru was judged to have got home by a short head.

As the King went to lead Minoru in through the

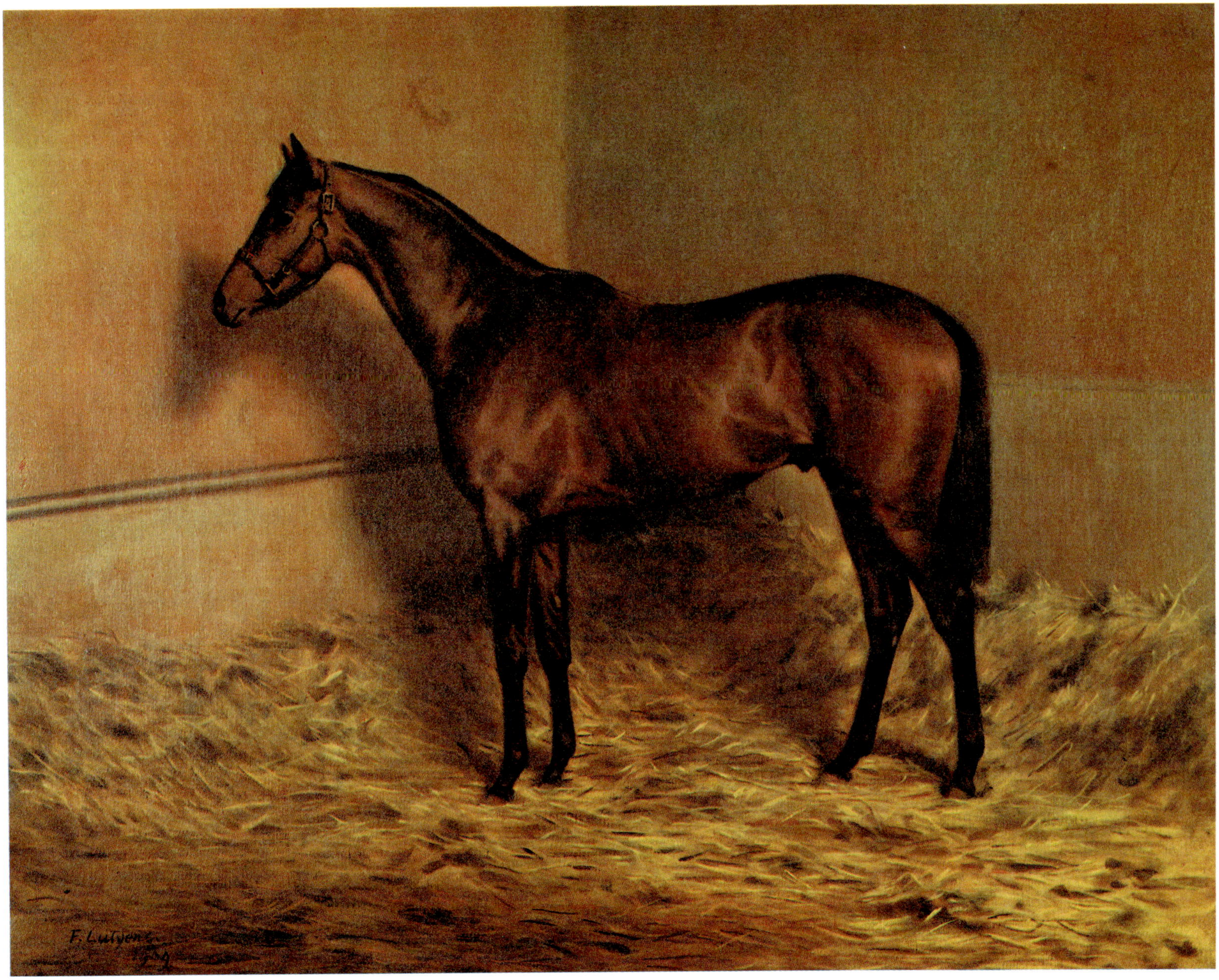


Frederick Lutyens: *Minoru*. 1909. Oil on canvas, 69.2 × 90.1 cm. Jockey Club, Newmarket

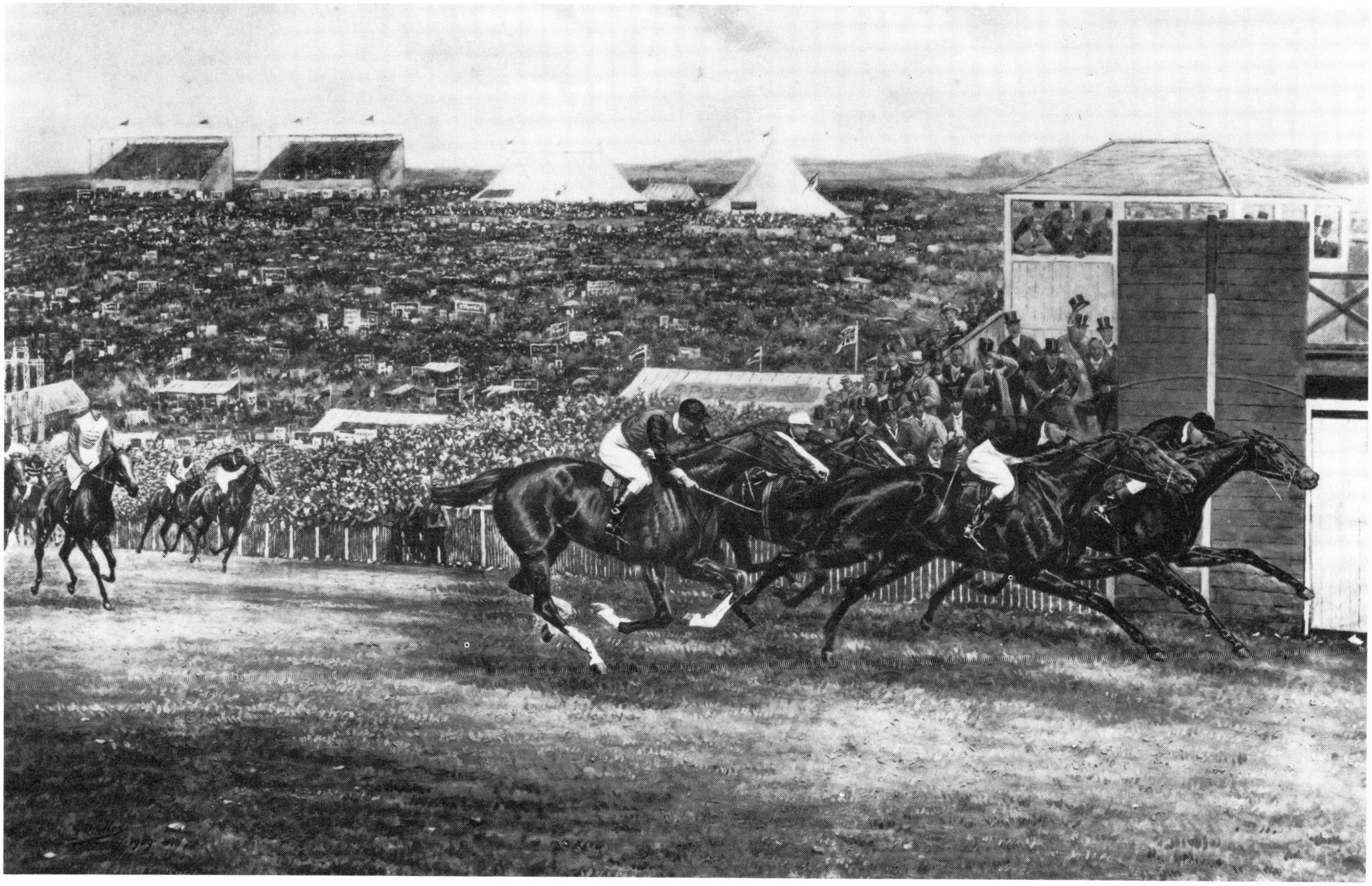

G. D. Giles: *The Finish of the 1909 Derby: Minoru, with Herbert Jones up, beating George Stern on Louviers.* Engraving, 48.2 × 77.4 cm. Jockey Club, Newmarket

surging crowd, a single powerful voice began to sing. Suddenly the whole enormous gathering stood still. As one, they joined in the National Anthem and 'God Save the King' rolled across the Downs in a chorus of emotion. It was the last Derby the King ever saw. That night he went back to host his traditional dinner for the Jockey Club, the table bedecked in the royal colours. Before another Derby came round, the King was dead and those anguished confrontations with Ireland, the suffragettes, Socialism, and, above all, the truculent empires of Europe were already looming.

Poor Minoru was caught up in the great cataclysm. He was allowed only two years at stud before being sold by Colonel Hall-Walker to the Russians. As the boat took him away to St Petersburg, his stock was low. The subsequent exploits of Bayardo and the mishap to St Martin had led the fancy to talk away the merits of the Derby winner. Yet his brief sojourn at stud was to produce the famous mare Serenissima, and through her the St Leger winner Tranquil, and ultimately Hyperion.

Minoru arrived in a Russia already seething. Within

two years there was war. In another three, revolution. In 1919, with Britain backing the White Russians against the Bolsheviks, a British sailor turned up with the White forces. He was leading two stallions and telling a strange tale. The two horses, he said, were Minoru and Aboyeur, winner of the 1913 Derby. Trapped in the revolutionary chaos, the sailor claimed he had harnessed them to a cart and driven 800 miles across Russia. From there, it is said, they were sent to Serbia. But times were too turbulent for men to know or care about bloodstock. Minoru finally disappeared from the pages of racing history. Yet who knows what descendants of Minoru may today be pulling the racing troikas round the packed snow circuit of the Moscow Hippodrome?

Frederick Mansfield Lutyens was one of the fourteen children of the splendid Victorian traveller, eccentric, and artist Charles Augustus Henry Lutyens (1829–1915). Frederick was for a time the tutor to his younger brother Edwin, later famous as the architect Sir Edwin Lutyens. Both boys were taught to draw by their father; they were made to view subjects through a piece of glass and outline them in crayon. Frederick seems to have been able to make a living as an artist entirely from commissions. Only two of his works are recorded in major exhibitions, both of them domestic scenes.

Most of his work for private patrons came from the military officers and friends who also bought his father's pictures, and there seems little doubt that he came to paint Minoru through family connections with the royal household. Edwin was already planning the new Delhi and Charles had painted Persimmon for King Edward in 1904, as well as producing a study of the King's shooting pony Iron Duke. In recent years, Frederick's pictures of Gadfly, a charger, and Filbert, a chestnut mare, were shown at an exhibition in Eastbourne, Sussex.

# A. G. Haigh

*1870–1963*

The Tetrarch
Bahram

By the time of Royal Ascot in the summer of 1913, English racing was in sore need of a lift to the spirits. For it had been as dark a season as any in the history of the English Turf.

There had been bitter words when Bowen Ismay's colt Craganour was adjudged to have lost the Two Thousand Guineas to Louvois, though the whole of Newmarket thought otherwise. More recriminations when his rider W. Saxby was 'jocked off' and John Reiff brought over from France to ride the favourite in the Derby. Then the tragic moment when Emily Davison dashed out in front of the field at Tattenham Corner to die in the suffragette cause. Finally, the sulphurous emotions unleashed when the Epsom stewards took it upon themselves to object to Craganour and then deprived him of the Derby victory in favour of the 100–1 outsider Aboyeur. Ismay, though a wealthy man – his family owned the White Star Line and had seen their *Titanic* go down the previous year – was not a member of the Jockey Club. His trainer, Jack Robinson, was an unfashionable hunter after handicaps. Motives had been impugned. Craganour, like some wounded albatross, was sold off to Argentina. It was time for the gods to relent.

So it was that the crowds at Ascot, waiting for the start of the Coventry Stakes in June of 1913, were granted perhaps the most astonishing vision ever seen on an English racecourse. Over the brow of the hill on the old course, quite alone, came a strange grey horse with great white spots. Many in the crowd assumed there had been a false start. But there was no mistake. They were seeing The Tetrarch – perhaps the fastest horse who ever ran.

It is hard now, when greys are quite common – indeed one holds the Epsom Derby record – to understand how unusual the 'Spotted Wonder' must have appeared. It was as though a gypsy-coloured horse had entered the paddock at Ascot. The Tetrarch was the result of a deliberate decision by the Irish breeder 'Cub' Kennedy to reintroduce the blood of Herod, which had wellnigh vanished from Britain, to be cherished only in France. He sent his mare Vahren to be served by Roi Hérode. The freakish-looking offspring of this mating, high and heavily quartered, with egg-shaped splotches of white all over his grey coat, was sold at Doncaster for 1,300 guineas to trainer Atty Persse. He had seen the yearling bouncing around the paddock at the Straffan Station stud.

As the winter of 1912–13 ended, Atty Persse could hardly believe what he was seeing on the home gallops at Stockbridge. The grey was leaving all his other horses for dead. Early in April, Persse decided to try him over 5 furlongs at level weights with one of his reliable handicappers, Captain Symons. The trial book reads: 'Won

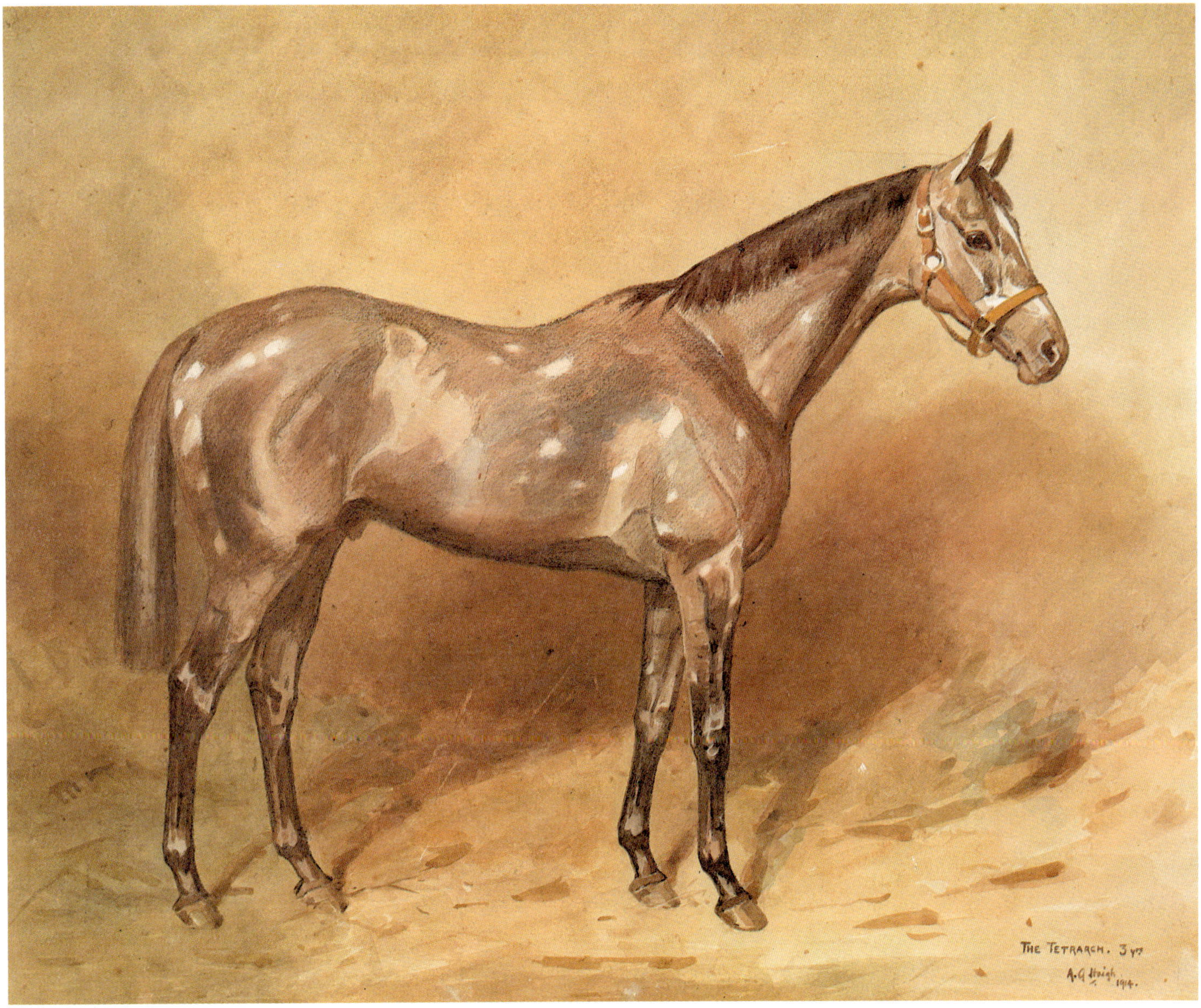


A. G. Haigh: *The Tetrarch*. 1914. Watercolour, 47.6 × 58.4 cm. National Horseracing Museum, Newmarket

pulling up in a canter.' A week later, Persse tried him again, this time giving Captain Symons a stone, and another promising two-year-old, Land of Song, a stone and a half. Again the verdict: 'Won in a canter.'

Persse's stable security was good enough for The Tetrarch to start at 9–2 for the Maiden Plate at the Newmarket Craven meeting. He lobbed home in what was to become a familiar unhurried style. At Epsom he won the Woodcote Stakes. There were still some sceptics. But then came the obliteration of the best of his generation at Ascot in the Coventry Stakes. A lone grey horse in any field seduces the eye. If he bursts towards the front the impression can be as lyrical as *Mazeppa*. Many of those who were at Ascot that day and wrote of it later, sometimes twenty or thirty years on, retained an image of prodigious speed beyond all comparison. Journalist Sidney Galtrey wrote: 'He came as something entirely new into my racing life, something to give colour to the sober tones of the conventional, something always to remember because he has never had an equal.' There was a special piquancy in such recollection, for The Tetrarch's career was to end before that season was out.

There was a heart-stopping moment at Sandown when another horse jumped right across him at the start and his jockey, Steve Donoghue, found himself many lengths down before he could get The Tetrarch under

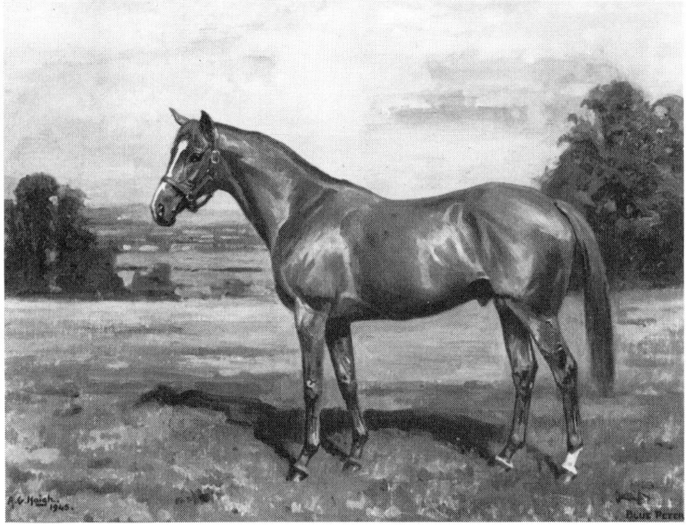

A. G. Haigh: *Blue Peter*. 1945. Oil on canvas, 54.6 × 74.3 cm. Jockey Club, Newmarket

way. For perhaps the only time in his life he really had to gallop, and he got up to win. The Tetrarch had six victories to his credit by the time he came to Doncaster to canter over the field and retain his unbeaten record in the Champagne Stakes. At the end of the season he was rated at 9 st. 10 lb. in the Free Handicap, 10 lb. clear of any other two-year-old. The Champagne was the last race of his life. He developed a habit of overreaching and rapping his off foreleg. He was 'pin-fired' to try and heal the damaged leg, but was not considered ready for the Two Thousand Guineas. Then just before the Derby he rapped himself again. He was retired to stud.

A. G. Haigh: *Bahram, with his jockey Freddy Fox and trainer Frank Butters*. 1935. Oil on canvas, 104 × 135.2 cm. Jockey Club, Newmarket

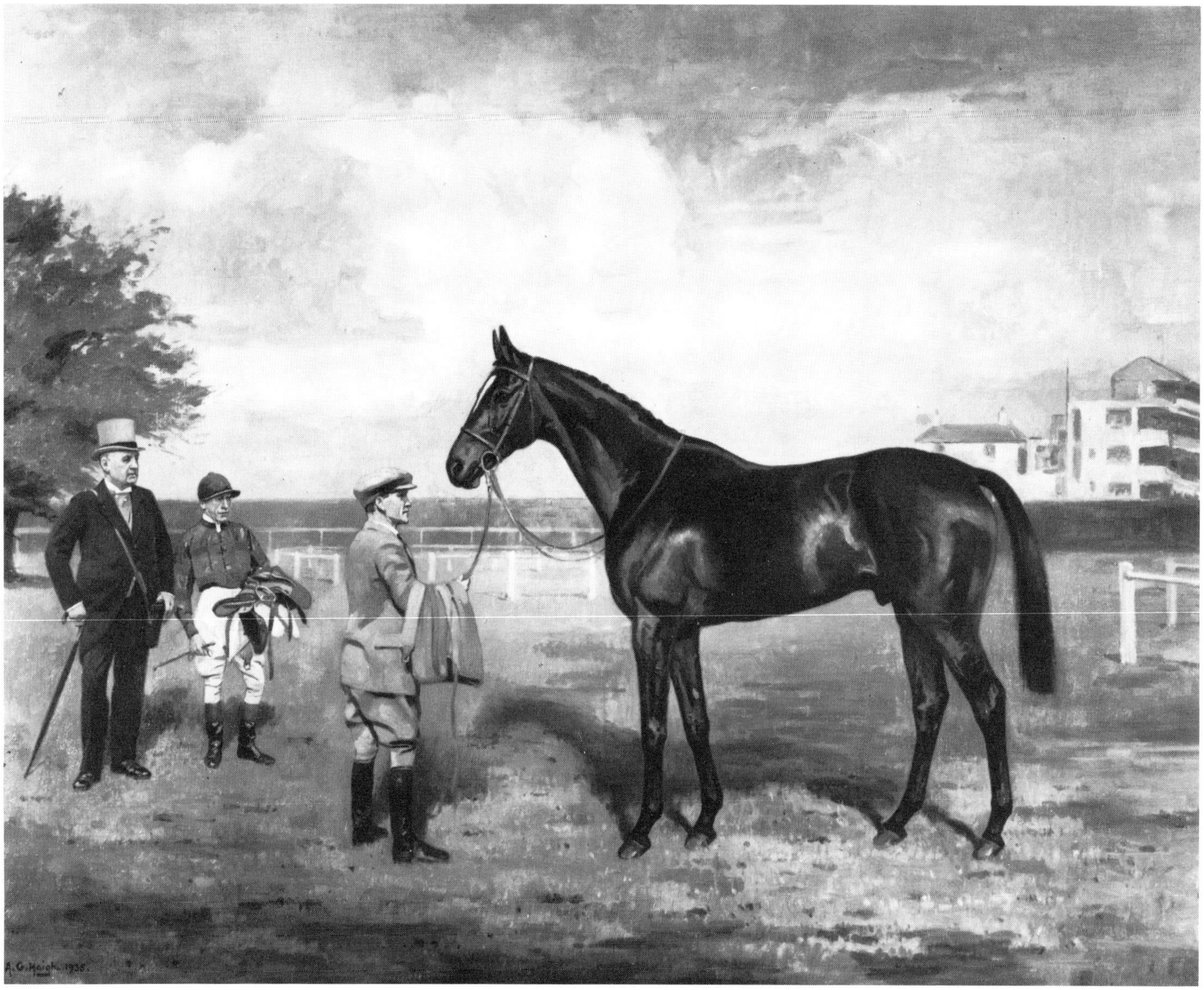

Amazingly, for such a fast horse, he straightway sired three stayers: the St Leger winners Caligula (1920), Polemarch (1921), and Salmon Trout (1924). In between came another grey wonder, his daughter Mumtaz Mahal, the 'Flying Filly', who dominated the two-year-olds of 1923 almost as completely as her parent had a decade before. And Mumtaz Mahal's daughter Mah Mahal bred Mahmoud, another flashing grey, who won the Derby of 1936 in what is still the record time.

Alfred Haigh was a painter whose straightforward and affectionate style kept him busy throughout an era when horse portraiture was seldom rewarding. He was still working in the 1950s when he was past 80 years old. Almost all his work seems to have been commissioned and remains in private collections. Born in Liverpool in 1870, he moved to Newmarket at the turn of the century and soon established a livelihood, becoming friendly with a number of trainers. He left Newmarket in 1907 for a working tour of India. On his return, he settled first in the Beaufort Hunt country in Gloucestershire, then later in Oxfordshire. He made two painting trips to the United States in the 1920s, via introductions to the Essex Hunt in Peapack, New Jersey.

His son Daniel Haigh recalls that his father absolutely refused to hold exhibitions and had an aversion to publicity. He explains that his father's businesslike method of working was first to sketch a plan of each picture and have it approved by the client. Then he would make three separate studies on quite a large scale, say 20 × 16 in., first of the horse itself in oil, then the people in oil or pencil, and finally the backgrounds in oil or watercolour. All were then combined in the final work.

Besides The Tetrarch, he certainly painted Dante, Airborne, Sunstar, Ocean Swell, Midday Sun, Serjeant Murphy, Manna, Music Hall, Verdict, Diomedes, Shaun Goilin, and Blue Peter, winner of the Two Thousand Guineas and the Derby in 1939. Haigh's picture of Bahram, the Aga Khan's Triple Crown winner of 1935, now hangs in the Jockey Club rooms at Newmarket. It is a lively study with stable-lad, trainer, and jockey all included against the Epsom background.

Bahram's career epitomized those practices which were to arouse such hostility against the Aga Khan. Bahram was unbeaten in nine races and had never been seriously tested when he won for the last time in the St Leger. His owner immediately retired him to stud, an action which in its day was regarded as lamentably commercial and unsporting, but set a trend which has continued to this day, whereby successful three-year-olds are removed to stud before they are within sight of maturity. Then, as war closed in on England in 1940, Bahram was bundled off to the United States along with Mahmoud and other notable stock from the Aga Khan's stud – a move which is often taken to mark the decisive shift of dominance in the bloodstock world from England to America.

As it turned out, unlike Mahmoud, Bahram was not a success at stud in the United States, and by 1946 he was shipped off to that gulag for failed or disgraced race-horses, Argentina. Only recently have breeders, especially in the United States, started to realize what a reservoir of high-quality sire lines are still running around the pampas of South America, and begun the process of acquiring them back.

# *Franklin Voss*

*1881–1953*

Man o' War
Sir Barton
Equipoise

August Belmont II made a greater sacrifice than he knew when, at the age of 65, he volunteered to aid the United States Expeditionary Force setting out for the battlefields of France during the First World War. In order to concentrate on his job as a supply officer, he decided to sell off all the foals from the 1917 crop at the famous Nursery stud. Among those foals was Man o' War, destined to be one of the greatest stars of the American Turf.

Franklin B. Voss's picture, with jockey Clarence Kummer up, captures the calm and assured power of the chestnut that his groom Will Harburt called 'de mostest hoss dat ever was'. Certainly Samuel D. Riddle struck the bargain of a lifetime when he bought Man o' War for $5,000. Four years later, Riddle really was handed a blank cheque by Texas cattle-baron William T. Waggoner and told to fill in whatever sum he wanted for Man o' War. But 'Big Red' was not for sale, despite other offers of $1 million.

Man o' War was beaten once as a two-year-old at Saratoga by Upset. Thereafter, he was invincible. In the season of 1920, with the men home from the war and the gambling 'blackout' virtually over, Man o' War electrified the crowds who came flocking back to the tracks. He broke five American records at distances from 1 mile to 1⅝ miles, and he had two superb encounters with another brilliant colt named John P. Grier.

When Man o' War came out for the first clash with Grier at Aqueduct, there were some doubts whether his trainer, Louis Feustel, had him fully fit. He was giving 18 lb. When they came to the mile post the two horses were neck and neck and it seemed Man o' War might go under, but one smack from jockey Kummer was enough to get his head in front and John P. Grier was finished. Man o' War won by 2 lengths. Then, in the Travers Stakes, he defeated Grier again. Man o' War was huge in height, stride, chest, and, above all, in personality. The crowds who saw him in that summer of 1920 constructed a legend around him that has lasted sixty years and more. Children's model horses and collectors' porcelain stallions are still cast in his image, as though no other horse has left footprints in the dirt.

Man o' War went to stud at the unprecedented fee of

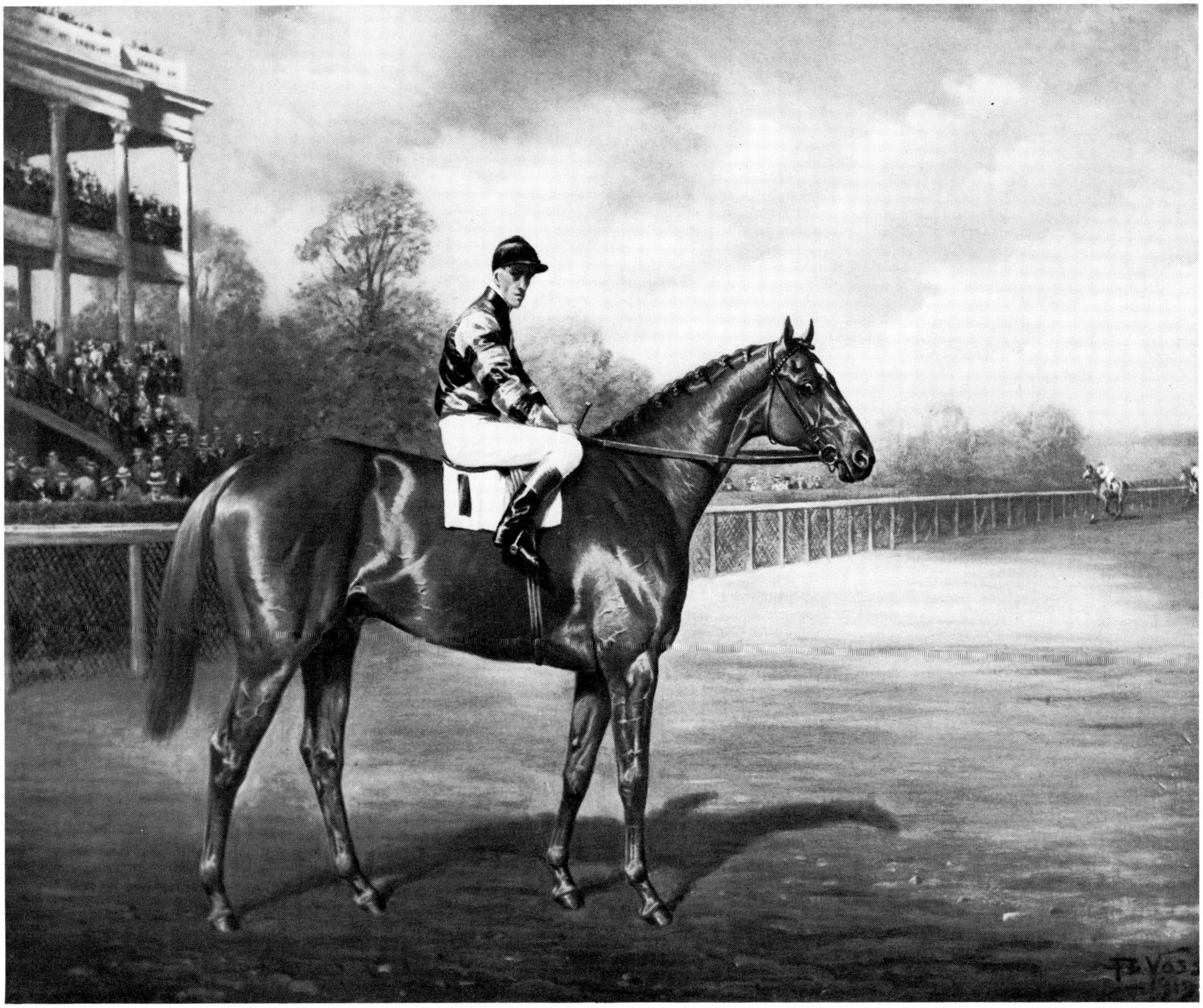

Franklin Voss: *Man o' War, with Clarence Kummer up*. 1919. Oil on canvas, 71.1 × 94.6 cm. National Museum of Racing, Saratoga Springs, NY

$5,000 per service and sired 64 stakes winners, including the American Triple Crown winner War Admiral, as well as Battleship, the extraordinary little horse who won the English Grand National in 1938. Standing at the Riddles' Faraway Farm, he lived to be 30 years old.

Man o' War's last race had been at Kenilworth Park in Canada in a match for $80,000 against Sir Barton, the Kentucky Derby winner of 1919 who had also taken the Belmont and Preakness. He belonged to the railroad heir Commander James K. L. Ross, and had won his previous four races before the Canadian show-down. As frequently happens in match racing, the contest was a

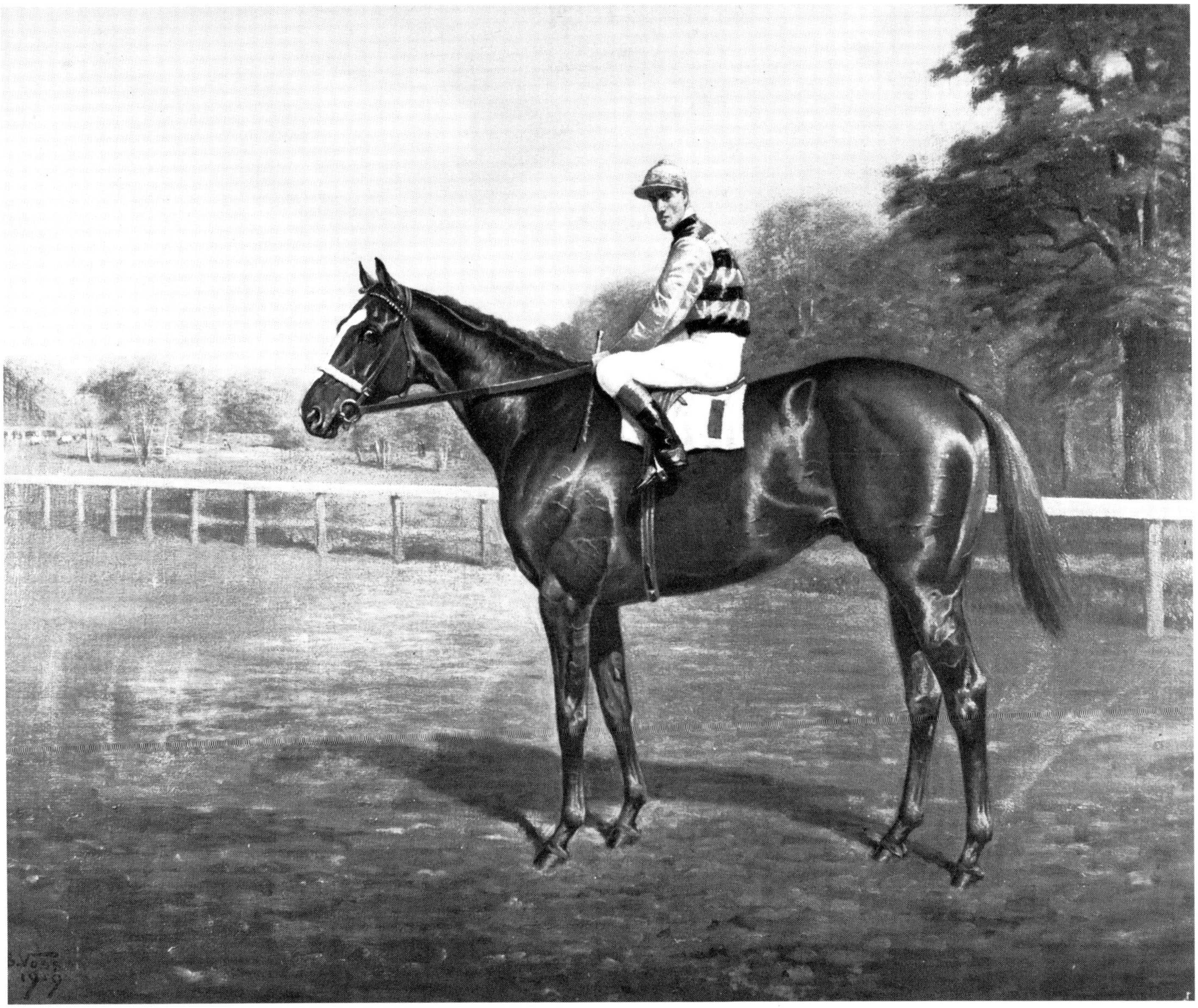

Franklin Voss: *Sir Barton, with John Loftus up*. 1919. Oil on canvas, 63.5 × 93.9 cm. National Museum of Racing, Saratoga Springs, NY

failure, with Sir Barton completely crumbling, though there were those who said, afterwards, that he had gone over the top. Indeed, he never won another race and was retired to stud.

Franklin B. Voss belonged to the Maryland gentry. His parents had moved down from New York and the family were brought up among the foxhunting clubs around Baltimore. Voss was to become the outstanding painter of that rare and elevated world, in which he himself participated until the day of his death. He fell from the saddle while out with the Elkridge-Harford Hunt in 1953, at the age of 72, and was dead when the first of his companions reached his side. He had hunted in England with the Duke of Beaufort and had become, in effect, private artist to the Whitneys, the Riddles, and the Vanderbilts in Maryland. Voss was no amateur, however. He had spent seven years in New York studying at the Art Students' League and the number of his known commissions stretches past the 500 mark. He had himself been a steeplechase rider and he was a friend of Alfred Munnings.

Voss painted the picture of Equipoise, the 'Chocolate Soldier', for the Whitneys. The dark chestnut stallion is set, for contrast, against the light colours of a pinto in the background, the scene radiating the summer warmth of the lovely white-railed paddocks which corral the city of Baltimore to this day. This is the country which rivalled Virginia and Kentucky in the development of the American thoroughbred. Equipoise was a true inheritor of the tradition. Tough and fast, he had Commando and Domino in his pedigree, and, despite losing most of his three-year-old season through injury, earned $338,000 in the lean years of the Depression. He broke the world record for the mile at Chicago's Arlington track.

Equipoise was Harry Payne Whitney's last great horse, and his owner died only days before Equipoise settled a family argument by beating Mrs Payne Whitney's Twenty Grand in the Pimlico Futurity in November 1930. As a four-year-old and a five-year-old, Equipoise won his first seven races each time. His story was written into a film, *Three Men on a Horse* of 1936, after he was disqualified, to the intense fury of the crowd, in the Metropolitan Handicap. He was the leading sire in America in 1942, and produced the Kentucky Derby winner Shut Out.

---

Franklin Voss: *Equipoise*. 1933. Oil on canvas, 91.4 × 106.6 cm. National Museum of Racing, Saratoga Springs, NY

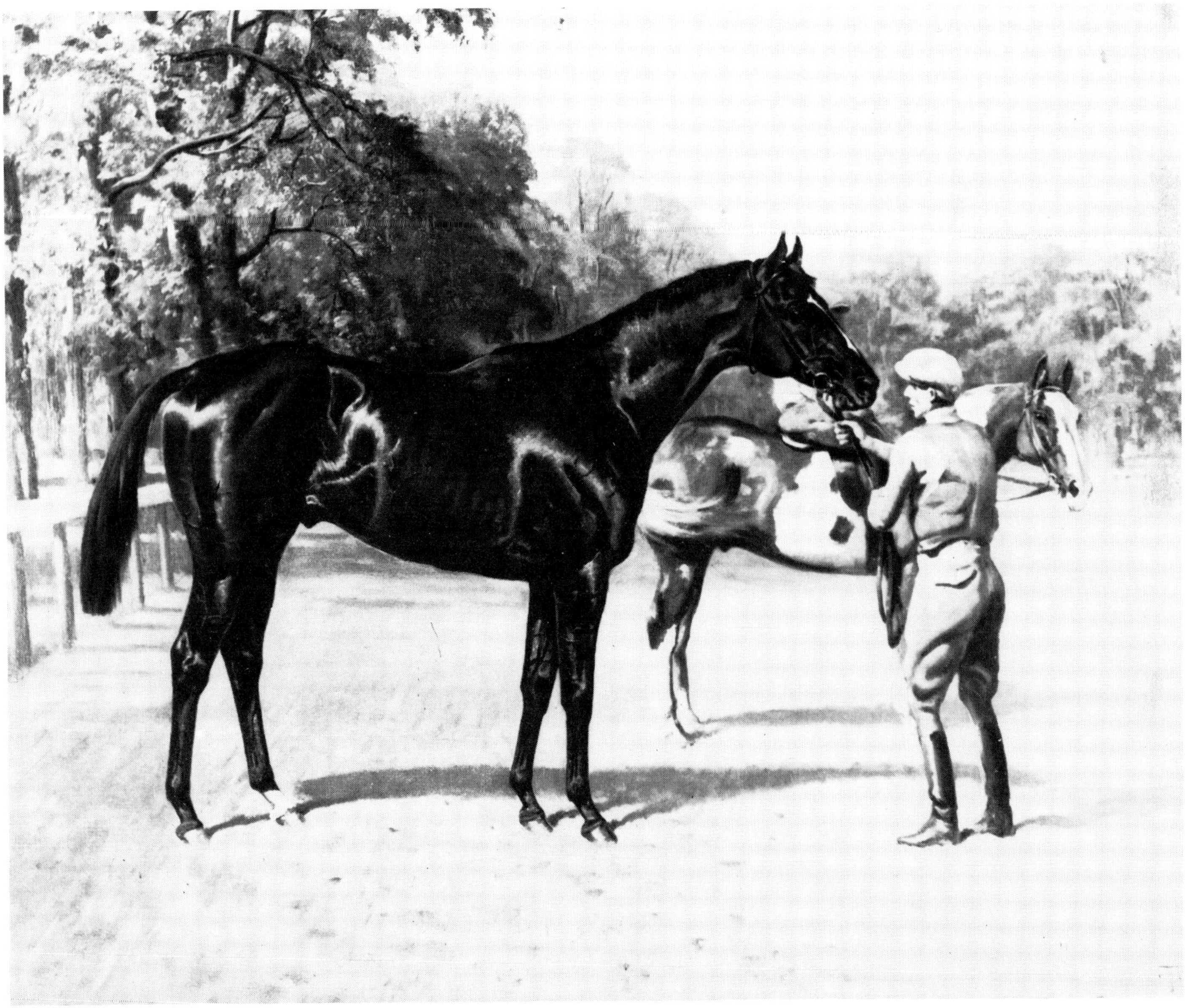

# *John Skeaping*

*1901–1980*

Hyperion
Brigadier Gerard

John Skeaping's life-size bronze of little Hyperion stands before a reredos of cypresses in a private shrine at Lord Derby's stud in Newmarket. The statue ripples with the arrogance for which Hyperion was famous. He was a national hero in England during the Depression of the 1930s. And forty years on, he was still remembered with affection by some unknown sentimentalist who came out and rugged up his effigy on a cold night. Next to Nearco, he has probably been, in England, the most influential stallion of modern times.

The two portly figures who dominated English racing between the wars, the Aga Khan and Lord Derby, both had contenders for the 1933 Classics, Felicitation and Hyperion. But it was a difficult time for Lord Derby. Immersed in the report on Indian policy which was to be published the following year, he was faced also with a crisis at his stables. The Hon. George Lambton, his trainer for forty years, had withdrawn once again into the illness and depression which had afflicted him periodically since a racing fall at Sandown in 1892. It was to lead to the two men parting company, with some bitterness, before the year was out. Hyperion was left, it seems, almost entirely in the care of the stable jockey, Tommy Weston. The horse had had an erratic two-year-old career, and even a thundering victory in bottomless mud for the Dewhurst Stakes was not enough to convince Mr Lambton of his merits.

Hyperion's 1933 campaign began with the Chester Vase, a contest in which he was displaying little interest until, for the first time in his life, and to the horse's evident astonishment, Weston clouted him. That one blow sufficed to wake him up not only for the Vase, which he won, but for the entire season. From that day on Weston plotted his Derby strategy, riding Hyperion in almost all his work, taking a hand in his training programme, and urging his merits on the Earl. Two days before the race, Lord Derby met Steve Donoghue at a press lunch, found he was without a ride at Epsom, and promptly hired him to set a pace for Hyperion on Thrapston.

The race went entirely according to plan. Donoghue sent Thrapston at a cracking gallop to Tattenham Corner. On cue, Weston and Hyperion took over to leave the rest of the field for dead down the entire length of the Epsom straight. Felicitation, who was later to defeat Hyperion in the 1934 Ascot Gold Cup, and Manitoba, who had defeated him as a two-year-old, were both among those beaten. Weston's greatest exertion came beyond the winning-post when it seemed he might find it impossible to stop his tearaway mount. Eventually, he hauled in enough reefs to turn him round and bring him back for Lord Derby to lead in before one of Epsom's largest-ever crowds.

An attack of colic on the way to Doncaster threat-

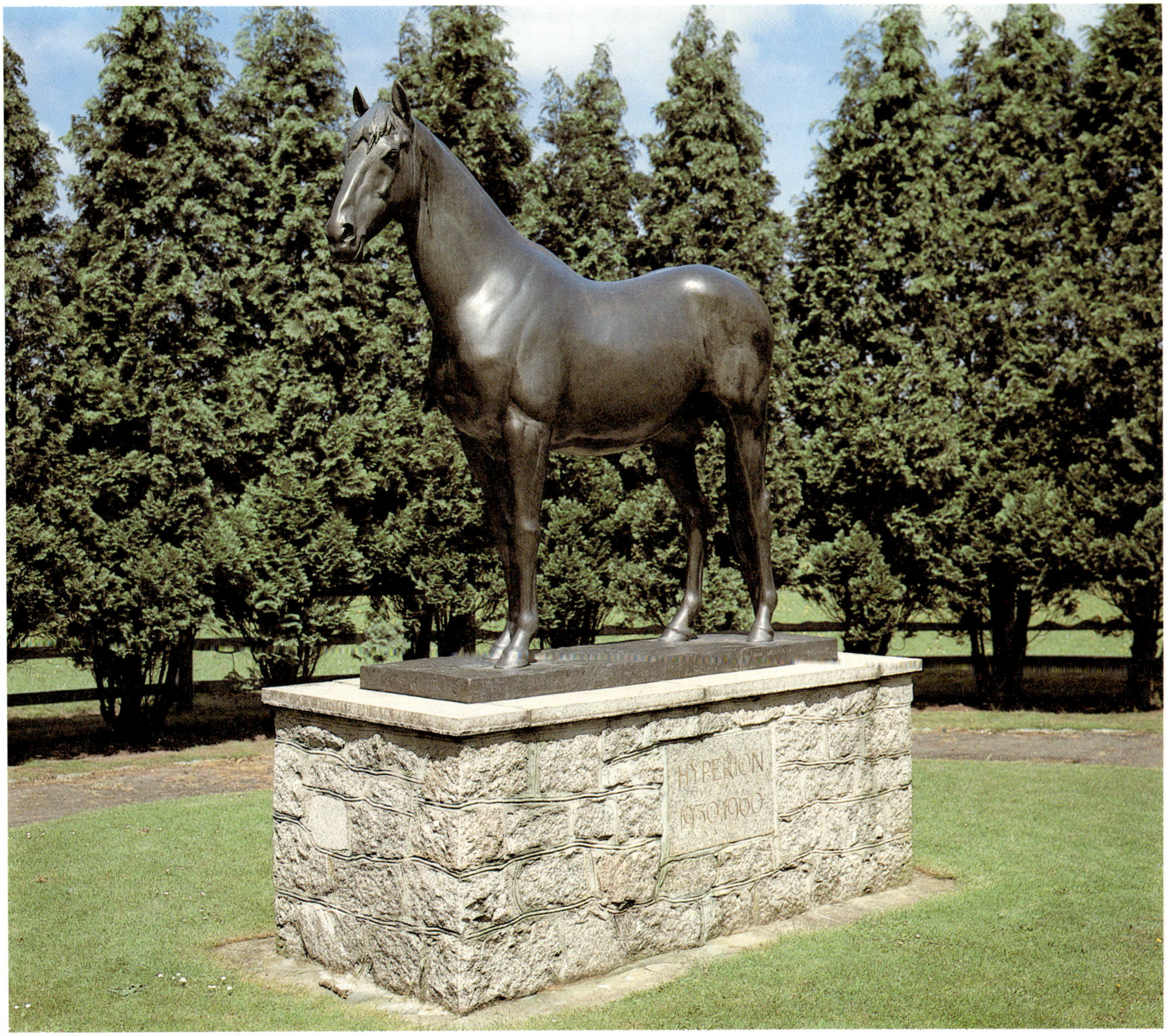


John Skeaping: *Hyperion*. 1961. Bronze, height 213 cm, length 236 cm (not including plinth). Stanley House, Newmarket

ened Hyperion's chances in the St Leger. But the head lad stopped the box and walked his charge round a field for half an hour. Then the blacksmith pricked a foot as the plates went on. But Hyperion was undeterred. Weston jumped him off and took the lead almost from the start. The Yorkshire crowd were treated to that rarest of sights: a champion winning the final Classic of the season and making almost every yard of the running for 14 furlongs. Felicitation was second.

Hyperion was a flaming chestnut, though both his sire Gainsborough and his dam Selene were bays. He was hardly 15 hands 1 inch when he won the Derby, and his four white feet made him seem even smaller. He retired to the Woodlands stud at Newmarket, and by 1941 had produced a Derby winner in Owen Tudor. Sun Chariot, his daughter, won the fillies' Triple Crown, and it is principally through the female line that he achieved his greatest successes at stud.

John Skeaping was not invited to sculpt Hyperion until after the horse's death in 1960. It was to be his first attempt at a life-size equine statue, and he was determined it should be accurate. First, he borrowed Hyperion's bones from the tank of chemicals at the Equine

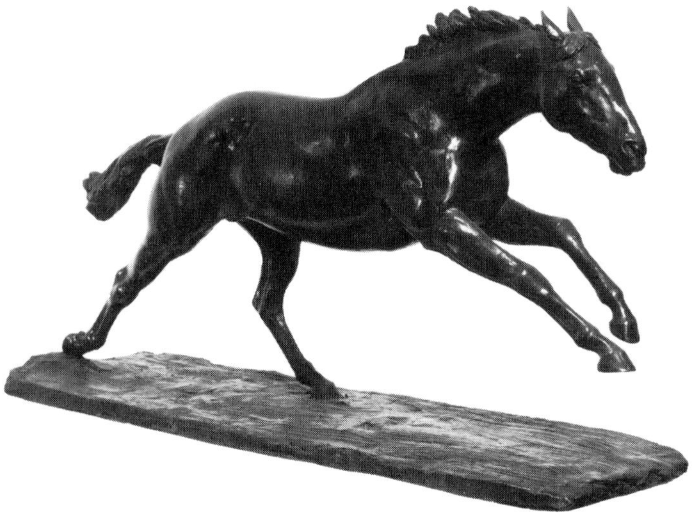

John Skeaping: *Secretariat at Full Stretch*. 1974. Bronze, height 22.9 cm, length 44.5 cm. Private collection

Research Station where they were being preserved, and had them delivered to his studio in Devon. Setting them up, he noticed that a bone behind the ear had at some time been fractured; the horse must have been stone deaf on one side ever after. Then Skeaping collected photographs, paintings, reminiscences from connections, and borrowed a living Hyperion look-alike. The first version collapsed in a heap of clay on the studio floor. Finally, after a year's work, the bronze was installed in Ozymandian grandeur beside the Snailwell Road in Newmarket, where, Skeaping was told, passing horses would whinny at it and mares in the adjoining paddock come up to make their overtures.

Although the statue of Hyperion and a number of Skeaping's other portraits in bronze have a classical precision, worthy of the hippodromes of ancient times, he also had a wonderful flair for the stirring evocation of horses in action. The smaller bronze of Secretariat pulsates with power, and the study *Hanging to the Left*, of the 1974 Travers finish in the United States when Holding Pattern beat Little Current, is incomparable. He was also a distinguished painter, and his action pictures, especially the gouaches, have a wonderful dynamism and excitement which has influenced many of the horse painters now working in England.

Brigadier Gerard was the result of a dream nurtured for forty years by his owner and breeder, John Hislop. When he was learning to ride as a boy, Hislop's riding mistress had fired his imagination with stories of the great filly Pretty Polly, who had won the distaff Triple Crown in 1904, and had then disappointed the racing public in England by losing to a rank outsider, Presto II, when dispatched to Longchamp for the express purpose of putting her French contemporaries in their place. Hislop determined to find a mare descended from Pretty Polly with whom he could breed a champion. And so it happened.

He bought Brazen Molly, a great granddaughter of Pretty Polly, for 400 guineas soon after the Second World War. She herself had a daughter, La Paiva, from whom John Hislop and his wife, Jean, decided to breed for the race-track rather than the sales. La Paiva's early foals showed no great distinction and the Hislops decided to look for a stallion, inbred to Fairway, who could be expected to get two-year-old winners, yet have Classic possibilities – and, above all, who would be cheap. They settled on Queen's Hussar.

The result was Brigadier Gerard, who was taken to the hearts of English racegoers like no other horse since the war, with the possible exception of Shergar. He was beaten only once in three years' racing, and in that time defeated some superb horses, such as Riverman, Mill Reef, and My Swallow. Unfancied, he won the 1971 Two Thousand Guineas. He was then withdrawn from the Derby because he was thought unlikely to act on the undulating Epsom track – a hard-headed but perhaps over-careful decision which allowed Mill Reef to challenge him for the affections of racing folk. The Brigadier won the Champion Stakes twice. His show-down with the 1972 Derby winner Roberto at York, in the Benson

John Skeaping: *The Last Furlong*. 1967. Gouache, 54.6 × 74.9 cm. Private collection

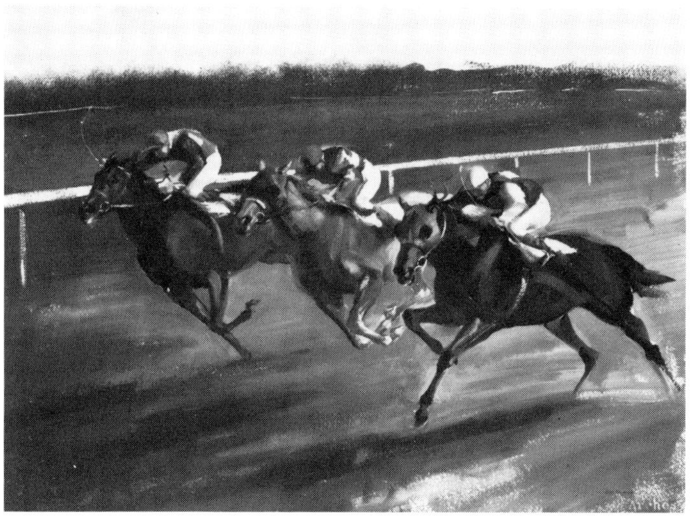

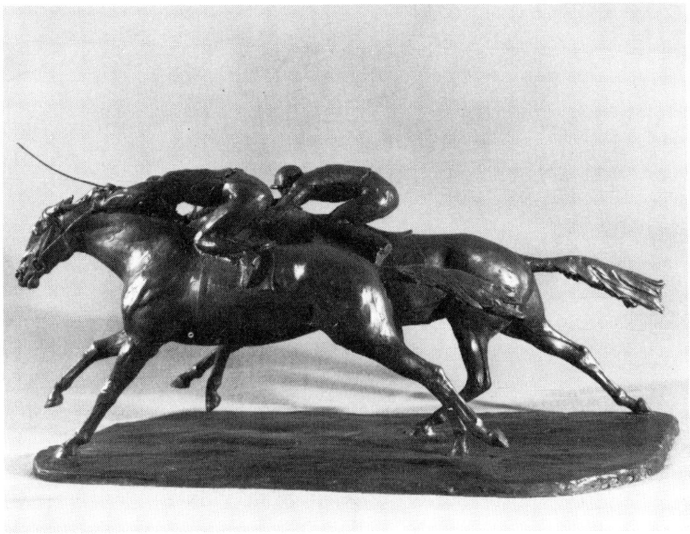

John Skeaping: *Hanging to the Left (The Finish of the 1974 Travers Stakes: Holding Pattern beating Little Current)*. 1975. Bronze, height 33.7 cm, length 67.3 cm. Private collection

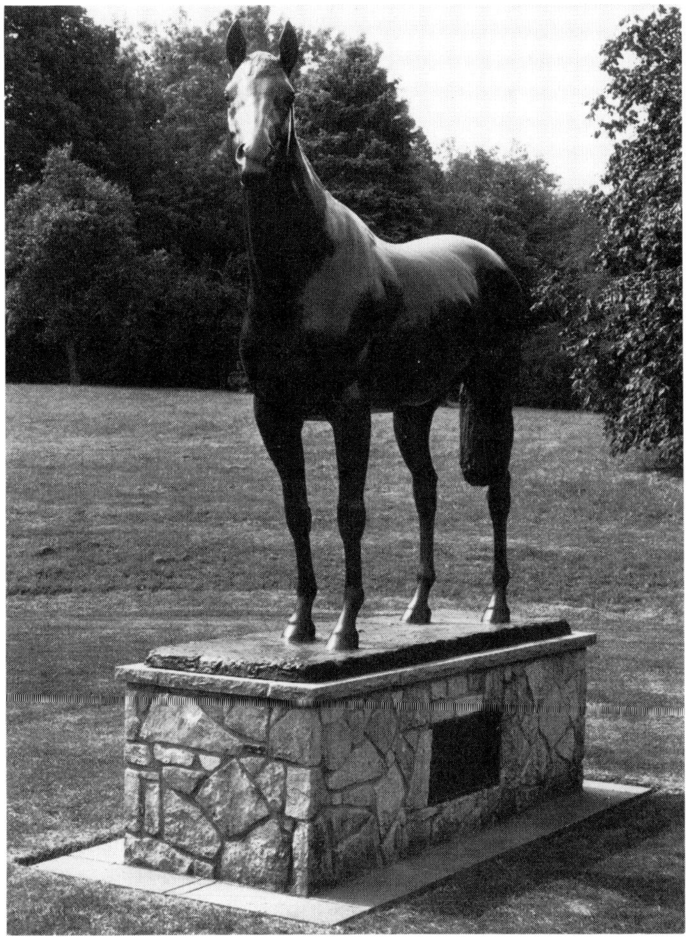

John Skeaping: *Brigadier Gerard*. 1972. Bronze, life-size. Private collection

and Hedges Gold Cup, was perhaps the most memorable race to be seen on the Knavesmire since Voltigeur took on The Flying Dutchman.

Three weeks previously, the Brigadier had won a hard race at Ascot for the King George VI and Queen Elizabeth Stakes. Roberto, forced home by Lester Piggott in the most unrelenting fashion at Epsom, had then flopped in the Irish Derby. It was no surprise, therefore, that Rheingold, second in the Derby and subsequent Prix de l'Arc de Triomphe winner, was much better fancied, not least by Lester Piggott, who gave up the ride on Roberto in order to partner Rheingold. The Panamanian jockey Braulio Baeza was brought over by trainer Vincent O'Brien to ride Roberto. He had never ridden in England before.

That day the traffic stretched from York almost the twenty-five miles back to Leeds, as the Yorkshiremen, who love to see a great horse, turned out for the race. Baeza, in the American fashion, jumped Roberto out of the stalls at a terrific pace and grabbed the lead from the first furlong. Entering the long York straight, jockey Joe Mercer moved Brigadier Gerard to challenge, but Roberto never faltered and a stunned crowd saw him pass the winning-post 3 lengths clear in record time.

It is possible that the Ascot race had taken too much out of the Brigadier, but some found it difficult to accept that he had been beaten by an animal who was regarded as a substandard Derby winner, and who was ugly and highly inconsistent to boot. There were all sorts of rumours about Roberto and his unconventional jockey at the time. But his subsequent record as a sire suggests that Brigadier Gerard had simply come up against a good horse on his best day.

John Skeaping was an old friend of John Hislop from the time they had been together in the Special Air Service during the Second World War, so it was natural that he should be asked to produce the statue of the Brigadier. This time, Skeaping had a live subject and, furthermore, he had seen the horse race a number of times, so the shifts and stratagems which had been required for the Hyperion bronze were superfluous. The Brigadier proved a perfect 'sitter' and Skeaping was able to take the most precise measurements of a horse whom he described as the most perfectly formed he had ever seen.

# *Sir Alfred Munnings*

*1878–1959*

Mahmoud
Cameronian
Solario
Davy Jones
Sun Chariot

'Grey horses were always my delight,' wrote Sir Alfred Munnings, 'my imagination stirred at the sight of them.' He was lucky enough to see in his lifetime one of only three grey colts who have ever won the Derby; and that was the outstanding Mahmoud, victor in 1936, in what is still the fastest-ever time.

As a child, Munnings had been fascinated by a picture of a grey horse which hung in the room where family prayers were held every morning, and it is hard not to see in the Mahmoud portrait an evocation of that picture as Munnings recalled it: 'a grey horse with a full eye, standing with a cloudy sky behind which emphasized its white form, the distance full of interest . . . it was painted directly and freshly, and the painter knew his craft and a horse well enough to please his clients'. That childhood vision still shines in this, one of the splendid paintings of Munnings's mature years.

Sir Alfred was himself an excellent horseman and judge of bloodstock, as well as a master of composition and colour. But, perhaps above all, he was able to capture the special atmosphere and excitements of the racecourse itself: the tensions of the start, the horses pulling-up against the skyline at Newmarket, jockeys in the weighing-room, and, as shown here at Epsom on Derby Day, the moments of concentration and isolation in the paddock as the blankets come off and the gladiators are prepared for the arena. Mahmoud's jockey is Charlie Smirke, and in the background is Taj Akbar, also carrying the Aga Khan's colours, with Gordon Richards about to mount.

Mahmoud was the less fancied of the Aga Khan's two runners in the Derby, despite having lost the Guineas by only a short head, for he carried on his dam's side one of the great speed blood lines. His second dam was Mumtaz Mahal, the 'Flying Filly' herself, by the grey The Tetrarch, who was widely thought to be the fastest horse ever seen on an English track. It was, therefore, assumed that Mahmoud would not stay the Epsom mile and a half. But on the day conditions suited him perfectly: very firm going and a pace, set by Thankerton, which verged on the frantic. Mahmoud hit the front more than 2 furlongs out and went on to win from Taj Akbar by 3 lengths – in 2 minutes $33\frac{4}{5}$ seconds. In 1940, Mahmoud formed part of the Aga Khan's controversial shipment of bloodstock to the United States, where he became champion sire and produced a string of fine brood mares.

Munnings's calm picture of Cameronian belies the tempestuous history of this bay son of Pharos. He was trained by Fred Darling at Beckhampton, but as the Two Thousand Guineas of 1931 approached, the stable were deceived by another of their string, Lemnarchus, in a late gallop. Lemnarchus showed such a turn of foot that the stable jockey, Freddy Fox, elected to ride him.

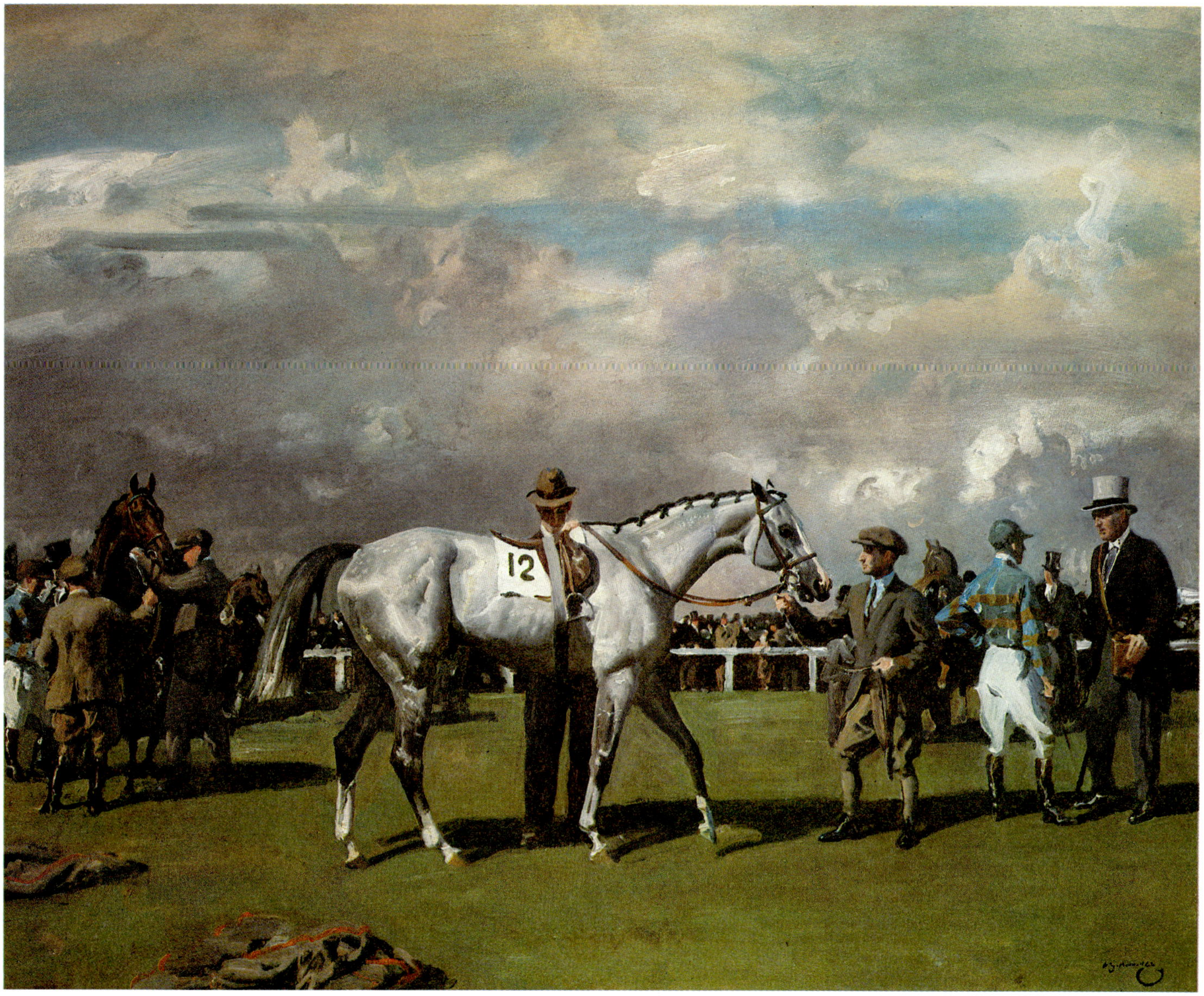


Sir Alfred Munnings: *Mahmoud, with Taj Akbar (l.), in the Paddock at Epsom before the Derby of 1936*. Oil on canvas, 63.5 × 76.2 cm.
Private collection

He turned out to be unable to stay a mile, and it was Cameronian who won. Fox made no such mistake in the Derby. Cameronian won by three-quarters of a length, thus giving his young owner, Mr John Dewar, a 'Blue Riband' with his first runner. Cameronian had been bred by Lord Dewar, his uncle, who in thirty years had never won the race. He had shown the foal, soon after it was born, to Edgar Wallace, the author, with the remark, 'He will win the Derby, but I may not live to see it.' Lord Dewar died in 1930.

Cameronian started as favourite for the St Leger, at 6–5 on, but the outcome was disaster. Journalist Sidney Galtrey wrote: 'I think of him coming in last of all, dead beat and, indeed, a pathetic sight. This could not be the horse that had won at Epsom and Ascot and had then been judiciously rested before entering on a graduated preparation for the last of the season's classic races. Here was a dead horse.' Galtrey was convinced Cameronian

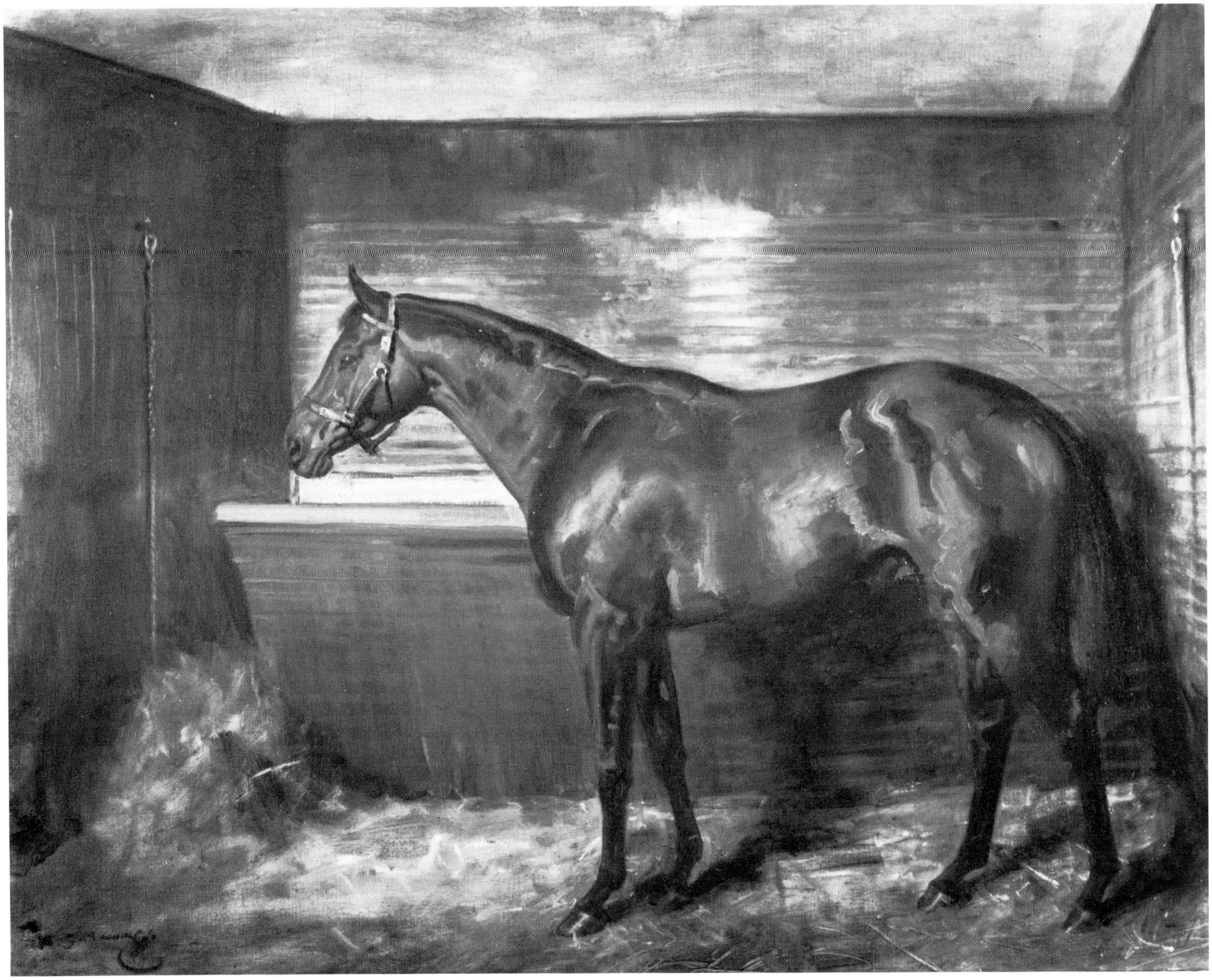

Sir Alfred Munnings: *Cameronian*. 1931. Oil on canvas, 69.8 × 90.1 cm. Jockey Club, Newmarket

had been 'got at': 'Fox found that his horse was crazy to begin with, so utterly unlike his real self. His madness could not be checked for so long as it lasted, though he took the horse to the outside, away from the rest in the hope that he would settle down. His way of settling down was to blow up so that he could not go on. The madness had passed off, leaving him a wreck of his true self.'

Fred Darling refused to put any 'sinister construction' on the episode, to use Galtrey's words. But it certainly took the horse a full year to recover. He ran a temperature above normal for twelve months, until in the October of his four-year-old career he came back to win the Champion Stakes. Cameronian was yet another horse who, after a sojourn at stud in England, was sold to Argentina.

Solario was one of the great stayers. He was beaten by Manna in the 1925 Derby, but had his revenge at Ascot and in the St Leger. On all three occasions there were excuses from the loser, with Solario having got his head entangled in the starting tapes and Manna breaking down in the St Leger. But when Solario came out as a four-year-old and won the Coronation Cup by 15 lengths, he banished all doubts. Journalist Quinny Gilbey wrote: 'After this victory he was described by many good judges as the horse of the century. . . . Shortly after this race he developed lameness and there were grave doubts whether he would be able to race in the Gold Cup at Ascot. By a superhuman effort, however, Reg Day got him to the post, though he could not give him anything like a preparation. Solario triumphed over all this, though he finished virtually on three legs.'

In July 1932, his owner Sir John Rutherford died and the horse came up for sale. He was bought by Lord Glanely's syndicate for 47,000 guineas in the face of some stiff American bidding. Solario was champion sire in 1937. Two of his sons, Midday Sun and Straight Deal, won the Derby. He died in 1945.

As with Seymour and Herring, it is fascinating to see Munnings's sketches and studies which formed the basis of the finished work. There is a set featuring Solario in the Clark Institute in Williamstown, Massachusetts. They were made at Newmarket in July 1926, complete with notes: 'Lovely horse with a kind eye,' Munnings has written beside one of the studies for the head. The Mares and Foals study too shows that he is trying to define quite precisely the stance, the colour highlights, and the light and shade. 'Hard and careful' is the phrase Munnings himself used for this stage of the work.

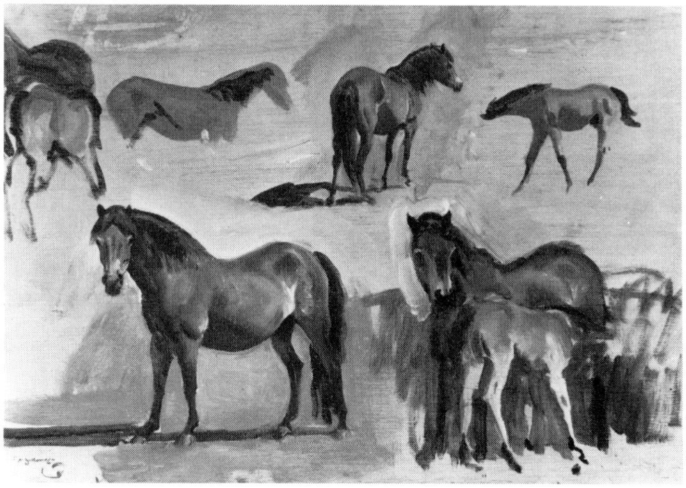

Sir Alfred Munnings: *Study of Mares and Foals*. *c*.1948. Oil on board, 40.6 × 61 cm. Private collection

Munnings described his method of working: 'I never started a large picture until I had painted smaller canvases of thirty by twenty-five inches or twenty-four by twenty inches. Of these, one or two might be worthy of a larger subject. My morning or afternoon subject planned – whichever it happened to be – with a fifty by forty inch canvas, I have sat or stood at the same place, in the same shadow of tree or fence, day by day, working out a picture, passage by passage. With canvas all set, a half bucket of water hung from the easel to steady it against a fitful breeze, palette and brushes ready.'

Sheltering under a large painting umbrella, he would work away until the frequent disaster of a change in the weather: 'No artist can tell a layman of the hopeless blight that falls upon him with such a change. He is doomed, beaten; but only for the moment. For the artist of experience there is a way out; he has with him his second canvas, his second string. Always in that flat cart nearby lay my other canvases, among them the grey subject, already well on its way, belonging to this same spot.' Like Herring, Munnings's grey skies and stormy backgrounds have a particular drama and force which is absent on sunnier days.

Davy Jones and his rider, Anthony Mildmay, became international celebrities after the Grand National of 1936. The new-fangled newsreel cameras carried the adventures of the day to the whole country, and across the seas to the Empire and the United States. Coming to the last jump, Davy Jones, a 100–1 outsider, seemed

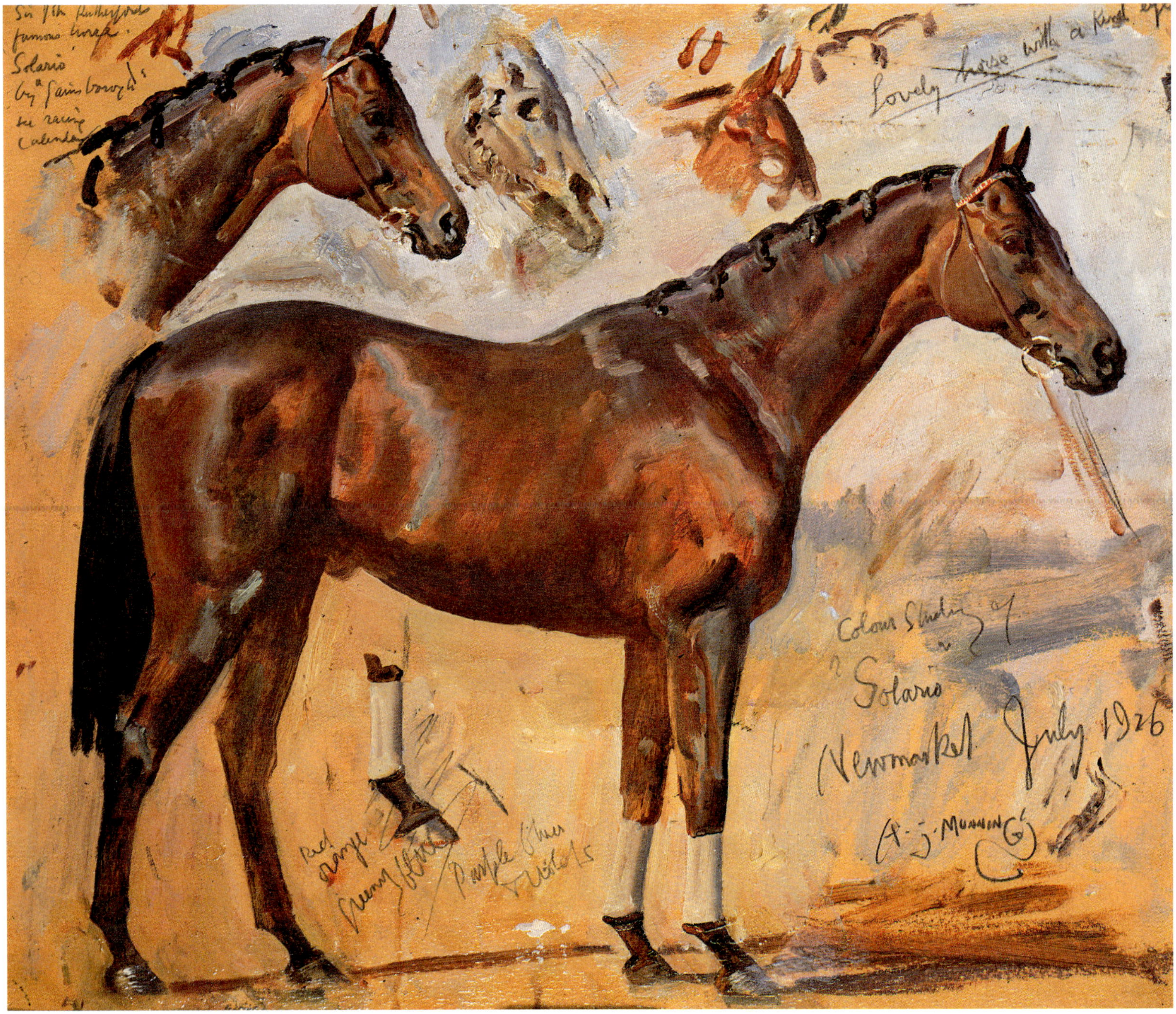


Sir Alfred Munnings: *Study of Solario*. 1926. Oil on board, 43 × 50.8 cm. Sterling and Francine Clark Art Institute, Williamstown, Mass.

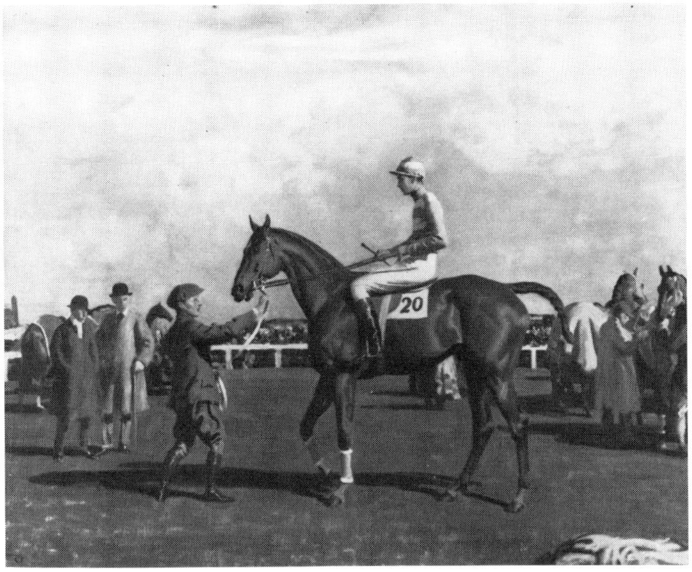


Sir Alfred Munnings: *Davy Jones, with Anthony Mildmay up.* 1937. Oil on canvas, 76.2 × 101.6cm. Private collection

certain to beat the previous year's winner, Reynoldstown. At the crucial moment, right underneath the cameras, the reins broke and Davy Jones ran out, scattering the spectators beside the jump, with Anthony Mildmay helpless. Reynoldstown went on to win. After the war, Mildmay was leading amateur for five seasons, until he was drowned in 1950.

Sun Chariot, all tacked up in Munnings's picture, won the fillies' Triple Crown in the war year of 1942, while leased to King George VI. She was an unruly female. When the King and Queen came down to Beckhampton to see her work, she rushed off into a ploughed field, went down on her knees, and started 'roaring'. In the Oaks, run at Newmarket because of the war, she careered all over the course at the start and was left a furlong or more. But Gordon Richards, her jockey, got her in hand again, and she was back in the bunch not long after they had gone a mile. She won by a length. In the St Leger, she was positively placid and beat Watling Street by 3 lengths. In nine races she was beaten only once, in a race at Salisbury, when Gordon Richards apparently could not get her to take hold of the bit.

Munnings, who had been blind in one eye since the age of 21, was chiefly responsible for restoring the prestige of the thoroughbred painter in England. He was knighted in 1944, and died in 1959.

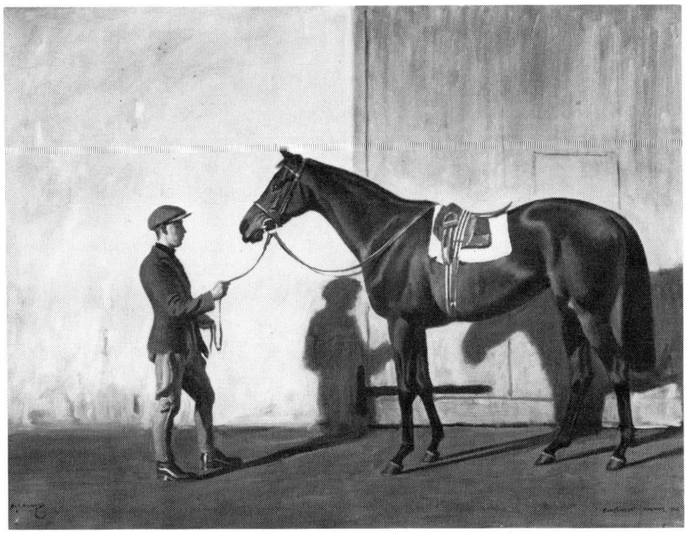

Sir Alfred Munnings: *Sun Chariot.* 1942. Oil on canvas, 54.6 × 74.9cm. Jockey Club, Newmarket

# Martin Stainforth

*c.1861–1952*

War Admiral
Trenton
Manfred

War Admiral was that rarest of creatures in racing: the outcome of a theoretically perfect mating which actually worked as planned. With his sire, Man o' War, representing Fair Play and his dam, Brushup, representing Domino and Ben Brush, War Admiral combined all three of the dominant lines of American stallions. He had a superb career as a three-year-old in 1937, taking the American Triple Crown with ease, only to fall from grace the following year in one of the most celebrated matches of the American Turf.

By the spring of his three-year-old career, War Admiral, a small brown colt, had shown himself fast and tough enough for his owner, Samuel D. Riddle, to overcome a lifetime's aversion to Churchill Downs and let him start in the Kentucky Derby. War Admiral led from start to finish and was never threatened. He then took the Preakness from Pompoon and the Belmont from Sceneshifter, despite putting up a daunting display of tantrums at the start and tearing off a chunk of his off forefoot in the process. He won all eight races that year and was undisputed champion.

But that same season another great horse – one year his senior – was establishing himself as a worthy rival in the public mind. Seabiscuit, a four-year-old son of Hard Tack by Man o' War, had stolen some of War Admiral's glory by running up a world winnings record, including seven straight victories. As the 1938 term began, the whole American racing world was agog for the decisive contest between the two great scions of Man o' War. But month after month went by and the two owners, Samuel D. Riddle with War Admiral, and Charles Howard with Seabiscuit, managed to avoid the showdown. First it was to be Belmont, then Laurel, then Boston where the two champions were to meet. Each time one or other was scratched.

Finally, on 1 November 1938, Alfred Vanderbilt succeeded in bringing the two to the starting-line at the Pimlico track in Maryland. It was a match with $15,000 added, winner takes all, over 9½ furlongs. This was a full 6 furlongs shorter than the distances War Admiral had been contesting that year, whereas for Seabiscuit it was positively a trial of stamina, for he had been running over a mile only. Straight from the off Seabiscuit's rider, George Woolf, grabbed the initiative and left War Admiral, normally a front runner himself, trailing 3 lengths behind. War Admiral fought back and at 6 furlongs was level. For half a mile they were neck and neck, until half-way down the final stretch the enormous Pimlico crowd saw War Admiral suddenly give way, to leave Seabiscuit 4 lengths clear at the post. It was a superb climax to one of the greatest seasons on the American track. War Admiral won his only race the following year before being retired for a successful stud career which made him leading sire in 1945.

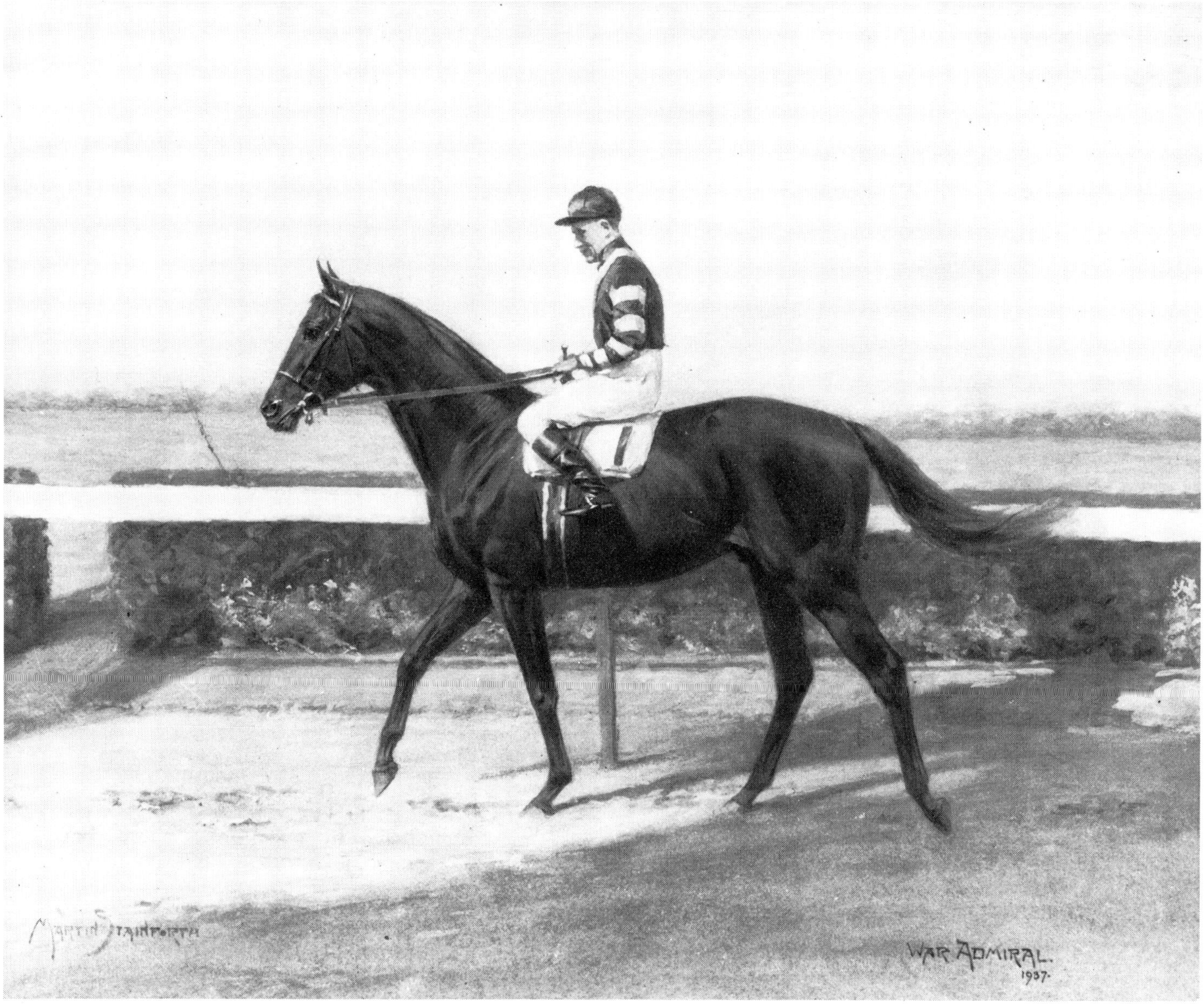


Martin Stainforth: *War Admiral, with Charley Kurtsinger up*. 1937. Watercolour, 31.1 × 39.3 cm. National Museum of Racing, Saratoga Springs, NY

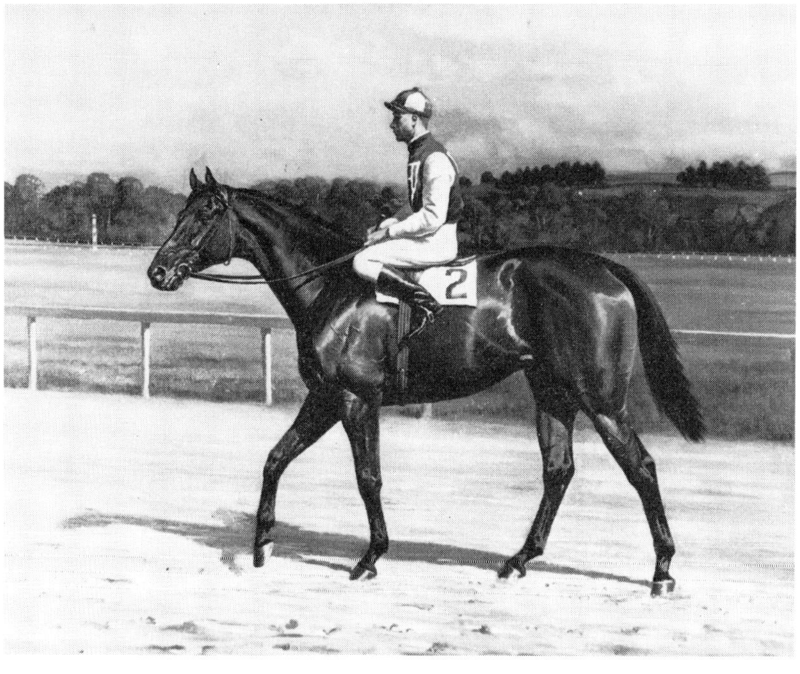

Franklin Voss: *Seabiscuit, with George Woolf up*. 1937. Oil on canvas, 76.2 × 91.4 cm. National Museum of Racing, Saratoga Springs, NY

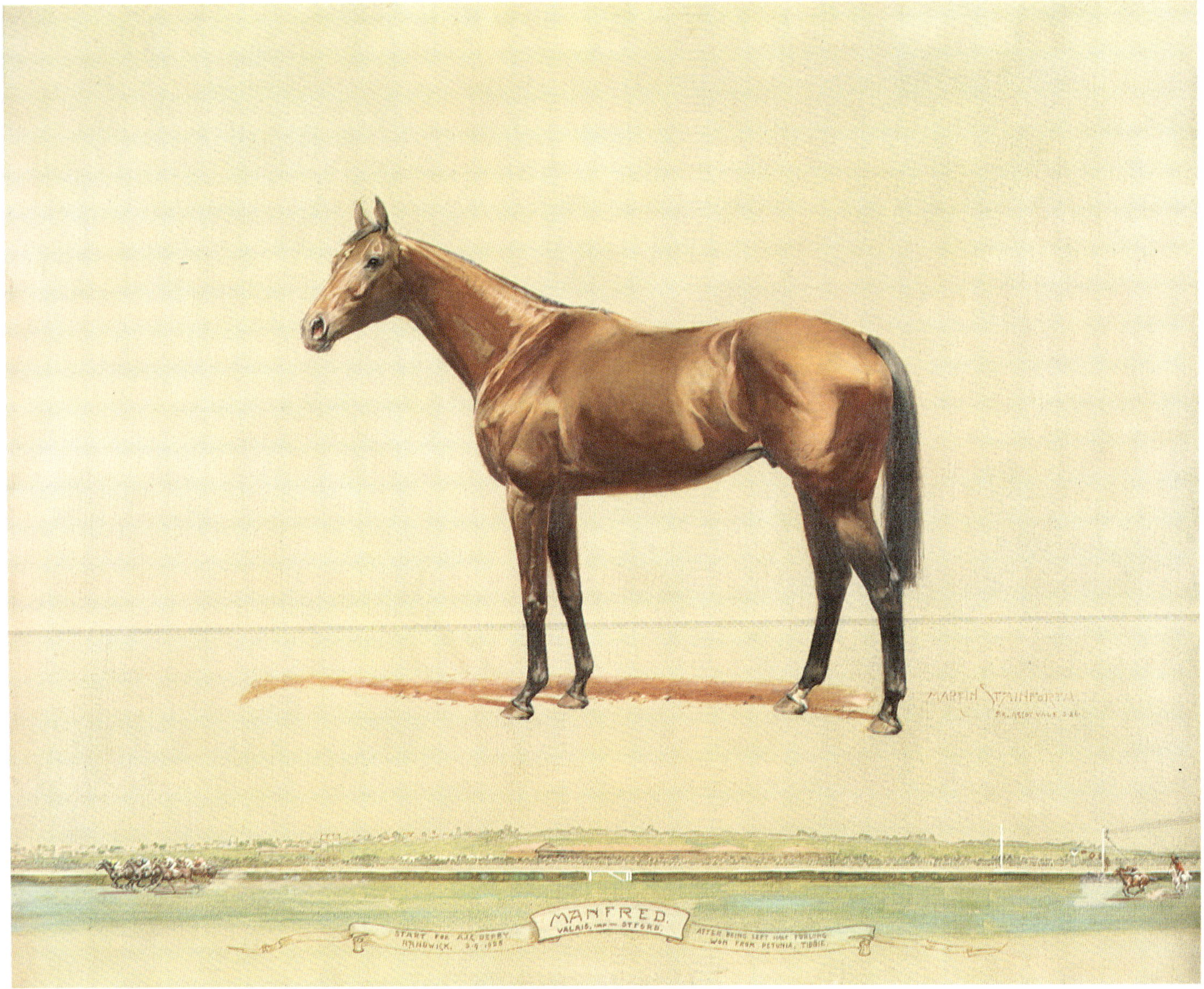


Martin Stainforth: *Manfred, Winner of the 1925 A.J.C. Derby, after being left Half a Furlong at the Start.* 1926. Oil on canvas, 73.6 × 87.6 cm. Australian Jockey Club, Randwick

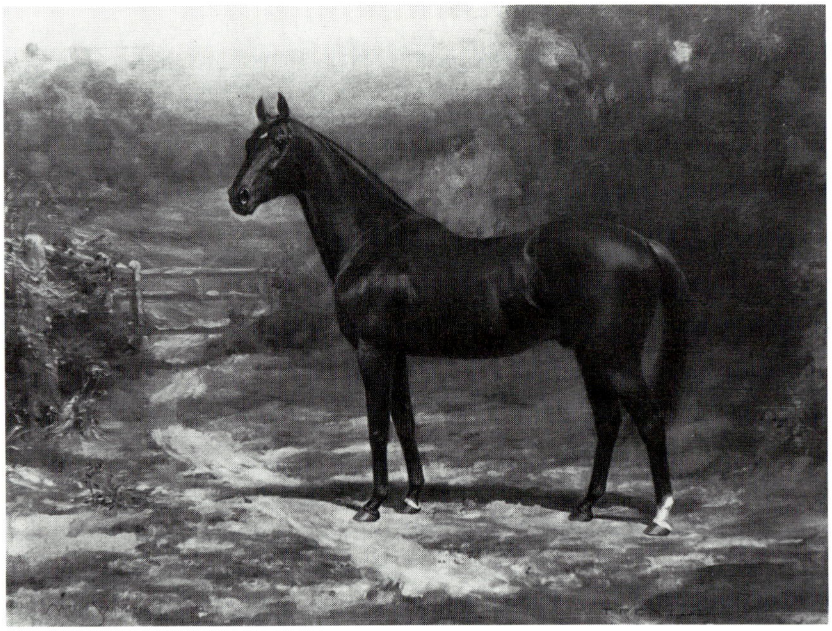

Martin Stainforth: *Trenton.* 1922. Oil on canvas, 72.4 × 90.1 cm. Australian Jockey Club, Randwick

Martin Stainforth was a truly accomplished artist who made his name in England, then Australia, and finally the United States before returning to die in obscurity in England. He was already in his late 40s, and a renowned engraver who had exhibited frequently at the Royal Academy in London, when he decided in 1908 to travel out to Australia where his brother had a cattle station in Queensland. He seems to have done little but lounge in the sun for three years until, in 1911, the death of his friend Douglas Fry left Australian thoroughbred owners devoid of any artist capable of recording their champions. A group of them prevailed on Stainforth to try his hand. Having never seriously painted horses, he took himself off to the Randwick track in Sydney and spent months studying the racers.

It was his avowed aim 'to upset the tradition of Herring and other old timers. They invariably depicted the thoroughbred with his muscles bulging out and his contour greatly accentuated by unaccountable light and shade. Every animal was shown with a ridiculously small head, tapering legs and tiny feet. To me they looked like fashion plates.' By contrast, Stainforth wanted to produce paintings both beautiful and useful: 'useful from the point of view that breeders and owners might have the opportunity of making my paintings a standard of comparison, or a standard of what our great Australian sires were in conformation'.

Stainforth was immediately and spectacularly successful. For nearly twenty years he painted all the great Australian thoroughbreds, from Trenton and Carbine through to Manfred, and remains unchallenged as the best equine painter ever to have worked in Australia. Trenton was Australia's champion sire in 1902, having raced for four seasons in both Australia and New Zealand in the 1880s. Like Carbine, he was by Musket, and he too was brought back to stand in England when already approaching 20 years old; both came from the Ithuriel line of Touchstone which had been almost lost in Europe.

When Stainforth was nearly 70 years old, the wanderlust struck him again, and he set sail for California. One of his last Australian commissions was the portrait of Manfred, the champion three-year-old of 1925, who won both the Australian Jockey Club Derby and the Victoria Derby. He took the Caulfield Cup the following year, and, in total, won eleven races worth nearly £29,000.

Stainforth had developed in Australia a wonderful flair for action painting, typified by his picture of the 1922 Australian Jockey Club Spring Stakes with Beauford beating Gloaming. The two horses were great rivals and Stainforth declared that he was painting the picture as a record 'of a historic event which no sportsman who saw it could ever forget'. It was this facility which brought him commissions in the United States. By the time he painted War Admiral, Stainforth was nearing 80, but there is still a splendid vigour in the canvas as the great Triple Crown winner steps down to the start.

Martin Stainforth: *The Finish of the 1922 A.J.C. Spring Stakes: Beauford beating Gloaming*. Oil on canvas, 61.6 × 174 cm. Australian Jockey Club, Randwick

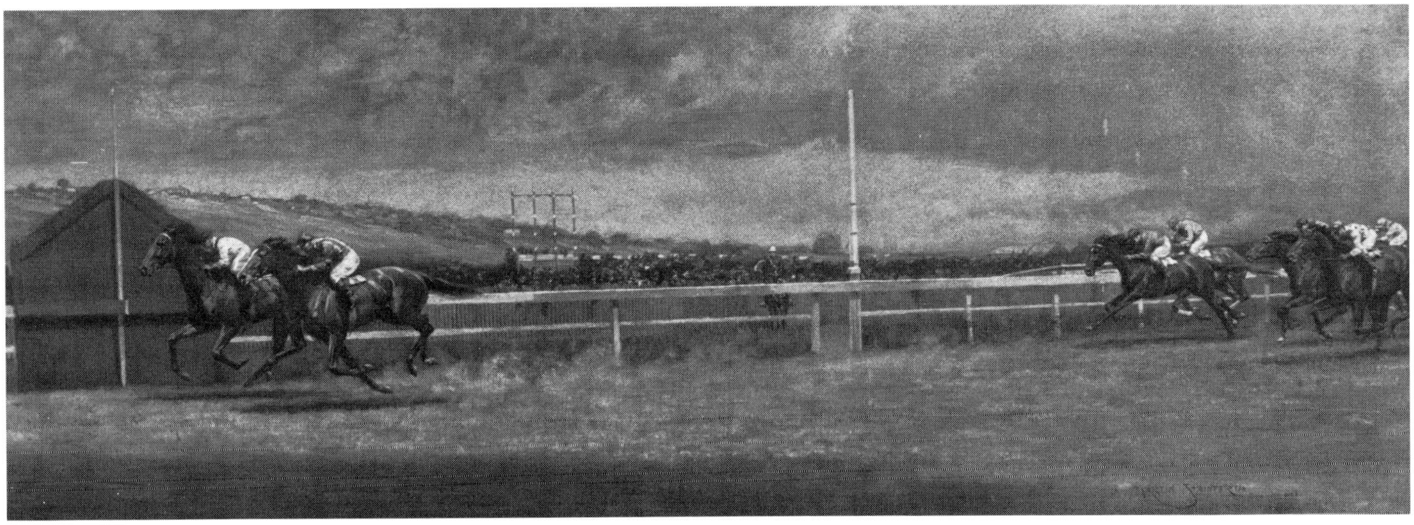

# W. S. Broadhead

*1888–1960*

Battleship
Nashua

Battleship was the most extraordinary son of Man o' War. He won over every distance from 5 furlongs on the Flat to $4\frac{1}{2}$ miles over jumps. In 1938 he became the first American owned and bred horse to win the Aintree Grand National, and one of the few entire colts ever to carry off the prize in that most daunting of contests.

He had his first win on the Flat in Florida at 2 years old, and his last at 4 years old in the Great Lakes Handicap at Hawthorne. He was then bought by Mrs Marion du Pont Scott, who spent the whole of 1932 supervising his schooling as a steeplechaser. With ten wins on the Flat in the United States, he clocked up another ten over jumps, including the Belmont Grand National. Mrs Scott next set her sights on the English Grand National. She knew the Ambrose Clarks, who had owned Kellsboro' Jack, winner of the race in 1933, and through them Reginald Hobbs, the Newmarket trainer. Battleship was shipped over to him. Hobbs campaigned the American horse hard in England and he recorded eighteen wins in two seasons, but Hobbs still did not consider him ready for the 1937 Grand National. Battleship had won four more times before the 1938 renewal date came round. It was to prove an epic Grand National.

Hobbs put up his 17-year-old son Bruce as jockey. The boy nearly came off at Becher's: 'Fred Rimell pulled me back into the saddle by the arse of my breeches,' recalls Bruce Hobbs, today himself a distinguished trainer of Flat racehorses at Newmarket. There was then a protracted and enthralling duel all the way from the Canal Turn between Battleship and the Irish horse Royal Danieli. In the punishing final straight at Aintree the two horses veered apart, but young Bruce Hobbs got Battleship up by no more than a neck to win the toughest steeplechase in the world.

It was reason enough for what turned out to be a national celebration. Battleship was returned across the Atlantic. Bruce Hobbs went with him. The horse had special quarters on the ship, with a patch of growing lucerne taken on board, from which a fresh cut was made each day. A regular flow of passengers came to visit him. When the ship docked in New York, there was a band waiting on the quayside, which played the national anthem as the hero was slung ashore. Standing

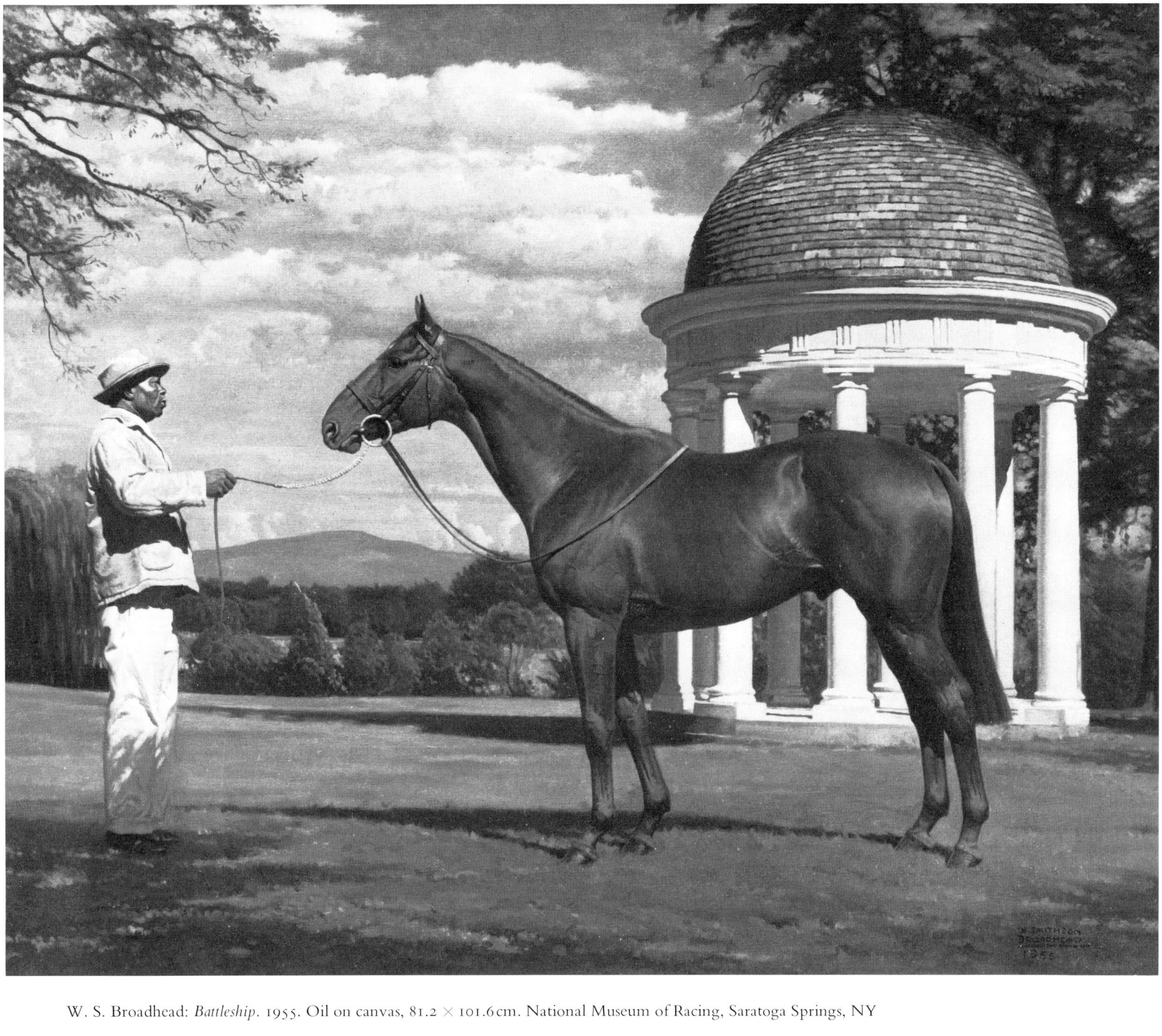

W. S. Broadhead: *Battleship*. 1955. Oil on canvas, 81.2 × 101.6 cm. National Museum of Racing, Saratoga Springs, NY

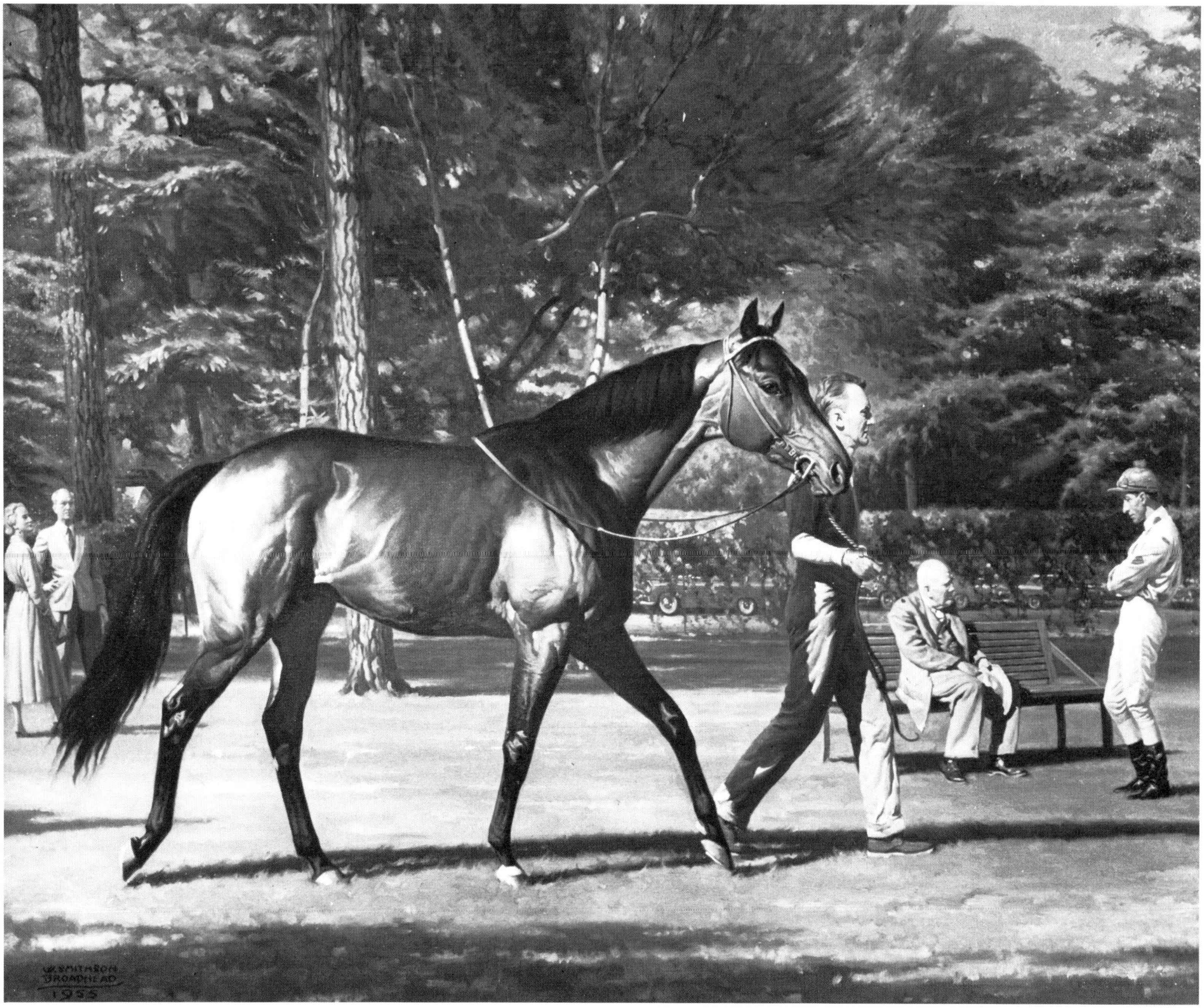

W. S. Broadhead: *Nashua at Saratoga, with jockey Eddie Arcaro in the Woodward Colours*. 1955. Oil on canvas, 91.4 × 110.4 cm. National Museum of Racing, Saratoga Springs, NY

at stud in Virginia, Battleship was not prolific, but he sired two champion American steeplechasers, Shipboard and War Battle.

W. S. Broadhead's picture of the stallion, painted back home in Virginia, shows a big and powerful horse. This must be an illusion – perhaps the handler is very short – for Battleship was certainly small, no more than 15 hands 2 inches, to such an extent that it was considered unlikely that he could cope with the great Aintree fences.

W. Smithson Broadhead lived in London and Sussex during the inter-war years. He exhibited seven times at the Royal Academy, between 1923 and 1937, before moving to the United States, where he has been highly valued as an equestrian artist. The Woodwards, a family steeped in sporting art, commissioned him to paint

Nashua, the first million-dollar racehorse. In 1955 and 1956, Nashua, a son of Nasrullah, had a series of contests with Mr and Mrs John W. Galbreath's Swaps. Kentucky versus California.

The Californian horse started with a victory over Nashua in the Kentucky Derby. Swaps had been carefully prepared by the Mormon partners Rex Ellsworth and Meshach Tenney, with a warm-up race at Kentucky the week before. Willie Shoemaker had Swaps in front all the way from the home turn and Nashua never got closer than half a length. Nashua won both the Belmont and the Preakness. Chicago's Washington Park then organized the 'Match of the Century' for $100,000, winner takes all. Nashua led from start to finish and fought off challenge after challenge from Swaps until – as is the way with match racing – one horse had given his all; the winning distance was a comfortable 6 lengths. Nashua and Swaps went to stud side by side at Spendthrift Farm in Lexington.

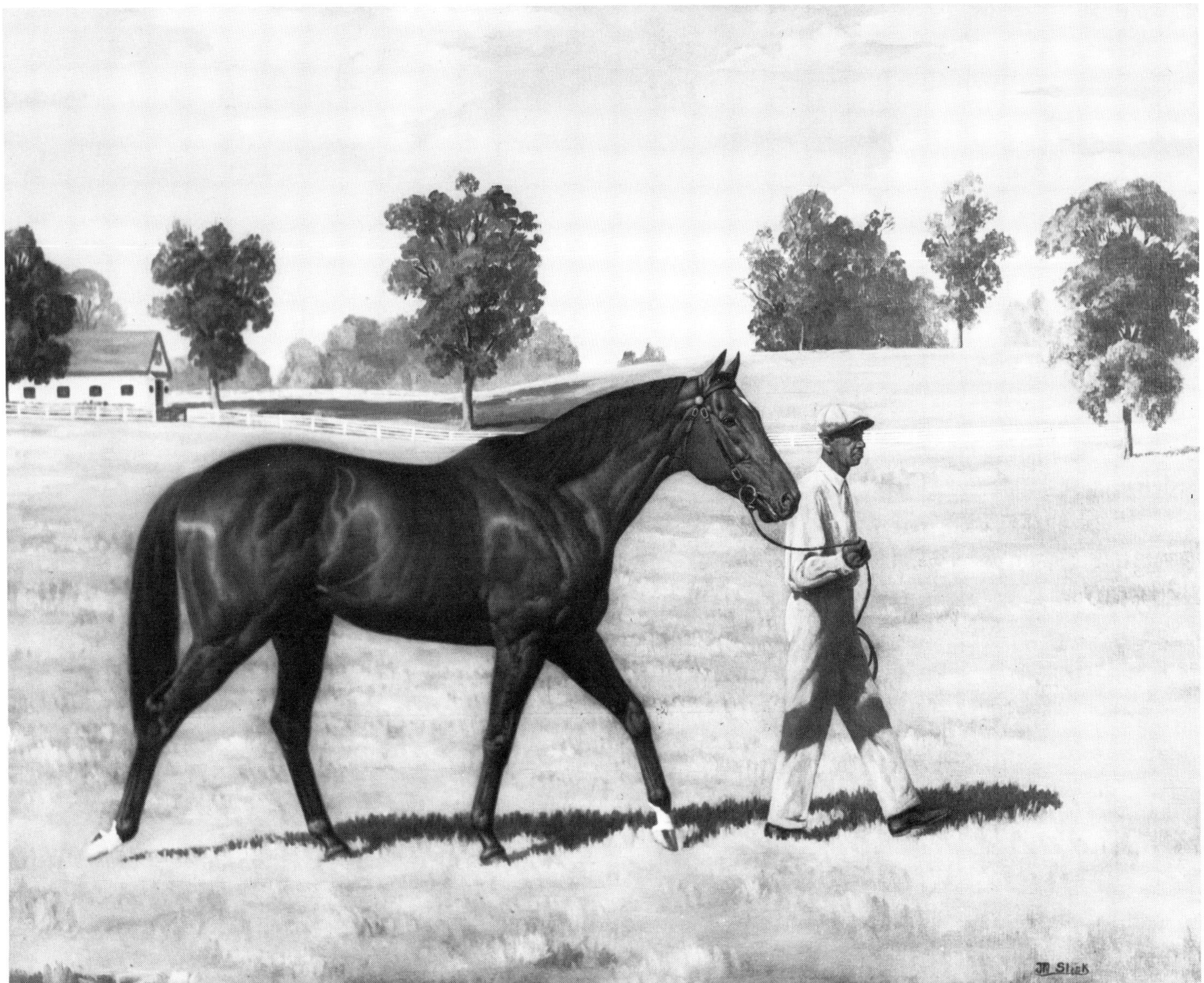

James N. Slick: *Swaps*. After 1956. Oil on canvas, 71.1 × 91.4 cm.
National Museum of Racing, Saratoga Springs, NY

# *André Marchand*

*1877–1951*

## Le Pacha

Racing in England and France during the summer of 1941 could hardly have presented a greater contrast. In England, the sport had retreated into a small enclave round Newmarket, while Winston Churchill was rallying the country for a long and lone struggle against Germany. Fred Darling sent out the last of his Derby winners, Mrs R. Macdonald-Buchanan's Owen Tudor, in a substitute race run over the Newmarket July course.

In France, it seemed, the war was over. The Third Reich ruled the Continent, with hostilities virtually at a standstill. Hitler had not yet plunged into the fatal adventure against the Soviet Union. The tribunes of Longchamp were once again dominated by Prussian accents and dotted with the grey uniforms. Racing flourished. And there were few if any Englishmen present to endorse the French view that Le Pacha, the champion of 1941, was one of the most handsome animals ever seen on a French racecourse. Henry Thétard, the French enthusiast, described him as 'a magnificent animal, as well as a superb racehorse. He was a dark bay with a proud head held high and a look of authority in his eye – and he stood out as a wonderful athlete.'

Le Pacha reeled off a string of victories in the big races of 1941 and always gave the crowds a tremendous thrill, for he hated galloping alone – as had his sire, Biribi – and consequently was always held up for a late run. The tactic failed him on one important occasion only, the Grand Prix de Saint-Cloud of 1942, when Djebel, the English Two Thousand Guineas winner of 1940, stole a run on him and got to the post with Le Pacha swooping just too late.

Le Pacha belonged to M. Philippe Gund, an art connoisseur as well as a fine judge of a racehorse. M. Gund commissioned André Marchand to paint this fine study of his champion, which indeed suggests that superbly made horse the wartime fancy so admired. Marchand was a Parisian who enjoyed some early success at the schools. A pupil of Édouard Détaille, with more than a hint of Munnings in his style, he had a considerable talent for animal painting of all sorts. Although he has one or two pictures in French galleries, he is nowadays an unjustly neglected artist.

His picture of the Grand Prix of 1931, with the Boussac and Rothschild horses Tourbillon and Taxodium in the foreground, and the windmill and the old stands behind, has an attractive summery quality. The race was won by Count de Rivaud's Barnevelot, shown in the spotted colours.

OPPOSITE ABOVE
André Marchand: *Le Pacha, with Paul Francolon up*. 1941. Oil on canvas, 34 × 44 cm. Private collection

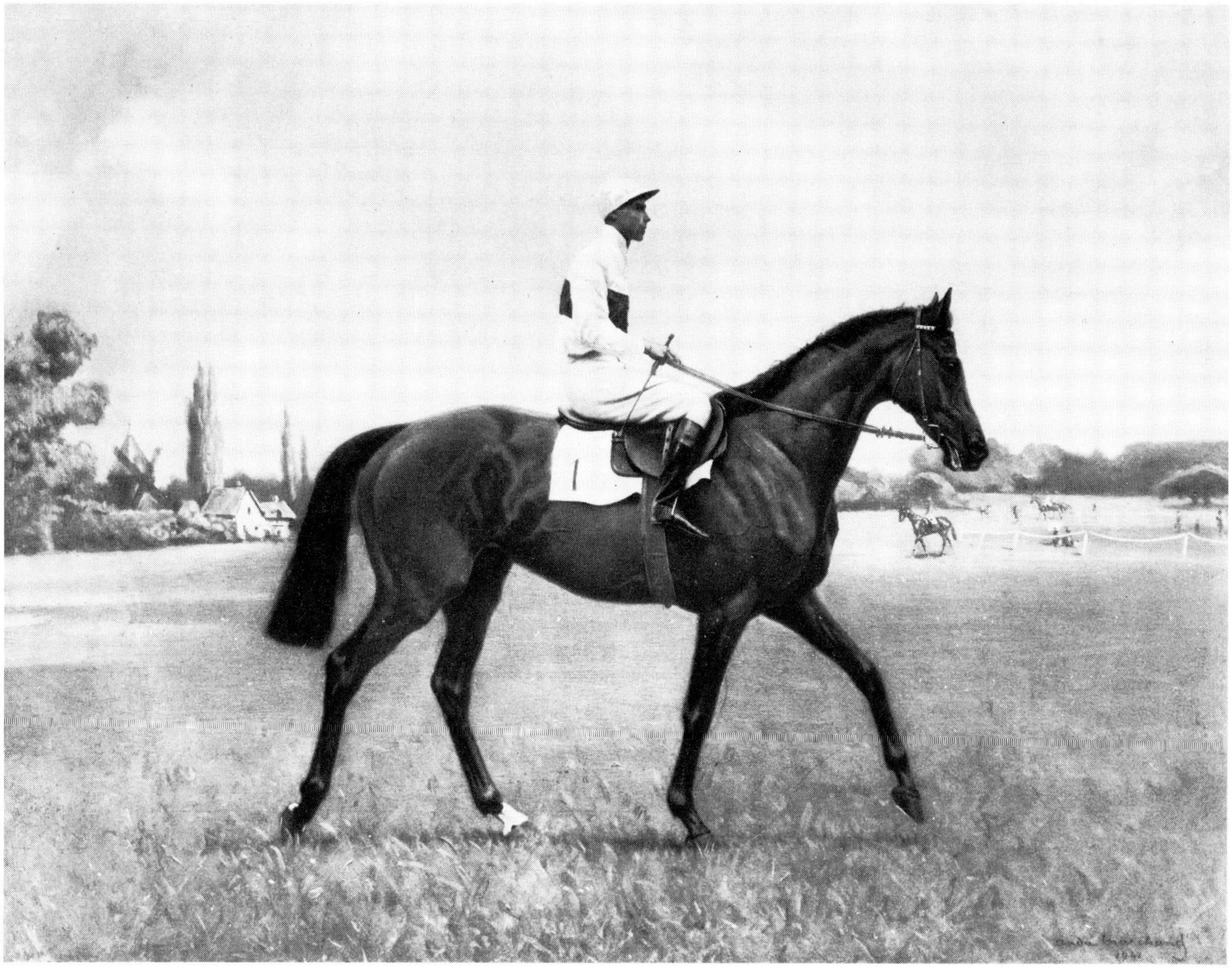

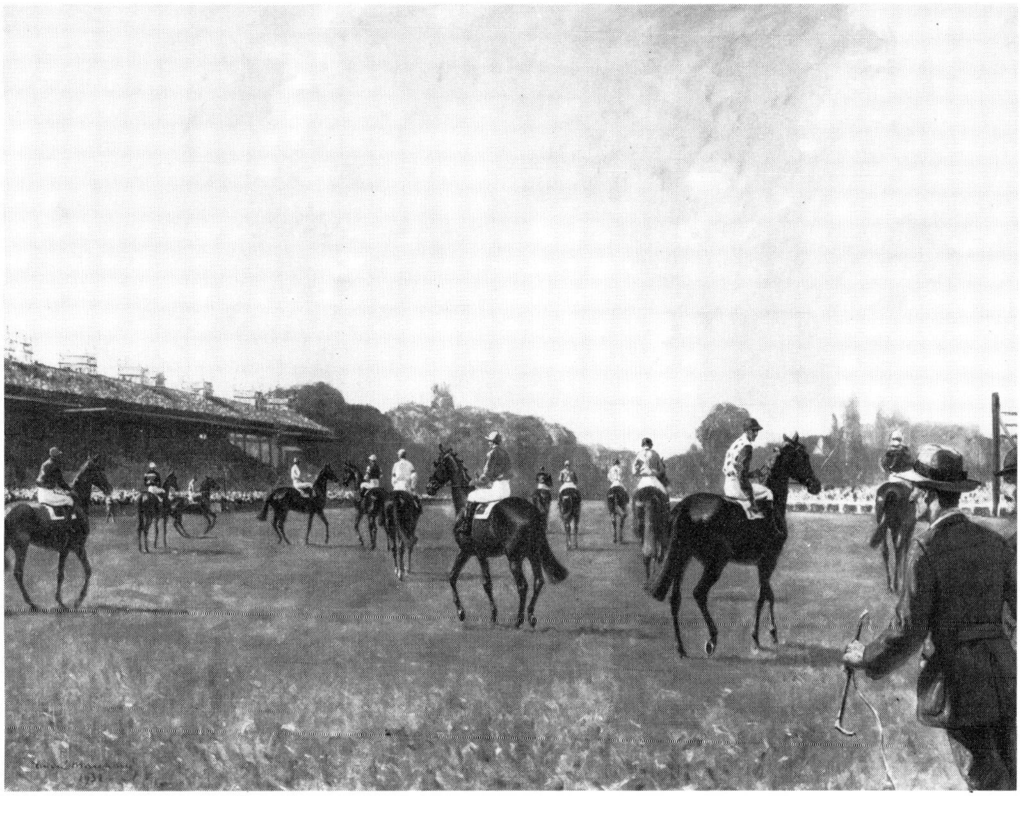

LEFT
André Marchand: *The Start of the 1931 Grand Prix*. 1932. Oil on canvas, 95 × 125 cm. Société d'Encouragement, Paris

# Susan Crawford

*born 1941*

Ribot
Mill Reef
Troy

Ribot was the ultimate tribute to the theories and genius of Federico Tesio, the great Italian breeder. Raised on the shores of Lake Maggiore at the Razza Dormello, with its fairy-tale views across the water to Isola Borromeo, Ribot left Italy to become arguably the most remarkable racehorse in Europe since the war. He won the Prix de l'Arc de Triomphe in 1955, then won it again the following year, when he also took England's premier all-age race, the King George VI and Queen Elizabeth Stakes at Ascot.

Tesio had spent much of his youth in South America, riding among the cattlemen of Patagonia. His thinking about the thoroughbred horse was unorthodox and, some would say, unscientific. But he was fascinated by the special qualities which he discerned in racehorses, particularly the nervous energy and the will to win. He wrote: 'In the last 50 yards of a race it is possible that the horse will be obliged to fight it out neck and neck. In this event, if both horses are of the same age and carry the same weight, the winner will be the one with the greater will to win – in other words, the one whose will-power can summon that increase in nervous "current" which will result in the winning burst of speed. The winner may even be of inferior physical build, provided his will to win be the stronger.'

He believed that this quality was handed over at the moment of conception: 'The atmosphere of intense sexual urge – which artificial insemination fails to provide – was intended by nature to accumulate a powerful charge of nervous energy which alone, when released through the sexual act, can result in an animal richer in will-power than his fellows, winner of all his battles and a successful producer.' Tesio also believed that this power was dissipated in racing and procreation, and could only be restored by rest. He was a believer in riding with the forces of nature in all respects. He had watched his mares scratching at the ground in the winter and he recognized the urge to migrate south which would have affected them in the wild. So he sent his horses to the south of Italy for the winter. He had strongly held theories of breeding, including the absolute necessity of reintroducing the blood of sprinters – or at least milers – into even the most perfect classic pedigrees.

Tesio had had a great success before the Second

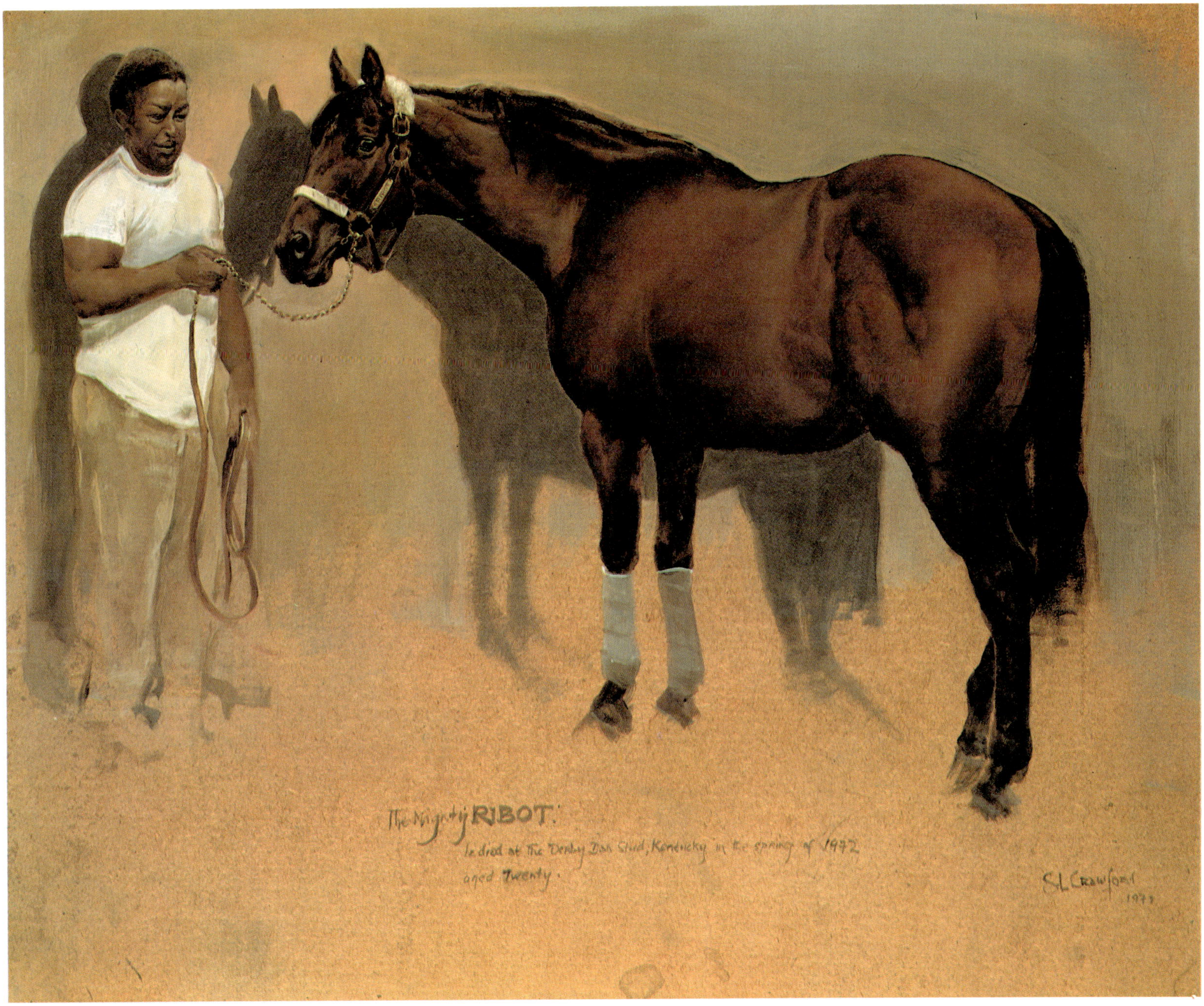


Susan Crawford: *The Mighty Ribot*. 1973. Oil on canvas, 50.8 × 60.9 cm. Woburn Abbey, Bedfordshire

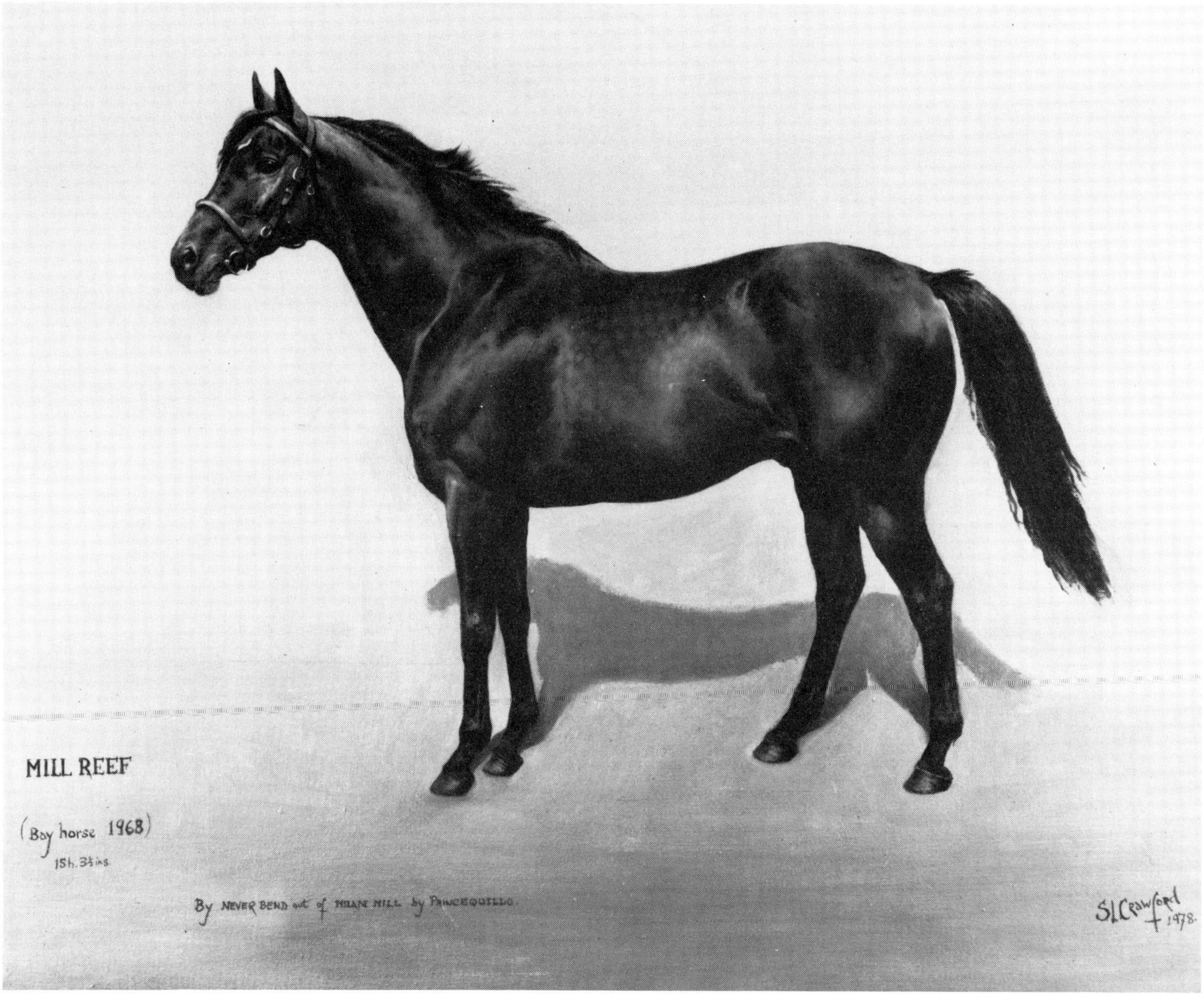


Susan Crawford: *Mill Reef.* 1978. Oil on canvas, 50.8 × 66 cm.
Paul Mellon Collection, Upperville, Virginia

World War with Nearco, who won the Grand Prix de Paris and was then brought to stud at Newmarket. But Ribot surpassed all of Nearco's achievements on the race-track. Susan Crawford's posthumous picture shows him at the end of his days at stud in Kentucky, a big bay of 16 hands with great depth and an honest eye.

Susan Crawford is a Scottish artist who studied in Italy and now paints on both sides of the Atlantic, attracting many discerning patrons. Her portraits of racehorses are rich, emotional, almost idolatrous, and her studies made against a neutral background have an impact which is reminiscent of studies by Herring. The portrait of Mill Reef, which she painted for his owner, Paul Mellon, glistens with the little horse's striking colour – 'a lovely deep mahogany bay,' as his trainer Ian Balding described it, 'even in mid-winter his coat had a gleam to it that was remarkable'.

Mill Reef, a son of Never Bend, bred in America by Paul Mellon, was a very fast two-year-old, winning the Coventry Stakes and the Gimcrack in 1970. The following year, in the Two Thousand Guineas, he came up against one of the best milers of all time, Brigadier Gerard, and was beaten. He then won the Derby untroubled, and the King George VI and Queen Elizabeth Stakes at Ascot. Ian Balding now aimed him at the Arc in Paris in October, giving him a rest by sending him off with an old horse, Aldie, down the distant vistas of the gallops at Kingsclere.

Balding recalled that the atmosphere at Longchamp was electric: 'more akin to that just before a Rugby football international than a race day'. Clapping broke out as Mill Reef came into the paddock. The applause was justified. Mill Reef, ridden by Geoff Lewis, won by 3 lengths and broke the track record. Standing at the English National Stud, he has also proved to be an outstanding sire. One of his sons, Shirley Heights, won the 1978 Derby for the Earl of Halifax.

Troy, trained by Dick Hern and ridden by Willie Carson, won the 200th Derby, in 1979, by 7 lengths, at that time the biggest margin for more than fifty years (since Manna). A dark bay son of Petingo, Troy had a rough time in the early stages of the race and was some 15 lengths behind when the field came down Tattenham Hill. But he produced an astounding burst of speed entering the straight, and came home alone, thus initiating an era of decisive Derby victories – Shergar, Golden Fleece, and Teenoso were to follow – the like of which has not been seen since the very early years of the race.

Troy went on to win the Irish Derby, the King George VI and Queen Elizabeth Stakes, and the Benson and Hedges Gold Cup at York. But once again the Prix de l'Arc de Triomphe at Longchamp proved too much for an English champion. He was defeated by the French filly Three Troikas. Troy was syndicated for more than £7 million to stand at Highclere stud in England. Sadly he died in 1983, just as his first progeny were reaching the racecourse.

Susan Crawford: *Troy, with Willie Carson up*. 1979. Oil on canvas, 71.1 × 91.4 cm. Private collection

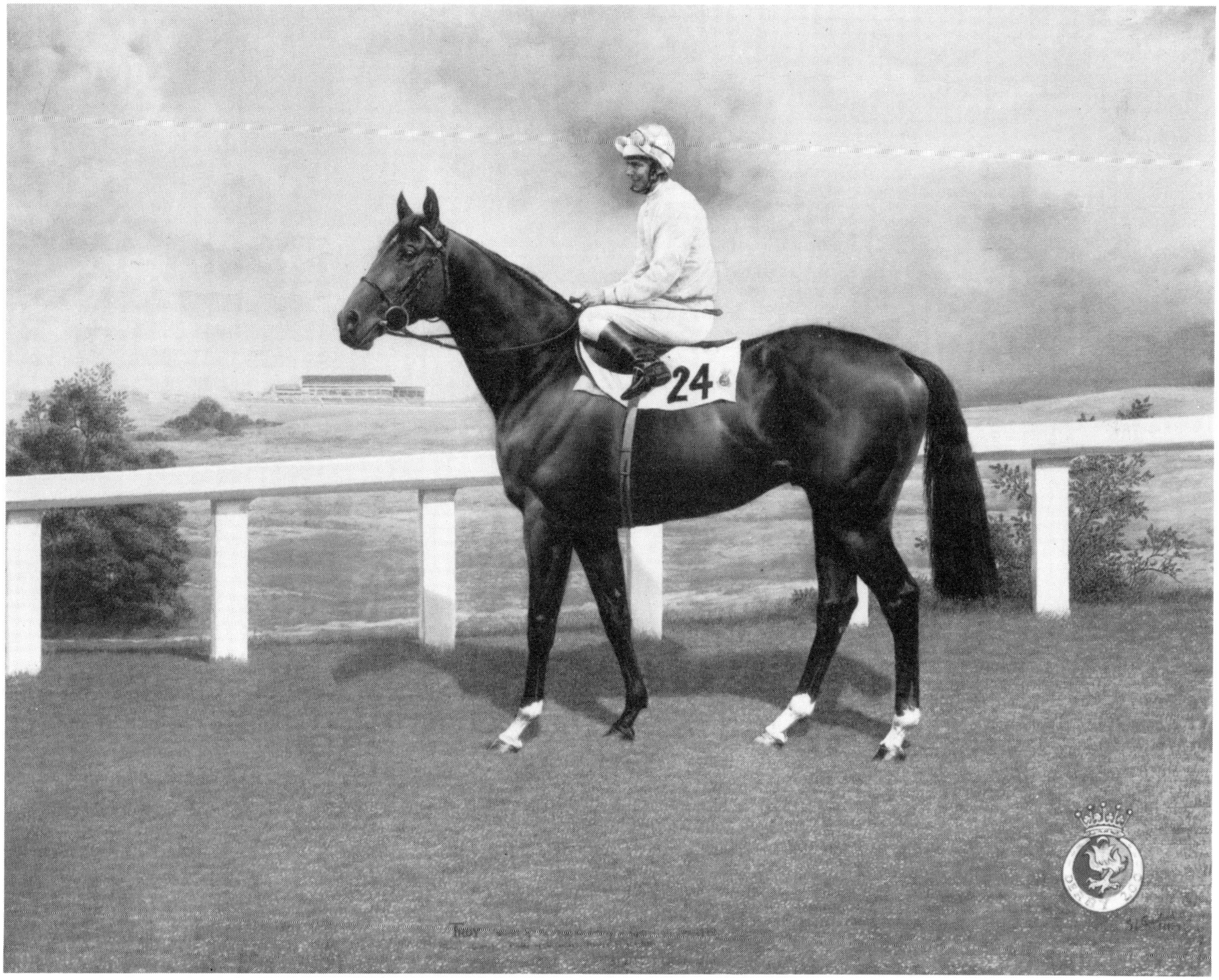

# *Liza Todd*

*born 1957*

## Northern Dancer

Northern Dancer, a small and burly bay horse, has proved to be one of the outstanding Classic sires of the twentieth century. His son Nijinsky is England's only post-war Triple Crown winner, and another son, The Minstrel, won both the English and Irish Derbys. He is also responsible for Lyphard, Nureyev, and Storm Bird, who have all been outstanding in Europe. Nijinsky, in turn, sired the very fast Derby winner of 1982, Golden Fleece.

Northern Dancer was bred in Canada by E. P. Taylor; he is by Nearctic, a son of Nearco, out of a Native Dancer mare, Natalma. As a two-year-old he made a name for his native country by winning the Coronation Futurity and then crossing the border to win the Remsen Stakes. In the following year, 1964, he was sent down to Churchill Downs for the Kentucky Derby, which he won by only a short head in a record time for the $1\frac{1}{4}$ miles. He went on to win the Preakness at Baltimore, but was deprived of the Triple Crown when he apparently failed to stay the $1\frac{1}{2}$ miles of the Belmont and was beaten by Quadrangle. There may have been some other explanation, for few of his progeny have showed any reluctance to race 12 furlongs, and Nijinsky won the 14-furlong St Leger.

He was retired to the Windfields stud-farm in Kentucky, syndicated for a figure of $2.4 million. Twenty years on, his owners were offered more than that for his services in his last years alone. They refused. By then his offspring had won well in excess of $10 million in prize-money and his tally of stakes winners was approaching the century.

Liza Todd's bronze has captured the assertive and extrovert personality for which Northern Dancer is known. A member of the celebrated American movie family, she began her training as a sculptress in England, at the Hornsey School of Art, and later moved to Los Angeles, to the Otis Art Institute. She has sculpted a number of notable thoroughbreds, including the champion stayer Properantes.

Liza Todd: *Northern Dancer*. Bronze, height 40.6 cm, length 51 cm. Private collection

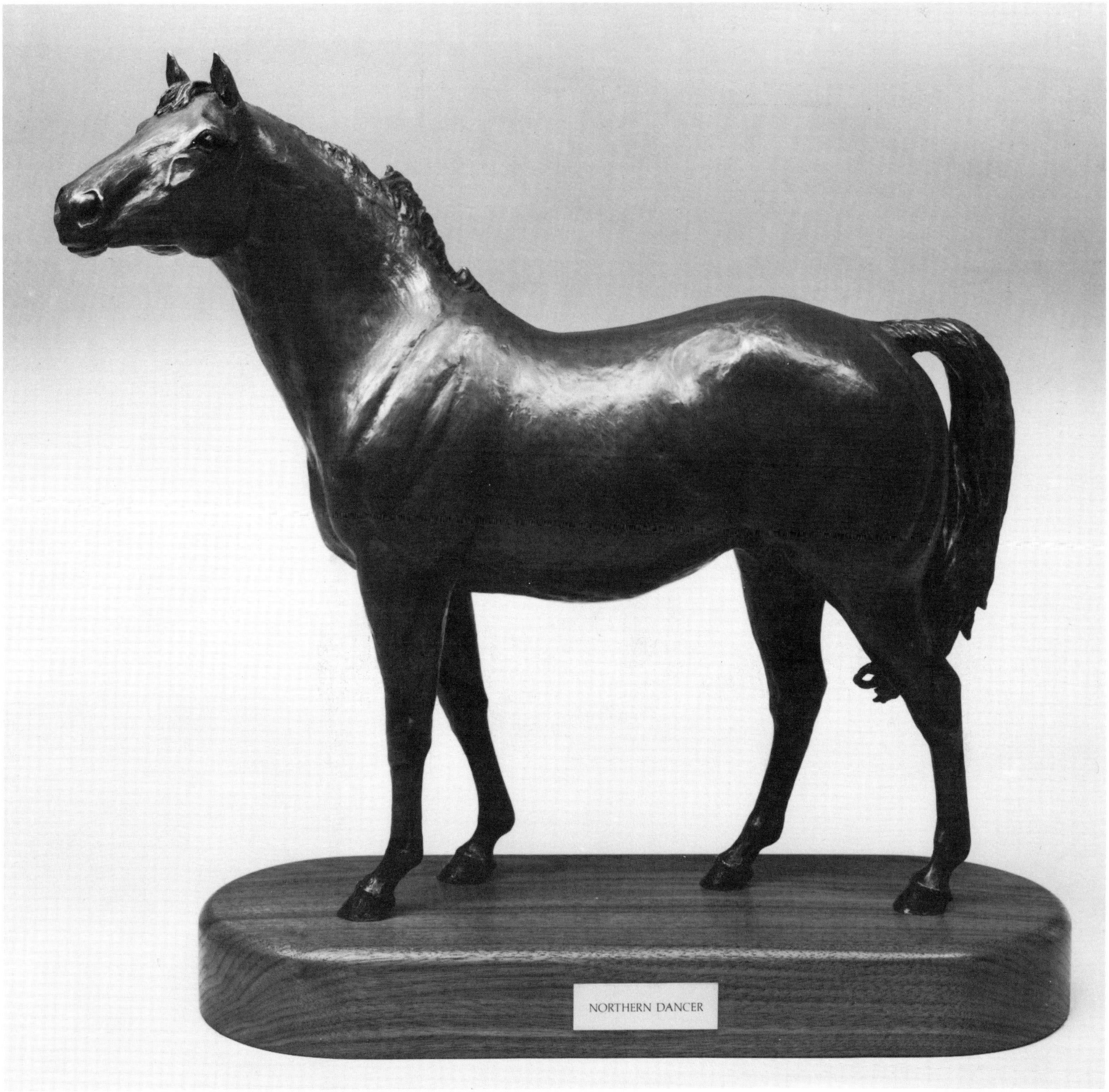
NORTHERN DANCER

# *Lionel Edwards*

*1878–1966*

## Arkle and Mill House

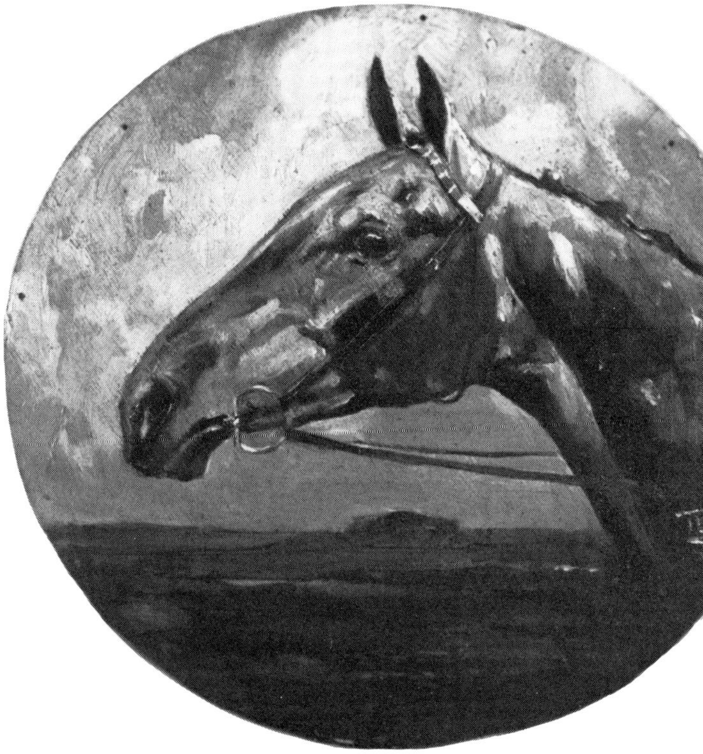

Lionel Edwards: *The Tetrarch*. 1941. Oil on wood, diameter 16.5 cm. St Peter's Church, Stockbridge, Hampshire

The two best steeplechasers in England since the Second World War were born in the same year, which was unlucky for Mill House, because the other one was Arkle.

Mill House had effectively a year's start on Arkle as a chaser. In 1963 he won the Cheltenham Gold Cup by 12 lengths, and also the King George VI Chase at Kempton and the Hennessy Cognac Gold Cup at Newbury. The manner of his victories throughout the fierce winter of 1962–3 was already producing comparisons with Golden Miller and Jock Whitney's Easter Hero, who had dominated steeplechasing in the decade before the war.

Arkle, a magnificent bay grandson of Nearco, was bred in Ireland by Mrs H. Baker. He was sold for 1,150 guineas at the Ballsbridge sales to Anne, Duchess of Westminster. She sent him to be trained by Tom Dreaper at Kilsallaghan, near Dublin. Arkle's merits soon became apparent and the annual Irish invasion of Cheltenham was enlivened in 1964 by the sure and certain knowledge that they had a champion who could defeat even the great Mill House. The contest for the Gold Cup, over Cheltenham's 3¼ miles, turned out to be one of the most memorable of all time.

Lionel Edwards's picture shows the pair at the second last fence with Arkle just leading. The battle continued to the final 100 yards of the uphill Cheltenham finish

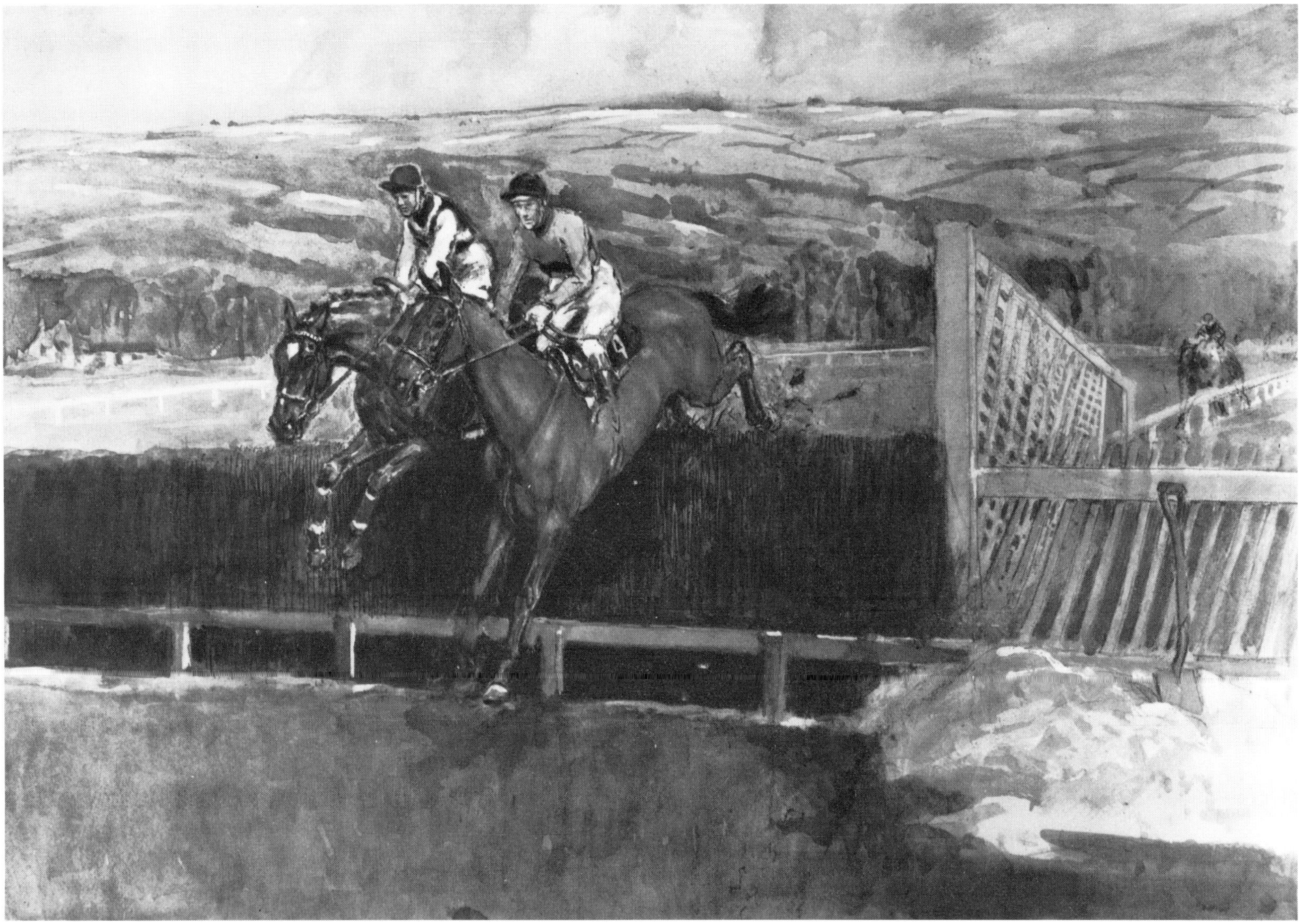

Lionel Edwards: *Arkle leading Mill House over the Second Last Fence in the Cheltenham Gold Cup of 1964.* Watercolour. Collection of Anne, Duchess of Westminster

before Mill House gave best. Arkle won by 5 lengths, with the third horse a further 25 lengths away. From that moment Arkle's superiority was unchallenged. He beat Mill House by 20 lengths in the Gold Cup of the following year, and then won it a third time by 30 lengths in 1966. He also won the Hennessy twice, as well as the King George and the Whitbread Gold Cup at Sandown, before an injury forced his retirement.

Lionel Edwards, a doctor's son from Chester, is principally known for his hunting scenes. Set against scudding skyscapes and rolling countryside, they are often spiced with touches of humour, rather in the manner of Henry Alken senior. Edwards was the keenest of hunting men himself, following stag, otter, and foxhounds with equal enthusiasm. He was a prolific book illustrator – he produced the illustrations for his own *Reminiscences of a Sporting Artist* – and he painted a number of racing scenes, both over the jumps and on the Flat. But perhaps his most unusual work in this field is the portrait of The Tetrarch painted in a roundel on the wooden screen in St Peter's Church in Stockbridge, Hampshire.

# *Richard Stone Reeves*

*born 1921*

Secretariat
Seattle Slew
Affirmed and Spectacular Bid
Dahlia
Allez France

Richard Stone Reeves has been valued above all other artists by the owners of the great thoroughbred champions of the post-war era. The roll-call of his patrons is sufficient witness: Phipps, Bunker Hunt, Firestone, Combs, Engelhard, Getty, as well as Alec Head, Lester Piggott, Vincent O'Brien, and Eddie Maple. The attraction of Reeves to the owner of a champion racehorse lies not only in his accuracy, but also in the shining hauteur which he bestows on his subjects. The portraits are celebrations of the monarch at rest, unruffled and aloof from the contest. The late Earl of Halifax, himself the possessor of a superb collection of works by the great sporting artists of the last three centuries, wrote of Reeves: 'His work in painting the thoroughbred horse is supreme in the world today.'

But for the best part of a generation, Reeves's work has remained the private delight of these wealthy owners. His paintings pass straight to the houses of his patrons; they are never seen in the auction room, and there are few examples on public view. The National Museum of Racing at Saratoga has some, including the picture of Secretariat shown here, and occasionally one can be seen at the Racing Scene gallery in New York, which is owned by his son. In recent years two volumes of reproductions have allowed a wider public their first glimpse of his work.

Even the best artists must wait for a truly great horse to appear, one that will present a fitting subject for their skills. Seymour had Flying Childers, Stubbs found Eclipse, Herring perhaps was not so fortunate. New Yorker Richard Stone Reeves has been lucky: Secretariat was the first international superstar in the age of world-wide racing and instant global communication. When he ran, the race was shown on television news bulletins in five continents. His picture was on the cover of news magazines, and his stud value was discussed in the pages of the *Financial Times* and the *Wall Street Journal.*

Secretariat is a huge slashing chestnut with three white feet. He is by Bold Ruler and is a grandson of Nasrullah. His dam was by Princequillo, an interesting reminder of the twists of fate which cross frontiers and oceans in modern racing. For the marriage of a Princequillo mare and a son of Nasrullah also produced one of England's great post-war champions, Mill Reef. Princequillo came, unfashionably, from a Belgian stallion, Prince Rose, who was moved to France in the uneasy lull before the Second World War and was safely cosseted there until his death in 1946. It was to be twenty-five years before the unique stamp of the big Belgian bay became clear at Churchill Downs and Epsom.

The exploits of Secretariat kept his fans on tenterhooks, for he was by no means invincible, losing five of his twenty-one races. But on his great days, it was as though one of the horses from the Apocalypse had

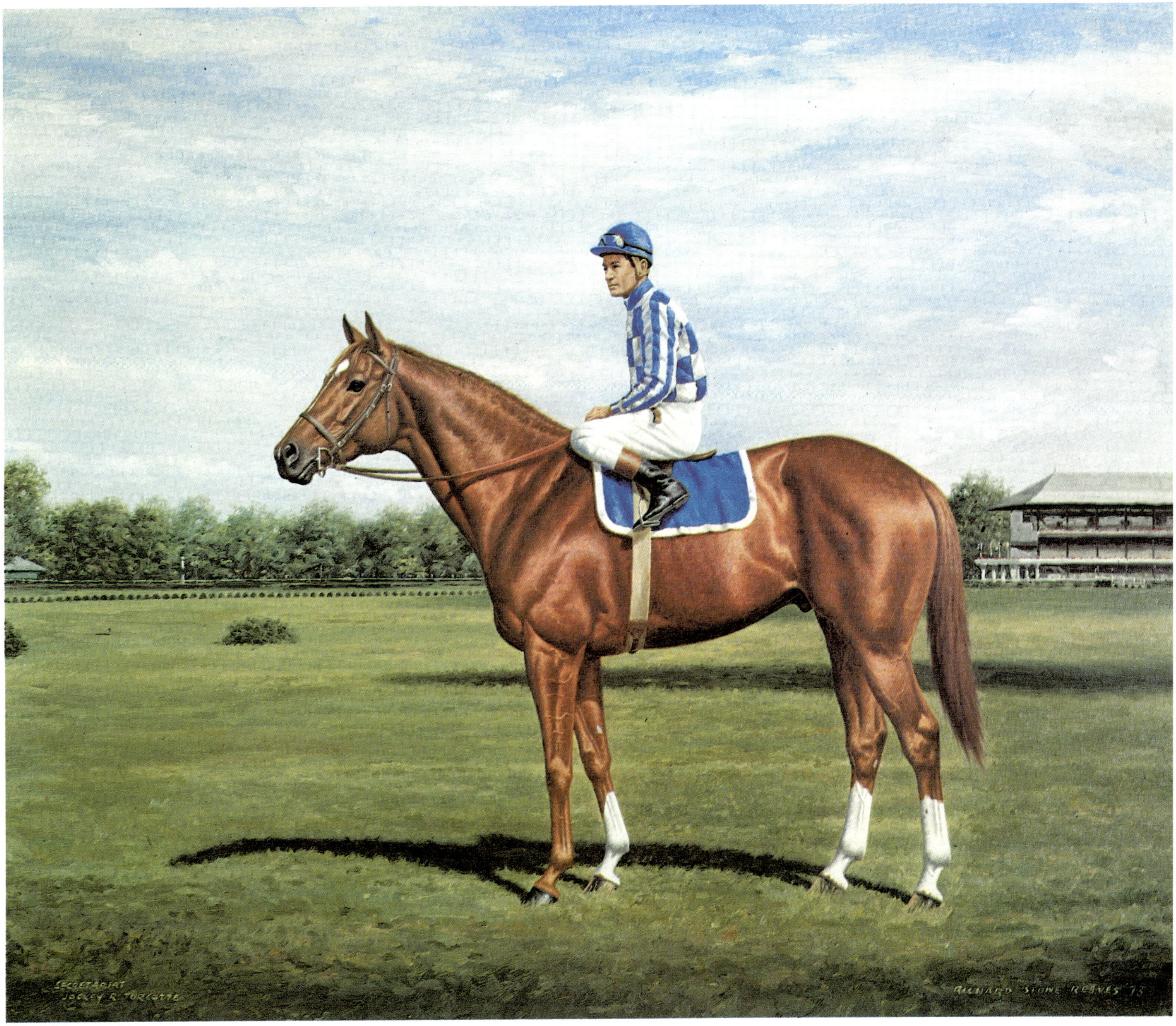


Richard Stone Reeves: *Secretariat, with Ron Turcotte up*. 1973. Oil on canvas, 57.1 × 66 cm. National Museum of Racing, Saratoga Springs, NY

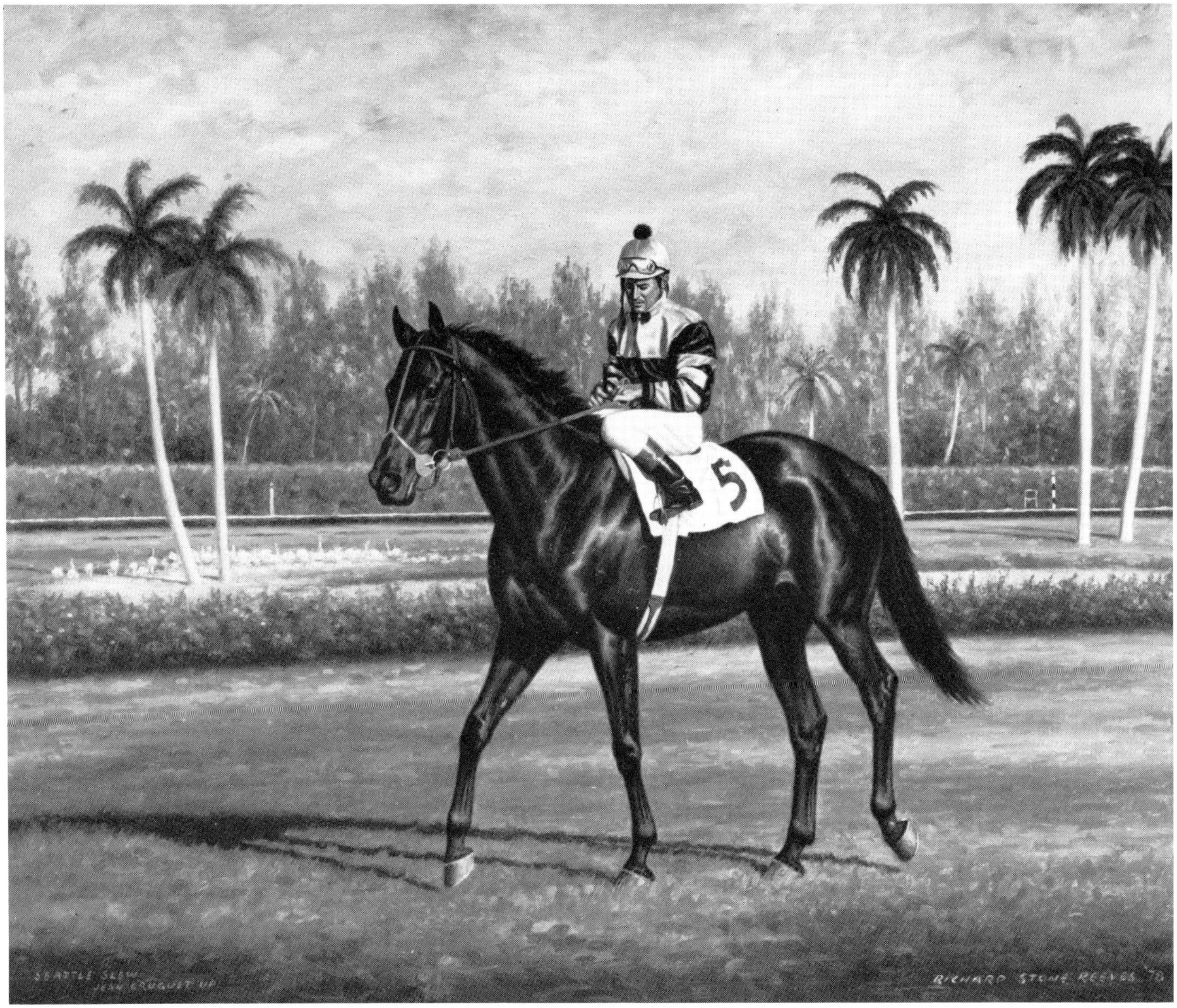


Richard Stone Reeves: *Seattle Slew, with Jean Cruguet up*. 1978. Oil on canvas, 50.8 × 60.9 cm. Private collection

descended, 'and a crown was given unto him and he went forth conquering and to conquer'. There was such a day at Belmont Park in 1973.

Secretariat had already won the Kentucky Derby in record time, and then the Preakness. It was twenty-five years since the last horse, Citation, had won the Triple Crown. There was a huge crowd agog to see if the feat of taking all three races against the nation's best three-year-olds, in just five weeks, was still possible. Secretariat chose that day to put on a supernatural performance. The stop watches, closely scrutinized in retrospect, as is the American style, confirmed the evidence of the awed spectators. Secretariat came out of the stalls fast, and, without check or pause, just proceeded to go faster and faster. In the wide Belmont stretch he was all alone, his rivals barely discernible in the distance. He won by 31 lengths, probably the greatest margin by which a Classic race has been won anywhere in the world. His time of 2 minutes 24 seconds for the $1\frac{1}{2}$ miles was, inevitably, a record. The consequence is that he would have left even a champion like Seattle Slew fifty yards behind.

Ron Turcotte, who had ridden Secretariat in all his races, was suspended during the week of the Canadian International, and Eddie Maple was in the saddle for the horse's last race. It was run in autumnal mist, through which the lights of the number-board and the illumination of the finishing-line suggested a dog track rather than a fit arena for a thoroughbred. But, once again,

Secretariat left his field floundering. He seemed to be still accelerating at the finish, as his rivals emerged from the gloom, with pursuit abandoned. His earnings in two seasons totalled over $1.3 million.

Four years later, in 1977, another Triple Crown winner appeared in America, Seattle Slew, the dark bay son of Bold Reasoning. He won the Kentucky Derby, after a bad break from the stalls, by 1¾ lengths, then equalled the record in the Preakness and streaked home in the Belmont. Thereafter, his career entered stormy waters. He was sent to California for what looked like an easy pay-day in the $300,000 Swaps Stakes at Hollywood Park and was beaten by J. O. Tobin. Then his owners took him away from trainer Billy Turner's barns in order to set up a private training establishment in Florida. The new trainer, Doug Peterson, fell out with the Slew's rider, Jean Cruguet, and 'jocked him off' in favour of Angel Cordero. Then Seattle Slew fell desperately ill with colitis.

But the horse came back as a four-year-old to take on the 1978 Triple Crown winner Affirmed and the champion from the West, Exceller. He beat Exceller over 1¼ miles in the Woodward and then went down to him by a short head in the Jockey Club Gold Cup over 1½ miles, when Affirmed pulled up after Steve Cauthen's saddle slipped. Affirmed too campaigned as a four-year-old and the Jockey Club Gold Cup of 1979 provided another of the superb contests of champions with which the 1970s were adorned in the United States.

Affirmed had duelled throughout his two- and three-year-old career with Alydar, including a desperate race for the Belmont, but had come out on top when it mattered, in the Classics of 1978. The following year he was faced with the strident claims of Spectacular Bid, the leading three-year-old, a grey son of Bold Bidder. From June onwards, the television commentators and the newspaper journalists had been working up the 'Race of the Century'. But the 'Race of the Century'

Richard Stone Reeves: *Affirmed beating Spectacular Bid, ahead of Coastal, in the 1979 Jockey Club Gold Cup at Belmont Park.* Oil on canvas, 45.7 × 76.2 cm. Private collection

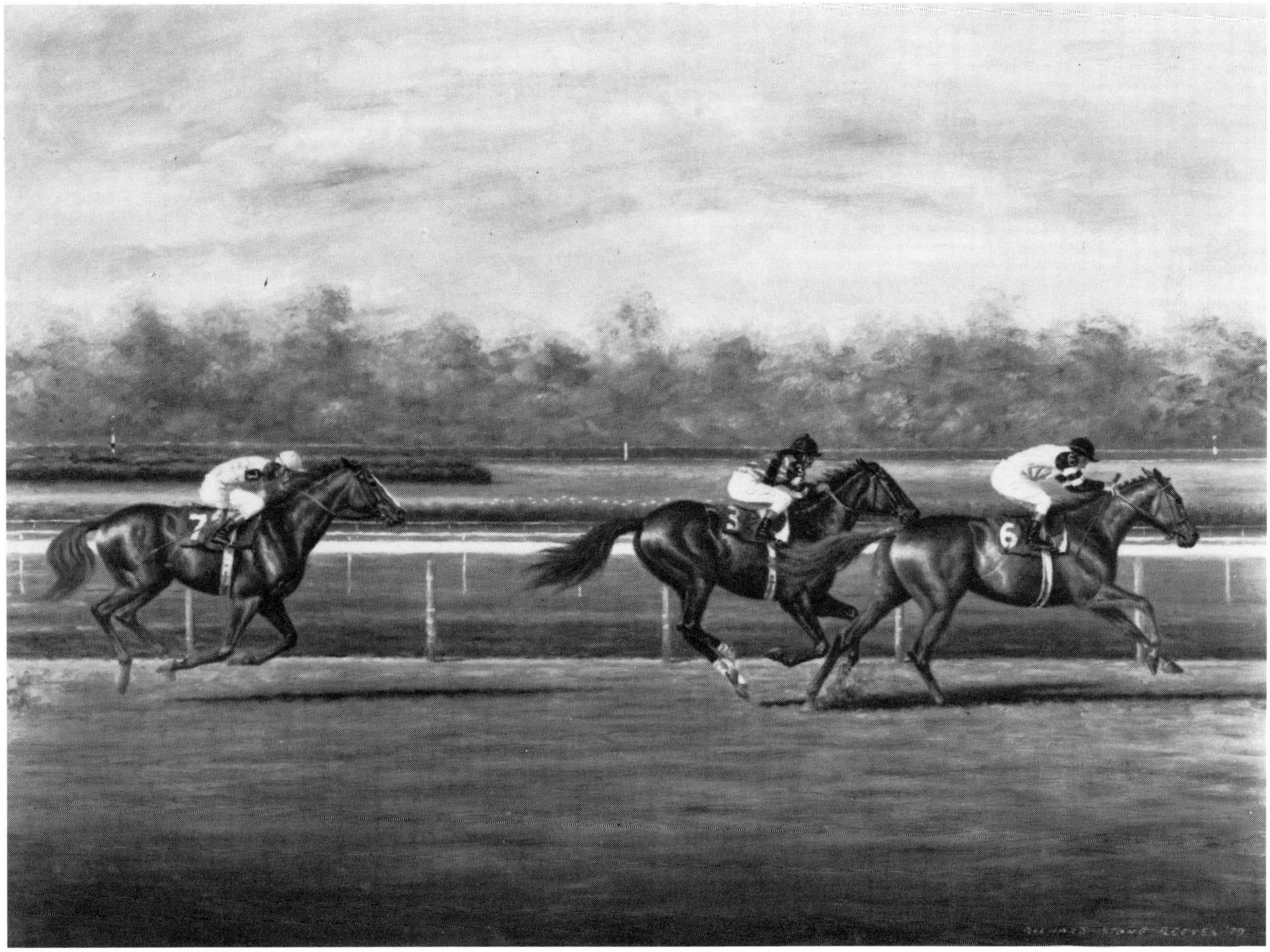

kept being postponed, until at last the two came out at Belmont Park for the Jockey Club Gold Cup in October.

Once again, there was a tinge of ill feeling around, for Steve Cauthen, who had ridden Affirmed to his Triple Crown, had been deposed in favour of Laffit Pincay on the grounds that Affirmed had become too strong for the teenage Cauthen. (America's loss was England's gain: Cauthen was captured by Robert Sangster to ride Barry Hills's horses in Europe, where he won with his first Classic ride.) Mr and Mrs Louis Wolfson, the owners of Affirmed, can feel justified, however, for Affirmed needed not only his own enormous courage but also every possible assistance to handle Spectacular Bid, ridden by Willie Shoemaker. Spectacular Bid challenged Affirmed repeatedly in the closing stages at Belmont, and twice it seemed that Affirmed would have to give best. But Pincay, who had always claimed Affirmed could not be beaten, was vindicated. Affirmed won and was retired to stud after three years of uninterrupted racing.

The 1970s also saw two outstanding French fillies, Allez France and Dahlia, who could take on and beat the colts at the highest level. Dahlia was the first truly international racehorse, beating the best in France, England, Ireland, and the United States. The Americans had the last look at her in Hollywood when she took her winnings past $1.5 million in the Turf Handicap. She had also won the Washington International. The Irish had seen her take the Irish Oaks, and the French the Grand Prix de Paris, though she was always in the shadow of Allez France on her home ground. But she loved England best of all.

The field for the 1973 King George VI and Queen Elizabeth Diamond Stakes at Ascot was one of the finest

Richard Stone Reeves: *Dahlia, with Bill Pyers up, at Ascot, 1973*. 1974. Oil on canvas, 81.2 × 96.5 cm. Private collection

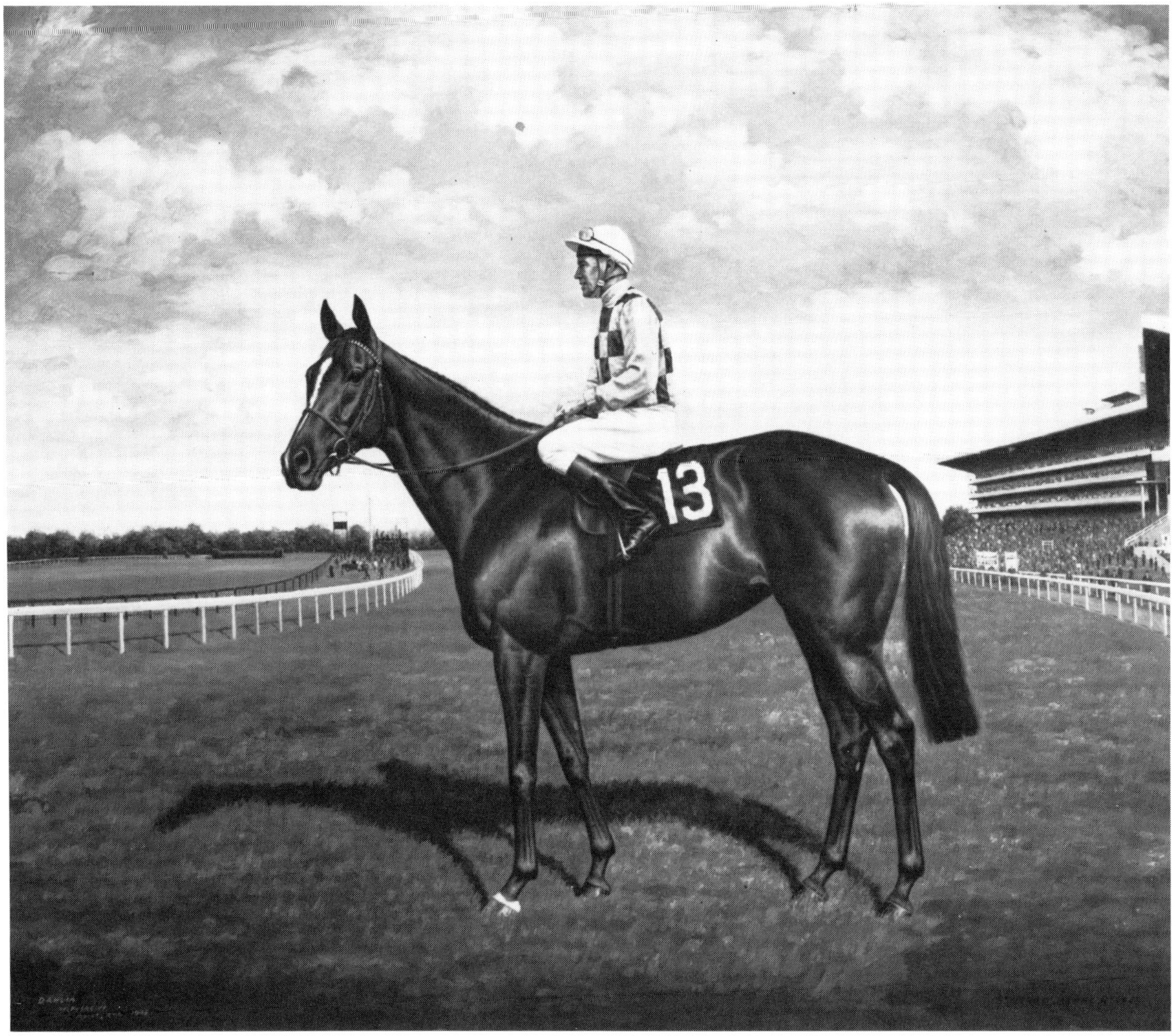

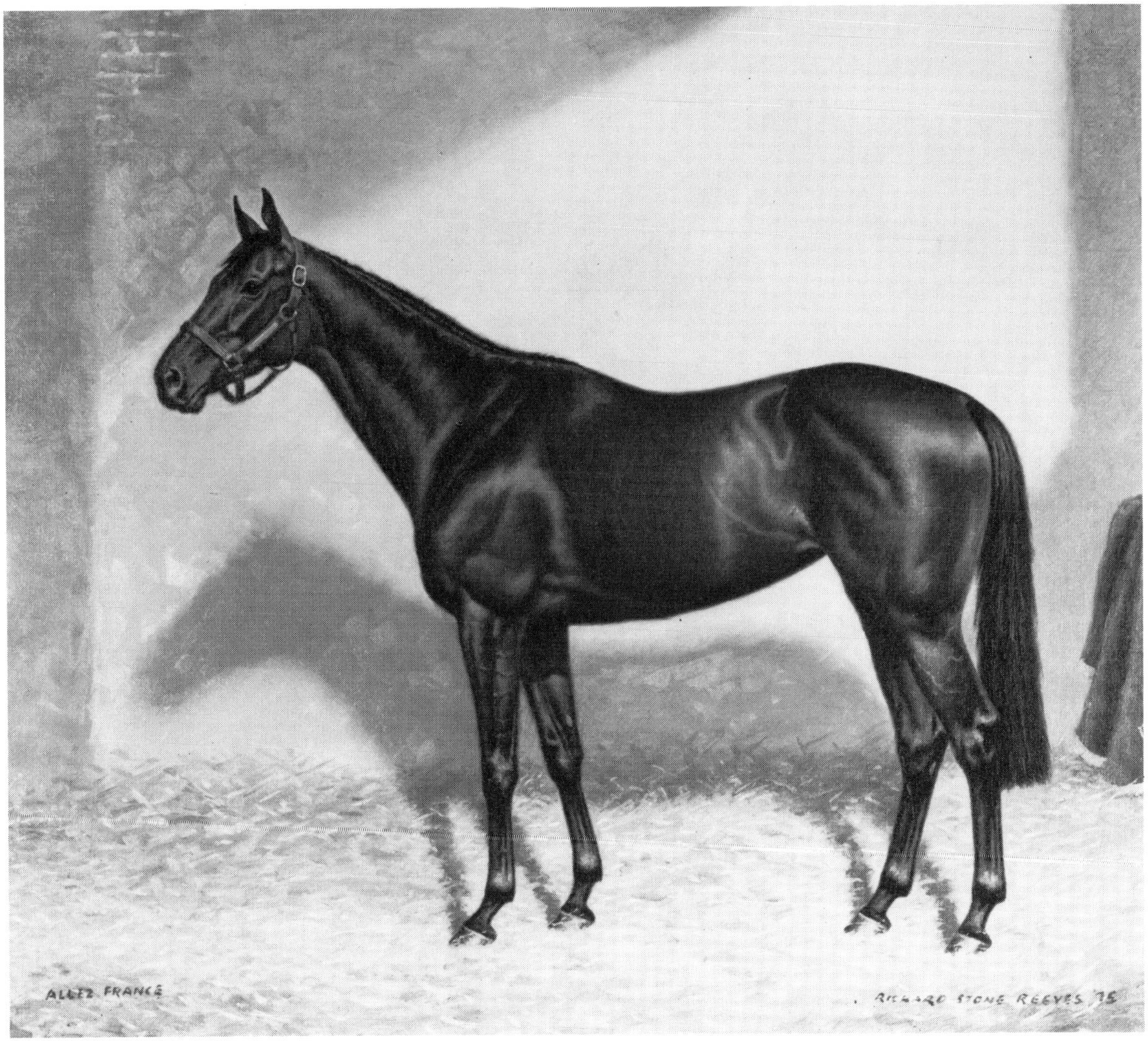


Richard Stone Reeves: *Allez France*. 1975. Oil on canvas, 40.6 × 50.8 cm. Private collection

in that most distinguished of England's all-age races. Dahlia was facing Roberto, the 1972 Derby winner and conqueror of Brigadier Gerard, Weaver's Hall, the Irish Derby winner, and Rheingold, who was to win that year's Prix de l'Arc de Triomphe. Dahlia beat them all, winning by 6 lengths in record time. The next year, Dahlia was back at Ascot beating the Derby winner Snow Knight. A month later, she was up in York to contest the Benson and Hedges Gold Cup, when she had no trouble in again accounting for Snow Knight and Imperial Prince.

As a five-year-old she defeated Grundy at York – a quite extraordinary performance. Grundy was not only a superb Derby winner, but had also lowered the Ascot King George record by 3 seconds in the titanic struggle with Bustino (see pp. 204–7). Dahlia had been third that day. At York, Piggott took Dahlia straight to the front on the long gentle bend which forms the first two-thirds of the race. Inexorably, he increased the pressure and, a quarter of a mile from home, Grundy cracked. He was beaten by 10½ lengths into fourth place.

Dahlia also won the Canadian International and the Man o' War Stakes at Belmont in her time, but the one horse she could not beat was her exact contemporary Allez France, Daniel Wildenstein's most unfeminine-looking filly. Allez France beat Dahlia six times, but the Wildenstein horse hated leaving French soil. She was twice beaten in the English Champion Stakes and also lost when she ventured to California for the Santa Anita National Thoroughbred Championship. In France, however, Allez France won three Classics and then, trained by Angel Penna and ridden by Yves Saint-Martin, won the Prix de l'Arc de Triomphe. Despite her defeats overseas, Angel Penna was convinced that he had had the good fortune to train 'the greatest filly ever to run in Europe'.

# *Leesa Sandys Lumsdaine*

*born 1936*

## Nijinsky

The stud-farms around Lexington, Kentucky, today cherish a clutch of champions trained in Ireland by Vincent O'Brien: Sir Ivor, Alleged, Storm Bird. But when O'Brien visits them, as he unfailingly does on his annual trip to the Keeneland sales, it is Nijinsky that holds a special place for him. The massive bay stallion, thundering round the elegant Claiborne paddock, is famous now as a sire, with the English Derby winner Golden Fleece among his sons. Nijinsky was a tremendous racehorse too, the only winner of the English Triple Crown in the best part of fifty years.

Vincent O'Brien had picked him out at the Woodbine sales in Toronto and persuaded Charles Engelhard to buy him. Unbeaten as a two-year-old, Nijinsky embarked in 1970 on one of the toughest campaigns in England of recent times.

Though he was nearly 17 hands, Nijinsky was very quick, and in the Two Thousand Guineas his jockey, Lester Piggott, felt he could have won at any point from quarter-horse distance onwards. As it was, he was in front 2 furlongs out at Newmarket and won by more than 2 lengths. Seeing his electrifying turn of foot that day, it was impossible to imagine that, five months on, he would be able to stay the 14 furlongs and more of the St Leger course at Doncaster. In the Epsom Derby he beat a very good horse in Gyr, and then went to The Curragh to take the Irish Derby. In the King George VI and Queen Elizabeth Stakes at Ascot he defeated the previous year's Derby winner, Blakeney.

The long straight on Town Moor at Doncaster has proved too much for some good horses in recent times – not least Shergar and Alleged – but Piggott rode Nijinsky with infinite care and produced him to beat Meadowville by a length. The victory appeared as smooth as glass. There seems no doubt, however, that the long Yorkshire Classic had got to the bottom of Nijinsky. He lost the Prix de l'Arc de Triomphe to Sassafras, and the Champion Stakes to a vastly inferior horse, Lorenzaccio – a defeat which Lester Piggott owns as gall and wormwood. But no horse in England has since come near to matching Nijinsky's record.

This portrait was presented to the Jockey Club at Newmarket by the winning Derby owner, a custom now observed only spasmodically. It is by the British artist Leesa Sandys Lumsdaine, who has painted a number of racehorses, including Arkle, Mill Reef, and Aldaniti. She was trained at Cheltenham Art College and travelled in both India and Africa before settling in the Borders region of Scotland. A number of her racing scenes have been reproduced as prints, including *Summer Silks* and *Winter Woollies*. She has an anecdotal style which in latter years has drawn much of its inspiration from the small dramas of the countryside and the farmyard, such as her amusing studies of pigs!

Leesa Sandys Lumsdaine: *Nijinsky, with Lester Piggott up*. 1970. Oil on canvas, 49.5 × 59.7 cm. Jockey Club, Newmarket

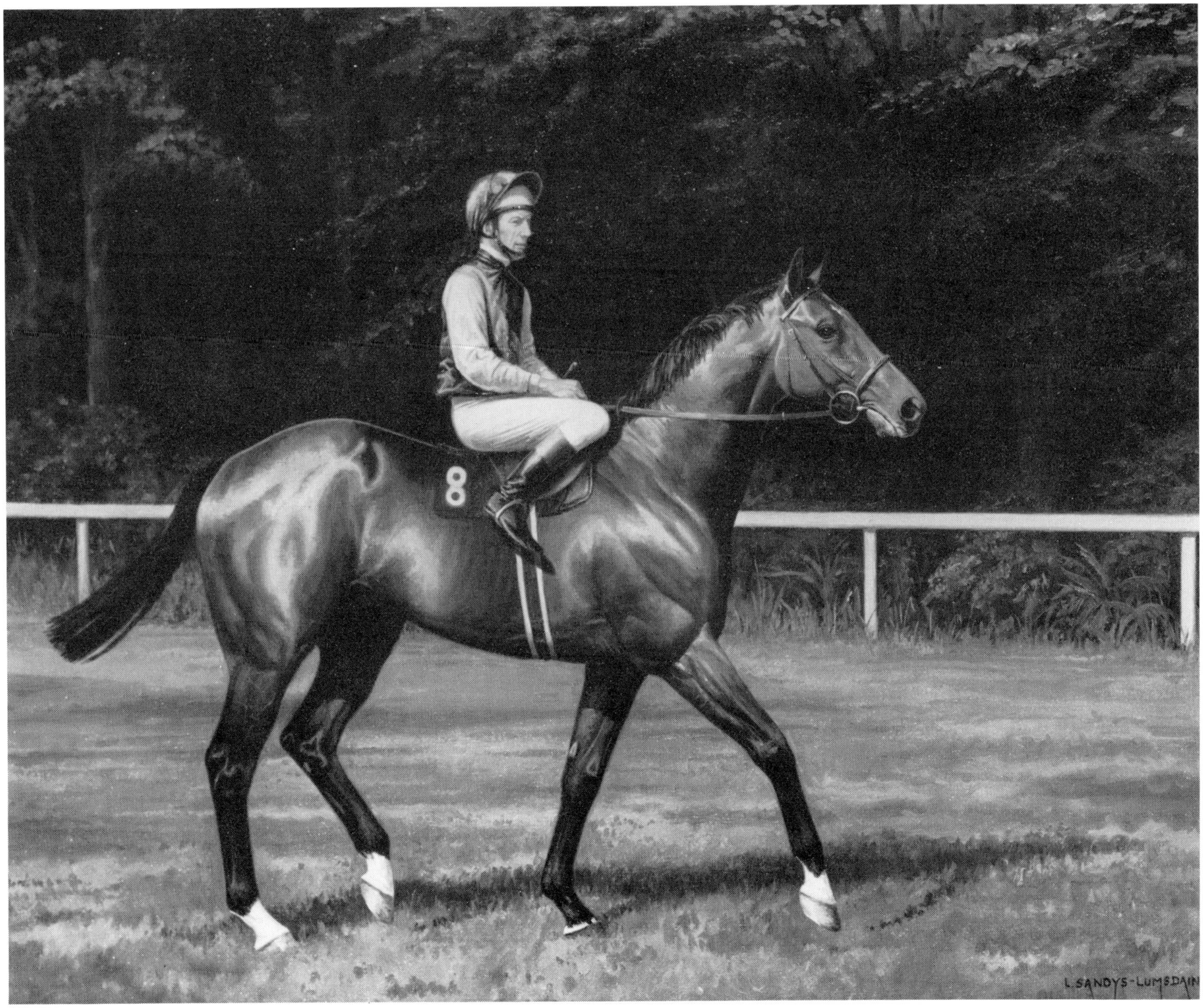

# *Gerry Cranham*

*born 1929*

Grundy and Bustino
Red Rum
Shergar

Gerry Cranham's photograph of Grundy and Bustino at Ascot in 1975 epitomizes that rare and supreme excitement of racing: two great horses, at the height of their powers, locked in combat at the finish. The superbly fit and muscled bodies, the strides matched at full stretch, above all that mysterious competitive will of the true champion are etched indelibly on the eye.

Often the great racehorses find no worthy opponents to try their mettle. 'Eclipse first, the rest nowhere,' was Dennis O'Kelly's famous cry in the eighteenth century. St Simon was never tested, nor was The Tetrarch. Hyperion did not meet a match when he was fully fit. In recent years Golden Fleece and Sea Bird II departed the scene without ever being fully tried. Brigadier Gerard and Mill Reef never met in their maturity. But when the day does come for the confrontation of true champions, the experience is sublime. Blacklock and Ebor's St Leger, Dungannon versus Rockingham, The Flying Dutchman versus Voltigeur – they all live down through the centuries. In recent times, American fans at Belmont were granted such a privilege when Spectacular Bid and Affirmed fought out their great battle (see p. 199).

Grundy and Bustino's moment came in the King George VI and Queen Elizabeth Stakes at Ascot, $1\frac{1}{2}$ miles at weight for age. Grundy had just won the Derby. Bustino had won the Coronation Cup at Epsom – the 'four-year-olds' Derby' – and the St Leger the year before. Grundy, by Great Nephew, was the warmest of chestnuts, compact, almost pretty, with a palomino mane and tail. He was unbeaten as a two-year-old, but as the 1975 season opened there was a fearful incident at Peter Walwyn's Seven Barrows yard at Lambourn. Another horse, Corby, frightened at Grundy's impatient caperings, lashed out and smashed Grundy's nose, splintering the bone. Almost impossibly, Grundy recovered in time to run second in the Two Thousand Guineas. He then won the English and Irish Derbys. It was time for the moment of truth for a three-year-old, the first encounter with older generations. Bustino was waiting.

Dick Hern, Bustino's trainer, has made the most telling use of pace-makers in his racing strategies, not least when the Queen's filly Dunfermline beat Alleged in the St Leger of 1977. For Bustino's contest with Grundy,

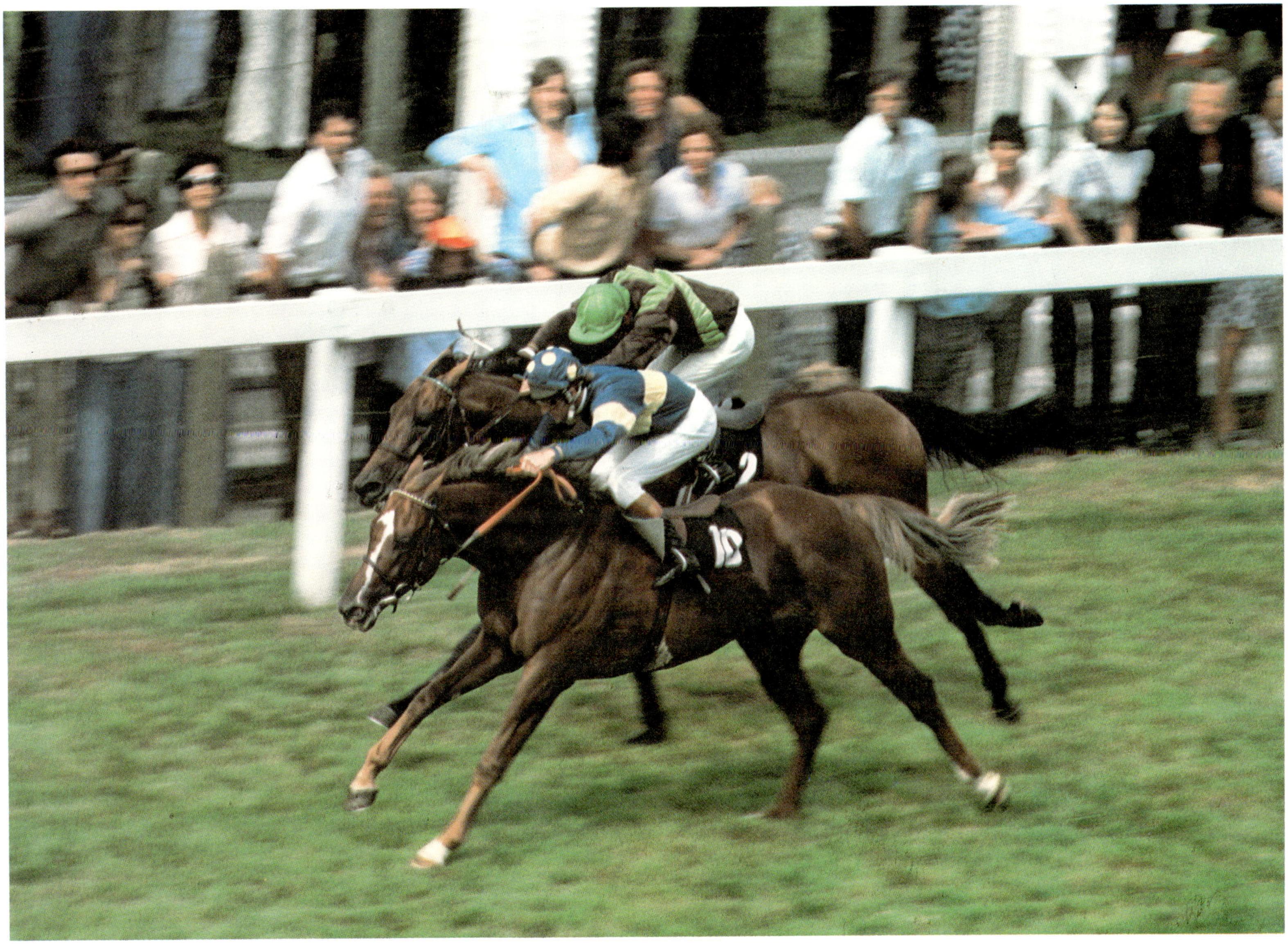

Gerry Cranham: *Pat Eddery on Grundy defeats Joe Mercer on Bustino in the 1975 King George VI and Queen Elizabeth Diamond Stakes at Ascot*

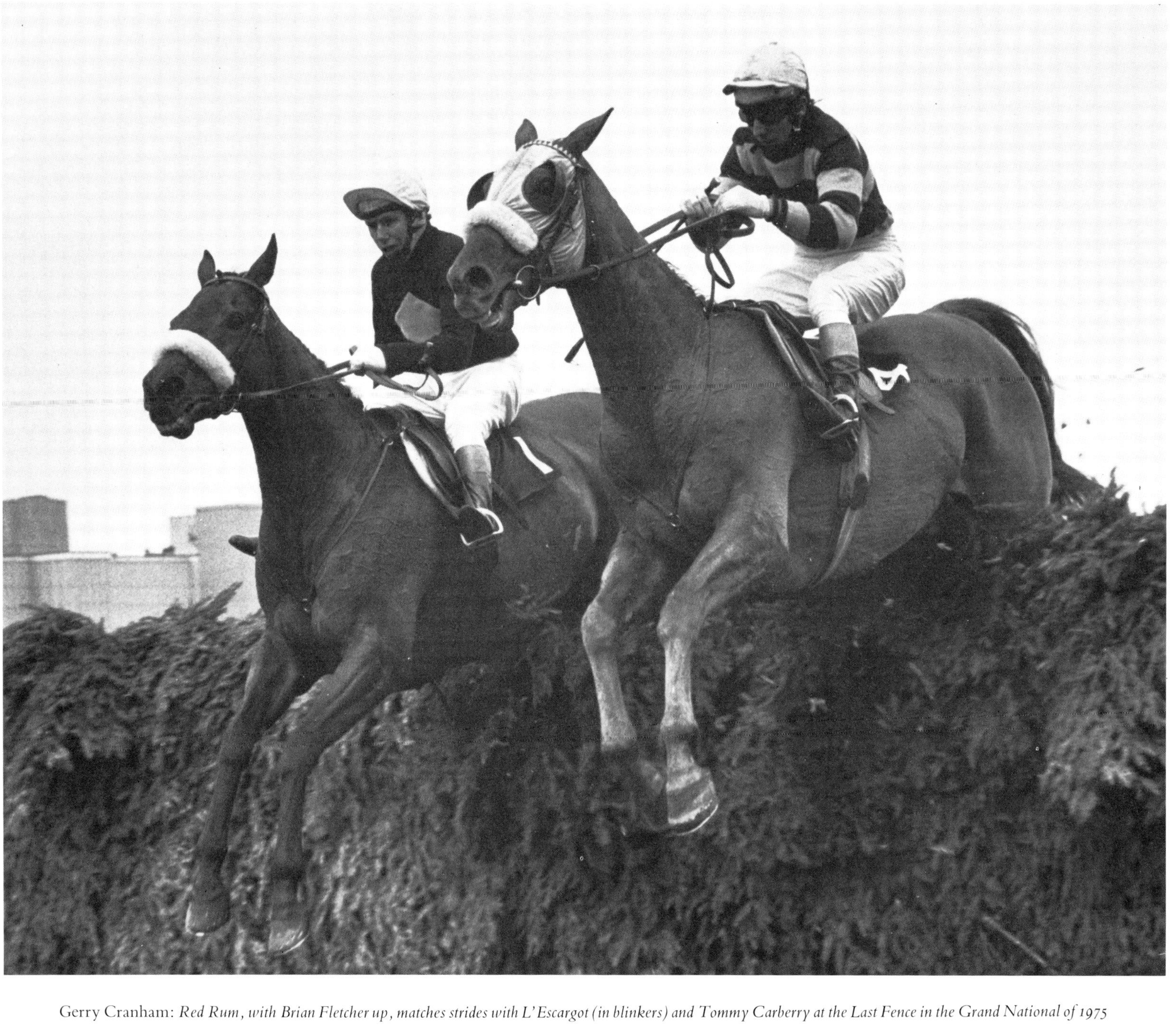

Gerry Cranham: *Red Rum, with Brian Fletcher up, matches strides with L'Escargot (in blinkers) and Tommy Carberry at the Last Fence in the Grand National of 1975*

Hern decided to run two pace-makers, Highest and Kinglet, to ensure that the Walwyn horse was searched to the very limit of his strength. Two other outstanding horses, Star Appeal and the mare Dahlia, were in the field. Fully half a mile out, Bustino slipped Grundy and went for home. Three lengths clear in the straight, it seemed he was beyond catching. But Pat Eddery gave Grundy a most punishing tattoo with the whip and got him up and past the four-year-old. Bustino came back. For the last furlong, the two were locked together until suddenly Bustino, at the end of his tether, gave best.

Gerry Cranham was first attracted by the colour and drama of racing when he was researching subjects for the new colour magazines which were being established in England in the 1960s. His own interests had been primarily in athletics and other sports, and he had worked for the American magazines *Sports Illustrated*, *Time*, and *Life*. But his eye for the unusual and illuminating angle – cameras placed under the jumps in steeplechasing, horses shot from the 'wrong' side as in the Grundy picture – as well as his instinct for the high point of a race and his patience (he waited beside one particular jump for four years before he shot a famous picture of Terry Biddlecombe taking a fall) have made him one of the world's outstanding racing photographers. This achievement was recognized when he became, in the wake of Cartier-Bresson, one of the first photographers to be the subject of an exhibition at the Victoria and Albert Museum in London.

Gerry Cranham's shot of Red Rum and the blinkered L'Escargot taking the last fence in the 1975 Aintree Grand National, every sinew and blood-vessel standing out, the jockeys locked in concentration, freezes the decisive moment of the race. L'Escargot, beaten by Red Rum the previous year, now had nearly a stone in hand, and, like only one other horse in five Grand Nationals, was able to defeat the champion in the long run-in.

Red Rum had passed through many hands before he ended up in trainer 'Ginger' McCain's yard behind a second-hand car lot at Birkdale on the Lancashire coast. His feet were poor: he had an affliction known as pedalosteitis. He had been running since he was 2 years old. He didn't seem to like soft going. McCain was taking a terrible 'flyer' when he paid 6,000 guineas for him at Doncaster sales in 1972. The gamble seemed to have failed when Red Rum turned out lame the very next day after McCain got him home. Red Rum's new owner, Noel le Mare, was already well past 80 years old when Red Rum arrived. He had dreamed of winning the National since he had caught the fever in Ascetic Silver's year, 1906. A fellow trawlerman in Fleetwood had introduced him to the sport.

But the eccentricity of McCain's stable, where the horses are trained only on the beach, great flat stretches of sand at the mouth of the Mersey where the tide takes the sea far out of sight, seemed to suit Red Rum. The first time he saw the ocean, he walked straight in chest deep. Ever after, he would dip his feet on the way home. For walking exercise he would scramble, spring, and slide up and down the sand-dunes, tuning his muscles as the Australian distance runner Herb Elliott used to do. The tendons were stretched, the loins and quarters were strengthened, yet the soft sand protected his fragile feet. His morning canter was always down a carefully harrowed pathway of sand, taken whenever the tide permitted.

The 1973 Grand National was a heart-stopping affair. Much of the sympathy went to Crisp, who was well clear two fences out, but, with 12 st. on his back, was hauled in yard by yard down Aintree's long straight. Red Rum, carrying 10 st. 5 lb., got up to snatch the race on the line. He was never again to have such an advantage. He beat L'Escargot in 1974 when they were the two top weights; lost to him the next year on 10 lb. worse terms; was beaten by Rag Trade, giving him 12 lb., in 1976; and then won again when he was 12 years old in 1977.

Red Rum was the greatest horse ever to run in the world's most gruelling race. He became a celebrity on a level with Hollywood stars, making personal appearances all over Britain, beginning with the night of his last triumph, when he walked up the steps of the Bold Hotel in Southport, down the red carpet, and graciously posed for photographers before listening to the victory speeches of his connections. The horse with the delicate feet had earned his retirement.

As Shergar entered the tree-lined paddock at Ascot for the King George VI and Queen Elizabeth Diamond Stakes in the summer of 1981, the huge crowd burst into spontaneous applause. It was in recognition of a horse who had won the hearts of racegoers almost entirely through one race – the Derby. With his great white blaze and his tongue lolling out, he had won the 'Blue Riband' more easily than any horse in memory. He was so far ahead that John Reid, coming with a run to take second place on Glint of Gold, for a moment thought he had won. Shergar won again at Ascot. But from then on his stars were crossed.

At Doncaster, for the St Leger in September, he looked hardly the god-like figure who had bestrode the summer. He was beaten and retired to stud in Ireland. From there, one black night in February 1983, he was kidnapped and spirited away, whether for money or out of some dark vengeance against his owner the Aga Khan has never become clear. At the time of writing, one of the greatest Derby winners of the age is still missing.

Gerry Cranham: *Shergar, with Walter Swinburn up.* 1981

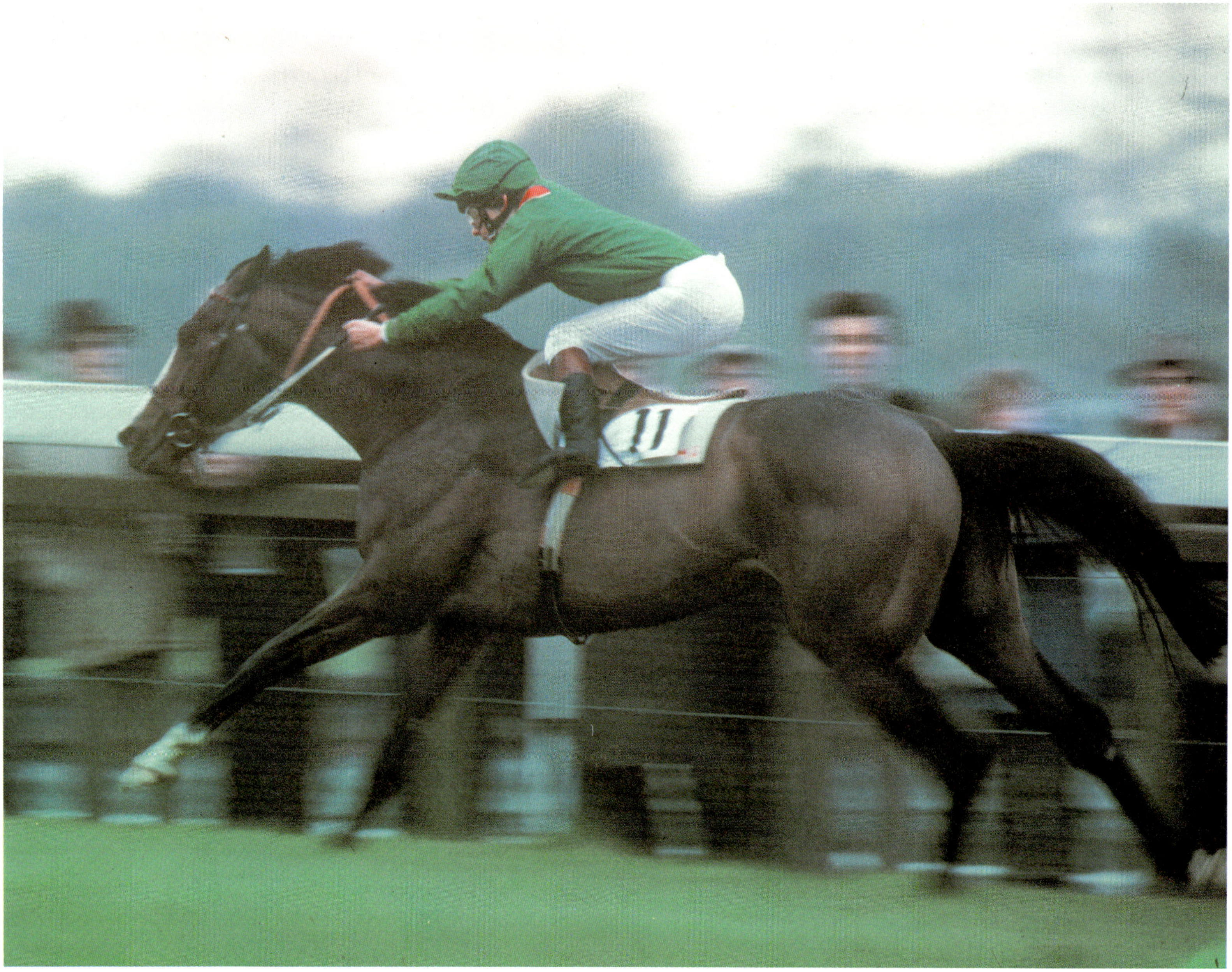

# Classic Winners

The races included here are for three-year-old colts and fillies, except for the Oaks, which is for three-year-old fillies only. The names of horses illustrated and featured in the text are printed in bold type.

## BRITAIN

| | Derby<br>Epsom<br>1½ miles | Oaks<br>Epsom<br>1½ miles | St Leger<br>Doncaster<br>1¾ miles |
|---|---|---|---|
| 1776 | | | Alabaculia |
| 1777 | | | Bourbon |
| 1778 | | | Hollandaise |
| 1779 | | Bridget | Tommy |
| 1780 | **Diomed** | Teetotum | Ruler |
| 1781 | Young Eclipse | Faith | Serina |
| 1782 | Assassin | Ceres | Imperatrix |
| 1783 | Saltram | Maid of the Oaks | Phenomenon |
| 1784 | Serjeant | Stella | Omphale |
| 1785 | Aimwell | Trifle | Cowslip |
| 1786 | Noble | The Yellow Filly | Paragon |
| 1787 | Sir Peter Teazle | Annette | Spadille |
| 1788 | Sir Thomas | Nightshade | Young Flora |
| 1789 | Skyscraper | Tag | Pewett |
| 1790 | Rhadamanthus | Hippolyta | Ambidexter |
| 1791 | Eager | Portia | Young Traveller |
| 1792 | John Bull | Volante | Tartar |
| 1793 | Waxy | Coelia | Ninety-three |
| 1794 | Daedalus | Hermione | Beningbrough |
| 1795 | Spread Eagle | Platina | **Hambletonian** |
| 1796 | Didelot | Parisot | Ambrosio |
| 1797 | Colt by Fidget | Nike | Lounger |
| 1798 | Sir Harry | Bellissima | Symmetry |
| 1799 | Archduke | Bellina | Cockfighter |
| 1800 | Champion | Ephemera | Champion |
| 1801 | **Eleanor** | **Eleanor** | Quiz |
| 1802 | Tyrant | Scotia | Orville |
| 1803 | Ditto | Theophania | Remembrancer |
| 1804 | Hannibal | Pelisse | Sancho |
| 1805 | **Cardinal Beaufort** | Meteora | Staveley |
| 1806 | Paris | Bronze | Fyldener |
| 1807 | Election | Briseis | Paulina |
| 1808 | Pan | Morel | Petronius |
| 1809 | Pope | Maid of Orleans | Ashton |
| 1810 | Whalebone | Oriana | Octavian |
| 1811 | Phantom | Sorcery | Soothsayer |
| 1812 | Octavius | **Manuella** | Otterington |
| 1813 | Smolensko | Music | **Altisidora** |
| 1814 | Blucher | Medora | William |
| 1815 | Whisker | Minuet | Filho da Puta |
| 1816 | Prince Leopold | Landscape | The Duchess |
| 1817 | Azor | Neva | Ebor |
| 1818 | Sam | Corinne | Reveller |
| 1819 | Tiresias | Shoveler | Antonio |
| 1820 | Sailor | Caroline | St Patrick |
| 1821 | Gustavus | Augusta | Jack Spigot |
| 1822 | Moses | Pastille | Theodore |
| 1823 | Emilius | Zinc | Barefoot |
| 1824 | Cedric | Cobweb | **Jerry** |
| 1825 | Middleton | Wings | **Memnon** |
| 1826 | Lap-dog | Lilias (renamed Babel) | Tarrare |
| 1827 | **Mameluke** | Gulnare | Matilda |
| 1828 | Cadland | Turquoise | **The Colonel** |
| 1829 | Frederick | Green Mantle | **Rowton** |
| 1830 | **Priam** | Variation | Birmingham |

| | *Derby* | *Oaks* | *St Leger* |
|---|---|---|---|
| 1831 | Spaniel | Oxygen | Chorister |
| 1832 | St Giles | Galata | Margrave |
| 1833 | Dangerous | Vespa | **Rockingham** |
| 1834 | **Plenipotentiary** | **Pussy** | **Touchstone** |
| 1835 | Mundig | Queen of Trumps | Queen of Trumps |
| 1836 | Bay Middleton | Cyprian | **Elis** |
| 1837 | Phosphorus | Miss Letty | Mango |
| 1838 | Amato | Industry | Don John |
| 1839 | Bloomsbury | Deception | Charles XII |
| 1840 | **Little Wonder** | **Crucifix** | Launcelot |
| 1841 | Coronation | Ghuznee | Satirist |
| 1842 | Attila | Our Nell | Blue Bonnet |
| 1843 | Cotherstone | Poison | Nutwith |
| 1844 | Orlando | The Princess | Faugh-a-Ballagh |
| 1845 | The Merry Monarch | Refraction | The Baron |
| 1846 | Pyrrhus the First | Mendicant | **Sir Tatton Sykes** |
| 1847 | The Cossack | Miami | Van Tromp |
| 1848 | **Surplice** | Cymba | **Surplice** |
| 1849 | **The Flying Dutchman** | Lady Evelyn | **The Flying Dutchman** |
| 1850 | **Voltigeur** | Rhedycina | **Voltigeur** |
| 1851 | Teddington | Iris | Newminster |
| 1852 | Daniel O'Rourke | Songstress | Stockwell |
| 1853 | **West Australian** | Catherine Hayes | **West Australian** |
| 1854 | Andover | Mincemeat | Knight of St George |
| 1855 | Wild Dayrell | Marchioness | Saucebox |
| 1856 | Ellington | Mincepie | Warlock |
| 1857 | Blink Bonny | Blink Bonny | Imperieuse |
| 1858 | Beadsman | Governess | Sunbeam |
| 1859 | Musjid | Summerside | Gamester |
| 1860 | Thormanby | Butterfly | St Albans |
| 1861 | Kettledrum | Brown Duchess | Caller Ou |
| 1862 | Caractacus | Feu de Joie | The Marquis |
| 1863 | Macaroni | Queen Bertha | Lord Clifden |
| 1864 | Blair Athol | Fille de l'Air | Blair Athol |
| 1865 | **Gladiateur** | Regalia | **Gladiateur** |
| 1866 | Lord Lyon | Tormentor | Lord Lyon |
| 1867 | Hermit | Hippia | Achievement |
| 1868 | Blue Gown | Formosa | Formosa |
| 1869 | Pretender | Brigantine | Pero Gomez |
| 1870 | Kingcraft | Gamos | Hawthornden |
| 1871 | Favonius | Hannah | Hannah |
| 1872 | Cremorne | Reine | Wenlock |
| 1873 | Doncaster | Marie Stuart | Marie Stuart |
| 1874 | George Frederick | Apology | Apology |
| 1875 | Galopin | Spinaway | Craig Millar |
| 1876 | Kisber | Enguerrande / Camelia | Petrarch |
| 1877 | Silvio | Placida | Silvio |
| 1878 | **Sefton** | Jannette | Jannette |
| 1879 | Sir Bevys | Wheel of Fortune | Rayon d'Or |
| 1880 | Bend Or | Jenny Howlet | Robert the Devil |
| 1881 | **Iroquois** | Thebais | **Iroquois** |
| 1882 | Shotover | Geheimniss | Dutch Oven |
| 1883 | St Blaise | Bonny Jean | Ossian |
| 1884 | St Gatien / Harvester | Busybody | The Lambkin |
| 1885 | Melton | Lonely | Melton |
| 1886 | **Ormonde** | Miss Jummy | **Ormonde** |
| 1887 | Merry Hampton | Rêve d'Or | Kilwarlin |
| 1888 | **Ayrshire** | Seabreeze | Seabreeze |
| 1889 | **Donovan** | L'Abbesse de Jouarre | **Donovan** |
| 1890 | Sainfoin | Memoir | Memoir |
| 1891 | Common | Mimi | Common |
| 1892 | Sir Hugo | **La Flèche** | **La Flèche** |
| 1893 | Isinglass | Mrs Butterwick | Isinglass |
| 1894 | Ladas | Amiable | Throstle |
| 1895 | Sir Visto | La Sagesse | Sir Visto |
| 1896 | **Persimmon** | Canterbury Pilgrim | **Persimmon** |
| 1897 | Galtee More | Limasol | Galtee More |
| 1898 | Jeddah | Airs and Graces | Wildfowler |
| 1899 | Flying Fox | Musa | Flying Fox |

| | *Derby* | *Oaks* | *St Leger* |
|---|---|---|---|
| 1900 | **Diamond Jubilee** | La Roche | **Diamond Jubilee** |
| 1901 | Volodyovski | Cap and Bells II | Doricles |
| 1902 | Ard Patrick | Sceptre | Sceptre |
| 1903 | Rock Sand | Our Lassie | Rock Sand |
| 1904 | St Amant | Pretty Polly | Pretty Polly |
| 1905 | Cicero | Cherry Lass | Challacombe |
| 1906 | Spearmint | Keystone II | Troutbeck |
| 1907 | Orby | Glass Doll | Wool Winder |
| 1908 | Signorinetta | Signorinetta | Your Majesty |
| 1909 | **Minoru** | Perola | Bayardo |
| 1910 | **Lemberg** | Rosedrop | Swynford |
| 1911 | Sunstar | Cherimoya | Prince Palatine |
| 1912 | Tagalie | Mirska | Tracery |
| 1913 | Aboyeur | Jest | Night Hawk |
| 1914 | Durbar II | Princess Dorie | Black Jester |
| 1915 | Pommern | Snow Marten | Pommern |
| 1916 | Fifinella | Fifinella | Hurry On |
| 1917 | Gay Crusader | Sunny Jane | Gay Crusader |
| 1918 | Gainsborough | My Dear | Gainsborough |
| 1919 | Grand Parade | Bayuda | Keysoe |
| 1920 | Spion Kop | Charlebelle | Caligula |
| 1921 | Humorist | Love in Idleness | Polemarch |
| 1922 | Captain Cuttle | Pogrom | Royal Lancer |
| 1923 | Papyrus | Brownhylda | Tranquil |
| 1924 | Sansovino | Straitlace | Salmon Trout |
| 1925 | Manna | Saucy Sue | **Solario** |
| 1926 | Coronach | Short Story | Coronach |
| 1927 | Call Boy | Beam | Book Law |
| 1928 | Felstead | Toboggan | Fairway |
| 1929 | Trigo | Pennycomequick | Trigo |
| 1930 | Blenheim | Rose of England | Singapore |
| 1931 | **Cameronian** | Brulette | Sandwich |
| 1932 | April the Fifth | Udaipur | Firdaussi |
| 1933 | **Hyperion** | Chatelaine | **Hyperion** |
| 1934 | Windsor Lad | Light Brocade | Windsor Lad |
| 1935 | **Bahram** | Quashed | **Bahram** |
| 1936 | **Mahmoud** | Lovely Rosa | Boswell |
| 1937 | Midday Sun | Exhibitionist | Chulmleigh |
| 1938 | Bois Roussel | Rockfel | Scottish Union |
| 1939 | **Blue Peter** | Galatea II | no race |
| 1940 | Pont l'Eveque | Godiva | Turkhan |
| 1941 | Owen Tudor | Commotion | Sun Castle |
| 1942 | Watling Street | **Sun Chariot** | **Sun Chariot** |
| 1943 | Straight Deal | Why Hurry | Herringbone |
| 1944 | Ocean Swell | Hycilla | Tehran |
| 1945 | Dante | Sun Stream | Chamossaire |
| 1946 | Airborne | Steady Aim | Airborne |
| 1947 | Pearl Diver | Imprudence | Sayajirao |
| 1948 | My Love | Masaka | Black Tarquin |
| 1949 | Nimbus | Musidora | Ridge Wood |
| 1950 | Galcador | Asmena | Scratch II |
| 1951 | Arctic Prince | Neasham Belle | Talma II |
| 1952 | Tulyar | Frieze | Tulyar |
| 1953 | Pinza | Ambiguity | Premonition |
| 1954 | Never Say Die | Sun Cap | Never Say Die |
| 1955 | Phil Drake | Meld | Meld |
| 1956 | Lavandin | Sicarelle | Cambremer |
| 1957 | Crepello | Carrozza | Ballymoss |
| 1958 | Hard Ridden | Bella Paola | Alcide |
| 1959 | Parthia | Petite Étoile | Cantelo |
| 1960 | St Paddy | Never Too Late II | St Paddy |
| 1961 | Psidium | Sweet Solera | Aurelius |
| 1962 | Larkspur | Monade | Hethersett |
| 1963 | Relko | Noblesse | Ragusa |
| 1964 | Santa Claus | Homeward Bound | Indiana |
| 1965 | Sea Bird II | Long Look | Provoke |
| 1966 | Charlottown | Valoris | Sodium |
| 1967 | Royal Palace | Pia | Ribocco |
| 1968 | Sir Ivor | La Lagune | Ribero |
| 1969 | Blakeney | Sleeping Partner | Intermezzo |
| 1970 | **Nijinsky** | Lupe | **Nijinsky** |

| | *Derby* | *Oaks* | *St Leger* |
|---|---|---|---|
| 1971 | **Mill Reef** | Altesse Royale | Athens Wood |
| 1972 | Roberto | Ginevra | Boucher |
| 1973 | Morston | Mysterious | Peleid |
| 1974 | Snow Knight | Polygamy | **Bustino** |
| 1975 | **Grundy** | Juliette Marny | Bruni |
| 1976 | Empery | Pawneese | Crow |
| 1977 | The Minstrel | Dunfermline | Dunfermline |
| 1978 | Shirley Heights | Fair Salinia | Julio Mariner |
| 1979 | **Troy** | Scintillate | Son of Love |
| 1980 | Henbit | Bireme | Light Cavalry |
| 1981 | **Shergar** | Blue Wind | Cut Above |
| 1982 | **Golden Fleece** | Time Charter | Touching Wood |
| 1983 | Teenoso | Sun Princess | Sun Princess |
| 1984 | Secreto | Circus Plume | |

## UNITED STATES

| | **Kentucky Derby**<br>Churchill Downs<br>$1\frac{1}{4}$ miles | **Preakness**<br>Pimlico Racecourse<br>$1\frac{3}{16}$ miles | **Belmont**<br>Belmont Park<br>$1\frac{1}{2}$ miles |
|---|---|---|---|
| 1867 | | | Ruthless |
| 1868 | | | General Duke |
| 1869 | | | Fenian |
| 1870 | | | Kingfisher |
| 1871 | | | Harry Basset |
| 1872 | | | Joe Daniels |
| 1873 | | Survivor | Springbok |
| 1874 | | Culpepper | Saxon |
| 1875 | Aristides | Tom Ochiltree | Calvin |
| 1876 | Vagrant | Shirley | Algerine |
| 1877 | Baden Baden | Cloverbrook | Cloverbrook |
| 1878 | Day Star | Duke of Magenta | Duke of Magenta |
| 1879 | Lord Murphy | Harold | Spendthrift |
| 1880 | Fonso | Grenada | Grenada |
| 1881 | Hindoo | Saunterer | Saunterer |
| 1882 | Apollo | Vanguard | Forester |
| 1883 | Leonatus | Jacobus | George Kinney |
| 1884 | Buchanan | Knight of Ellerslie | Panique |
| 1885 | Joe Cotton | Tecumseh | Tyrant |
| 1886 | Ben Ali | The Bard | Inspector B. |
| 1887 | Montrose | Dunboyne | **Hanover** |
| 1888 | Macbeth II | Refund | Sir Dixon |
| 1889 | Spokane | Buddhist | Eric |
| 1890 | Riley | Montague | Burlington |
| 1891 | Kingman | no race | Foxford |
| 1892 | Azra | no race | Patron |
| 1893 | Lookout | no race | Comanche |
| 1894 | Chant | Assignee | Henry of Navarre |
| 1895 | Halma | Belmar | Belmar |
| 1896 | Ben Brush | Margrave | Hastings |
| 1897 | Typhoon II | Paul Kauvar | Scottish Chieftan |
| 1898 | Plaudit | Sly Fox | Bowling Brook |
| 1899 | Manuel | Half Time | Jean Bereaud |
| 1900 | Lieut. Gibson | Hindus | Ildrim |
| 1901 | His Eminence | The Parader | Commando |
| 1902 | Alan-a-Dale | Old England | Masterman |
| 1903 | Judge Himes | Flocarline | Africander |
| 1904 | Elwood | Bryn Mawr | Delhi |
| 1905 | Agile | Cairngorm | Tany |
| 1906 | Sir Huon | Whimsical | Burgomaster |
| 1907 | Pink Star | Don Enrique | Peter Pan |
| 1908 | Stone Street | Royal Tourist | Colin |
| 1909 | Wintergreen | Effendi | Joe Madden |
| 1910 | Donau | Layminster | Sweep |
| 1911 | Meridian | Watervale | no race |
| 1912 | Worth | Colonel Holloway | no race |
| 1913 | Donerail | Buskin | Prince Eugene |
| 1914 | Old Rosebud | Holiday | Luke McLuke |

| | *Kentucky Derby* | *Preakness* | *Belmont* |
|---|---|---|---|
| 1915 | Regret | Rhine Maiden | The Finn |
| 1916 | George Smith | Damrosch | Friar Rock |
| 1917 | Omar Khayyam | Kalitan | Hourless |
| 1918 | Exterminator | { War Cloud<br>{ Jack Hare Jun. | Johren |
| 1919 | **Sir Barton** | **Sir Barton** | **Sir Barton** |
| 1920 | Paul Jones | **Man o' War** | **Man o' War** |
| 1921 | Behave Yourself | Broomspun | Grey Lag |
| 1922 | Morvich | Pillory | Pillory |
| 1923 | Zev | Vigil | Zev |
| 1924 | Black Gold | Nellie Morse | Mad Play |
| 1925 | Flying Ebony | Coventry | American Flag |
| 1926 | Bubbling Over | Display | Crusader |
| 1927 | Whiskery | Bostonian | Chance Shot |
| 1928 | Reigh Count | Victorian | Vito |
| 1929 | Clyde Van Dusen | Dr Freeland | Blue Larkspur |
| 1930 | Gallant Fox | Gallant Fox | Gallant Fox |
| 1931 | Twenty Grand | Mate | Twenty Grand |
| 1932 | Burgoo King | Burgoo King | Faireno |
| 1933 | Brokers Tip | Head Play | Hurryoff |
| 1934 | Cavalcade | High Quest | Peace Chance |
| 1935 | Omaha | Omaha | Omaha |
| 1936 | Bold Venture | Bold Venture | Granville |
| 1937 | **War Admiral** | **War Admiral** | **War Admiral** |
| 1938 | Lawrin | Dauber | Pasteurized |
| 1939 | Johnstown | Challedon | Johnstown |
| 1940 | Gallahadion | Bimelech | Bimelech |
| 1941 | Whirlaway | Whirlaway | Whirlaway |
| 1942 | Shut Out | Alsab | Shut Out |
| 1943 | Count Fleet | Count Fleet | Count Fleet |
| 1944 | Pensive | Pensive | Bounding Home |
| 1945 | Hoop Jun. | Polynesian | Pavot |
| 1946 | Assault | Assault | Assault |
| 1947 | Jet Pilot | Faultless | Phalanx |
| 1948 | Citation | Citation | Citation |
| 1949 | Ponder | Capot | Capot |
| 1950 | Middleground | Hill Prince | Middleground |
| 1951 | Count Turf | Bold | Counterpoint |
| 1952 | Hill Gail | Blue Man | One Count |
| 1953 | Dark Star | Native Dancer | Native Dancer |
| 1954 | Determine | Hasty Road | High Gun |
| 1955 | **Swaps** | **Nashua** | **Nashua** |
| 1956 | Needles | Fabius | Needles |
| 1957 | Iron Liege | Bold Ruler | Gallant Man |
| 1958 | Tim Tam | Tim Tam | Cavan |
| 1959 | Tomy Lee | Royal Orbit | Sword Dancer |
| 1960 | Venetian Way | Bally Ache | Celtic Ash |
| 1961 | Carry Back | Carry Back | Sherluck |
| 1962 | Decidedly | Greek Money | Jaipur |
| 1963 | Chateaugay | Candy Spots | Chateaugay |
| 1964 | **Northern Dancer** | **Northern Dancer** | Quadrangle |
| 1965 | Lucky Debonair | Tom Rolfe | Hail to All |
| 1966 | Kauai King | Kauai King | Amberoid |
| 1967 | Proud Clarion | Damascus | Damascus |
| 1968 | Dancer's Image | Forward Pass | Stage Door Johnny |
| 1969 | Majestic Prince | Majestic Prince | Arts and Letters |
| 1970 | Dust Commander | Personality | High Echelon |
| 1971 | Canonero II | Canonero II | Pass Catcher |
| 1972 | Riva Ridge | Bee Bee Bee | Riva Ridge |
| 1973 | **Secretariat** | **Secretariat** | **Secretariat** |
| 1974 | Cannonade | **Little Current** | **Little Current** |
| 1975 | Foolish Pleasure | Master Derby | Avatar |
| 1976 | Bold Forbes | Elocutionist | Bold Forbes |
| 1977 | **Seattle Slew** | **Seattle Slew** | **Seattle Slew** |
| 1978 | **Affirmed** | **Affirmed** | **Affirmed** |
| 1979 | **Spectacular Bid** | **Spectacular Bid** | Coastal |
| 1980 | Genuine Risk | Codex | Temperance Hill |
| 1981 | Pleasant Colony | Pleasant Colony | Summing |
| 1982 | Gato del Sol | Aloma's Ruler | Conquistador Cielo |
| 1983 | Sunny's Halo | Deputed Testamony | Caveat |
| 1984 | Swale | Gate Dancer | Swale |

FRANCE

## Prix du Jockey Club

Chantilly

1½ miles

| | |
|---|---|
| 1836 | Franck |
| 1837 | Lydia |
| 1838 | Vendredi |
| 1839 | Romulus |
| 1840 | Tontine |
| 1841 | Poetess |
| 1842 | Plover |
| 1843 | Renonce |
| 1844 | Lanterne |
| 1845 | FitzEmilius |
| 1846 | Meudon |
| 1847 | Morok |
| 1848 | Gambetti |
| 1849 | Experience |
| 1850 | St Germain |
| 1851 | Amalfi |
| 1852 | Porthos |
| 1853 | Juvence |
| 1854 | Celebrity |
| 1855 | Monarque |
| 1856 | Lion |
| 1857 | **Potocki** |
| 1858 | Ventre St Gris |
| 1859 | Black Prince |
| 1860 | Beauvais |
| 1861 | Gabrielle d'Estrees |
| 1862 | Souvenir |
| 1863 | La Toucques |
| 1864 | Bois Rousse |
| 1865 | Gontran |
| 1866 | Florentin |
| 1867 | Patricien |
| 1868 | Suzerain |
| 1869 | Consul |
| 1870 | Bigarreau |
| 1871 | no race |
| 1872 | Revigny |
| 1873 | Boiard |
| 1874 | Saltarelle |
| 1875 | Salvator |
| 1876 | Kilt |
| 1877 | Jongleur |
| 1878 | **Insulaire** |
| 1879 | Zut |
| 1880 | Beauminet |
| 1881 | Albion |
| 1882 | Dandin / St James |
| 1883 | Frontin |
| 1884 | Little Duck |
| 1885 | Reluisant |
| 1886 | Sycomore / Upas |
| 1887 | Monarque |
| 1888 | Stuart |
| 1889 | Clover |
| 1890 | Heaume |
| 1891 | Ermak |
| 1892 | Chêne Royal |
| 1893 | Ragotsky |
| 1894 | Gospodar |
| 1895 | Omnium II |
| 1896 | Champaubert |
| 1897 | Palmiste |
| 1898 | Gardefeu |
| 1899 | Perth |
| 1900 | La Morinière |
| 1901 | Saxon |
| 1902 | Retz |
| 1903 | Ex Voto |
| 1904 | Ajax |
| 1905 | Finasseur |
| 1906 | Maintenon |
| 1907 | Mordant |
| 1908 | Sea Sick / Quintette |
| 1909 | Negofol |
| 1910 | Or du Rhin II |
| 1911 | Alcantara II |
| 1912 | Friant II |
| 1913 | Dagor |
| 1914 | Sardanapale |
| 1915–18 | no race |
| 1919 | Tchad |
| 1920 | Sourbier |
| 1921 | Ksar |
| 1922 | Ramus |
| 1923 | Le Capucin |
| 1924 | Pot au Feu |
| 1925 | Belfonds |
| 1926 | Madrigal |
| 1927 | Mon Talisman |
| 1928 | Le Corrège |
| 1929 | Hotweed |
| 1930 | Château Bouscaut |
| 1931 | Tourbillon |
| 1932 | Strip the Willow |
| 1933 | Thor |
| 1934 | Duplex |
| 1935 | Pearlweed |
| 1936 | Mieuxce |
| 1937 | Clairvoyant |
| 1938 | Cillas |
| 1939 | Pharis II |
| 1940 | Quicko |
| 1941 | **Le Pacha** |
| 1942 | Magister |
| 1943 | Verso II |
| 1944 | Ardan |
| 1945 | Coaraze |
| 1946 | Prince Chevalier |
| 1947 | Sandjar |
| 1948 | Bey |
| 1949 | Good Luck |
| 1950 | Scratch II |
| 1951 | Sicambre |
| 1952 | Auriban |
| 1953 | Chamant |
| 1954 | Le Petit Prince |
| 1955 | Rapace |
| 1956 | Philius II |
| 1957 | Amber |
| 1958 | Tamanar |
| 1959 | Herbager |
| 1960 | Charlottesville |
| 1961 | Right Royal |
| 1962 | Val de Loir |
| 1963 | Sanctus |
| 1964 | Le Fabuleux |
| 1965 | Reliance |
| 1966 | Nelcius |
| 1967 | Astec |
| 1968 | Tapalque |
| 1969 | Goodly |
| 1970 | Sassafras |
| 1971 | Rheffic |
| 1972 | Hard to Beat |
| 1973 | Roi Lear |
| 1974 | Caracolero |
| 1975 | Val de l'Orne |
| 1976 | Youth |
| 1977 | Crystal Palace |
| 1978 | Acamas |
| 1979 | Top Ville |
| 1980 | Policeman |
| 1981 | Bikala |
| 1982 | Assert |
| 1983 | Caerleon |
| 1984 | Darshaan |

# *Selective Blood Lines*

The names of horses illustrated and featured in the text are printed in bold type.

## BYERLEY TURK

- Jigg
  - Partner
    - Tartar
      - Herod
        - Florizel
          - **Diomed**
            - Sir Archy
              - Timoleon
                - **Boston**
                  - **Lexington**
            - Duroc
              - **American Eclipse**
        - **Highflyer**
          - **Rockingham**
          - Sir Peter Teazle
            - Walton
              - Partisan
                - **Mameluke**
        - Woodpecker
          - Buzzard
            - Castrel
              - Pantaloon
                - Windhound
                  - Thormanby
                    - Atlantic
                      - Le Sancy
                        - Le Samaritain
                          - Roi Hérode
                            - **The Tetrarch**
            - Selim
              - Langar
                - **Elis**
              - Sultan
                - Glencoe
                  - Vandal
                    - Virgil
                      - Hindoo
                        - **Hanover**
                - Bay Middleton
                  - **The Flying Dutchman**
          - **Dragon**
- **Basto**

## GODOLPHIN ARABIAN

- Cripple
  - **Gimcrack**
- Cade
  - Matchem
    - Conductor
      - Trumpator
        - Sorcerer
          - Comus
            - Humphrey Clinker
              - Melbourne
                - **West Australian**
                  - Australian
                    - Spendthrift
                      - Hastings
                        - Fair Play
                          - **Man o' War**
                            - **War Admiral**
                            - **Battleship**
                - **Sir Tatton Sykes**
          - Smolensko
            - **Jerry**

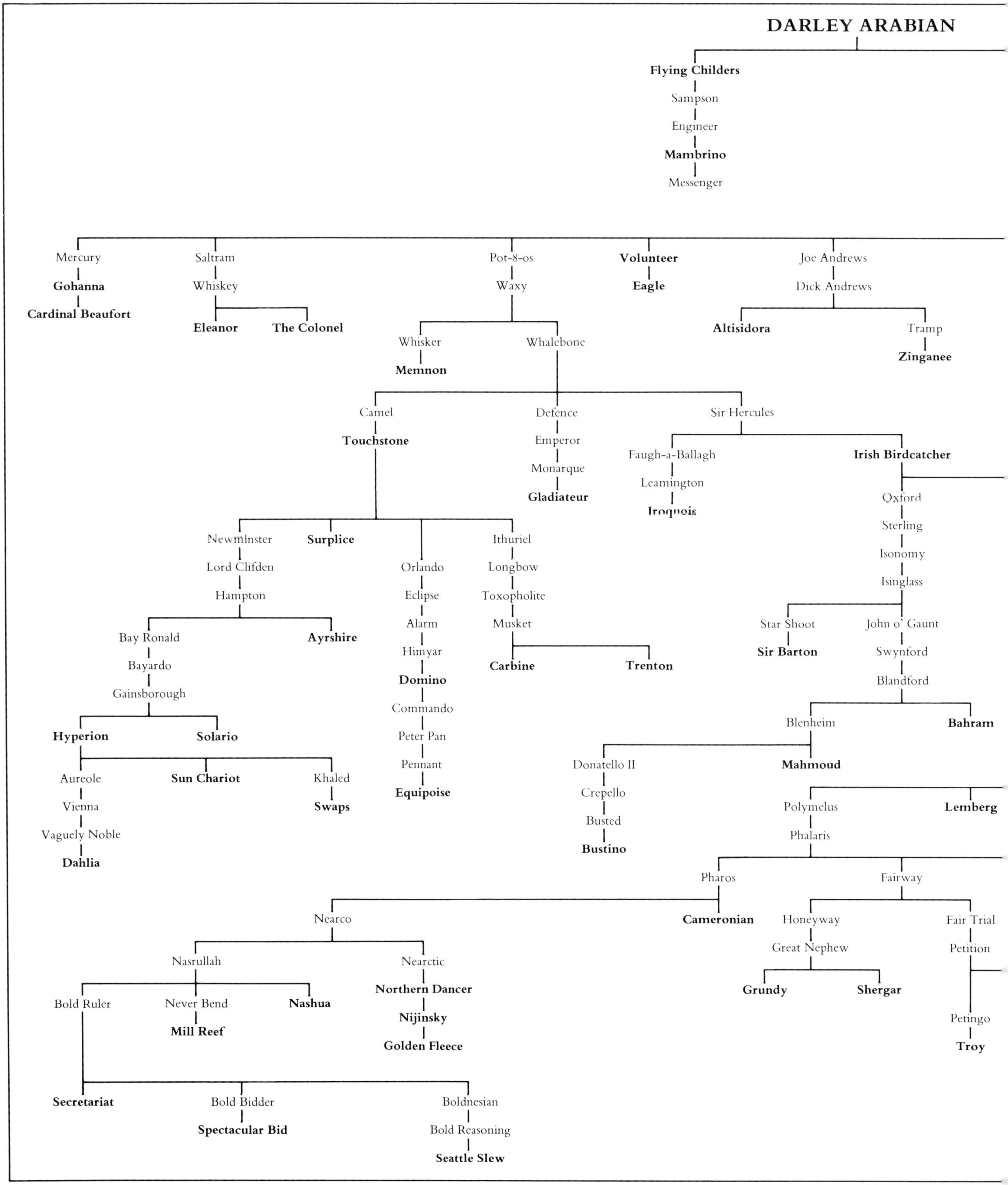
DARLEY ARABIAN
Flying Childers
Sampson
Engineer
Mambrino
Messenger
Mercury
Gohanna
Cardinal Beaufort
Saltram
Whiskey
Eleanor
The Colonel
Pot-8-os
Waxy
Volunteer
Eagle
Joe Andrews
Dick Andrews
Altisidora
Tramp
Zinganee
Whisker
Memnon
Whalebone
Camel
Touchstone
Defence
Emperor
Monarque
Gladiateur
Sir Hercules
Faugh-a-Ballagh
Leamington
Iroquois
Irish Birdcatcher
Oxford
Sterling
Isonomy
Isinglass
Newminster
Lord Clifden
Hampton
Surplice
Orlando
Eclipse
Alarm
Himyar
Domino
Commando
Peter Pan
Pennant
Equipoise
Ithuriel
Longbow
Toxopholite
Musket
Carbine
Trenton
Bay Ronald
Bayardo
Gainsborough
Ayrshire
Hyperion
Solario
Aureole
Vienna
Vaguely Noble
Dahlia
Sun Chariot
Khaled
Swaps
Star Shoot
Sir Barton
John o' Gaunt
Swynford
Blandford
Blenheim
Bahram
Donatello II
Crepello
Busted
Bustino
Mahmoud
Polymelus
Phalaris
Lemberg
Pharos
Fairway
Nearco
Cameronian
Honeyway
Great Nephew
Grundy
Shergar
Fair Trial
Petition
Petingo
Troy
Nasrullah
Nearctic
Northern Dancer
Nijinsky
Golden Fleece
Bold Ruler
Never Bend
Mill Reef
Nashua
Secretariat
Bold Bidder
Spectacular Bid
Boldnesian
Bold Reasoning
Seattle Slew

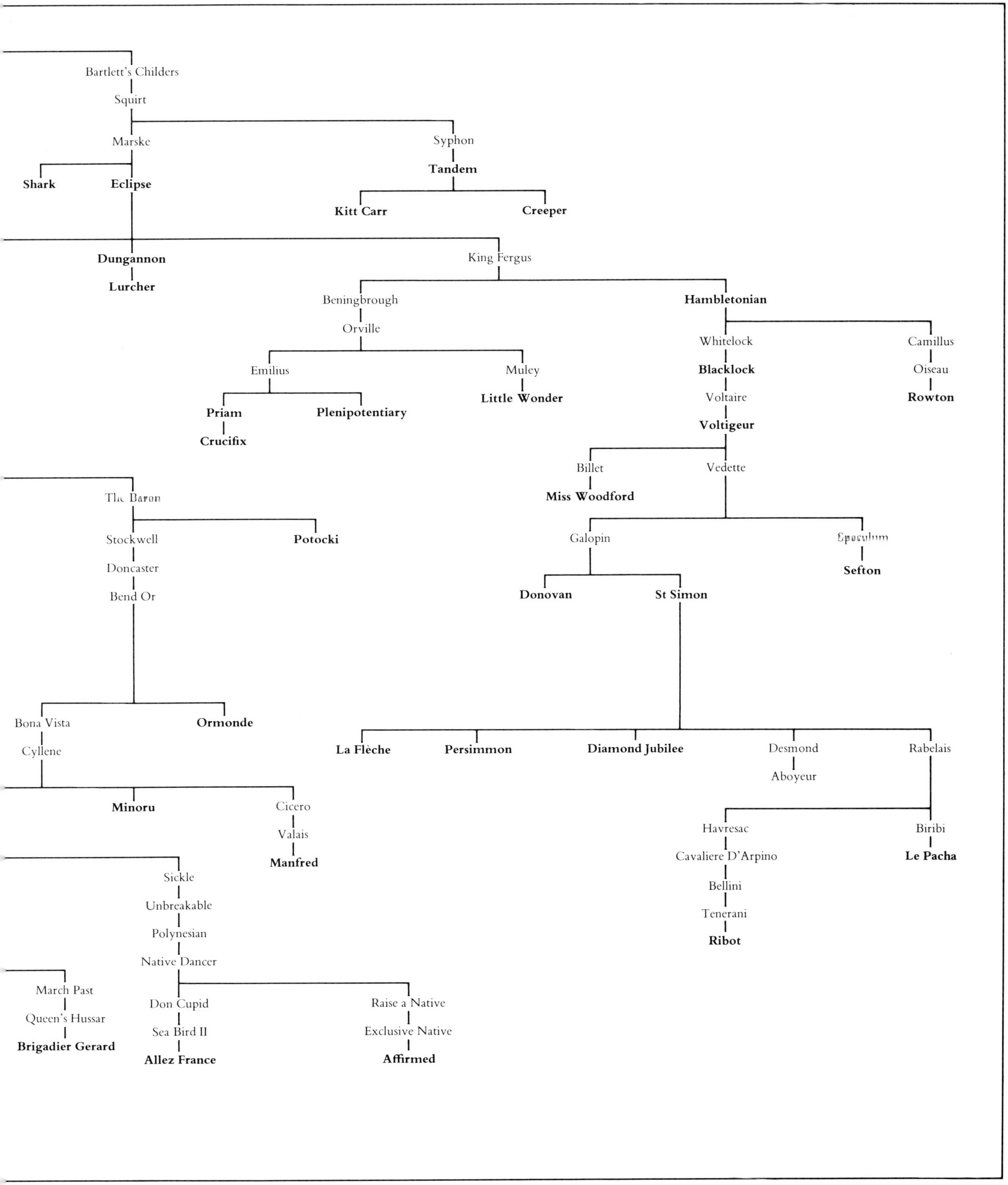
Bartlett's Childers
Squirt
Marske
Syphon
Shark
Eclipse
Tandem
Kitt Carr
Creeper
Dungannon
King Fergus
Lurcher
Beningbrough
Hambletonian
Orville
Whitelock
Camillus
Emilius
Muley
Blacklock
Oiseau
Little Wonder
Voltaire
Rowton
Priam
Plenipotentiary
Voltigeur
Crucifix
Billet
Vedette
The Baron
Miss Woodford
Stockwell
Potocki
Galopin
Speculum
Doncaster
Sefton
Bend Or
Donovan
St Simon
Bona Vista
Ormonde
Cyllene
La Flèche
Persimmon
Diamond Jubilee
Desmond
Rabelais
Aboyeur
Minoru
Cicero
Havresac
Biribi
Valais
Cavaliere D'Arpino
Le Pacha
Manfred
Sickle
Bellini
Unbreakable
Tenerani
Polynesian
Ribot
Native Dancer
March Past
Don Cupid
Raise a Native
Queen's Hussar
Sea Bird II
Exclusive Native
Brigadier Gerard
Allez France
Affirmed

# *Bibliography*

From the earliest days the racing world has benefited from the painstaking efforts of countless men and women who have recorded the careers and achievements of many thousands of thoroughbreds.

Weatherby's *The Racing Calendar* and *General Stud Book*, started in 1773 and 1803 respectively, are unbroken tablets. *Baily's Racing Register* contains the most precise details from 1709 – the very first meeting at York contains the splendid note, 'The third [race] was a dead heat between Button and Milkmaid; but the riders being guilty of foul play in running, and afterwards fighting on horseback, the plate was given to Brisk.'

From the days when the *Sporting Magazine* began at the end of the eighteenth century there has been a wonderfully vivid seam of anecdote and history preserved in print. Contemporary writers like Roger Mortimer and Peter Willett continue the tradition, providing an erudite and diverting commentary on the horses of our time.

Painters of the racing scene have been less fortunate. Almost a century ago Sir Walter Gilbey made available an invaluable collection of biographical material in his *Animal Painters of England*, but anybody interested in the work of sporting painters is still obliged to delve deep for random evidence which chance has preserved. For the period up to 1870, the most useful single source for research and identification of racehorse pictures is the *Sporting Magazine*. One must also be grateful for the records of the great galleries like Messrs Fores and Messrs Ackermann, and for the remarkable archive of Christie's.

There are important works on the best-known racing painters, such as Major Guy Paget's *The Melton Mowbray of John Ferneley*, Basil Taylor's *Stubbs*, Reginald Grundy's *James Ward, R.A.*, and, most recently, Oliver Beckett's *J. F. Herring & Sons*. For many years the magazine *British Racehorse* (now *European Racehorse*) has published valuable articles on individual painters, and the British Sporting Art Trust, formed in 1977, has circulated a number of illuminating monographs. More generally, Judy Egerton's superb catalogue of the Mellon Collection stands out, and Stella Walker's *Sporting Art* is a seminal volume.

Eileen P. Loder produced in 1978 a bibliography of racing which is as comprehensive as can be. However, it is hoped that a selected bibliography specifically related to the subject-matter of the present book will prove useful.

### Journals and Periodic Reference Books


*Baily's Magazine*, vols. 1–126, 1860–1926
*Bell's Life in London*, vols. 1–64, 1822–86
*Directory of the Turf*, vol. 1, 1961, nine editions to 1984
*European Racehorse* (formerly *British Racehorse*), vol. 1, 1949, published five times per year
*Fores Sporting Notes and Sketches*, vols. 1–29, 1884–1912
*General Stud Book* (Weatherby's), vol. 1, 1803, since 1845 published every four years
*The Racing Calendar* (Weatherby's), vol. 1, 1773, published weekly
*Ruff's Guide to the Turf*, vol. 1, 1842, published annually
*Sporting Magazine*, vols. 1–156, 1792–1870


### Other Publications


Aga Khan, H.H. the. *Memoirs*. Cassell, 1954
Alken, Henry. *The Beauties and Defects in the Figure of the Horse*. S. & J. Fuller, 1816
Allen, G. D. R. *A Sire Line Chart of the Derby, the St Leger, the Prix du Jockey Club, the Grand Prix de Paris, 1890–1964*. J. A. Allen, 1965
Apperley, Charles, *see* 'Nimrod'
Axe, Prof. J. Wortley. *The Horse*, 9 vols. Gresham, 1907
Axthelm, Pete. *The Kid*. Bantam Books, 1978 (A biography of the jockey Steve Cauthen)

Baerlein, Richard. *Nijinsky*. Pelham Books, 1971
*Baily's Racing Register*, 3 vols. Baily Brothers, 1845
Beckett, Oliver. *J. F. Herring & Sons*. J. A. Allen, 1981
Bland, Ernest. *Flat Racing since 1900*. Andrew Dakers, 1950
Booth, Stanley. *Sir Alfred Munnings*. Sotheby Parke Bernet, 1978
Boucat, Sir James Penn. *The Arab: the Horse of the Future*. Gay & Bird, 1905
Bourg, Ross du. *The Australian and New Zealand Thoroughbred*. Michael Joseph, 1980
Broke, Lord Willoughby de (ed). *Steeplechasing*. Seeley Service, 1954
Browne, Capt. T. H. *History of the English Turf*, 2 vols. H. Virtue, 1931

Cheney, John. *An Historical List of all Horse-matches run*. (London) 1727–50
Chetwynd, Sir George. *Racing Reminiscences and Experiences of the Turf*. Longmans, Green, 1891
Chifney, Samuel. *Genius Genuine*. (London) 1792
Connor, Patricia, and Lionel Lambourne. *Derby Day 200*, exhibition catalogue. Royal Academy of Arts, London, 1979
Cook, Theodore A. *A History of the English Turf*, 3 vols. H. Virtue, 1905
Cuming, E. D. *George Morland*. A. & C. Black, 1910
Custance, Henry. *Riding Recollections and Turf Stories*. Edward Arnold, 1894

Darling, Sam. *Reminiscences*. Mills & Boon, 1914
Day, William. *Reminiscences of the Turf*. Richard Bentley & Son, 1886
—— *Turf Celebrities I have known*. L. V. F. White, 1891
Dighton, Adair. *My Sporting Life*. Grant Richards, 1934
Dixon, Henry, *see* 'The Druid'
Donoghue, Steve. *Autobiography*. Collins, 1938
'The Druid' (Henry Dixon). *The Post and the Paddock*. Piper Stephenson, 1856
—— *Silk and Scarlet*. Rogerson & Tuxford, 1859

Edwards, Lionel. *Reminiscences of a Sporting Artist*. Putnam, 1947
Egerton, Judy. *British Sporting and Animal Paintings 1655–1867, in the Paul Mellon Collection*. Tate Gallery Publications, 1978

—— and Dudley Snelgrove. *British Sporting and Animal Drawings 1500–1850, in the Paul Mellon Collection*. Tate Gallery Publications, 1978

Fairfax-Blakeborough, John. *Malton Memories and I'Anson Triumphs*. Truslove & Bray, 1925
—— *Sykes of Sledmere*. Phillip Allen, 1929
—— *Northern Turf History*, 5 vols. J. A. Allen, 1948
Fletcher, Brian. *My Rum Life*. Viking Books, 1977
Fletcher, J. S. *The History of the St Leger Stakes*. Hutchinson, 1902
Francis, Dick. *Sport of Queens*. Michael Joseph, 1957

Galtrey, Sidney. *Memoirs of a Racing Journalist*. Hutchinson, 1934
Gaunt, William. *Stubbs*. Phaidon Press, 1977
Gilbey, Quinny. *Racing for Fun*. Hutchinson, 1936
Gilbey, Sir Walter. *Animal Painters of England*, 3 vols. Vinton, 1900
Gill, James. *Racecourses of Great Britain*. Barrie & Jenkins, 1975
—— *Bloodstock*. Elm Tree Books, 1977
Graham, Clive, and Bill Curling. *The Grand National*. Barrie & Jenkins, 1972
Grundy, C. Reginald. *James Ward, R.A.* Otto, 1909

Hammond, William. *The Gentleman's Most Accomplished Jockey*. (London) *c.*1750
Hawkins, Christopher. *The Race of the Century*. George Allen & Unwin, 1976
Herbert, Ivor. *Arkle: the Story of a Champion*. Pelham Books, 1966
—— *Red Rum*. Arrow Books, 1977
Heron, Roy. *Cecil Aldin: the Story of a Sporting Artist*. Webb & Bower, 1981
Hieover, Harry. *The Pocket and the Stud*. Longmans & Roberts, 1857
Hislop, John. *The Turf*. Collins, 1948
—— *The Brigadier*. Secker & Warburg, 1973
Hodgman, George. *Sixty Years on the Turf*. Grant Richards, 1903
Humphris, Edith Mary. *Life of Fred Archer*. Hutchinson, 1923
—— *Life of Matthew Dawson*. H. F. & G. Witherby, 1928

Jones, Capt. Adrian. *Memoirs of a Soldier Artist*. Stanley Paul, 1933

Kent, John. *Racing Life of Lord George Bentinck*. William Blackwood & Sons, 1892
—— *Records and Reminiscences of Goodwood and the Duke of Richmond*. Sampson Low, Marston, 1896

Lambton, George. *Men and Horses I have known*. Eyre & Spottiswood, 1924
Laverty, Colin. *Australian Colonial Sporting Painters*. The David Ell Press, Sydney, 1980
Lawrence, John. *World of Racing*. Purnell, 1970
Loder, Eileen P. *Bibliography of the History and Organisation of Horse Racing and Thoroughbred Breeding in Great Britain and Ireland*. J. A. Allen, 1978
Logan, Guy B. H. *The Classic Races of the Turf*. Stanley Paul, 1931
Lyle, R. C. *Royal Newmarket*. Putnam, 1945

Marsh, Richard. *A Trainer to Two Kings*. Cassell, 1925
Meysey-Thompson, R. F. *Reminiscences*. Edward Arnold, 1898
Millar, Oliver. *British Sporting Painting 1650–1850*, introduction to exhibition catalogue. Hayward Gallery, London, 1974
Mortimer, Roger. *The Jockey Club*. Cassell, 1958
—— *The History of the Derby Stakes*. Cassell, 1962
—— *The Flat*. George Allen & Unwin, 1979
—— Richard Onslow, and Peter Willett. *Biographical Encyclopaedia of British Flat Racing*. Macdonald & Jane, 1978
Munnings, Sir Alfred. *An Artist's Life*. Museum Press, 1950
—— *The Second Burst*. Museum Press, 1951
—— *The Finish*. Museum Press, 1952
Muybridge, Eadweard. *Animal Locomotion*. University of Pennsylvania, 1887

'Nimrod' (Charles Apperley). *The Chase, the Turf, and the Road*. John Murray, 1837
—— *The Life of John Mytton*. R. Ackermann, 1837
Noakes, Aubrey. *Ben Marshall*. F. Lewis, 1978

Orchard, Vincent. *Tattersalls*. Hutchinson, 1953
—— *The Derby Stakes 1900–1953*. Hutchinson, 1954
Ormond, Richard. *Sir Edwin Landseer*, exhibition catalogue. Philadelphia Museum of Art, Tate Gallery, London, 1982
Orton, John. *Turf Annals of York and Doncaster*. H. Southeran, 1841
Osbaldeston, George. *Squire Osbaldeston: his Autobiography*, ed. E. D. Cuming. John Lane, 1926

Paget, Guy. *The Melton Mowbray of John Ferneley*. Edgar Backus, 1931
—— *Sporting Pictures of England*. Collins, 1945
Pendred, G. L. *Clifton Tomson*. Privately published, Nottingham, 1978
Pick, William. *Pedigree and Performance of the Most Celebrated Racehorses*. (York) 1785
*Pick's Authentic Historical Racing Calendar*. (York) 1768
Porter, John. *Kingsclere*. Chatto & Windus, 1896
Portland, Duke of. *Memories of Racing and Hunting*. Faber & Faber, 1935

Ramsden, Caroline. *Ladies in Racing*. Stanley Paul, 1973
Reeves, Richard Stone, and Patrick Robinson. *Decade of Champions*. Michael Joseph, 1980
Richardson, Charles. *Racing at Home and Abroad*, 2 vols. London & Counties Press, 1923
Rickman, Eric. *On and Off the Racecourse*. George Routledge & Sons, 1937
Roberts, Keith. *Degas*. Phaidon Press, 1982
Robertson, William H. P. *The History of Thoroughbred Racing in America*. Prentice-Hall, 1964
Rous, Henry John. *On the Laws and Practice of Horse Racing*. Baily Brothers, 1850

Sasse, F. H. *Theme on a Pipe Dream*. J. A. Allen, 1969 (Derby blood-lines)
Scott, Alexander. *Turf Memories of Sixty Years*. Hutchinson, 1925
Skeaping, John. *Drawn from Life*. Collins, 1977
Sloan, Tod. *Tod Sloan, by Himself*. Grant Richards, 1915
Sparrow, Walter Shaw. *British Sporting Artists*. John Lane, 1922
—— *A Book of Sporting Painters*. John Lane, 1931
Stewart, Lt.-Col. P. D. *Training the Racehorse*. Stanley Paul, 1952

Taunton, Theodore. *Famous Horses with Portraits*. Sampson Low, 1895
Taunton, Thomas Henry. *Portraits of Celebrated Racehorses*. Sampson Low, 1887
Taylor, Basil. *Stubbs*. Phaidon Press, 1971
Taylor, Desmond. *Edwin Cooper of Beccles, 1785–1833*. F. Lewis, 1981
Tesio, Federico. *Breeding the Racehorse*. J. A. Allen, 1958
Thétard, Henry. *Histoire et secrets du turf*. Robert Laffont, 1947
Touchstone, S. F. *History of Celebrated English and French Thoroughbred Stallions and French Mares, 1764 to 1887*. John C. Nimmo, 1890
Trarieux, Jean. *Journal d'un homme de courses*. Fayard, 1971
Trench, Charles Chenevix. *A history of Horsemanship*. Longman, 1970

Voigt, Charles Adolph. *Famous Gentleman Riders*. Hutchinson, n.d.

Walker, Stella A. *Sporting Art*. Clarkson N. Potter, 1972
Wentworth, Baroness. *Thoroughbred Racing Stock and its Ancestors*. George Allen & Unwin, 1938
Wilder, F. L. *English Sporting Prints*. Thames & Hudson, 1974
Willett, Peter. *The Thoroughbred*. Weidenfeld & Nicolson, 1970

# Index

Page numbers printed in bold type indicate the main references for the artists and racehorses which are featured in the text and whose names appear in the section headings. The entry for a horse which is illustrated, whether by a painting, a sculpture, or a photograph, includes in italic type within brackets the name of the artist who produced the work, the title of which can be found as a sub-entry under the artist's name. Thus the entry for the colt Affirmed, for example, shows that he is featured on pp. 199–200 and is illustrated in a painting by Richard Stone Reeves. Reference to the entry for Reeves shows that the title of the painting is *Affirmed beating Spectacular Bid*, reproduced on p. 199.

# *Acknowledgements*

The author and publishers would like to thank Carolyn Alexander and Richard Stone Reeves; Arthur Ackermann and Sons Ltd., Christie's, A. C. Cooper Ltd., The Courtauld Institute of Art, Frost and Reed Ltd., Richard Green Galleries, and The Tryon Gallery, London; Colourlabs International, Newmarket; and Christie's, New York.

They are grateful to all those museum authorities, institutions, and private owners who have kindly allowed their works to be reproduced, and they have endeavoured to credit all known persons holding copyright or reproduction rights for the illustrations in this book.

The works of André Marchand are © A.D.A.G.P. Paris 1984, and those of Raoul Dufy are © S.P.A.D.E.M. Paris 1984.

Thanks are also due for permission to reproduce the following photographs: pages 11, 53 (below), 149, 150 (above and below), 151 (right) by gracious permission of Her Majesty The Queen; 105 (above left and below) by gracious permission of Her Majesty Queen Elizabeth The Queen Mother; 127 (left) by courtesy of the Museum of Fine Arts, Boston, purchased, S. A. Denio Collection; 39, 152, BBC Hulton Picture Library; 27, 28, 107 (above) by courtesy of the Trustees of the British Museum; 58, The Trustees of the Rt. Hon. Olive, Countess Fitzwilliam's Chattels Settlement, by kind permission of the Lady Juliet de Chair; 81 (above) by courtesy of Cox and Company, London; 41 (below), 205, 206, 208, photo by Gerry Cranham; 169 by kind permission of the Earl of Derby; 61 (above) by permission of the Syndics of the Fitzwilliam Museum, Cambridge; 14, Goodwood Estate Company Ltd.; 171 (right) by kind permission of Mr and Mrs John Hislop (photo by Elizabeth Williams, Oxford); 40, 60, 63 (above), 73 (above and below), 74 (above right and left, below left), 79, 102 (above), 114, 115, 117 (below), 137, 142, 151 (left), 153, 154, 155, 157, 158, 162 (above and below), 174, 177 (right), 203 by kind permission of the Stewards of the Jockey Club; 141 (below), The Mansell Collection; 36 (above), The National Galleries of Scotland (photo: The National Trust for Scotland); 59, The National Trust; 33 (below), The National Trust for Scotland; 193 by courtesy of the Newmarket Gallery, New York; 46, photo by courtesy of Mrs J. O'Brien; 189 by kind permission of the Marquess and Marchioness of Tavistock and the Trustees of the Bedford Estates; 67 (above and below), 68, 69, 112, 138 by kind permission of Tattersalls Ltd.; 195 by kind permission of Anne, Duchess of Westminster; 194, photo by Elizabeth Williams, Oxford; 12, 20, 49, 50 (above left), 51 (right), 109, 131, Yale Center for British Art, Paul Mellon Collection; 117 (above), 119 by kind permission of the Marquess of Zetland.